THE ART OF
POLITICAL MURDER

Also by Francisco Goldman

The Long Night of White Chickens
The Ordinary Seaman
The Divine Husband

THE ART OF
POLITICAL MURDER

WHO KILLED THE BISHOP?

FRANCISCO GOLDMAN

Grove Press
New York

Parts of this work have appeared in
The New Yorker and the *New York Review of Books*.

Published simultaneously in Canada
Printed in the United States of America

FIRST EDITION

ISBN-10: 0-8021-1828-3
ISBN-13: 978-0-8021-1828-8

Grove Press
an imprint of Grove/Atlantic, Inc.
841 Broadway
New York, NY 10003

Distributed by Publishers Group West

www.groveatlantic.com

07 08 09 10 11 12   10 9 8 7 6 5 4 3 2 1

Por los que creyeron. For the believers.

And in memory of
Darinel Domingo Montejo, José Mérida Escobar,
Mama Lotti, and others unnamed

No hay nada más injusto que lo justo.
Nothing is more unjust than what is just.
—Lope de Vega

Neighborhood of the Murder

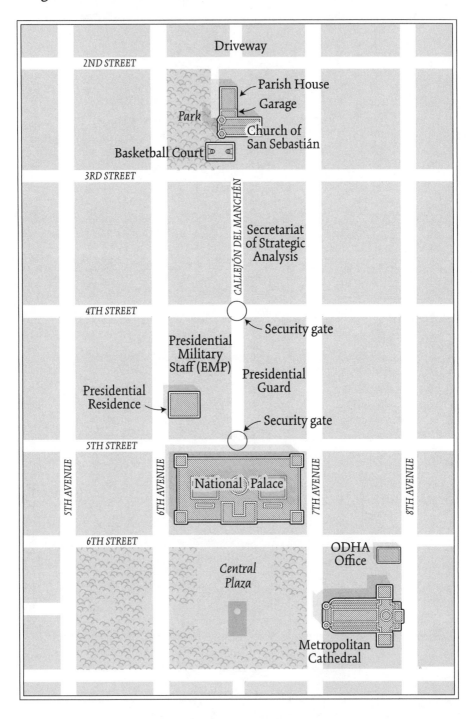

San Sebastián Parish House

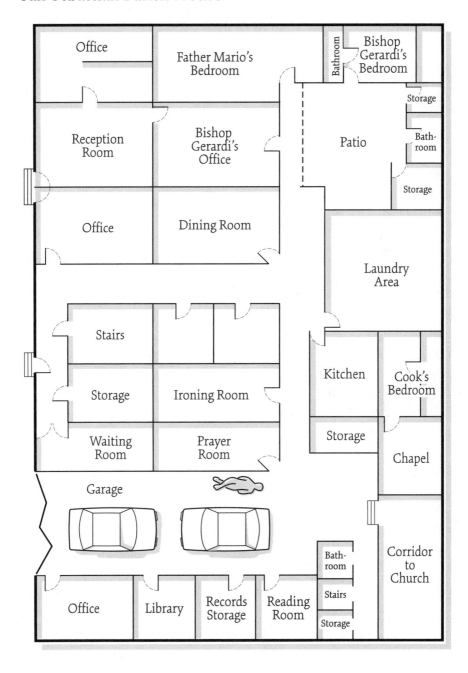

Office

Father Mario's Bedroom

Bathroom

Bishop Gerardi's Bedroom

Storage

Reception Room

Bishop Gerardi's Office

Patio

Bath-room

Storage

Office

Dining Room

Laundry Area

Stairs

Kitchen

Cook's Bedroom

Storage

Ironing Room

Storage

Waiting Room

Prayer Room

Chapel

Garage

Corridor to Church

Office

Library

Records Storage

Reading Room

Bath-room

Stairs

Storage

Contents

Bishop Juan Gerardi Conedera (1922–1998)

I
THE MURDER
APRIL 26, 1998

1

ONE SUNDAY AFTERNOON, a few hours before he was bludgeoned to death in the garage of the parish house of the church of San Sebastián, in the old center of Guatemala City, Bishop Juan Gerardi Conedera was drinking Scotch and telling stories at a small gathering in a friend's backyard garden. Bishop Gerardi's stories were famously amusing and sometimes off-color. He had a reputation as a *chistoso,* a joker. "In a meeting with him, you would get this whole repertoire of jokes," Father Mario Orantes Nájera, the parish's assistant priest, told police investigators two days later. "I wish you could have known him." Guatemalans admire someone who can tell *chistes.* A good *chiste* is, among other things, a defense against fear, despair, and the loneliness of not daring to speak your mind. In the most tense, uncomfortable, or frightening circumstances, a Guatemalan always seems to come forward with a *chiste* or two, delivered with an almost formal air, often in a recitative rush of words, the emphasis less in the voice, rarely raised, than in the hand gestures. Even when laughter is forced, it seems like a release.

Guatemalans have long been known for their reserve and se-cretiveness, even gloominess. "Men remoter than mountains" was how Wallace Stevens put it in a poem he wrote after visiting "alien, point-blank, green and actual Guatemala." Two separate, gravely ceremonious, phantasmagoria-prone cultures, Spanish

Catholic and Mayan pagan, shaped the country's national character, along with centuries of cruelty and isolation. (At the height of the Spanish empire, ships rarely called at Guatemala's coasts, for the land offered little in the way of spoils, especially compared with the gold and silver available in Mexico and South America.) In 1885, a Nicaraguan political exile and writer, Enrique Guzmán, described the country as a vicious, corrupt police state, filled with so many government informers that "even the drunks are discreet"—an observation that has never ceased to be quoted because it has never, from one ruler or government to the next, stopped seeming true.

Bishop Gerardi was a big man, and still robust, though he was seventy-five years old. He was over six feet tall and weighed about 235 pounds. He had a broad chest and back; a prominent, ruddy nose; and thick, curly gray hair. After the murder, his friends recalled not only his sense of humor and affection for alcohol but also his voracious reading, his down-to-earth intelligence, and a nearly clairvoyant understanding of Guatemala's notoriously tangled, corrupt, and lethal politics, which made him by far the most trusted adviser on such matters to his superior, Archbishop Próspero Penados del Barrio, a less worldly figure. Soon after Penados was named archbishop, in 1983, he had recalled Gerardi from political exile in Costa Rica. As the founding director of the Guatemalan Archdiocese's Office of Human Rights (Oficina de Derechos Humanos del Arzobispado de Guatemala), which was usually referred to by its acronym, ODHA—pronounced OH-dah—Gerardi became one of the Catholic Church's most important and visible spokesmen and leaders.

The gathering in the garden on that last afternoon of Bishop Gerardi's life was a celebration of the completion of *Guatemala: Never Again,* a four-volume, 1,400-page report on an unprecedented investigation into the "disappearances," massacres, murders, torture, and systematic violence that had been inflicted on the population of Guatemala since the beginning of the 1960s, decades during which right-wing military dictators and then military-dominated civilian governments waged war against leftist guerrilla groups. An estimated 200,000 civilians were killed during the war, which formally ended in December 1996 with the signing of a peace agreement monitored by the United Nations. The Guatemalan Army had easily won the war on the battlefield, but making peace with the guerrillas had become a political and economic necessity. Still, the Army was able to dictate many of the terms of the agreement and engineered for itself and for the acquiescent guerrilla organizations a sweeping amnesty from prosecution for war-related crimes. This "piñata of self-forgiveness" was an ominous beginning for an era supposedly based on such democratic values as the rule of law and access to justice, as well as demilitarization.

The peace agreement endorsed a truth commission sponsored by the UN—the Historical Clarification Commission—which was intended to establish the history of the crimes of the previous years. But many human rights activists, including Bishop Gerardi, who had participated in the peace negotiations, doubted that the UN commission would be able to provide a thorough accounting of events. The commission was not permitted to identify human rights violators by name or assign responsibility for killings. Testimony given to the commission could not be used for future prosecutions. As a counterweight, under Gerardi's guidance, ODHA had initiated a parallel and supportive investigation, the Recovery of Historical Memory Project (Recuperación de la Memoria Histórica), known as REMHI (REM-hee), which in April 1998 produced *Guatemala: Never Again*. Bishop Gerardi wrote an introduction to the report.

On Wednesday, April 22, Bishop Gerardi, along with Ronalth Ochaeta, a thirty-three-year-old lawyer who was the executive director of ODHA, and Edgar Gutiérrez, the thirty-six-year-old coordinator of REMHI, held a press conference to brief reporters on the general content of *Guatemala: Never Again*. When a reporter asked if they were taking extra security precautions, Gerardi ceded the microphone to Gutiérrez, and turned to whisper in Ochaeta's ear, "*Qué vaina*," which is not exactly translatable, but in this context meant something like, "Damn." Shortly after the murder, Ochaeta saw a newspaper photograph that captured the instant after that whispered exclamation. The bishop had just settled back in his chair, a look of grim preoccupation on his face.

The next evening, Thursday, April 23, Bishop Gerardi and his associates invited journalists and influential personages to a dinner in the Archbishop's Palace in the sprawling Metropolitan Cathedral complex, near the church of San Sebastián. That night, copies of the first two volumes of *Guatemala: Never Again*—"The Impact of the Violence" and "The Mechanisms of Horror"—were handed out. While the guests dined, Bishop Gerardi explained REMHI's methodology, and afterward he took questions. Over a two-year period, he said, some 800 people had undergone intensive training for interviewing and collecting testimony for the investigation. Operating from thirteen regional centers, the "reconciliation facilitators" had spanned out across the country. Guatemala's population is at least 60 percent Mayan Indian, and the Maya, the rural peasantry especially, had borne the brunt of the war's carnage. Well over half of the interviews for *Guatemala: Never Again* had been conducted in fifteen Mayan languages and the rest in Spanish.

On Friday, April 24, *Guatemala: Never Again* was formally presented in the cathedral. The cavernous house of worship—an austerely sturdy, earthquake-scarred, 150-year-old neoclassical edifice—was packed with diplomats, politicians, members of nongovernmental organizations, former guerrillas, journalists, human rights activists, and others. The only body not represented that it would seem should have been was the government of the president of Guatemala, Álvaro Arzú Irigoyen.

Television screens were installed in the two aisles off the nave of the cathedral so that the people sitting and standing there could watch the ceremony at the altar. Despite the gravity of the report, the mood was quietly jubilant. To many it seemed as if Guatemala really was on the verge of a new era. Only twelve days earlier President Arzú had announced on national television that the country had been removed from the UN Human Rights Commission's list of the world's worst human rights violators, a status it had held for nineteen years and which had led to UN sanctions, intrusive observer missions, and periodic suspensions by the U.S. Congress of military aid (although covert and other forms of military assistance, through the CIA and surrogate nations such as Taiwan and Israel—which, for example, built the Guatemalan Army an ammunitions factory—had continued).

Along with the peace accords, the end of Guatemala's position as a pariah state cleared the way for renewed foreign aid and assistance. And now the Church, through REMHI, was initiating a truthful accounting of the past—an accounting that, Bishop Gerardi had stressed on many occasions, was crucial for repairing the country's shredded social fabric and for ensuring that human rights abuses would no longer be protected by an official culture of silence and lies or by a legal system that effectively gave certain institutions and sectors of society carte blanche to commit crimes.

In the cathedral that evening, bishops from every diocese that had been involved in REMHI were assembled at the altar. (Only one of twelve dioceses had declined to participate.) A Lutheran pastor was also invited to speak. "When we began this task, we were interested in learning, in order to share, the truth," Bishop Gerardi said in his speech, "to reconstruct the history of suffering and death, discover the motives, understand the how and why. Portray the human drama, share the pain, the anguish of thousands of dead, disappeared, and tortured. . . . The REMHI project has been a door thrown open so that people can breathe and speak in liberty, and for the creation of communities of hope. Peace is possible, a peace that arises from the truth for each and every one of us."

After the ceremony, there was a reception in the Archbishop's Palace. The crowd, including some 600 of the people who had worked on REMHI in the field, pressed into one of the old colonial-style patios for a traditional repast of tamales and coffee, and to congratulate Bishop Gerardi. Edgar Gutiérrez soon noticed that Gerardi had withdrawn to the end of a corridor alongside the patio and was standing in the shadow of one of the arches, silently observing the crowd. Gutiérrez approached and asked if he felt overwhelmed by so many people. The bishop answered, somewhat vaguely, "It's turned out to be a wonderful night. Hopefully it won't rain." Then he asked, "And you, Edgar, have you made arrangements to leave the country with your family, to go study somewhere until the waters here calm down?"

"They're not calm, Monseñor?" asked Gutiérrez.

"Well, they'll be much more agitated when they finish reading REMHI."

"So then I still have time, Monseñor," said Gutiérrez, with a touch of bravado.

During the final weeks and days of his life, Gerardi had several times warned his young associates to take precautions. He had urged Ronalth Ochaeta to explore the possibility of a scholarship to study at a European university, or to look for a job with an international organization. But Gerardi seemed much less concerned about his own safety. Guatemala, after all, remained a fervently Catholic country, despite a surge in conversions to evangelical Protestantism, particularly during the last decades of the war. Gerardi may have assumed, as everyone else around him apparently did, that his status as a highly visible eminence in the Catholic Church protected him.

SUNDAY, APRIL 26, THE LAST DAY of Bishop Gerardi's life, began normally enough. Margarita López, for more than twenty years the cook and housekeeper at the parish house, served him morning coffee—strong, the way he liked it—in his room. Bishop

Gerardi slept in a simple wood-frame bed. A crucifix hung on the wall above it, and his dentures were in a glass of water on a nightstand. The room was sparely furnished, with bookshelves, a desk, a stereo, and a television set in the corner. Bishop Gerardi donned his robes, pulled on his heavy bishop's ring, and gave the seven AM Mass. Afterward he was visited by his nephew Javier and Javier's children. The assistant priest, Father Mario, later recalled how absorbed the bishop was while watching the children play Nintendo in his room. Father Mario, who was then thirty-four and had shared the parish duties for eight years, was among the first to notice how unusually Bishop Gerardi was dressed that day, in blue jeans and a red-checked shirt instead of his black suit and collar.

At about eleven that morning, Ronalth Ochaeta came to the church of San Sebastián to pick Gerardi up and take him to El Encinal, a wooded hillside residential community overlooking Guatemala City, where Dr. Julio Penados, the archbishop's brother, was giving the celebration for REMHI. They first drove to Ochaeta's house to collect Ochaeta's wife and children—the bishop's "grandchildren," as he liked to say. Ochaeta, a small, stocky man with a cherubic mestizo face, had been working at ODHA for nearly ten years, and Gerardi, it was often remarked, had come to regard him as a kind of son. On the way to the party, Gerardi excitedly recounted impressions of the events of Friday night, and said, "Now I can retire in peace." He played with Ochaeta's children, giving them pieces of chocolate as a prize if they could reproduce the funny faces he made.

The guests at that final Sunday afternoon celebration were mostly colleagues from ODHA and family members. Many recalled later that "Monse"—short for Monseñor—was in an ebullient mood, and they commented on the unaccustomed informality of his clothes. He wore a beige jacket over his jeans. Monse looked, a woman guest told him, as if he'd suddenly shed ten years. There was festive banter, drinks, and, later, bowls of stewed garbanzos and beef. The sky was a brilliant placid blue, the air fresh and fragrant with the smell of pine and eucalyptus trees.

Naturally, when people who were there recount what they remember about that afternoon, they emphasize details that in hindsight seem charged with premonition. And so they recall that at one point Bishop Gerardi said to Ronalth Ochaeta and Edgar Gutiérrez, "You two shouldn't go around together so much. They'll say you're *huecos*"—Guatemalan slang for homosexuals. When the laughter subsided, he insisted he was serious. "Remember, now is when the smear campaigns begin," he warned.

They recall that the main subject of conversation, of course, was the REMHI report. "Now we know what happened, but we don't know who gave the orders," Bishop Gerardi remarked at one point. "I think we need to begin another little project," a new report on "the intellectual authors" of the war's atrocities. He let those words sink in, then cackled mischievously. And Gutiérrez responded, "Ay, Monseñor, if we do that they'll kill us for sure."

And they recall that Edgar Gutiérrez's small son fell from a swing made from a rubber tire suspended by a rope from a tree and cut his lip open badly and that the other children were shouting, "There's blood! There's blood!" and that it was after that, around four-thirty, that the party slowly began to break up. Gutiérrez's mother-in-law, who was visiting from Mexico, was so perturbed by Bishop Gerardi's warnings that she decided that afternoon to take her three grandchildren back with her to Mexico City.

Ronalth Ochaeta, with his wife and two children in the car, drove Bishop Gerardi back to his home at the church of San Sebastián, in a still mostly residential neighborhood in Zone 1. (Guatemala City is demarcated into numbered zones, most encompassing several neighborhoods—*colonias* or *barrios*—which often have names of their own.) San Sebastián was only a few blocks north of the central plaza fronting the cathedral and the recently renamed Palace of Culture—formerly the National Palace, the seat of so many dictatorships. Between San Sebastián and the palace was the presidential residence. They reached the church sometime between five-thirty and five-forty-five. "Don't you have Mass?" Ochaeta asked. The bishop said that Father Mario was giving the six o'clock Mass. They spoke a bit about a trip Gerardi was to take to a conference in Mexico on Wednesday, and Ochaeta assured him that everything was arranged. Bishop Gerardi got out of the car, turned to wave good-bye, and went inside the parish house.

IF BISHOP GERARDI REALLY was contemplating retirement—he occasionally mentioned the possibility, although most people seem to think that he was too energetic and involved in his work, and too important a figure to Archbishop Penados and the Church, to go through with it—the completion of *Guatemala: Never Again* would have represented a logical and triumphant capstone to more than five decades in the priesthood. The son of Italian immigrant merchants, Gerardi had spent most of his first twenty years as a priest serving poor, mostly Indian, rural parishes until being called to Guatemala City, where he worked for two extremely conservative and politically powerful prelates in succession—Archbishop Mariano Rossell and Cardinal Mario Casariego—and served a stint as Chancellor of the Curia. His appointment as bishop of the northern diocese of Verapaz in 1967 coincided with the years of the Second Vatican Council (1965) and the Latin American Episcopate's Medellín Conference (1968), seminal gatherings that committed the Church to a greater openness and its clergy, at the latter conference especially, to a worldlier role, responsive to the needs of the poor.

What to some seemed like aspects of a radical new theology—reforming the liturgy to make it more accessible, for example—must have seemed like practical good sense to the young Bishop Gerardi. The Verapaz diocese ranged over rugged cloud-covered mountains, subtropical rain forests, and rich coffee-growing slopes. It had long served the spiritual needs of a small oligarchy made up of the owners of coffee plantations, many of whom were descended from nineteenth-century German immigrants, at the expense of a rural population of mostly Q'eqchi Maya Indians. For centuries, on the rare occasions when Catholic Masses were given in their isolated communities, the Q'eqchi, many of whom didn't even speak Spanish, heard them in Latin. Bishop Gerardi pioneered the implementation of Mayan-language Masses. He encouraged his priests to learn Q'eqchi and trained and sponsored Q'eqchi-speaking catechists and other lay teachers. "Our Church feels deeply challenged by the reality and situation lived by our indigenous peoples," Gerardi wrote in 1973. "Effectively we find ourselves faced with a situation of exploitation, marginalization, illiteracy, endemic illnesses, poverty, and even misery; all of which amount to a state of injustice, and reveal a state of sin. This situation, seen by the light of our faith, invites us to return to the nucleus of the Christian message, and to create in ourselves the intimate consciousness of its true meaning and exigencies."

Reading over some of the pastoral letters and other writings produced by Gerardi in those and later years, I was struck by how he balanced a traditional sense of pastoral mission—seeking and preaching the mystery of salvation in the example of Christ—with a commitment to the poor. "The suffering of Christ in his mystical body is something that should cause us to reflect. That is to say, if the poor are out of our lives, then, maybe, Christ is out of our lives." The inclusion of that "maybe" was characteristic. Nobody ever described Bishop Gerardi as dogmatic.

In 1980, Gerardi, who had become bishop of the Quiché diocese, in the country's most populous Indian province, escaped an assassination attempt. He nearly became the second bishop to be murdered in Central America within a year. (During the preceding five centuries only one other bishop, in the seventeenth century, had been slain.) Another outspoken and influential prelate associated with liberation theology, El Salvador's Arch-

Bishop Gerardi in Quiché, circa 1975

bishop Oscar Romero, had recently been assassinated by gunmen linked to El Salvador's ruling, far-right ARENA party.

Guatemala's internal war had by then been going on, with various degrees of heated and bloody intensity, for eighteen years. The war was a consequence of a coup engineered by the CIA in 1954 against Jacobo Arbenz, only the second democratically elected president in Guatemala's history. Arbenz had passed an agrarian reform law to alleviate the inequities of a system that he called, in his inaugural address, "feudal." Privately owned uncultivated land—far from all of it—was expropriated and redistributed to landless peasants. Some of the land was expropriated from the country's largest single landowner, the United Fruit Company. The Arbenz government reimbursed United Fruit, though at the deflated prices the company had declared the land to be worth for tax purposes.

United Fruit wielded considerable influence inside the Eisenhower administration through some important personal connections, particularly the Dulles brothers, John Foster and Allen. As Stephen Schlesinger and Stephen Kinzer explained in *Bitter Fruit,* an account of the 1954 coup and its aftermath, John Foster Dulles, the U.S. secretary of state, had negotiated a favorable railroad transportation deal for United Fruit in Guatemala when he was a senior partner in the New York law firm of Sullivan and Cromwell. Allen Dulles, who had also done legal work for United Fruit, was director of the CIA. But the most important motive behind the coup was U.S. government fears of communism. Arbenz had legalized the Party in 1952. (It was quite small, with only a few hundred active members, almost none of whom had much influence.) First the Truman and then the Eisenhower administrations misconstrued the politics behind the Guatemalan government's actions, refusing to acknowledge that Arbenz was essentially a nationalist, with no proven ties to Moscow. And so, on the heels of a similar operation in Iran, in which Prime Minister Mosaddeq was deposed, the CIA's first covert regime-change program in Latin America—which included strident allegations about the imminent establishment of a Soviet military beachead—was soon under way. After several months of economic sabotage, psy-ops maneuvers, threatening gestures by the U.S. military, and an actual invasion by a small rebel force armed and trained by the CIA, Arbenz agreed to resign and asked for political asylum in the Mexican embassy. Guatemala was handed over to an extreme right-wing faction of plantation owners and political leaders who founded their own paramilitary death squads, and to the Guatemalan Army, which was backed by the United States. Arbenz's land-reform policy was reversed and many of its proponents and beneficiaries were murdered. The Guatemalan Army eventually became the most brutal, corrupt, and criminal military institution in the western hemisphere.

Five years after Arbenz was removed as a force in Latin America, the Cuban revolution inspired a new concern about the region. Following an aborted military revolt led by a handful of

Arbenz-era officers in 1960, the Eisenhower administration made the fateful decision to beef up the Guatemalan Army's intelligence units, thus engendering a clandestine apparatus of state terror and crime over which eventually even the United States would lose control. A pair of young soldiers—Lieutenant Yon Sosa and Luis Turcios, both of whom had received elite U.S. military training outside Guatemala—took to the countryside to wage guerrilla war against what they described as "tyranny and humiliation." The uprising had some early support from the now-outlawed Guatemalan Communist Party, but was quickly put down. Although the cause of armed revolution survived, the number of guerrilla forces in Guatemala in the 1960s never exceeded several hundred; yet a counterinsurgency campaign supported by the United States (it was called "counter-terror") had killed some 10,000 civilians by the end of the decade. An especially tragic paradox of that time was that while the Alliance for Progress program sponsored by President Kennedy sought ways to identify and support young moderate democratic reformers in Guatemala—even, in the 1960s, bringing them to the United States to study—Guatemalan security forces and death squads, backed by the United States, murdered those same reformers after they returned and began to practice what they had learned. By the 1970s, two-thirds of the people who'd been sent to study in the United States had been killed.

As the possibilities for peaceful change were cut off by violent repression, the ranks of the mostly Marxist guerrillas swelled. Guatemala's internal war, like the other conflicts soon to follow in Central America (in El Salvador and Nicaragua especially), was usually depicted in the context of rivalry between the United States, the Soviet Union, and Cuba, and local causes were downplayed, but in fact it was essentially a war to protect an entrenched elite. By the early 1980s, the Guatemalan Army's highest-ranking officers had become wealthy. Almost all the death squads operating in Guatemala were linked to the Army, although their activity was regularly blamed on rogue right-wing extremists. Either you supported military dictatorship and the oligarchy or you were regarded as a leftist.

One of my relatives in Guatemala, a politically conservative, devout Catholic physician, known for his nonpartisan commitment to public health issues, was forced to take his family into exile in the 1970s. The barefoot doctors he had trained to deliver essential medical treatment, such as dysentery pills, to the rural poor were being murdered by the Army, which also confiscated a small public clinic he'd built with international donations in the Ixil Triangle town of Nebaj, in a rugged corner of northern El Quiché.

ON JANUARY 31, 1980, El Quiché literally flamed up into the world's consciousness when thirty-seven Mayan peasants occupied the Spanish embassy in Guatemala City to call attention to the violence being inflicted on their communities. Guatemalan security forces stormed the embassy, provoking an inferno that killed all but one of the protesters, as well as embassy staff members and others trapped inside the building. Among the dead was the father of the future Nobel Peace Prize–winner Rigoberta Menchú. That night the sole surviving Indian protester was kidnapped from his hospital bed and killed. His corpse was flung onto the campus of the University of San Carlos, the national public university, before dawn.

The massacre in the Spanish embassy precipitated an international outcry, and Spain broke off diplomatic relations with Guatemala. Not long afterward, a campaign of terror against the Catholic Church that wouldn't abate for years was launched throughout the misty mountain towns, villages, and hamlets of El Quiché, which was populated mostly by Maya. In the departmental capital, Santa Cruz, the seat of Bishop Gerardi's diocese, the mutilated corpses of two Church catechists were discovered hanging outside a small radio station. Convents were strafed with machine-gun fire and attacked with grenades. As the fighting against guerrillas intensified in *el antiplano,* the mountainous central highlands, the Army seized and occupied church buildings, parish houses, and convents, turning them into barracks and interrogation and torture centers. Statues of saints were draped in military camouflage and olive green, as if to remind parishioners to whom they really owed their obedience, at least if it was earthly salvation they sought. The Spanish priest from the village of Chajul, in the Ixil Triangle, was ambushed and murdered. In Joyabaj, Father Faustino Villanueva was assassinated at his desk. Sometimes, after the Army had finally vacated a church parish or convent building, people would leave lighted candles outside for the restless spirits of those who had been murdered inside.

In THE ONCE BUSTLING town of Nebaj, the Army placed a machine-gun nest in the belfry of the church, overlooking the plaza. A few years later, in 1984, I rode the bus from Guatemala City to Nebaj with my friend Jean-Marie Simon, a photographer and journalist who was also a courageous investigator for human rights organizations such as Americas Watch and Amnesty International. In Nebaj we visited a tiny community of nuns who were still residing in a rustic little convent house in the middle of a complex of colonial-era church buildings that the Army had occupied. A nun placed a small tape recorder on a table and we listened to the faint sobs and screams from torture sessions the nuns had recorded through their adobe walls at night. At the time, the Army and civilians who had been pressed into service in rural militias—called civil patrols—were bringing captured Indian refugees down from the mountains by the truckload and settling them in bleak camps, rows of pine shacks with zinc roofs. The camps were called "model villages" and given Orwellian names such as New Life. We accompanied the nuns to the town market to buy food staples and multicolored plastic plates and cups for the refugees. The nuns selected plates and cups in every color but green—the Army's color, one explained in a lowered voice. It was a subtle protest, unlikely to be noticed by the refugees or the Army, but who dared risk anything more?

For years, experts on Guatemala's internal war have argued over how much blame the guerrillas, in particular the faction called the Guerrilla Army of the Poor (Ejército Guerrillero de los Pobres, or EGP), deserved for the violence. Did they, by moving among the population and promising protection they were unable to provide, make the Army's actions inevitable? The guerrillas certainly bear some responsibility. But the Guatemalan Army also had its own agenda, one that, in the early 1980s, foreclosed any chance of a peaceful or negotiated settlement to the war. A national-security-state mentality relegated the entire Mayan *altiplano* into an area in need of the Army's own extremely thorough brand of transforming authority.

For as long as possible, Bishop Gerardi sought to maintain a prudent distance from both the guerrillas and the Army. But on one occasion, often recounted since his murder, he confronted the commander of the Quiché military zone. The Army, he told the commander, was killing many more people than the guerrillas were. In its zeal, Gerardi warned, the Army was falling into lawlessness and was driving people into the arms of the guerrillas. The commander responded by asking for Bishop Gerardi's cooperation—meaning that Gerardi should, for example, identify guerrilla collaborators in his parish. He refused, and the Army began to regard him as its enemy. Demetrio Toj, a lay teacher and radio announcer who was abducted by the Army and tortured but somehow managed a spectacular and extremely rare escape, told ODHA that at one point his tormentors had demanded to know "where Gerardi hides the weapons." Not long after the kidnapping of Toj, Gerardi was warned by villagers in San Antonio Ilotenango that soldiers were preparing an ambush for him. He was guided out of the village by an alternative mountain path at night, under cover of darkness.

Following the escape from death in San Antonio Ilotenango, Bishop Gerardi perhaps lost his nerve. "When you feel death at your door, it paralyzes you," he once confided to Edgar Gutiérrez. Gerardi decided to close the El Quiché diocese, a decision that would long haunt him. But it was an act of protest as well as fear, perhaps partly intended to draw the attention of Cardinal Casariego, an old-fashioned, conservative prelate who assiduously cultivated his relationships with the wealthy and powerful and who used to bless Army tanks with Holy Water. Cardinal Casariego kept silent about the repression, even about the murders of his own priests. His emphatic anticommunism appears to have made him an uncritical supporter of the Army.

The exit of the clergy from El Quiché only deepened the province's isolation while doing nothing to impede the slaughter, and Bishop Gerardi and Próspero Penados, who was then bishop of San Marcos, soon traveled to the Vatican, where, in a private meeting, they informed Pope John Paul II about the situation. The pope was moved by what they said and wrote a public letter to the Guatemalan Episcopal Conference strongly condemning the violence against the civilian population and the persecution of the Church: "I share your sorrow," the pope wrote, "over the tragic accumulation of suffering and death that weighs, and shows no sign of abating, over so many families and your ecclesiastical communities, debilitated not only by the murders of more than just a few catechists, but also of priests, in the darkest circumstances, in vile and premeditated ways. I am particularly saddened by the grave situation in the diocese of El Quiché, where, because of multiple criminal acts and death threats against ecclesiastics, the community remains without religious assistance."

Cardinal Casariego must have felt that open letter as a stinging rebuke. Guatemala's conservative rulers and elites were infuriated. Wasn't Pope John Paul II a symbol of anticommunist resistance all over the world? Why was he siding with the "communists" in El Quiché?

Although Bishop Gerardi asked for a new assignment and permission not to return to Guatemala, the pope ordered him to reopen the El Quiché diocese. Gerardi obeyed, but at the Guatemala City airport he was met by a military contingent that denied him entrance into the country and put him on a plane to El Salvador. Bishop Quezada Toruño, who had gone to the airport with other Church delegates to meet Gerardi's flight that day, recalled years later—by then he was Cardinal Quezada—that it had been his impression that only their presence had prevented the soldiers from taking Gerardi away and probably killing him.

In El Salvador, as soon as he landed, Gerardi was warned by the country's centrist Christian Democratic president, Napoleon Duarte, that assassins were waiting for him. Gerardi flew on to Costa Rica, where he endured three years of anguished exile. Three months after the El Quiché diocese was reopened without him, a priest there was murdered. Before the war was over, more priests, nuns, and religious workers would be "martyred" by violence in El Quiché than in any other diocese in the Americas.

In 1982, a military coup ousted General Lucas García as president of Guatemala and replaced him with General Efraín Ríos Montt, an evangelical Protestant who launched an infamous scorched-earth counterinsurgency campaign in the highlands. There were hundreds of massacres. Over 600 villages and hamlets were burned to the ground, an estimated 70,000 people were killed, and perhaps as many as 1 million refugees fled into the mountains and over the borders. For Gerardi, those were years of helpless depression and guilt at being so far from the fray. They were also years, some people have said, of solitary heavy drinking. But Ríos Montt was overthrown in 1983 by General Óscar Mejía Víctores, and when Cardinal Casariego died later that year the pope named Próspero Penados del Barrio the new archbishop of Guatemala. Penados was a unifying figure for a badly divided Church. He discarded his predecessor's limousine and chauffeur for a Toyota, which he drove himself.

General Ríos Montt had on many occasions openly antagonized and defied Pope John Paul II. For example, Ríos Montt made it a point, on the eve of the pope's first visit to Guatemala, in 1983, to ignore papal pleas for clemency and execute several "subversives" who had been sentenced in special military tribunals that didn't include defense attorneys. In a sorely needed gesture to the Church, General Mejía Victores reluctantly allowed Archbishop Penados to summon his old friend Gerardi back from exile.

ODHA, which Archbishop Penados established in 1989, with Bishop Gerardi as its head, was the first grassroots human rights organization in Guatemala capable of operating on a national scale. Many Guatemalans trusted the Church as they did no other institution—although others, of course, despised it. In any case, the Church was the only organization that could overcome the cultural limitations of the United Nations truth commission, which was why Bishop Gerardi conceived the REMHI project. Guatemala's modern Maya speak twenty-three indigenous languages and dialects, and many do not speak Spanish as a second language. Many of the Maya communities were in military zones where a climate of repression still prevailed long after the fighting had stopped. Tens of thousands of Maya who abandoned their homes during the years of terror, fleeing into remote mountains and forests, had for years been living in semi-clandestine communities—"resistance communities"—inside the country and over the border in Mexico, and also in refugee camps. Bishop Gerardi understood that most Maya villagers wouldn't feel secure cooperating with UN investigators, many of whom were foreigners, unless the Catholic Church could first help dispel deeply ingrained inhibitions and fears against speaking out.

The REMHI report—whatever its flaws as strict social science—was by far the most extensive investigation of the war's toll on the civilian population that had ever been attempted. *Guatemala:*

Never Again identified by name a quarter of the war's estimated civilian dead (the 50,000-plus names fill the fourth volume) and documented 410 massacres, which are defined as attempts to destroy and murder entire communities. Most of the massacres occurred between 1981 and 1983, but some took place as late as 1995. There were also over 1,500 violent killings of three or more civilians at one time. The report compiled estimates of the numbers of refugees created by the war, of widows and orphans, of victims of rape and torture, and of the disappeared. It drew on the testimony of victims, survivors, and combatants from both sides of the conflict, as well as on declassified U.S. government documents. The report also included an examination of its own methods of collecting information, reflecting on such challenges and pitfalls as the unreliability of memory and the passage of time. It analyzed the war's historical background, its impact on communities, its strategies and mechanisms. One chapter cast some light on the most feared and mysterious of the state's entities, Military Intelligence, usually referred to as G-2. (The terminology was adopted from the U.S. Army's classification system: G-1, Personnel; G-2, Intelligence; G-3, Logistics; etc.) The report described the structure and functions of its various units, one of which was devoted to sexual spying (gathering information on cheating husbands or employing prostitute-spies to compromise opponents). Where it had the evidence to do so, *Guatemala: Never Again* identified military units responsible for crimes, and in numerous cases named individuals. The report concluded that the Guatemalan Army and associated paramilitary units, such as the rural civil patrols, were responsible for 80 percent of the killings of civilians, and that the guerrillas had committed a little less than 5 percent of those crimes.

The authors of the REMHI report attempted to describe and illustrate the logic behind what they called "the inexplicable." But numbing numerical estimates, analysis of tactics and causes, and even journalistic reconstructions of specific massacres could "explain" only so much. Bishop Gerardi, as he'd once told Edgar Gutiérrez, had wanted a report that would "enter readers through their pores" and move them. Thus there were hundreds and hundreds of pages of direct testimony distributed throughout the text:

The señora was pregnant. With a knife they cut open her belly to pull out her little baby boy. And they killed them both. And the muchachitas [little girls] playing in the trees near the house, they cut off their little heads with machetes. Case 0976, Santa María Tzejá, Quiché, 1980.

They killed them with machetes, they killed them by strangling and with bullets. They picked up the children by their legs and smashed them against a tree, and the tree they smashed the children against, that tree died, because of so many children smashed against that tree so many times, well the tree died. Case 3336 Río Negro, Rabinal, Baja Verapaz, 1982.

On the 19th of March 1981 the Army came to the village of Chel, and took from the church the 95 people praying there, and they took them down to the river at the edge of the village, and there they massacred them with knives and bullets. The rest of the people were frightened and they fled into the mountains where they were pursued by helicopters. The responsible ones were the Army and the civil patrols. Case 4761, Chel, Chajul, Quiché.

When I looked, they were calling the people to come together and they were ordering them into a church that is there and I stayed hidden where I was, watching everything that was happening, until I saw that no one was left outside, men, women, old people, children, they put them in the church. When I looked, they were closing the doors and then they poured gasoline around and then they set it on fire. That's the testimony I've come to give. Case 977, Santa María Tzejá, Quiché. 1982.

I don't know if it was a captain or a lieutenant who arrived with the soldiers and said, "We're going to finish off this village because this village is with the guerrillas." By one in the afternoon they'd finished killing everyone and only the women and children were left. And then the lieutenant said, "We better kill the women and children so that no one will be left."

They killed the women and children with bombs [grenades], because there were so many children; and as they had pretty young women in that town, well then the soldiers separated out those women. They formed into three groups, and got to work killing those poor people, but the soldiers had their way with the young ones, it was the lieutenant who started fucking around with the poor muchachas [young women]. The two-year-olds were all pressed together into a tight ball, and they were set on fire all pressed together, into a ball, all the children were burned. Case 6070 Petanac, Huehuetenango, 1982.

Josefa [Acabal] was talking with Eulalia [Hernández] when the soldiers came and surrounded the house. They cut up the señoras with knives, they killed them, five people in all. When the corpses were on the ground they started burning the house, they threw the corpses on the fire. Case 4912, Xix Hamlet, Chajul, Quiché, 1983.

The burning fat runs outside, look, how the fat of the poor women runs. It looks like when it rains and the water runs in the gutters. The fat runs like that, pure water. And what's that? I thought as I went in, and pure fat was coming out of those poor women, pure water comes out. Case 6070, Petanac, Huehuetenango, 1982.

A reader might emerge from those pages ready to believe the Guatemalan Army guilty of any crime it might ever be accused of. That would later pose a problem for those who had to investigate and prosecute the case of Bishop Gerardi's murder. They would have to resist drawing prejudicial conclusions emotionally rooted in the savagery of the recent past.

In 1998, when the REMHI report appeared, no Guatemalan military officer had ever been convicted or imprisoned for a crime related to human rights, although a few cases had resulted in convictions against low-level soldiers and members of militias. Some major cases had been stalled in the courts for years, and the amnesty decreed by the peace accords was meant to prevent any more such cases from going forward. But under international law there were conditions in which the amnesty might one day be breached or partially overturned, and *Guatemala: Never Again,* it would later seem obvious, helped to make those conditions seem within reach. Bishop Gerardi had let it be known that evidence collected by REMHI would be made available to people who might later seek justice against either the military or the guerrillas, should circumstances permit.

So the REMHI report introduced unpredictable and unforeseen dynamics into Guatemala's postwar climate. It loudly initiated a public conversation—responsible for 80 percent of the war's crimes!—that the Guatemalan Army and its allies had not expected to have to tolerate, certainly not *within* the country. By anticipating the looming, more authoritative report sponsored by the UN, and by breaking taboos against speaking out and assigning blame, REMHI posed a direct challenge to the amnesty and to the Army's uncontested position at the center of Guatemalan society. There was much at stake in preserving that position. Initially empowered as protectors of the country's oligarchy and of the United States' cold war goals, the Army had became a power unto itself, its officer corps constituting an elite social class that looked after its own interests.

But how could murdering Bishop Gerardi in retaliation for the REMHI report—two days *after* its publication—have served those interests?

2

Soon after arriving at the parish house on that final Sunday evening of his life—after Ronalth Ochaeta dropped him off—Bishop Gerardi, without even changing his clothes, went out again. Father Mario later recounted that when he left his bedroom for the six o'clock Mass, on the short walk down the corridor to the sacristy and the church, he passed the garage and saw that both of the bishop's vehicles—a beige Toyota Corolla and a white VW Golf—were parked there. When he headed back to his room about forty-five minutes later, the VW Golf was gone. But there was nothing unusual about that. As he did every Sunday night, Bishop Gerardi had picked up his sister Carmen at her home —the same house where they'd spent their childhood, in Candelaria, one of the city's oldest and most venerable barrios. The Gerardis had grown up across the street from the home of the Nobel Prize–winning novelist Miguel Angel Asturias, whom they had known as children. There was a statue of Asturias in a traffic island in front of the two houses.

Bishop Gerardi and Carmen went to the home of their nephew Javier, where they watched television and had a simple dinner of *plátanos*, beans, and cheese. Then the bishop drove his sister back to Candelaria, arriving there—as she was able to recall later, because she'd asked him the time—at twenty minutes before ten. They lingered in the car awhile, talking, before saying good-bye.

Carmen watched her brother drive off in the direction of the church of San Sebastián. At that hour, investigators later calculated, with the streets empty of traffic—by day they were usually impossibly jammed—it was a drive that the bishop could have made in five minutes, and probably in no more than eight.

So a few minutes before ten, Bishop Gerardi drove up Second Street and turned left into the driveway that runs between the San Sebastián complex and a tree-filled park. The complex includes, in a row, a Catholic school building, the parish house, the garage, and the church. The park is traversed by a paved walkway leading from Sixth Avenue to the raised plaza in front of the church doors. At night, the park is dark and quiet, and the neighborhood, which bustles by day, because it is so close to the downtown business area and government buildings, is mostly deserted. Shops were shuttered, offices and school buildings were empty, and the heavy wooden doors of faded residences were securely locked. San Sebastián is an old parish, dating nearly to the founding of the city in the late eighteenth century, but the church itself, which is of modest size, with two bell towers, one at each corner, was twice destroyed by earthquakes and twice rebuilt during the past century. A remnant of the colonial era, a statue of the Virgin of Sorrows of Manchén, her chest pierced by numerous swords, her pale polychrome face ethereally sad, lips parted to expel a gentle sigh of pain, stands in a side chapel.

A dead-end side street, Callejón del Manchén, extends two blocks, between Third and Fifth streets, from alongside the church of San Sebastián to the rear of the old National Palace. At the intersections of Callejón del Manchén and Fourth and Fifth streets, guarded security gates protect the presidential residence, which is situated between them. The very wealthy and patrician President Arzú, who is descended from Spanish colonial viceroys and archbishops, was the first Guatemalan president to choose to live in his own home instead of in the presidential residence, which was being used for business and formal ceremonies. Also inside those gates were the headquarters of the Guatemalan Army's Presidential Guard and the Estado Mayor Presidencial (EMP), or Presidential Military Staff. In recent decades there was probably no city block in all of Central America more forbidding or generally feared than that one on Callejón del Manchén, where the EMP and its notorious military intelligence unit, formerly known as El Archivo, were situated. The EMP and the Presidential Guard, aside from overseeing the personal security of the president and his family, sheltered, among its approximately 500 members, an elite anti-kidnapping commando unit. During the war years, there were rarely any survivors of the EMP's interrogation and torture sessions. (According to declassified U.S. documents, Guatemalan Military Intelligence—G-2—and the Archivo, though technically separate, worked hand in hand.) Looming on the other side of Fourth Street, just outside the gates and only about 200 feet from the church, is the modern white-concrete and black-glass multi-story building of the Secretariat of Strategic Analysis (SAE), a government information-gathering agency that up until 1998, at least, was also integrated into the military's intelligence structure.

So the church of San Sebastián is located in an interesting neighborhood, inside an Army security perimeter. The park itself, it would turn out later, when investigators and journalists subjected it to anthropological scrutiny, was its own complex and busy little world of sometimes clashing subcultures. Local office workers came to the park for lunch or snacks purchased from the food stands lining the sidewalks, or to sit on a park bench for a contemplative shoeshine. Young lovers snuggled on the shaded benches along the paved paths in the afternoons. During the day, *lavacarros*, car washers, plied their trade alongside the park, filling their plastic buckets with water from the fountain. Some of the car washers were alcoholic indigents, but most were not, and almost all belonged to a union that collected small dues at an office downtown where classes were offered on such subjects as how to negotiate prices with customers.

But the park was also a place where tribes of teenagers and small gangs of delinquents staked out and sometimes fought over territory—tough high school kids, heavy-metal *rockeros,* petty thieves, *pushiteros* who sold drugs, and even a gang of druggy alleged satanists who always wore black and who sometimes burst into the church to interrupt Masses, shouting obscenities. Young athletes came to play basketball and *fútbol* in the little basketball court near the Chapel of the Eternal Father, on the Third Street side of the church. Later Father Mario would tell police investigators that the smell of marijuana often pervaded the parish house because of the youths smoking outside, in front of the parish house door, and that sometimes they smoked crack. It was naturally assumed, given the character of the neighborhood, and its nearness to the seat of government and military security and intelligence installations, that some of the park's denizens, the vendors, shoeshine men, car washers, and petty criminals, must be *orejas*—ears, informers.

On any given night, as many as fourteen homeless men and a woman or two would take shelter in the covered walkway alongside the parish house garage, or on the plaza in front the church entrance, which was commonly referred to as the "atrium." They slept in beds made from old cardboard and tattered blankets that they folded and stored by day between the beams of the concrete overhang or in other nooks of the church property. Like Guatemala's narco traffickers, gang members, and sports heroes—or like the Turks in *Don Quixote de la Mancha,* "who have the custom of naming themselves according to the flaws or virtues that each possesses"—the indigents had nicknames: Carne Asada (Grilled Meat), Chalupa (Lollipop), El Gallo (Rooster), El Monstruo (Monster), El Árabe, El Canche (Blondie), Ronco (Hoarse One), El Loquito (Little Crazy Man), more than one El Chino (Chinaman), and so on. That was how they were known among themselves and to the police, though most others referred to them, and to such indigents generally, as *pordioseros*, after the beggars' cry "For the sake of God," and as *bolitos*, little drunks. "My *bolitos*," Bishop Gerardi used to say, and they in turn called him *jefe*. ("Another of my *bolitos* died last night," a neighbor recalled the bishop lamenting on the sidewalk one morning.) The indigents were also called *charamileros*, from the name for pharmaceutical alcohol mixed with water that most of them drank, a concoction also known as a *quimicazo*, which sped them toward oblivion and death. Pure alcohol mixed with dirty water from the basin of the park's fountain was claimed by some to be a particularly potent *quimicazo*.

That Sunday evening, two of the park's indigents—Rubén Chanax Sontay, better known as El Colocho (Curly), and El Chino Iván Aguilar—were in Don Mike's, a small liquor-and-grocery store around the corner from the church. Unlike the owners of other, similar *tiendas* in the neighborhood, Don Mike didn't conduct his business through lowered gates after dark. Customers could gather there, small as the store was, lean against the counter sipping beer or soft drinks, and watch the small portable television set that was mounted in a corner.

Rubén Chanax would later tell police investigators that he was originally from the *altiplano* town of Santa Cruz, Totonicapán, and that he'd been living in the park for about four years, since shortly after his discharge from the Army. He was a doe-eyed, Mayan-featured youth of twenty-four, small but muscular, with wavy-bristly black hair rather than the curls suggested by his nickname, and a quiet, self-contained manner. Alone among the indigents who slept in front of the church, he didn't drink alcohol or take drugs. He said that when he first arrived at the park, four years earlier, he was a drinker, but that under Bishop Gerardi's influence he'd stopped. (A somewhat dubious claim, I think, but who knows?) He earned his living as one of the park's *lavacarros*, though because he wasn't in the union, the other car washers wouldn't allow him to fill his plastic buckets at the park's fountain. Bishop Gerardi, who does seem to have taken some interest in him—buying him new sponges and cloths, for instance —used to let him come into the Chapel of the Eternal Father to fill his buckets from the tap in its little garden.

El Chino Iván, taller, skinny, lighter-skinned, and a far more truculent character than Rubén Chanax, was a petty thief, a *cristalero*—one of those who smash automobile windows to steal radios and such. He drank and used drugs, including crack and pills known as *piedras*, stones. He'd turned up in the park a year before the murder, after his parents expelled him from their home, and ever since he had been coming and going, disappearing for weeks, then returning. He had been sleeping in the park for the past month.

Rubén Chanax and El Chino Iván had spent part of that Sunday in their own idle ways, the former going to see a movie in the afternoon and wandering the city, the latter mostly hanging out at a downtown video-game parlor called Indianapolis. At about seven o'clock that night Rubén Chanax came into Don Mike's— the little shop's real name was Arrobeteria San Sebastián—where he found El Chino Iván watching a Chuck Norris movie on TV. The Chuck Norris movie was to be followed, on Channel 3, by the adventure thriller *Congo*.

Rubén Chanax bought a prepackaged cup of dehydrated ramen noodles and took it back into the park, where, in front of the church, he built a small fire and boiled water in a tin can to make the soup. After his supper, he hurried back to Don Mike's to watch *Congo*. Chanax was a passionate moviegoer, a denizen of the cheap downtown movie theater complexes. Later he would explain that because he'd already seen *Congo* several times and knew how it turned out, he'd left the store before the movie ended, crossed the street, and headed into the darkened park to sleep. He recalled that the clock in Don Mike's said it was a little before ten. The station manager at Channel 3 later confirmed that *Congo* had ended at five minutes after ten.

Near the park entrance Rubén Chanax saw a couple sitting on a bench in the shadows. He ascended the park's slight incline through the darkness, toward the parish house garage. The soft lights outside the garage were on. The church sacristan, when he went home at night, would leave the lights on for Bishop Gerardi if he was out, and Gerardi would turn them off when he returned. Next to the garage doors, on the side closest to the church, there was a grated window. Rubén Chanax climbed onto its ledge and reached up into the beams, where his blanket and the cardboard he slept on were stored. In the more exposed church "atrium" several of the indigents were already asleep, laid out in a row like rag-covered bundles, bodies close together for warmth.

Chanax liked to sleep in a corner in front of the garage, sheltered by the concrete overhang. Lately he'd been sharing that space with El Chino Iván. But sleeping there meant having to get up whenever a vehicle, always Bishop Gerardi's Toyota or VW Golf—Father Mario didn't drive—came into or out of the garage. The garage door was made of hinged, black-painted steel panels that were pulled open and closed laterally, accordion-like, along a rail at the top. The garage door could be opened only from the inside, and there was a smaller door in one of the panels that Bishop Gerardi, when he was the driver, would first have to unlock and enter through. Leaving his car idling in the driveway, he'd step in through the small door, haul the cumbersome and noisy garage door open, get back into the car, and drive it inside. Apparently, he always opened and closed the garage door himself. He never accepted help.

As Rubén Chanax laid out his bedding, he said later, the small metal door to the garage suddenly scraped open. Illuminated by the lights inside the garage, a man in his twenties stood framed in the doorway. Chanax described the man as dark-skinned, of medium height and build, and strikingly muscular. He had large eyes, strong features, a light beard, and a mustache. But the most striking thing about him was that he was naked from the waist up. Guatemala City is a mountain-plateau city, and the nights can be chilly. People don't go around shirtless, as they might in the hot lowlands and on the coasts.

Chanax asked the half-naked man if a car was about to come out. The man answered, "*Simón, ese*"—a somewhat gangsterish phrase meaning, "Yeah, man." At that moment, a police patrol car drove up Second Street, and the shirtless man stepped back into the little doorway, pulling it partly shut, and stood frozen, watching through the trees and darkness as the patrol car turned left onto Sixth Avenue and continued past the park and the church. Then the shirtless man stepped out again and ran to Second Street, where he veered right, toward Seventh Avenue. He wore jeans, Chanax would tell the police investigators later that night, and black boots with yellow soles, probably Caterpillar brand boots. About five minutes after the shirtless man left, Chanax saw him return, walking up Second Street, but now he was buttoning on a long-sleeved shirt; he turned onto Sixth Avenue. Chanax said the shirt was white.

El Chino Iván later said that he left Don Mike's about five minutes after Rubén Chanax, when *Congo* was over. He was already inside the park when he realized that he'd left his cigarettes behind in the little shop. El Chino Iván said that before turning back to retrieve them, he saw Chanax speaking, in front of the garage, to a man who was naked from the waist up.

Moments later, in front of the church, another of the indigents, Marco Tulio, shared a plastic bag of food with El Chino Iván. Rubén Chanax said that he joined them there. At about eleven o'clock every night, representatives from Eventos Católicos, a charity organization that delivered simple meals to the homeless around the city, stopped at San Sebastián. But much earlier that Sunday night, investigators would learn later from the indigents, a stranger had turned up at the park bearing a special offering: Kraft cheese sandwiches and three uncapped liter bottles of beer—"not the normal thing," according to El Chino Iván.

Some of the *bolitos* would claim later that the beer and food must have been spiked with a soporific, because they quickly became drowsy and fell into a heavy sleep. This was why, they said, they hadn't heard or seen anything unusual that happened in and around the garage. They couldn't even remember Bishop Gerardi returning in his white VW Golf.

El Chino Iván, who had not grown accustomed to lying on the hard pavement, exposed to the elements, was usually a restless sleeper, but that night, he said, soon after partaking of the purportedly drugged leftovers from Marco Tulio's plastic bag, he fell into a deep sleep that was undisturbed until six in the morning, when police and investigators from the prosecutors' office roused him. That was when El Chino Iván would describe his own encounter with the no-longer-shirtless man. After he'd gone back to Don Mike's for his forgotten cigarettes—he said that Don Mike handed them to him through the now lowered gates—and was headed back into the park, he came on the same half-naked man he had spotted talking to Rubén Chanax minutes before, except now the stranger was wearing a shirt that El Chino Iván described as light beige with light brown checks. According to El Chino Iván, the stranger said, "*Compadre,* sell me a cigarette." El Chino Iván handed him two cigarettes, and the stranger gave him a one-quetzal bill, worth about fifteen cents (El Chino Iván later turned the bill over to the police), and said, "*Buena onda, gracias*"— roughly, "Cool, dude, thanks." Then he left again, this time heading out of the park and down Sixth Avenue, in the direction of the presidential residence.

The question of whether it was really only a few minutes, or quite a bit longer, between the moment when El Chino Iván turned back for his cigarettes and the time when he returned to the park, would come to obsess ODHA's investigating attorney, Mario Domingo. It was one of many nagging, seemingly small mysteries related to the crime, and one that Mario Domingo would not solve, at least to his own satisfaction, for another five years.

Rubén Chanax said that he hadn't partaken of the allegedly spiked food and drink. He and El Chino Iván lay down to sleep in their usual space in front of the garage, and when the man from Eventos Católicos arrived that night, before eleven, to bring the indigents their meals, he rose to receive his, quickly devoured it, and went back to sleep. The man from Eventos Católicos said later that the only unusual thing he noticed that night, apart from how soundly the *bolitos* were sleeping, was that the light inside the garage was on.

Don Mike, whose real name is Miguel Angel Hércules Garcia, and who was thought by park locals to be an informer, had little to say about the events of the night of the murder. He would claim, in his first statements, that he had closed his shop before nine-thirty, and that El Monstruo Jorge and Pablo el Loquito had been inside earlier, watching the movie. He claimed not to know anyone who went by Rubén Chanax's nickname, El Colocho, but he said it was possible that, if he saw such a person, he would recognize him. Later Don Mike would refuse to say very much more to investigators and certainly not to journalists. Whenever any of the latter came to his shop to talk, he would withdraw into the back room.

The *bolitos* El Monstruo Jorge and Pablo el Loquito didn't seem to have anything useful to communicate to investigators about that night either. But no one will ever be able to discover if it was simpy alcohol and drugs that erased whatever memories they might have had or if simple fear played a role. Within just a few years the two indigents, like virtually all of the other *bolitos* who were sleeping outside the parish house on that Sunday night—with the exception of Rubén Chanax and El Chino Iván— would be dead.

* * *

USUALLY, ON ARRIVING back at the San Sebastián parish house on Sunday nights after his dinner with his family, Bishop Gerardi would phone Juana Sanabria, the parish administrator and his longtime close friend, to let her know that he had arrived safely. On Saturday nights, Bishop Gerardi customarily dined with Juana Sanabria and her teenage daughter in their home, and then they would watch a movie starring Cantinflas, the classic Mexican comedian, on television. Perhaps nobody was closer to Bishop Gerardi than Juana Sanabria and her daughter. But sometimes Bishop Gerardi forgot to call, so when ten o'clock passed that Sunday without any message, Juana Sanabria at first tried to reassure herself that there was no reason to worry. She couldn't restrain her anxiety, however, and, at ten-thirty she phoned the parish house. For the next hour or so, Juana Sanabria said, she phoned every fifteen minutes, and then, worried about disturbing Father Mario, she gave up.

For a long time it was generally believed that Juana Sanabria had called the bishop's private line, in his bedroom, which was why, according to Father Mario, he couldn't hear it ringing. But the sacristan said that the telephone in the bishop's bedroom could be heard throughout the house. Later, Juana Sanabria testified that she had called three different numbers at the parish house that night. She understood the dangers that came with having published the REMHI report, and she'd noticed, that last Saturday night when Bishop Gerardi was in her home, that he was preoccupied, so much so that he hadn't even stayed for the Cantinflas movie, which always made him laugh. Juana Sanabria would testify that when neither Bishop Gerardi nor anybody else answered any of the parish house phones on Sunday night, she was overcome with fear and foreboding, and began to weep.

At about half past midnight, perhaps somewhat earlier, the front door of the parish house opened and Father Mario stepped out in his bathrobe and pajamas. Rubén Chanax told investigators later that morning that the priest called out to the row of sleeping *bolitos:* "*Muchá*"—which can be short for *muchacho,* or *muchacha,* or, as in this case, the plural of those (boys, or youths)—"did any of you see who came in or went out?" One of the *bolitos,* who was known as El Pitti, and who liked to drink only lethal *quimicazo* and so had forgone the presumably spiked beer, answered, "Don't worry, Father, Monseñor went in a while ago."

Rubén Chanax said that he got up from his blanket and approached Father Mario and told him that he'd seen a *muchacho* come out of the garage and that this *muchacho* had been naked from the waist up. According to Chanax, the priest said, "Ah, then stay here, because I've phoned the police." Chanax's many subsequent testimonies would never vary regarding what he told the priest, but the first police investigators dispatched to the scene of the murder would report Father Mario's own account of that moment following his discovery of the body in the garage: "He went to the parish house door, interrogating the '*bolitos*' who slept in the external part, to the right of the garage, if they had seen anyone coming in or out, the interrogated answering in the negative." Two days later, in a declaration given to the special prosecutor assigned to the case, the priest would again give the impression that the *bolitos* had answered by saying they had seen nothing unusual, leaving Chanax out of his account. But Father Mario's two subsequent declarations, on May 15 and on July 22, would coincide, at least in that one respect, with Chanax's.

Father Mario later told investigators that he had spent Sunday afternoon, after the midday Mass, in his bedroom, watching television and dining on his favorite food, fried chicken delivered from Pollo Campero, a popular fast-food chain. After the evening Mass, he took his eleven-year-old German shepherd, Baloo, for a brief walk in the park. A female parishioner who'd attended the Mass asked to speak with him, and he brought the dog inside and went back and spoke to the woman for about ten minutes. At about that time, the choir members who'd sung in the evening Mass left the church. Back in his bedroom, Father Mario changed into his pajamas at his usual hour, around seven-thirty, and went to the parish house kitchen to take medicine for a severe migraine condition. In the kitchen he spoke briefly to Margarita López, the cook, and to the sacristan, Antonio Izaguirre. Usually Margarita López, after serving breakfast, had Sundays off and went to spend the day with her family, but on this Sunday, because of a bad chest cold, she had stayed in the parish house. She and the sacristan shared an evening meal and Margarita López retired to her bed. Around eight-thirty, the sacristan went home. Father Mario fed Baloo, washed up, sat down at his computer, and logged on to the Internet. At about twenty minutes before ten, he said, he turned on the air conditioner and watched television in bed. (In later statements, he would say he was wearing headphones.) A Spanish television show that he wanted to see was on at ten-thirty. He watched the news, but drifted off to sleep, he calculated, at around ten-twenty. He woke half an hour later, turned off the television and lights, and went back to sleep.

At around midnight, Father Mario said, he turned over in bed and was awakened by a light shining through the glass pane over his bedroom door. "Maybe you turn over in bed," he explained during that first statement to prosecutors in the parish house two days after the murder, "and *púchica*"—the inoffensive, popular version of another common though more vulgar exclamation: *puta*! (whore)—"what's going on, and then I said, what's going on, and I got up, right, and I went to turn off the light and I said to myself, Monseñor forgot to turn off the light again." Bishop Gerardi was supposed to turn off the light in the corridor when he got home. But when Father Mario went out, leaving Baloo behind in his room, he saw that more lights were on at the end of the corridor. "And that," he said, "seemed strange to me." The corridor, about thirty feet long, ran the length of the house, from the bedrooms of Father Mario and the bishop, past two small patios, the kitchen, and the cook's bedroom, directly into the garage, which is in an open area at the end of the house that connects to the church. The priest continued: "But look, *licenciado*"—the proper form of address for a lawyer—"sometimes, maybe because of the affection you feel for someone, you don't want to believe that the dead person is that person, right, and so in the first place, like I told you, I didn't recognize him, you saw how he was, right, he was unrecognizable, so I didn't recognize him, and with so many *bolitos* here coming inside . . ."

When Father Mario stepped into the garage, he found Bishop Gerardi lying on his back in a pool of blood between the Toyota Corolla and the wall. His mouth was open and his brutally battered face was covered with blood. His legs were crossed at the ankles, and his hands, "his *manitas*," said Father Mario to the investigators from the prosecutors' office two days later, "his little hands were, I don't know how they were but yes, right, his little hands were how you saw them, he had them like this"—crossed at the wrists and resting on his chest—"and that did seem strange to me, the way he had them crossed, just the way you saw him, that's how I found him, and also, the sweater was there." Near a water tank in the garage, a blue sweatshirt had been left on the floor. A triangular concrete paving stone lay not far from the body and some blood. There was blood everywhere.

Father Mario said that he thought, "Maybe there was a fight here inside, and one of the *bolitos* died." He said that he then went back down the corridor to the front door of the parish house, which was double-locked as always, and he unlocked it and stepped out and that was when he "asked the *bolitos* if they'd seen anything, some fight, some argument or anything, and they said no Father, don't worry Father, Monseñor went in a while ago, and then that's what *killed* me, and I went to my room to get a flashlight, because I didn't think the light was sufficient, not in the garage or anywhere, and I went back and shined it in his face until I realized it was him, and when I realized it was him, I phoned Monseñor Hernández, the chancellor of the Curia."

First, though, he woke the cook, Margarita López, knocking on her door. "Margarita, I told her, 'They killed Monseñor.' And then the cook came out and she went to see, she'd been here working for Monseñor for as long as he'd been here, she was his servant, and it was really terrible for her, she began to cry."

AT ABOUT ONE O'CLOCK in the morning, Ronalth Ochaeta was awakened by the ringing of the telephone in his living room. It wasn't uncommon for the Ochaetas to receive calls in the middle of the night, anonymous voices speaking insults and threats or making weird, menacing sounds. Usually Ronalth's wife, Sonia, got up to disconnect the phone, but this time she didn't want to get out of bed, so Ronalth did. Instead of unplugging the phone, he answered it, and he was surprised to hear the voice of Dr. Julio Penados, who asked how he was, where he was, and then said, "I don't know how to tell you this . . ." Ochaeta's first thought was that Archbishop Penados must have died. "They killed Juanito," Penados said.

What? How? Impossible?

"They attacked him when he was coming into his house and killed him."

Ronalth Ochaeta said he was on his way to San Sebastián, and he hung up. A moment later the phone rang again. It was Dr. Penados, telling him to stay put, that he was sending his son Fernando over to pick him up. In a daze, Ochaeta went back into the bedroom. Sonia was sitting on the bed with the lights on. "What happened?" she asked, and he answered calmly, "They killed Monseñor," and added, a moment later, "*Hijos de la gran puta*"—sons of a big whore. Sonia wailed, "I'm afraid! Don't go, please don't go!" and began to sob.

From far away on the Tulum Zu highway, empty of traffic at that hour, he heard the engine of a speeding car and knew it was Fernando Penados, on the way to pick him up.

*   *   *

FERNANDO PENADOS, the archbishop's twenty-eight-year-old nephew, had been awakened by his father and told of the murder of Bishop Gerardi. The bishop had been Fernando Penados's mentor. Fernando's family had always hoped that he would become a priest. As an unruly teenager with all too secular interests he'd even been sent to live in the Archbishop's Palace in the cathedral, where his family arranged for him to have a seminarian as a roommate. "To see if he could influence my behavior," Penados would tell me later. "But in the end I didn't comprehend much of the process in which I was immersed. And the seminarian decided to leave the seminary." Penados, who kept his hair short, almost in a crewcut, and wore dark sunglasses all the time and T-shirts that showed off a weight lifter's biceps, had an improbably grandiloquent but often playful way of speaking. It wasn't until he was twenty and went to work for Bishop Gerardi at ODHA that he found what felt like a true calling.

When describing his years working under Bishop Gerardi, Fernando Penados frequently used the phrase "my formation." Investigating human rights cases was "a part of my formation," as was this or that memorable conversation, beginning with the two-hour monologue Bishop Gerardi had delivered on Guatemalan political realities during what was supposed to have been his job interview in 1990. Bishop Gerardi frequently took trips abroad to represent ODHA in various international forums, and Fernando Penados occasionally accompanied him. He relished the closeness they shared on those trips, especially on the long flights to Europe. "They were a part of my formation, those ten hours in the air, something I took advantage of," he said. "Talking about how he saw the Army, the war, the civilian sector, the inner workings of the Church, always accompanied by a pair of *wiskitos*." They would sip their whiskeys and talk, Penados said, "about the everyday problems that arise. Well, maybe not so everyday. For example, when I was working with him there was a period when I was going through a divorce. I talked about how difficult it was within my family, which was so conservative. He was at my wedding. I was married by the archbishop and two priests, in the cathedral. They really had me roped up!" He felt that Bishop Gerardi understood him and gave him helpful advice.

Investigating human rights cases for ODHA was probably the best education in criminal investigation that could be had in Guatemala. By the time he was twenty-three, Fernando Penados had been involved in some of the country's most notorious and murkiest crimes, including the murder, in 1990, of the young anthropologist Myrna Mack Chang, who was stabbed twenty-seven times on a downtown street in a political execution faked to resemble a crime of passion or drug-frenzied robbery. Mack was murdered primarily because her research on the war's impact on highland Maya communities, especially internal refugees such as those living in the resistance communities hidden deep in the mountains, had brought her to the Army's attention. (The Army denied the existence of the resistance communities.) The extraordinary investigation and unprecedented court fights that followed, driven by the relentless perseverance of Myrna's sister Helen Mack, had resulted in the arrest, trial—after twelve judges resigned from the case because of death threats—and conviction, in 1993, of the "stabber," Noél Beteta, an Army sergeant and operative in the EMP's covert intelligence unit, the Archivo.

The Myrna Mack case was at that time the last known instance in which a Guatemalan police homicide detective had dared to investigate evidence pointing to the Army's participation in a political murder. The detective, José Mérida Escobar, was a young officer known for his firm character and exceptional tenacity. José Mérida had selected another young police detective, Julio Pérez Ixcajop, to be his assistant, and they soon received warnings from a policeman who knew that Noél Beteta was the killer and that he was from the EMP's Archivo. The policeman told them to be careful, "because there are some things that should be investigated, and others not." When José Mérida persisted, he began receiving threats. He was demoted and then arrested on false charges of dereliction of duty. At his departmental hearing, he revealed that he'd discovered evidence of the Archivo's involvement in Myrna Mack's murder. A few weeks later, in October 1990, José Mérida was assassinated in a park across the street from the National Police headquarters. He took four bullets in the face. A platoon of armed police standing nearby looked on. "They left him to die like a wounded animal," another former criminal investigations police officer would testify before the International Court of Human Rights, in San José, Costa Rica, years later.

The National Police was no place to learn how to be a homicide detective. Fernando Penados took courses in various aspects of criminology sponsored by the FBI and by the French and Spanish governments, and then, in 1996, when he was twenty-six, he left ODHA to take a job as subdirector of investigations in the Public Ministry—more or less the Guatemalan equivalent of the U.S. Department of Justice—a job from which he soon resigned, because, as he put it, "there were too many criminals working there." At the time of Bishop Gerardi's murder, he was teaching at the National Police Academy, as well as studying business administration at Rafael Landívar University.

That Sunday night—or Monday morning, by then—after Penados picked Ronalth Ochaeta up at his home (he said he found Ochaeta in a nearly catatonic state), he drove the less than four miles to the church of San Sebastián in about four minutes. They rode in silence, although finally Penados asked, "What do you think?" and traded a few observations, such as that the church was only a block from the headquarters of the EMP. But it seemed impossible that the Army would dare to murder the bishop. Fernando Penados was on the verge of weeping, and Ochaeta said, "Now isn't the time." He said that they had to stay calm, that they would need all their wits.

It was about one-twenty-five when they reached the church. The police and firemen (the latter have the job of collecting dead bodies in Guatemala, and function as ambulance drivers too) had arrived and were inside the garage. There was more than one Japanese compact parked among the cars in the drive. The door of the parish house was answered by Ana Lucía Escobar, a pretty young woman known as La China. Ana Lucía was a member of the household of Monseñor Efraín Hernández, the chancellor of the Curia, and she was destined for a lasting role in future speculations about the crime. Fernando Penados asked Ana Lucía— he'd known her since childhood—"*¿Qué pasó?*" and remained behind a moment, talking with her, while Ronalth Ochaeta went into the house. Ochaeta walked down the corridor connecting the priests' bedrooms to the kitchen and garage, which was already full of people. The cook, Margarita López, intercepted him, wailing, "*¡Se nos fue! ¡Se nos fue!*" He's been taken from us! Just then Father Mario approached. Father Mario was a bulky, phlegmatic, yet refined-looking person, and he had a serene expression on his thin-lipped, pale face. His eyes were magnified by the lenses of a large pair of designer glasses. "And without my having asked him anything," Ochaeta recalled later, the priest launched into his story of how he had found the bishop's body—the light that woke him, the body he hadn't recognized, and so on. "There he is, lying in the garage, do you want to see him?" asked the priest. Ochaeta said no, and turned into the kitchen, where Monseñor Hernández was huddled with two other priests.

As CHANCELLOR of the Curia—something like the chief administrator of the archdiocese—Monseñor Efraín Hernández was third in the Church hierarchy, behind Archbishop Penados and Bishop Gerardi. His parish was El Calvario, a massive old church located at Eighteenth Street and Seventh Avenue, in one of downtown Guatemala City's busiest and seediest districts. Monseñor Hernández shared the parish house with his longtime cook, Imelda Escobar, and several of her relatives, including her daughter, Ana Lucía, and a nephew named Dagoberto Escobar. It was

Dagoberto who, around midnight, had answered the phone when Father Mario called about the bishop's murder. Monseñor Hernández had been asleep since around ten. When he came to the phone, he asked Father Mario, whom he had known since Mario was a child, if he had called the police and firemen. When Father Mario answered that he hadn't, Hernández told him to do so immediately.

Ana Lucía Escobar, La China, said later that she was awoken by her mother, and that she dressed as quickly as she could, and that she then drove Monseñor Hernández, along with her cousin Dagoberto, to the church of San Sebastián. She said that she remembered glancing at the digital clock in the car and noting that it was a little past midnight, and that they made the drive quickly.

After telephoning Monseñor Hernández, Father Mario made other calls, to his parents and to friends in Houston, Texas, where he often went for medical treatment. He phoned the distraught Juana Sanabria at ten minutes past midnight. When Father Mario told her that the bishop had been killed, and that he was in the garage, she suggested that maybe he was only badly wounded, but the priest repeated that Monseñor was in the garage, and said that she should come immediately and to bring her parish house keys. "I fell apart and couldn't utter a word," she would recount later, "and my legs went weak, and my body wouldn't respond, the news had such a horrible impact, and then I said, Father, I don't feel well." So he told her to stay where she was. She turned on the radio and sat listening to the live coverage from San Sebastián that soon commenced. But first she had her daughter phone the bishop's nephew, Axel Romero, a lawyer, who remembered receiving the call at precisely twelve-fifteen. Romero phoned Father Mario at the parish house to verify the terrible news, and the priest asked him to come right over.

When Monseñor Hernández arrived at San Sebastián, Father Mario led him into the garage. Hernández asked the priest if he'd given the bishop the last rites, and when he answered that he had not, Hernández performed the holy sacrament.

Ana Lucía Escobar told me later, over the telephone, in her small, softly melodic voice, that Monseñor Hernández then came to get her in the parish office. "He took me by the arm and walked me down the corridor, and he said, 'Monseñor is dead, do you want to see him?' At first I said yes, but when we got there, and I saw the blood, I said no, and went back." Ana Lucía was put to work making telephone calls to inform church authorities and others of the bishop's death. First she phoned Archbishop Penados. Ronalth Ochaeta's cell phone was turned off. Then she phoned Dr. Julio Penados. Using a church directory that was in the office, she phoned bishops, members of the Episcopalian Conference, and other parish priests. The people who received those calls telephoned others in turn and the news of Bishop Gerardi's murder, invariably met with exclamations of incredulity and shock, was quickly relayed throughout the city, the country, and beyond. Telephone records would reveal that one of the calls from the parish house was made to a pay phone outside a military academy in San Marcos. The likeliest explanation was that it was a wrong number: the pay phone's number was only one digit off from the telephone number of the Bishop of San Marcos, Álvaro Ramazzini. Still, the day after news of the mysterious call appeared in a newspaper, the phone itself vanished, torn from its post.

Monseñor Hernández sent Ana Lucía to pick up Father Maco, Marco Aurelio González—"the priest with the two Saint Bernard dogs," as Ana Lucía described him—at the church of La Candelaria, because the priest didn't drive.

At twelve-forty AM, the firemen of Substation 2 had received a telephone call from Father Mario, who didn't identify himself, informing them of a dead body in the San Sebastián parish house. Five minutes later, a detachment of firemen left in an ambulance.

At twelve-forty-eight, Father Mario finally phoned the police. He and one of the *bolitos,* El Monstruo Jorge, waited outside the church, and when they saw a police car passing in front of the park—it was now ten past one—they shouted and waved their arms, but the car kept on going. Five minutes later the firemen arrived and went into the garage, where they found Monseñor Hernández praying beside the bishop's body. One of the firemen also knelt to pray.

The police arrived fifteen minutes later. A video taken by firemen provides a relatively composed look at what would, within half an hour, be a chaotic and overrun crime scene. The camera moves as slowly as a deep-sea diver's cinematography around the garage, which is illuminated by fluorescent lights. The white VW Golf is parked on the right side of the garage, behind the beige Toyota. The bishop is lying on his back in the narrow space between a potted palm by the garage wall and the front tire of the Toyota. There is a large pool of blood around his head. His body is partially covered by a rumpled white sheet, and the cuffs of his jeans and his big shoes, the left foot crossed oddly over the right, protrude from underneath. There is a smaller pool of blood on the floor near the VW's front door, which is slightly ajar. The triangular concrete chunk lies beside it on the polished, speckled stone floor, close to an upright, empty Pepsi bottle. Crumpled pages of newspaper are strewn about. Two vivid, parallel streaks of blood on the floor lead away from the VW to where the body lies, ending at the bishop's shoes. The blue sweatshirt is on the floor. And a few feet from the body, near the bishop's head, planted as if it were the last step of someone lifting off into flight, there is a bloody footprint.

In the kitchen, the refrigerator had been left open, and it appeared that at least one of the intruders had drunk from a half-filled pitcher of orange juice that had been full when Margarita López had gone to bed that night. A half-eaten raw hot dog was found in the dirt of one of the potted palms in the garage. An assistant prosecutor assigned to the case would deduce later that night that the piece of hot dog might have been left there by a stray cat that was frequently seen about the house.

* * *

DURING HIS YEARS as executive director of ODHA, Ronalth
Ochaeta often displayed a temperamental and pugnacious personality that struck some as supercilious. He made enemies and,
sometimes, mistakes. But he also, as the coming months would
show, often made headway where a more restrained or passive
personality might not have. When Ochaeta stepped into the
kitchen of the parish house, Monseñor Hernández, a small,
plump figure with a rabbit-like face and slanted, almond-shaped
eyes, said to him, "This is what happens for trying to investigate
the past." And Father Maco, the priest whom Ana Lucía had gone
to pick up at La Candelaria, said, "Yes, I was never in agreement
with that." Ochaeta snapped, "You were never in agreement with
anything that Monseñor did, so don't give me stories." Monseñor
Hernández broke in, "Well, what are you going to do now?" And
Ochaeta answered, incredulously, "What am *I* going to do? You
mean what are *we* going to do!" A third priest, a Spaniard whose
surname was Amezaga, a Church conservative, stared at Ochaeta
and then said, "But you in ODHA have the experience and should
know what to do."

Then a furious Fernando Penados stormed into the kitchen
and said, "Ronalth, come out here! These people are already altering the crime scene! They're shit! I asked them to widen the area
inside the security cordon and they don't want to!"

The first policemen to arrive had hung yellow tape around an
area enclosing the body and the two cars. Even the bloody footprint had been left outside the perimeter of that first cordon, as
well as other footprints at the back of the garage. Various crime-
scene specialists had arrived soon after, as had the lawyer Axel
Romero, the bishop's nephew, among many others. People were
walking around the body, and into and out of the garage and
parish house. Some were even ignoring the yellow tape, stepping over it, and eventually it was knocked down. The tape itself

became stained with blood. People tracked blood throughout the house.

Fernando Penados shouted at the police, ordering that the cordon be made wider. They obeyed, but then moved it back again. "Of course, later they made it much bigger," Penados recalled later, "but by then the crime scene was totally contaminated." Penados went outside and began shouting and kicking at the somnolent *bolitos* to wake them up, because surely they had seen or heard something.

THE CROWD GREW. Edgar Gutiérrez, from ODHA, was there, as was Helen Mack. Years before, Gutiérrez, who was an economist, had worked for a foundation with Helen's sister Myrna, the young anthropologist murdered by the EMP's Archivo. Before her sister's death, Helen Mack, whose physical resemblance to the character Peppermint Patty in "Peanuts" was often remarked on, was a shy, sheltered real-estate agent from a religiously devout Chinese-Guatemalan family. She belonged to the ultraconservative Roman Catholic order Opus Dei, no less. Helen Mack was still working in real estate and finance, but she was also the founding director of the Myrna Mack Foundation. Her long and still ongoing pursuit of justice for her sister's murder had made her Guatemala's most formidable and admired human rights activist. Intelligent and seemingly fearless, Mack projected a focused and even cold implacability along with the most disarming emotional vulnerability, often breaking into heartrending tears when discussing her sister's murder or having to address the press after yet another discouraging reversal in the courts. Eloquent in public, in private she was usually considerate and kind but also straightforward, blunt, and often astonishingly salty. In that way she resembled Bishop Gerardi, with whom she'd worked closely over the years. Fernando Penados liked to say that it was his dream to one day be head of the Presidential Guard, but only when Helen Mack became president.

Jean Arnault, the French head of the United Nations Peace Verfication Mission, which was assigned to monitor Guatemala's compliance with the Peace Accords, also arrived on the scene. The multinational mission, which was referred to by its Spanish acronym, MINUGUA (min-U-gwa), was a ubiquitous presence in Guatemala. Arnault was accompanied that night at San Sebastián by Cecilia Olmos, a Chilean working at MINUGUA's headquarters in Guatemala City, and Rafael Guillamón, a veteran investigator from Spain with years of expertise in Arab counterterrorism. Guillamón, who was in his early forties, was broad-shouldered and compact, with a scruffy reddish beard. He was MINUGUA's chief police investigator, and he and his small team of two other agents reported solely to Jean Arnault.

The prosecutors of the Public Ministry were assigned cases according to a numeric rotation system, and that weekend Prosecution Unit 6, which was led by Otto Ardón Medina, was on duty. Gustavo Soria, one of the assistant prosecutors from Unit 6, had arrived at San Sebastián shortly before his boss that night. Ardón, a lugubrious, retiring man, mostly hung back and watched the younger, comparatively sleek and self-confident Soria direct the police.

Outside the garage, the groggy indigents told the police that Rubén Chanax had information. He was the only one among them who didn't drink, they said, and so he'd "seen everything." Chanax told the prosecutors and the police about the shirtless man who'd stepped out of the garage. He was whisked away to a police station, and his long journey as a protected witness, in the custody of the National Police and the Public Ministry, began.

Back inside the house, Ronalth Ochaeta was struck by Father Mario's seemingly preternatural serenity, and by how neatly dressed he was, all in black, in a black leather jacket, his hair looking recently washed and combed. He abruptly asked the priest what had happened, and Father Mario again launched into his story. Later, when Ochaeta asked if he could use the bathroom in the priest's bedroom, Father Mario said no, and directed him to another bathroom in the house. Ochaeta watched Father Mario going into his bedroom and thought it was odd, the way he opened the door just enough to be able to slide in sideways.

The attorney general, the head of the Public Ministry (a presidential appointee), arrived and embraced Ochaeta. *"Hijos de puta,* this has all the marks of *los de allí enfrente,"* he said—"of those from just over there." He obviously meant the EMP's military intelligence unit. He telephoned another prosecutor from his office, Fernando Mendizábal de la Riva, who came to the church and, soon after arriving, remarked to Rafael Guillamón, MINUGUA's chief investigator, "This looks like the work of *esa gente*—those people." In Guatemala such euphemisms are easily understood. But Mendizábal de la Riva was known to be a friend of General Marco Tulio Espinosa, who until his recent promotion to head the Army High Command had been the head of the EMP, and was now seen as the most powerful figure in the Guatemalan Army. So even people with powerful political appointments, like the attorney general, and a friend of the Army's most powerful general, were capable of spontaneous observations that later they would most likely deny having made. Even politically compromised and complicit people do not always behave predictably, just as, of course, the most disciplined and intricately plotted crime does not always turn out exactly according to design.

Nery Rodenas, the coordinator of ODHA's legal team, lived well outside the city with his wife and small children, and he didn't have a telephone, so someone from ODHA drove to his house and brought him back to San Sebastián. Rodenas had studied law at the public university, San Carlos, at the same time as Ronalth Ochaeta. But while Ochaeta made his name in political circles as a member of the University Students' Association, Rodenas was the leader of a Catholic students' group. He had converted from Protestantism to Roman Catholicism as a teenager. Tersely soft-spoken, Nery Rodenas had the melancholy eyes, rosebud mouth, plump cheeks, and somewhat stiff but gentle air of a clerk in a Botero painting. Of all his colleagues at ODHA—at least the ones I was to get to know—Rodenas was the only devout, practicing Catholic.

Nery Rodenas reached the church of San Sebastián sometime between two and two-thirty in the morning and pushed his way through the crowd gathered in front of the garage door. All around him people were weeping, or conversing in hushed tones, or taking notes and snapshots as Gustavo Soria and the police worked inside the now re-expanded security cordon. Rodenas turned around and saw a man—short, brown-complexioned, with a mustache—taking photographs with a flash, and he realized that he had seen him before. The man wasn't a photojournalist. Rodenas had seen him in the old colonial city of Antigua, at the trial of the accused murderer of a twenty-year-old milkman named Haroldo Sas Rompich.

THE PRESENCE of the short man who was taking photographs was one of hundreds of threads of evidence that would eventually be woven into the investigation and prosecution of the murder of Bishop Gerardi, Guatemala's "crime of the century"—the most important, and certainly the most bizarrely spectacular, passionately contested, and convoluted legal case in the country's history. Years later Rodenas and others would still be pulling on that particular thread, investigating and debating its significance.

One day in February 1996, President Álvaro Arzú, not even a month into his term as president, and his wife had been horseback riding through the countryside near Antigua, accompanied by their EMP bodyguards in a caravan of vehicles and horses, when the milkman Sas Rompich drove into their path in the 1984 Isuzu pickup in which he made his daily rounds. It is possible that Sas Rompich was at least a little drunk. Earlier, he'd stopped at a small country store to drink a few beers to help lighten a hangover, and now he was on his way to the farm where he picked up his milk.

Captain Byron Lima, of the EMP Presidential Guard, alertly rode his horse into the path of the oncoming pickup, holding out his hand for the driver to stop, but the pickup kept on coming forward, and the horse reared, throwing its rider, who broke his arm. The pickup then crashed into a parked car by the side of the road. Apparently confused and panicked, the milkman accelerated, then rocked into reverse, and another officer jumped onto the pickup's running board and reached in for the ignition, trying to bring the vehicle under control. Someone else shot out the rear tires. A guardsman drove his car against the front of the pickup, blocking it, and someone went right up to the pickup with a nine-millimeter pistol in his hand, reached in through the window, and fired three bullets into the milkman, including one into his ear, killing him instantly.

The government subsequently announced that the president's bodyguards had heroically prevented an attempted double assassination of President Arzú and his wife. No one could deny that the milkman had given the first couple a scare. The first lady had turned and galloped her horse into a nearby field, leaping a fence. In the past, the declaration of a threat to the president would have been enough to put an end to the matter. The legal system, the press, and all relevant actors would have asked no more questions. But in the new climate established by the Peace Accords people were willing to entertain the idea that the president's security guards might have displayed a reckless disregard for human life, perhaps even committed murder.

ODHA lawyers represented the victim's family at the trial of the guardsman, Sergeant Major Obdulio Villanueva, who was accused of having murdered the milkman. Mario Domingo's account of the incident, which was also the prosecution's, as narrated above, was based on the testimony of the sole civilian witness: a youth who was out riding his bicycle when, as he was about to overtake the slow-moving presidential caravan, he was ordered to dismount and walk alongside.

At the trial, members of the EMP and other military types crowded the courtroom. The short, dark photographer that Nery Rodenas saw the night of Bishop Gerardi's murder had turned up daily to focus his camera on the people from ODHA and others who had come to observe the unprecedented trial of a member of the president's security force. He was also seen outside the courthouse photographing the license plates of automobiles. Suspecting that the photographer was not a journalist, Ronalth Ochaeta asked the judges at the trial to demand that he identify himself. The photographer's identification card revealed that he was from the EMP. In the end, Obdulio Villanueva received a five-year sentence for the murder of the milkman. ODHA had asked for the maximum penalty under the circumstances, thirty years.

That night in the church of San Sebastián, Nery Rodenas sought out Ronalth Ochaeta and Fernando Penados and told them that there was a man from the EMP taking pictures inside the garage. When Jean Arnault, the head of MINUGUA, dispatched his investigators to look into the matter, the photographer identified himself as a member of the director of the National Police's advance security. By then, Nery Rodenas and some of the others had noticed that the photographer wasn't alone. A tall, thin man who wore a red baseball cap, with the bill pulled low over his face, accompanied him. Later the man was seen in the park, talking into a portable radio.

Ángel Conte Cojulún, the director of the National Police, arrived at San Sebastián at three in the morning. When he was informed that his advance security had been inside the parish house taking photographs, he responded that he didn't have any advance security. Accompanied by the MINUGUA investigators, Conte Cojulún went to speak with the suspicious men, who insisted on talking with him alone. After a few minutes, the two men left the park, and Conte Cojulún spoke to Fernando Penados. "Listen, Fernando, they're with the EMP," he said. "Don't make such a big deal out of it."

* * *

AT SOME POINT during that long night, Helen Mack and the bishop's protégés from ODHA, Ronalth Ochaeta, Edgar Gutiérrez, and Fernando Penados, huddled together on the ground in one of the inner patio gardens of the parish house and had a conversation, which, as the situation developed over the next few days, resulted in a decision that ODHA should form its own team to document the case. Experience had taught them that it would be naive to assume that an investigation conducted by the government would not be biased, or that it would go after the most obvious suspects, the people in the Army, or with ties to the Army, most threatened by the REMHI report.

The idea that ODHA should form its own team seems to have been Helen Mack's. She also suggested that night that forensic anthropologists from ODHA should attend the autopsy of the bishop's body. ODHA teams were participating in the exhumations of clandestine graves and massacre sites then being conducted throughout the country, and Ochaeta phoned two of the forensics specialists.

Ronalth Ochaeta and Edgar Gutiérrez agreed that they shouldn't leave the parish house until the bishop's body was taken to the morgue. "I just sat there," Ochaeta recalled. "I'd get up, sit down, get up. Edgar too. Nobody said anything. I think an hour, an hour and a half went by. We just looked at each other without saying anything."

Helen Mack, though, was in constant motion. She had gone to fetch her friend Dr. Mario Iraheta, a respected forensics specialist, and bring him to San Sebastián. Now she came to sit with the men from ODHA. "*Chafas cerotes hijos de la gran puta,*" she burst out. *Chafas* is slang for military officers; *cerotes* is a common Guatemalan vulgarism, something like little pieces of shit. "*Chafas cerotes hijos de la gran puta!*" she repeated several times. "*Estos pisados fueron*—those assholes did it." Then she took out her cigarettes and sat smoking in silence.

In the parish house garage, Dr. Iraheta worked alongside Dr. Mario Guerra, head of forensics for the Judicial Morgue. They carefully washed the murdered bishop's wounds, cleaning the blood from the face, which had received repeated blows with some hard object—apparently, the triangular chunk of concrete —delivered with almost inconceivable ferocity. The most obvious wounds were fractures in both cheeks and around and across the nose, bloody bruises over the right eye, and multiple bruises in the back of the skull. The left ear was a particularly excoriated mass. On the bishop's neck there were bloody scratches that indicated a struggle—marks that might have been caused if the zipper of his jacket was pulled against his skin while he fought to free himself, or perhaps when a thin gold chain, affixed to a religious medal, was torn from around his neck.

Bishop Gerardi had apparently received the first blows as he emerged or was pulled from the car. Axel Romero discovered a lens from the bishop's eyeglasses in the pocket on the inside of the door on the driver's side. There was blood inside the car, and grains of concrete. The keys were missing, and the Public Ministry towed the car away that night. Later, when ODHA was told that they could take the car back, Nery Rodenas went to get it, bringing the spare set of keys left behind at the parish house. When the car's ignition was turned on for the first time since the night of the bishop's death, the air conditioner and radio came on simultaneously. The bishop hadn't had the chance to turn either off. The assailants must have reached in, switched the ignition off, and yanked out the keys.

Sometime before dawn, when the firemen took Bishop Gerardi's body to the morgue, Ronalth Ochaeta and Edgar Gutiérrez walked over to the ODHA offices. They had to prepare a statement. In a few hours, people would be awakening to the shocking news of Bishop Gerardi's murder. Everyone—the press, the government, the diplomatic community, all of Guatemala—would be waiting for the reaction of the Catholic Church and of ODHA. They had to think about what they were going to say.

Father Mario said later that he approached a crime-scene specialist from the Public Ministry, asked for permission to clean up the garage, and was told to go ahead. Margarita López; the sacristan, Antonio Izaguirre; and Julio Trujillo, whose job it was to tend to the venerated statue of the Virgin of Sorrows of Manchén, set to work mopping up the bishop's blood and cleaning the garage. Trujillo found more bloody footprints in the entrance of one of the little offices at the back of the garage, but he was told to keep mopping, and he did.

When the cleaning up of the garage—the destruction and washing away of evidence that might have still remained at the crime scene despite the earlier chaos and carelessness—became a scandal in the press, Father Mario repeatedly insisted that someone from the Public Ministry had told him that it was OK. The priest couldn't identify that person by name but said he was a tall man with a beard. By then Father Mario had become the focus of much speculation and suspicion, public and private. So when no one from the Public Ministry stepped forward to take responsibility for the "error," or to identify the "bearded man," many assumed that the priest was lying, and that he had ordered the cleanup of the garage entirely on his own.

Edgar Gutiérrez told me later that while he realized that people say the opposite about Father Mario's demeanor that night, he personally did see the priest quietly weeping. Others described feeling strangely chilled when, after Bishop Gerardi's body was taken to the morgue and the garage and house had been mopped and cleaned, the priest emerged from the parish house, expressionless, immaculately dressed and groomed, to walk his German shepherd, Baloo, in the park.

Margarita López laid the bishop's robes out on his bed, and later that morning Father Mario took the clothing to the funeral home. He oversaw the dressing of the bishop's corpse and assisted the undertakers in reshaping the ruined face so that it would resemble the living one as much as possible.

At about six in the morning El Chino Iván, roused from his night of soporific-induced deep sleep, had told the police of his encounter with the shirtless man, and had handed them the quetzal bill that he said the stranger had paid him in exchange for two cigarettes. Then El Chino Iván slipped away, disappearing into the city. Two days later, he would turn up at MINUGUA's office, claiming that he feared for his life, and soon after he joined Rubén Chanax in the subterranean life of a protected witness in the custody of the Guatemalan police.

Meanwhile in the early morning hours of April 27, in the Public Ministry, Rubén Chanax was giving the first of his many official statements. He wouldn't get a chance to sleep until ten o'clock that night, twenty-fours after he had walked out of Don Mike's. Along with the prosecutors, observers from MINUGUA, and the director of the police, three of the young men from ODHA were present for Chanax's interrogation. He seemed a little frightened but calm, Nery Rodenas recalled, and clearly wasn't muddled by alcohol or drugs. Once again, Chanax described the shirtless man. He had brown skin, big eyes, a big round face, a wide mouth, a small mustache, a light beard, and curly hair, cut short, "military-style." When challenged by his interrogator about the haircut, Chanax insisted that he had spent thirty months in the Army and could recognize a military haircut when he saw one. According to El Chino Iván's later testimony, the shirtless man's hair was not curly, and he didn't have a beard.

Rubén Chanax told his interrogators that about ten nights earlier a man known to the indigents as El Chino Guayo had turned up at the church to sleep, and that he'd asked what time Bishop Gerardi usually returned to the parish house at night. Chanax claimed to have answered that he didn't know. El Chino Guayo was described by some of the other indigents as a crackhead with a violent temper who sometimes started loud fights outside the parish house. The police went to El Chino Guayo's house at six in the morning, and though the youth, the son of an Army man, was in some ways an interesting character, he turned out to be the first of many apparently false leads.

WHEN THE PARISH HOUSE was finally calm and empty of people, Otto Ardón, his assistants, and some police specialists were able to conduct a more relaxed and relatively thorough inspection. They found blood drops in a little room by the garage where ironing was done, and more on the wall outside it. They found specks and small stains of blood on other walls; there were still more traces of blood that they missed and that ODHA would find later.

The evidence recovered from the garage that morning included the discarded sweatshirt, which would turn out to have some bloodstains and a few human hairs; the concrete chunk, also bloodstained; some sheets of rumpled newspaper; and a few fingerprints and handprints that might be related to the crime.

As they were leaving San Sebastián for the morgue that morning, the MINUGUA investigators were startled to hear one of the few female indigents, a woman known as Vilma, chanting in a slurred way that the bishop had been murdered by *huecos*—homosexuals.

THE AUTOPSY got under way at about nine in the morning. Dr. Mario Guerra, head of forensics for the morgue, and the other doctors who performed and observed it were hardly facing a deep forensic mystery. "Fourth-degree facial cranial trauma" was listed as the official cause of death. A fracture and cuts on one thumb, plus the marks on his neck, seemed to indicate that Bishop Gerardi had put up a brief, furious struggle.

On the back of the bishop's head were four distinct punctures, in the shape of an arc. Rafael Guillamón, who monitored the autopsy for MINUGUA, thought they looked like marks left by a blow delivered with "brass knuckles."

The assistant prosecutor, Gustavo Soria, came into the autopsy room and said that an anal swab—to check for signs of recent homosexual penetration—was to be performed on the bishop's body. "Orders from above!" said Soria. When Guillamón recounted this story to me many years later, he snorted sardonically that the orders, coming from Military Intelligence, of course, were from General Espinosa, the former commander of the EMP who had recently been promoted to head of the Army High Command. "Soria worked with Military Intelligence," Guillamón said.

Was Guillamón correct? People had turned up that night, at the church and elsewhere, he said, like actors walking onto a stage to perform their roles. Some knew their roles in advance. Maybe others had arrived at the church, assessed the situation, and quickly understood what their roles should be. But were some of the people whose actions later seemed suspicious merely grossly incompetent? Were some fated to be suspected because of their intrinsic oddness, or because they had other secrets and vulnerabilities? Who were the actors in the crowd outside and inside the church of San Sebastián that night? Were any of the indigents and *bolitos* actors in the sense that Guillamón meant? Was Vilma, the female indigent chanting that the bishop had been murdered by "fags," an actress? The chancellor of the Curia or La China—Ana Lucía Escobar? The parish-house cook? Even someone from ODHA? And who had the important "offstage" roles? General Marco Tulio Espinosa ("the most powerful man in the Army")? Or even President Arzú? All would eventually be targets of suspicion.

It was obvious, at least if the accounts of both Rubén Chanax and El Chino Iván were true, that the man without a shirt had meant to be seen, or did not mind being seen, by at least two of the park's indigents when he stepped out of the garage that night. He left a sweatshirt behind on the floor. Was that to make it seem as if the terrible act of violence had somehow involved an act of love or lust? So that later, when witnesses spoke up, it would suggestively connect the shirtless man, the sweatshirt on the floor, the murdered bishop? But why, if it really was the same man, did he come back minutes later wearing a shirt? And where did the stranger go?

Those were some of the questions, based on the most obvious early information available, that were contemplated in the first hours and days after the murder, which made headlines across the world. Denunciations of the crime and calls for justice poured in from political and religious leaders, including Pope John Paul II. It was widely assumed, of course, that the bishop was killed in retaliation for the REMHI report, though it was hard to believe that his enemies could respond with such reckless brutality, no matter how threatened or angered they were.

How realistic was it to expect that the murderers would ever be brought to justice? Guatemalans had only to look at the region's recent history of "unimaginable" homicides to feel discouraged. Though a UN truth commission in neighboring El Salvador had confirmed what had been widely alleged since the crime occurred, that Archbishop Romero had been murdered by government assassins, no charges had ever been brought in that case, nor had any serious criminal investigation been sustained. To the north, in Mexico, the murder of Cardinal Posadas in 1993 remained unsolved, as did the assassination of the reformist presidential candidate, Luis Donaldo Colosio, in 1988. The more shocking the crime, it seemed, the more powerful or powerfully connected the criminals, and in Latin America powerful people almost never end up in prison.

Nevertheless, as Ronalth Ochaeta said in the statement given to reporters that first morning, it was inconceivable that a crime of such magnitude could occur only hundreds of feet from some of the government's most sophisticated security units and surveillance apparatus and remain unsolved for long.

II

THE INVESTIGATION
THE UNTOUCHABLES AND
THE DOG-AND-PRIEST SHOW

Peace would then be a form of war, and the State a means of waging it.
—Michel Foucault, "Truth and Power"

1

THE CHURCH OF SAN SEBASTIÁN was my mother's church when she was young. During her adolescence she gave handwriting lessons in its school for boys. When I was an infant, my grandparents and my mother brought me to the church of San Sebastián to be baptized. My mother married an American from a Jewish-Ukrainian immigrant family, and though I spent my early childhood bouncing between Guatemala and the United States (and between religions) I grew up mostly in Massachusetts. In the 1980s, when my grandparents were no longer alive, I returned to Guatemala frequently and lived in their house, once for an unbroken stretch of about two years, in an upstairs apartment that had belonged to my unmarried great-aunt. I was in New York in the spring of 1998 and followed the story of Bishop Gerardi's murder and its repercussions from there. By late summer the case had taken several astonishing turns, culminating with the controversial arrest, on July 17, of Father Mario, whose behavior the night of the murder had immediately aroused suspicion. Margarita López, the cook, was also arrested, and Father Mario's aged German shepherd, Baloo, was taken into police custody. A renowned Spanish forensics expert claimed to have discovered evidence of dog bites on Bishop Gerardi's skull.

The murder, which had at first seemed like a clear-cut political crime—a consequence of the REMHI report—had become a baroque story of perhaps perverse human passions. The mysterious shirtless man who appeared at the garage door was widely perceived to be a player in some as yet unresolved homosexual drama. As a writer I couldn't resist, and toward the end of August I took a sort of assignment from *The New Yorker* to write an article about the case. An editor said that the magazine would take it "on spec." I had to pay my own way, but I would receive a letter from *The New Yorker* that I could use as a press credential, and if eventually the magazine did want to publish the story, I would be paid for it and my expenses would be reimbursed.

GUATEMALA CITY is a uniquely ugly place. The mid-nineteenth-century American travel writer John Lloyd Stephens described it as "a mere speck in the middle of a vast plain," but by 1998 it was a sprawling, choked, polluted, impoverished, claustrophobic metropolis with a population of 3 million and a level of so-called ordinary crime and a homicide rate that made it, even though Guatemala's civil war was over, one of Latin America's most dangerous and violent cities. Its best feature is its horizon: on a clear day, immense volcanoes seem to loom so near that you might think it an illusion, as if the light possesses a magnifying quality. Sometimes the volcanoes belch plumes of black smoke, covering the city in ashes, or a crater glows like a flaming planet in the night sky.

The first night I was in the city, a Saturday, I waited until eleven, maybe a little later, to take a taxi to the church of San Sebastián. I wanted to begin there at the same time of day that Bishop Gerardi had his final encounter in the garage. It can take an hour to drive the twelve blocks or so to the church from the Hotel Spring, the inexpensive pension where I was staying, because the traffic is so bad, but at night the darkened, empty blocks glide by. Late at night, downtown Guatemala City resembles a vast, grimy old cemetery. The streets are shadowy, with steel gates pulled down over the fronts of shops and businesses, making them look like long, deserted rows of dilapidated tombs.

The taxi dropped me off, and I stood outside the dark park, which ascends gently upward toward the church. I took a few tentative steps into it and stopped to stare at a bulky human figure silhouetted against the backdrop of the parish house, in the muted glow of a light over the door. The figure seemed to be staring back at me. I retreated to the sidewalk, annoyed at myself. Then I turned, walked back into the park, and stopped again. The figure came toward me. It was a young policeman in a bulletproof vest. He had a partner, also in uniform and with a similar vest, who had been sitting in the shadows, out of view. Laid out in a row of darkened humps, sleeping under ragged blankets in front of and near the metal garage door, were the *bolitos*, looking just as they must have that night when Bishop Gerardi drove his white VW Golf inside for the last time.

Suddenly a white van with scratchy rock music coming from a speaker on its roof drove up Second Street and stopped at the foot of the drive. One of the policemen ambled down to the van and returned with a young man carrying two plastic bags filled with rice and beans. He was from Eventos Católicos, the charity that brought food to the *bolitos* at night.

The indigents woke up, and one of them shouted, then another, a domino effect of waking *bolitos*. I saw their wild-haired heads turning, eyes blinking open in grime-blackened faces as they pushed themselves up off their cardboard beds.

"¡La *policí-í-í-í-a*!" one began to taunt, voice thick with false fright and real mockery. "¡Ayyy! ¡Ayyy! ¡La *policí-í-í-í-a*!" And then another, in a sarcastic singsong, cawing, "We didn't see a thing! ¿*Nosotros*? Us? Who, *us*? We didn't see *aaaanything*. We don't know *aaaanything*." Were these really the same *bolitos* who were in the park the night Bishop Gerardi was killed? I had been told that the *bolitos* had scattered to other parks, or dropped from sight. But some of them, apparently, had drifted back.

The next morning, Sunday, the previous night's howling wraiths were sitting quietly on benches, looking like circus clowns who'd been shot out of cannons and stunned into a stupor by a hard landing. Car washers worked along the sidewalks. Bright orange flower petals had dropped from towering *fuego del bosque* trees and were spread prettily over the grass and concrete pathways. Since the murder, the park, which now had a twenty-four-hour police presence, had become a favorite make-out spot for adolescents. A female *bolito,* frumpy and dirty, with a sagging face and feral black hair, was sitting against the wall of the parish-house garage. She looked something like that inebriated woman, despondent and dazed, in the café in the famous Degas painting. She said her name was Vilma. This was the Vilma the investigators from MINUGUA had heard muttering about homosexuals having killed Bishop Gerardi.

The beloved bishop's murder, followed by the arrest of Father Mario, and innuendos about a homosexual crime of passion, had, of course, hit like a succession of earthquakes in the old parish of mainly middle-class and poor residents, of old-fashioned manners and morality, where scandals are buried secrets within families. Father José Manuel, Father Mario's replacement, a trim young man with a reserved and thoughtful air, told me that attendance, especially after the arrest, had fallen off drastically, though it was starting to come back now. "There's been so much confusion," he said.

None of the people I approached as that morning's Baptism Mass let out wanted to discuss the crime or its impact on the parish. Only a man selling cotton candy would venture an opinion. Father Mario had been a very punctual priest, he told me, and would have finished the Mass half an hour earlier than Father José Manuel had. "And I'd be over at the church of the Recolección by now," he said, "selling to the people arriving for the noon Mass."

That afternoon, I had lunch with a friend of a friend of mine in New York, Andy Kaufman, who had spent several years in Guatemala as a founding member of a forensics team that conducted some of the first exhumations of massacre sites in the country. Andy had also worked with MINUGUA and had helped ODHA set up its own exhumation unit. His friend was close to people in ODHA and was familiar with their version, though not the details, of the Gerardi case. During the four months since the murder, ODHA and the prosecutors from the Public Ministry had been, under great pressure, investigating the crime and pursuing theories about it, building their competing narratives. ODHA, Andy's friend said, was firmly convinced that it had been a political assassination, most likely carried out by the military. Apparently, ODHA had some evidence of its own, including credible anonymous tips and a possible key witness who, unfortunately, neither ODHA nor anyone else could find. Nobody at ODHA believed the scenario involving dog bites, or that Father Mario had been the murderer.

After lunch that Sunday, I strolled through the mildly crowded downtown streets, thinking over what Andy's friend had told me. I stopped at the Metropolitan Cathedral, where a Mass was in session, and stood at the side of the altar, behind a faded velvet cordon. A man was playing an organ and there was a choir consisting of a small number—five? eight? I no longer remember —of mostly middle-aged and elderly women of very humble appearance. One was dressed partially in Indian garb, with a woven shawl around her shoulders. She seemed prematurely withered and gaunt, her black hair roughly cut and greasy-looking. I especially remember the way she kept glancing at me, this stranger who was watching her and the choir too intently, her eyes filled with nervous fear. Her fear ignited, or rather revived, mine, like the disease the Indians call *susto*, a "fright" that you can catch like a cold, fear leaping from someone's glance into your own, a low-grade contamination that felt so familiar that it was just like stepping back into the past, into the Guatemala of the war years and its suffocating atmosphere of paranoia.

*   *   *

I KNEW THAT I NEEDED to gain the confidence of people at ODHA, but it was not an opportune moment. A reporter from the *Miami Herald* had recently published a story alleging that Father Mario was a homosexual, citing an anonymous source close to ODHA. I learned later that the reporter had quoted from an off-the-record conversation, or so his source insisted. In any case, the incident had caused problems for ODHA, especially within the Church, and it fed a long-standing distrust of journalists, both Guatemalan and foreign. Andy Kaufman's contacts were more immediately helpful at the offices of the UN mission, MINUGUA, and I quickly found an ally there in Cecilia Olmos, who had gone to San Sebastián the night of the murder with Jean Arnault, the director of MINUGUA, and Rafael Guillamón, its chief investigator. Olmos was a Chilean woman in her forties with a leonine mop of reddish hair. If the UN mission couldn't help Guatemalans solve the Gerardi case, she said to me one day, then she didn't see what reason it had for being in the country.

The ODHA office was in a Spanish colonial building nearly two centuries old in the Metropolitan Cathedral complex, two blocks from the headquarters of the Presidential Guard and four blocks from the church of San Sebastián. Its massive double wooden doors—they looked more like the gates to a medieval castle—opened onto a courtyard paved with rough gray stones where vehicles were parked. Visitors buzzed an intercom in the blackened stone frame of the entrance and, once admitted through a small door set in one of the larger ones, stepped into a vestibule where a receptionist sat behind bulletproof glass. An open corridor with a red-tiled roof ran around an interior courtyard, with offices, workrooms, and storage areas opening onto it.

On my first visits to ODHA I met with Ronalth Ochaeta, who was friendly enough and reasonably forthcoming, but careful. He phrased his answers to my questions as if he expected to see them

Ronalth Ochaeta (front right), carrying the coffin of Bishop Gerardi

printed in a newspaper the next day. He did, however, let me hang around a bit, and one day he introduced me to Fernando Penados, who was in charge of the murder investigation and was obviously the key person for me to talk to. But Fernando came off as intimidating and hermetic, and he rebuffed my first attempts to interview him. I got around that with the help of Cecilia Olmos, who fed me morsels of information from MINUGUA that I could drop. This went on for a while, until Fernando finally, he told me later, said to some of his colleagues, "How has that *pisado*—asshole—found out so much?" Which led to what would become many, many conversations.

Fernando Penados's tough-guy air seemed at odds with his upbringing as a possible prince of the Church, although it was leavened by a good-natured charm. There was also, I eventually realized, an impressionable side to Fernando—a touch of immaturity and romantic or overheated imagination—but he was hardly a naïf. He told me that during the discussions between ODHA and the Church about forming an independent team to investigate the bishop's murder, he had proposed two options. "One, we can form a team that will be able to conduct a real criminal investigation," he had said. "People with incredible experience in investigating cases, but who, because of their past, have their vulnerable points. If we pay them well, these people will find the person who came out of the garage without a shirt. Or, two, we can form an ODHA type of team, with clean, trustworthy people. People who don't have experience in criminal investigations." The Church authorities, said Fernando, "in the very logical and wise explanations that they gave me," decided, of course, that they couldn't pay the sort of people he was talking about. "They said, 'We'll have an ODHA-type team just to document the case.'"

ODHA supported many groups—REMHI, people working on legal and educational projects and on mental health programs for victims of the war's violence, exhumation teams—and the legal office under which Fernando's investigators worked had the smallest budget of any of them. His team, which had only four members, was called, half jokingly, Los Intocables, the Untouchables, which accurately evoked their youthful spirit of adventure while poking some ironic fun at their ambitions. Two of the Untouchables, Arturo Aguilar and Arturo Rodas, were physically large young men. Aguilar was a law student at Rafael Landívar University, a Jesuit school. He was only twenty and still lived at home with his parents, but he'd been doing volunteer work at ODHA since his adolescence. During a year as a high school exchange student in Madison, Wisconsin, he'd joined the football team, where he played center. Arturo Rodas was a childhood friend of Fernando's who was working as the manager of a gas plant in Quezaltenango when Fernando contacted him. His nickname, inspired by his girth and pharaonic features, was El Califa. He was conservative in appearance, while the other Arturo, "El Gordo" Aguilar, was a devotee of indie rock and the writings of Charles Bukowski and wore an earring, close-cropped hair, and baggy grunge attire. They made a comical sight sitting side by side in the front seat of OHDA's old Suzuki Samurai mini-jeep, like a pair of Babar the Elephant detectives.

The Untouchables' fourth member, Rodrigo Salvadó, was a tall, thin twenty-two-year-old anthropology student who had been working with REMHI's exhumation team one day when Fernando was leaving the ODHA courtyard in a jeep, on his way to the morgue, and realized he didn't have any cigarettes. He would need to smoke at the morgue, because of the stench, and when he spotted Rodrigo smoking in the courtyard, he leaned out the window and asked if he wanted to join his team, and if so to get in the car. Rodrigo was handsome, with a long black ponytail, and the others had nicknamed him El Shakira, after the famous Colombian singer who was at the time raven-haired. The son of academic

The ODHA lawyer Mario Domingo, with two Untouchables, Rodrigo Salvadó and Arturo Aguilar

parents with leftist affiliations in the 1970s and 1980s, Rodrigo had lived on the run with his mother when he was a boy, continually changing houses in the political underground and in exile over the border in Chiapas and Mexico City before returning to Guatemala. Many of his parents' relatives and friends were killed or had "disappeared." Rodrigo was a remarkably unflappable and easygoing young man with a quiet, quick wit.

Fernando had in the beginning perceived the mission of the Untouchables as collecting information that could be used to assess the claims of the prosecutors and the police, who had shown themselves to be more than reluctant to seriously investigate or follow up any lead that might implicate the Army, or to advance the scenario that Bishop Gerardi's murder had a political motive. But before long Fernando, along with ODHA's legal team, realized that instead of playing a merely defensive role, they might be able to make a case against the true killers. A lot of information flowed through ODHA. People who had something to say about the Gerardi case, whether their motives were sincere or mendacious, their information helpful, mistaken, or designed to mislead, seemed to contact the Church before contacting anyone else.

Investigating Bishop Gerardi's murder quickly became an obsession and a way of life for the Untouchables, but one that merged with their usual lives—essentially those of young, unmarried, middle-class men who were far from puritanical or pious. After work nearly every day they would gather in a bar or nightspot, huddled together at a table over beers, eternally talking, it seemed, about the case, while, on occasion, young women made caustic comments over their shoulders before moving off in search of more attentive companions. "You go to bed thinking about this case," Fernando once told me. "And at night you dream about it. And when you wake up in the morning, you're still thinking about it."

THE TRAIL OF EVIDENCE that ODHA's investigators and lawyers would follow began on April 28, the day before Bishop Gerardi's funeral, as a crowd of 20,000 people marched through the streets of Guatelmala City in protest against the murder. That afternoon, Mynor Melgar, who had recently joined ODHA as coordinator of its legal team, replacing the less experienced Nery Rodenas, after having served in the Public Ministry for most of the 1990s, was summoned to the office of the chancellor of the Curia. Melgar, a dark-skinned, broad-shouldered man with black hair combed straight back, large languid eyes, and a mustache, had a quiet, confident, seen-it-all affability. Though still in his early thirties, he was renowned as a prosecutor of human rights cases. He had been the special prosecutor in the Myrna Mack murder case, winning an unprecedented thirty-year conviction against Noél Beteta, the EMP operative who had stabbed the young anthropologist to death. In another unprecedented case, he'd won a murder conviction against Ricardo Ortega, a violent young carjacker protected by military officers who ran a car-theft ring.

Waiting in the chancellor's office that day was the parish priest from the church of El Carmelo, in a working-class barrio in Zone 7. His name was Gabriel Quiróz, and he was obviously frightened and distressed. Father Quiróz told Melgar that as he was dressing to assist in the funeral ceremonies at the cathedral that morning, a man had come to see him. The man, who seemed nervous, said that he was a taxi driver and that on April 26 he'd been working the night shift. Sometime after ten—he wasn't sure of the exact time—he'd driven past the church of San Sebastián and had seen a white Toyota Corolla parked nearby. Several men were gathered around the Toyota, including a man who was naked from the waist up. The Toyota's license-plate number had four digits —the kind of number, the taxi driver knew, that was usually assigned to police cars or other official vehicles. The taxi driver thought a bust of some kind was going on, but the next day, when the murder of Bishop Gerardi was all over the news, he realized that he must have seen the shirtless man whom witnesses had described to the police. He had come to Father Quiróz because he didn't know what to do.

Father Quiróz didn't know the taxi driver's name, nor did he recall ever having seen the man before. Maybe the taxi driver hadn't given his name, or the priest, startled and himself frightened by the visit, hadn't registered it. The taxi driver was light-skinned, with a mustache, a bit overweight, said the priest, and he apologized, because that was all he could remember. But he had the slip of paper on which the taxi driver had written the number of the license plate, and he handed it to Melgar, who unfolded it and read the hurried scrawl: P-3201. The priest told Mynor Melgar that when he walked the taxi driver to the door, he saw a white taxi waiting outside, with at least one other man inside it.

Melgar passed the piece of paper to Ronalth Ochaeta, who gave the number to the interior minister the next day, asking that it be checked out.

"Why does a person passing in a taxi memorize a license-plate number?" Fernando Penados asked, rhetorically, one day in early September, after I'd been in Guatemala for two weeks. "First, the hour. And second, because this person is no tame dove. The taxi driver notices these things because he has his past." Fernando said that the taxi driver told the priest that he had once been arrested on a drug charge. Someone with that kind of experience tends to notice the same things that a good policeman does. If that sort of person sees a group of men and another man wearing no shirt standing by a car—indeed, the kind of car undercover policemen frequently use—on a dark street late at night, that person will memorize a license-plate number.

Four months after first learning of license-plate number P-3201, ODHA was still hunting for the taxi driver, hoping that he was not already dead. The taxi driver was the mystery witness Andy Kaufman's friend had mentioned.

OTTO ARDÓN was appointed special prosecutor in the case. ODHA was granted co-plaintiff status, as legal representatives of Bishop Gerardi's family and the Church. Thus ODHA was, theoretically, a partner of the prosecution. But what ODHA soon discovered about Ardón's past did not inspire confidence. Until recently he had been a lawyer for the Guatemalan Air Force, and he was related to military officers. In 1996, when he was on a team prosecuting soldiers accused of massacring over 300 civilians, he was removed from the case after relatives of the victims complained that he blatantly favored the defense. (Mynor Melgar had eventually taken over as prosecutor of that case.) Indeed, many people began to suspect that Bishop Gerardi's murder had occurred on the date it did because those who planned the crime knew that the investigation would fall to Ardón. He had only two assistant prosecutors working under him on the Gerardi case, including Gustavo Soria. By contrast, a case involving corruption and contraband rackets had twenty investigators assigned to it.

Rubén Chanax and El Chino Iván, the two indigents who were taken into custody the night of the murder, had given conflicting descriptions of the shirtless man, which resulted in quite different composite sketches of the "suspect." Nevertheless, the sketches had been widely published in the Guatemalan press as the face of Bishop Gerardi's murderer. Chanax's and El Chino Iván's perusal of mug shots led to the arrest, three days after the murder, of Carlos Vielman, a young, alcoholic, sometime indigent. At the police lineup in which Vielman was presented to the witnesses, hidden in a row of other young men, Chanax said that the man without a shirt was not among them, but El Chino Iván positively identified Vielman as the man he had sold cigarettes to that night. Vielman was much shorter than the man both witnesses had earlier described, and he had tousled curly hair. One side of his face was grotesquely swollen from a dental infection. He seemed nearly retarded and had been imprisoned in the past, most recently for public drunkenness, though for only about five days. He had been released from jail less than a week earlier, and had celebrated by embarking on a drinking binge that lasted up to the moment of his arrest.

During the initial interrogation of Vielman, Otto Ardón had bellowed at him: "Confess that in the moment in which Monseñor Juan José Gerardi Conedera was entering the parish house . . . at about ten at night, you attacked him with a piece of concrete with which you gave him several blows until you caused his death!" Vielman, apparently utterly bewildered, responded with the same words throughout the interrogation: "I don't know what you're talking about!"

It was almost inconceivable that Vielman, who was lame in one arm, could have wielded the heavy chunk of concrete. The church of San Sebastián was far from his usual stomping grounds by the bus terminal. And what reason could he have had for murdering Bishop Gerardi? Robbery didn't seem a plausible motive. The bishop's gold ring and his wallet with fifty dollars inside it had been left on his person. The only things that were missing were the keys to the parish house and to the bishop's car, the chain from around his neck, and his cheap plastic Casio watch.

ODHA checked out Vielman's alibi, which seemed solid. After sweeping up, as he often did, in La Huehueteca, a little cantina near the bus terminal, he'd been paid with a bottle of cheap cane liquor, which he shared with other indigent friends, and then he had slept there. Nevertheless, Otto Ardón continued to insist that Vielman was the perpetrator. Ardón may simply have been eager to arrest anyone and perhaps hoped that Carlos Vielman would provide an adequate scapegoat. Or perhaps he really was as incompetent as Edgar Gutiérrez said he was. Gutiérrez had been educated in Mexico as an economist and was responsible for much of the REMHI report's shape and content. His gentle, soft-spoken demeanor belied an intensely cerebral and complex personality. Gutiérrez's public calls for Ardón's removal poisoned relations between ODHA and the prosecutors, although it is hard to imagine that a spirit of collaboration could ever have flowered between them.

The lethargic, seemingly diffident Ardón—the prosecutor bore a remarkable resemblance to an unsmiling Alfred E. Neuman, the cartoon character who is the face of *Mad* magazine—had been bemoaning to everyone his unlucky fate in drawing such a high-profile, implicitly dangerous case. He let it be known that he had nothing to gain from prosecuting it, that it would be bad for his career. Sometimes, in a tone of weary bravado, he said the pressures and complications of the case didn't allow him to sleep at night.

VERY QUIETLY, HARDLY NOTICED, FBI agents had slipped into the country a few days after the murder and were aiding Ardón and the prosecutors. Rubén Chanax had passed a polygraph test the FBI administered in which the only question he was asked was if he had seen a shirtless man step out of the garage. El Chino Iván refused to take the test.

In late May, Ardón sent pieces of evidence to the FBI laboratories in Washington, D.C., to find out if the blood or hairs found in the blue sweatshirt corresponded to Vielman's, or if any traces of Vielman's body fluids or DNA were on the bishop's clothes. The results of all those tests would be negative. It was to be an ongoing routine in the investigation. Guatemalan prosecutors would send evidence and samples to Washington and then wait with bated breath for the results, which on every occasion disappointed them. One reason was that the prosecutors were often requesting the wrong kind of information. There was a great deal of Bishop Gerardi's blood in the garage, tracked all over the house, and left in traces on the walls, but there was not much in the way of incriminating evidence waiting to be discovered in it. And a great deal of potentially crucial evidence had been lost. The single, rather small, bloody footprint found by the bishop's body, the first and seemingly most promising piece of evidence, was never matched, at least not publicly or officially, to the footwear of any named suspect or witness.

President Arzú responded to the crime by appointing a High Commission of notables, including Rodolfo Mendoza, the minister of the interior, to whom Ronalth Ochaeta had passed the license-plate number. The Church declined to participate, arguing that the work of investigating the crime should be left to those who were presumably better qualified: the police and prosecutors. The Church feared being trapped into sanctioning an official whitewash. It did not go unnoticed that military regimes of the past had typically responded to crises by appointing a political commission.

President Arzú, who was notoriously thin-skinned to begin with, was on the defensive. In his first public interview about the case, published in *Prensa Libre,* the country's largest newspaper, Arzú pointed out that just days before in New York City a priest who had done social work in the Bronx had been murdered. "Why should the image of our country be stained," he said, "and not that of the United States, when these two acts are equally reprehensible and painful?" Throughout the 1980s, when Guatemala was frequently sanctioned for its human rights record, Army and government spokespersons had customarily responded by pointing to the crime rate in New York City and indignantly asking why the UN, American liberals, and human rights organizations weren't asking for sanctions against the United States as well.

DURING THOSE FIRST DAYS and weeks after the murder, the small team of UN investigators led by Rafael Guillamón, who reported directly to MINUGUA's chief, Jean Arnault, quietly tried to identify and track down some of the indigents who had slept outside the San Sebastián parish house on the night of the murder. The exact number will probably never be known, but it seems that perhaps eight, though more likely ten or twelve, *bolitos* were sleeping in the open plaza in front of the church and by the garage that night.

Four nights after the murder, on April 30, three of the *bolitos*— El Chalupa, El Cachimba, and El Árabe—on their way out of the park to buy a bottle of alcohol, had reportedly been accosted by a group of men who had roughly interrogated and beaten them and even attempted to pull them into a white Mercedes Benz. On another night, shots were said to have been fired into the park.

Some of the *bolitos* had surprising backgrounds. Two of them, Marco Tulio Rivera and his brother Héctor, were the sons of a former director of the National Police. Marco Tulio had been thrown out of military school as a youth for drunkenness, but Héctor was a civil engineer who had graduated from the military officers' training academy. Héctor would stay drunk for two months or so, living in the park, then would turn up sober on a highway building crew in the mountains, and then would repeat his odd cycle. He was one of those who said he'd slept through everything the night of the murder. Vilma's "husband," the *bolito* known as Ronco, was also an ex-soldier and claimed to be on the run from a mysterious pursuer.

The *bolitos* were hardly reliable interview subjects, fogged by drugs and drink and, on the night of April 26 specifically, by whatever soporific they had unwittingly ingested in their unlikely gift basket of cheese sandwiches and beer. Some may have pretended to remember less than they knew, some more. But Rafael Guillamón culled a number of interesting details from the *bolitos*. Years later, when the case finally went to trial, some of what he learned would seem hauntingly pertinent. Several of the *bolitos* might have been able to provide important corroborating testimony, had they still been alive. El Canche, Marco Tulio, and El Pitti, whose real name was Arni Mendoza Jeréz, claimed to have at least glimpsed the shirtless man who had stepped out of the garage. El Canache said that he was muscular, a common soldier type. Most notably, in light of evidence that would eventually emerge, Marco Tulio and El Canache both mentioned seeing a large black vehicle, which one of them identified as a Jeep Cherokee.

El Canache, who disappeared soon after his conversation with MINUGUA, said that he ran into El Chino Iván at a Burger King in downtown Guatemala City the day after the murder, and that El Chino Iván was clearly distressed. He told El Canache that he'd been hungry the previous night, and that finding the little door to the garage left open had entered through it and walked all the way to the parish-house kitchen, where he'd eaten from the refrigerator. Guillamón believed that was the likeliest explanation for the half-empty pitcher of orange juice in the kitchen and the piece of hot dog in the potted plant next to the bishop's body.

The day after the encounter in the Burger King, El Chino Iván's father phoned MINUGUA's investigators to say that his son had information about the Gerardi case and that he was frightened. El Chino Iván—who was tall, fair-skinned, and well spoken—soon turned up at MINUGUA headquarters and told Rafael Guillamón that Rubén Chanax had told him that he was with G-2, Military Intelligence. He said that Chanax often boasted about his knowledge of weaponry and that he had said that in ninety days a *limpieza social,* or social cleansing, of the park—an operation, usually carried out by police, in which undesirables were "eliminated"—was going to begin. El Chino Iván asked for protection. His father wanted him to go to the United States, but it was his immediate fate to pass into the custody of the police as a protected witness alongside Rubén Chanax.

When Guillamón interviewed Chanax, he asked about El Chino Iván's assertion that he worked for G-2. Chanax admitted telling him that, but said that he'd been lying. He only wanted to frighten his friend, to keep him from robbing and breaking into cars near the park. Chanax said that he had been shanghaied into the Army when he was sixteen, like so many other poor Guatemalan boys. He remembered the names of his commanding officers and squad leaders. There was really no reason to doubt that he had a military past, and that, like some of the others who lived in the park, he had drifted into the life of the homeless after being discharged.

Later Chanax told someone else in MINUGUA that El Chino Iván worked for military counterintelligence.

Were these claims simply fantasies and boasts? Apparently Chanax did not repeat them to Otto Ardón and his prosecutors or to the police.

THE FIRST PIECE OF EVIDENCE that pointed, however circumstantially, to a military connection to the crime was the license-plate number that the taxi driver had given to Father Quiróz. The minister of the interior had asked Ronalth Ochaeta for the name of the witness who had taken down the plate number, claiming that without this information he couldn't attempt to identify its owner. But Arturo Aguilar and Rodrigo Salvadó had already hired, with Ochaeta's permission, a *tramitador,* someone whose job it is to undertake bureaucratic procedures—guiding paperwork through red tape, knowing when to grease a palm—on behalf of others, an occupation that is a Latin American institution. The *tramitador* took care of the necessary business at the registry of motor vehicles and discovered that the license-plate number had once been attached to the Chiquimula military base.

The Chiquimula base had been shut down the year before, and the vehicle that bore license-plate number P-3201, a pickup truck, was now registered to the Army High Command in Guatemala City. ODHA passed this information to the commission appointed by President Arzú, and from one day to the next, according to Ronalth Ochaeta, all records of the plate vanished except for the documents ODHA had in its possession. When Ochaeta complained that the Arzú commission was not cooperating in regard to the information, the Defense Ministry issued a statement explaining that the pickup had been sold, but then was forced to acknowledge that the pickup had been sold *without* the license plates. Finally it was acknowledged that one of the two plates numbered P-3201, which should still have been in the possession of the Army High Command, was missing.

On April 28, the same day Mynor Melgar learned of Father Quiróz's encounter with the taxi driver, an anonymous telephone call had been received by a receptionist at the archbishop's office. A woman said to tell Archbishop Penados to investigate "Colonel Lima Oliva," and then she said, "Investigate the Limas." She described herself as a friend of the archbishop and of Monseñor Quezada, a prominent bishop with a conservative reputation, but she would not give her name. This was just one of countless anonymous tips that reached ODHA. The legal team and the Untouchables had quickly learned that information arriving in this manner was often intended to mislead, and so far almost none of it had proved useful.

There was no Colonel Lima Oliva in ODHA's database. But there was a Captain Byron Lima Oliva in the EMP's Presidential Guard. Indeed, he was the officer who had been thrown from his horse and broken his arm during the incident in 1996 that cost the milkman Sas Rompich his life. And there was a recently retired Colonel named Byron Disrael Lima Estrada, who turned out to be the father of the young Lima in the EMP. Colonel Lima Estrada lived in the Colonia Lourdes, a comfortable neighborhood where military officers make their homes. The retired colonel was said to run a little grocery store out of his garage.

Colonel Lima Estrada was a most unlikely shopkeeper. In 1988, he had commanded the Chiquimula military base—the same base to which plate number P-3201 had formerly been assigned. That immediately caught ODHA's eye. The colonel had had an exemplary military career during the cold war period. A number of files on him held by the U.S. Defense Department and the CIA had been declassified, and the records were posted on the National Security Archive Web site maintained by George Washington University. Colonel Lima Estrada was an anticommunists' anticommunist and a legendary counterinsurgency officer. The colonel's visceral hatred of communists was explained by his painful personal history: his father, a military officer who had led a lethally repressive operation against university students after the coup in 1954, was assassinated by left-wing guerrillas in the 1960s. Lima Estrada was a graduate of Guatemala's Escuela Politécnica, the training academy for Army officers. He had studied at the U.S. Army's School of the Americas, and also took an elite U.S. military course in counterespionage and "special operations" in Panama.

During the 1970s, Lima Estrada was an officer in the Regional Telecommunications Center, a special political-intelligence unit inside the presidential palace, described in the National Security Archive as a predecessor of the EMP's "notorious 'Archivo.'" By 1981 he'd been promoted to the rank of colonel. According to one declassified U.S. intelligence report, in the early 1980s Colonel Lima Estrada "was extremely successful as commander of the most important Mil Zone (20 Quiché)." Apparently he'd assumed his command in El Quiché just after Bishop Gerardi had closed the diocese there. At least five massacres of Mayan peasants by the Guatemalan Army occurred under Colonel Lima Estrada's command in El Quiché. In an interview given to the *Wall Street Journal* in 1981, the colonel named Napoleon and Hitler among his heroes. Later he commanded an airborne special forces unit that played a central role in counterinsurgency campaigns and also, according to the National Security Archive, "founded an elite 'Kamikaze' Counterinsurgency Tactical Unit to carry out political executions and other hits, directed by the president and his key intelligence advisers." Those advisers met in secret to decide the life and death of Guatemalans under the auspices of a group known as CRIO (Centro de Reunión de Información y Operaciones) that was later revived, according to the National Security Archive, under the government of General Mejía Víctores, which took power after a coup against General Ríos Montt in 1983.

During that era of massacres in the countryside, the Guatemalan Army received fulsome public support from President Ronald Reagan, who famously declared General Ríos Montt the victim of "a bum rap." In 1983, three Guatemalan U.S. Aid workers were killed, and even the U.S. ambassador said that they had been murdered "by the presidential intelligence unit, the 'Archivo,' in reprisal for recent U.S. pressure on human rights in Guatemala." From 1983 to 1985, in the government of General Mejía Víctores, Colonel Lima Estrada was the director of Military Intelligence, G-2. In 1999, less than a year after the murder of Bishop Gerardi, the National Security Archive procured and published an extraordinary dossier, a "logbook" kept by G-2 of death-squad operations in the years when Colonel Lima Estrada was at the agency's head, documenting the cases of 183 murdered civilians, with individual photographs, from August 1983 to March 1985. That example of G-2's zeal for record keeping might seem puzzlingly self-incriminating, though it is hardly the first instance in world history of criminally repressive and even murderous government entities displaying an earnest faith in the self-absolving guarantees of bureaucratic procedure and order.

Soon after Guatemala's first democratically elected civilian president in decades, Vinicio Cerezo, came to power, in 1986, Colonel Lima Estrada found himself languishing in the military backwater of the Chiquimula base, in the dry eastern lowlands. He seemed to be out of the game, far from the remaining war zones or the internecine machinations of the capital, where Defense Minister General Héctor Gramajo was consolidating his own position and pushing aside hard-line officers whom he considered excessively hostile to Guatemala's democratic opening. From Chiquimula, Colonel Lima Estrada soon emerged as one of the leaders of a failed coup against President Cerezo's government. His punishment was to be sent to the country's embassy in Peru as military attaché, where he continued to be involved in coup plotting from afar, and then to Nicaragua. The declassified reports also reveal that charges of corruption were leveled against Colonel Lima Estrada only two weeks before the attempted coup. It was alleged that in the mid-1980s he had participated with two other officers in defrauding the Army of 1.5 million quetzales, and this at a time when the national currency still had a strong value against the dollar.

Colonel Lima Estrada, by his institution's standards, had had a spectacular career, yet he had never been promoted to the rank of brigadier general. The reason, according to declassified reports, was political. "Lima is very strong-willed and highly outspoken," wrote the author of a U.S. intelligence report. "That coupled with his very conservative philosophy and ideology makes him a bit dangerous in a budding democracy." He belonged to a group of influential active and retired Military Intelligence officers known informally as the Cofradía (as the secretive religious brotherhoods in Mayan villages and towns are also called), and to the larger, and official, group of retired officers and war veterans known as AVEMILGUA (Association of Military Veterans of Guatemala). It was on behalf of the latter organization that the colonel had turned up to testify to the truth commission after the Peace Accords in 1996. That had been a defiant performance. When the commission members turned on their tape recorders at the beginning of the session, the colonel opened his jacket and showed them an electronic device he was carrying. "I'm recording also," he said. He denied, during that brief, blustery session, that during the war the Guatemalan Army had been guilty of any illegal transgressions against the lives or physical integrity of anyone whatsoever. The retired officers met regularly with General Marco Tulio Espinosa, the head of the Army High Command, to discuss their concerns about how the Peace Accords might affect the Army and the officers who had fought and won the war, especially given the increasingly vehement, amnesty-defying calls for a reckoning and prosecution of past human rights violations.

Another tip, two tips really, linking Colonel Lima Estrada to the Gerardi murder would filter down to both OHDA and MINUGUA from, I learned later, his sister-in-law, in whom his wife had confided. The wife was distraught because she had overheard a conversation between her husband and other retired officers in the little store in Colonel Lima's garage. She heard the officers say to her husband, shortly before the murder, "*No te rajes,* Lima," or, "Don't get cold feet on us." And she'd heard her husband reply, "We had to do much worse things during the war." The day after the murder he got very drunk. When the wife realized the significance of what she had heard, she went to her sister, Meche, who told the story to her doctor, Carlos Pérez Avedaño, who in turn told two friends. One of those friends phoned ODHA. The other, an architect named Sergio Búcaro, brought the information directly to President Arzú, who was his friend and neighbor. Arzú told Búcaro to go to the EMP. A few months later, Búcaro was named Guatemala's ambassador to the Vatican. Rafael Guillamón at MINUGUA believed that Búcaro had been rewarded for keeping silent about what he knew.

There was not nearly as much information available about the colonel's son, Captain Byron Lima Oliva. He was one of the young officers in charge of President Arzú's security detail. About thirty, tall, dark, athletic, handsome, possessed of a striking intensity and verbal facility, he was said to be well regarded by most of his fellow officers, but he was also dogged by rumors of a dangerous emotional volatility. He was a former Kaibil special-forces soldier who had first seen combat at the age of seventeen in some of the campaigns of the 1980s. The Kaibiles are an elite commando force known for their cruelty. Their motto is, "If I go forward, follow me. If I stop, urge me on. If I turn back, kill me." Their involvement in massacres of civilians is well documented, and REMHI's report recommended that they be disbanded.

Captain Lima had belonged to the controversial anti-kidnapping commando unit of the EMP to which his father, the retired colonel, reportedly served as an adviser. Given the inability of the police and the Public Ministry to confront Guatemala's skilled, ruthless kidnapping rings, the EMP had been called on to perform much of the police work in high-profile or especially delicate cases. Alhough many kidnapping rings were known to involve military men and police, the unit had some successes, but it had also been implicated in disappearances and was accused of making off with ransom payments.

The Untouchables discovered that on April 26, the Sunday that Bishop Gerardi was murdered, Captain Lima had flown into Guatemala City on American Airlines flight 927 from Argentina via Miami, landing at one in the afternoon. (He had been in Argentina arranging advance security for a presidential visit.) Captain Lima claimed, in a statement to prosecutors, that he had been with a friend, Erick Urízar, in a bar called the Sports Grill until eleven-thirty that night, and had gone directly from the bar to his barracks in the EMP headquarters, arriving around midnight. But ODHA had conducted a check of credit-card receipts and discovered that, although the captain had indeed been in the bar, he had paid his bill at eight-twenty-two. Captain Lima then explained that although he had paid the bill at the earlier hour, he and Urízar had run into two people they knew and had sat with them in the bar until eleven-thirty. On another occasion, he said that after arriving back at EMP headquarters, he had eaten cake with someone there at around eleven. Other EMP members would give conflicting accounts of whether and when they had seen Captain Lima that night. He claimed that he didn't learn of Bishop Gerardi's murder until the next day, despite his having spent that night in the barracks, within blocks of the church of San Sebastián.

A month after Bishop Gerardi's murder, Captain Byron Lima Oliva was sent to Cyprus as the sole Guatemalan member of an Argentine military detachment of UN peacekeepers.

THE CHURCH WANTED to keep its distance from President Arzú's High Commission, but Ronalth Ochaeta and Edgar Gutiérrez, accompanied by Helen Mack, attended some of the sessions. One of these sessions, they discovered when they arrived, was intended to be a serious discussion of the case against Carlos Vielman, the alcoholic indigent who was still under arrest. "We became very belligerent," Ronalth told me later. They derided the case, and one of the commission members, Gustavo Porras, a former guerrilla ideologue who had been a key architect of the Peace Accords and who was now President Arzú's personal secretary, responded defensively. Porras looked like a caricature of a nineteenth-century radical intellectual: thin, pallid, arrogant, with a large bulb of a forehead. He began to speculate that the bishop's murder might have arisen from a plot inside the Cofradía, the brotherhood of mostly retired Military Intelligence officers, to destabilize President Arzú's government. Gutiérrez answered that this could be, but only if they had employed the logistical advantages, infrastructure, and the authority of the EMP. This led to more heated words, the exact nature of which is in dispute. Ronalth Ochaeta recalls that Jean Arnualt had to physically step in, trying to calm the angry men. Soon afterward, the High Commission ceased to meet or even to exist.

ODHA believed that the early evidence and leads in the case—the unexplained presence of the two men from the EMP at San Sebastián on the night of the murder, the license-plate number, the activity the taxi driver had glimpsed on the street by the church, the anonymous tips about the Limas—indicated that the murder was carried out by, or at the very least aided by, a clandestine intelligence unit, most likely from within the EMP. But some members of President Arzú's inner circle were convinced that they had access to far better information than was available to ODHA. They knew that a different spin could be put on the crime, shifting responsibility from the Army to the Church. In this version, which would soon be developed by prosecutors, the murder was a domestic crime of passion, *un lío de homosexuales*. That is how, according to witnesses, it was described by none other than General Marco Tulio Espinosa, the head of the Army High Command, at a cabinet meeting the morning after the murder. This piece of highly confidential information, for the moment too explosive and too disrespectful to be made public to a shocked, grieving, largely Catholic nation, was passed by President Arzú and members of his government and military officers to influential businessmen and media figures. It went through diplomatic back channels and soon began sprouting, in whispers and innuendo, everywhere.

The homosexual angle was played up most grotesquely by Mario Menchú, an abrasive, hustling defense lawyer of little particular accomplishment or renown who offered his services, at no charge, to the indigent Carlos Vielman. As a defense lawyer, he could hardly have been more ineffective, but he displayed a talent for getting himself into the newspapers, and he also aroused suspicions. Instead of asking that Vielman's friends from the cantina La Huehueteca be called to testify about his client's whereabouts on the night of the murder—the most obvious defense—why did Menchú take another tack?

"I've been consulting medical forensics specialists," the agitated lawyer announced at an impromptu press conference, "and they say these kinds of crimes have something to do with passion. Why? Because the aggressor causes the total destruction of the face and head, true? Even the destruction of the genital organs. How many blows did Monseñor Gerardi receive in his face? . . . This also has something to do with, for example, the sexual deviations, . . . such as homosexuality, necrophilia, eating cadavers, pedophilia." Menchú implied that the deviant he had in mind was Father Mario. "Why don't they want to interrogate Mario Orantes?" he asked. "Why doesn't he want to help?" He said that an exhumation of the body and an examination of the bishop's genitals would prove his theory.

Mario Menchú's innuendos about Father Mario's sexual proclivities elicited a predictable uproar and condemnation. But the comments also sent doubt and comic titillation rippling through the vast, irreverent world of whispered rumor and gossip, probably the most effective form of media in a largely illiterate country. And

Church spokesmen barely responded. Edgar Gutiérrez and others at ODHA already considered the crime-of-passion scenario to be a key element of the crime itself: not just a smoke screen but a trap set to ensnare the Church in such a way that the more the Church leaders and ODHA struggled against the charges, the more they would end up debilitating and dividing themselves. This was because the Church had serious vulnerabilities, and its enemies in the Army knew about them. As Edgar Gutiérrez remarked in an interview, "Mario Menchú says out loud what Military Intelligence is saying in whispers."

In early June, Fernando Linares Beltranena, a conservative lawyer who had made his reputation defending accused military officers and narco traffickers and who also wrote a regular column for *Prensa Libre*, became the first of what would soon be a number of journalists and commentators to discuss the putative crime of passion and the possibility that Bishop Gerardi had been a homosexual. Linares wrote a column that was a particularly strained piece of devil's advocacy: "Is it defamatory to describe Bishop Gerardi as a presumed homosexual?" he asked. "How do the homosexuals feel, whether confessed or in the closet, that their lifestyle should be called an insult or a dishonor? If there were a pro-gay association in Guatemala, they would have protested by now, like the American group defending Versace, recently killed in Miami. It's true that priests take a vow of chastity, but not of castration, and their natural sexual impulse stays alive. . . . The dishonor to Gerardi is his cruel and vile assassination, not the suggestion of his presumably practicing a certain lifestyle."

Dina Fernández, an influential columnist and editor at *Prensa Libre* and a graduate of Columbia University's School of Journalism—I'd met her when she was a student there, and we'd become friends—had been responsible for *Prensa Libre*'s publishing, in its Sunday magazine, a summation of the REMHI report that appeared on the day the bishop died. She had recently given birth to her first child and was trying to be more cautious about what she wrote. Since the murder—and the columns she'd published in response to it—an armed bodyguard had been accompanying her everywhere. But she couldn't stop herself from answering Linares's column with a furious one of her own: "It awakens suspicions that the crime-of-passion version came, with the speed of lightning, from the most powerful man in the Army." She was referring to General Marco Tulio Espinosa and his alleged comments about the murder being a consequence of a homsexual squabble. "As was to be expected, the calumnies made the murder seem banal, anesthetizing those who didn't want to see it as the political step backward it implies," Fernández wrote. "Find a copy of REMHI and read Noél de Jesus Beteta's confession of his assassination of the anthropologist Myrna Mack: there it is explained very well how crimes planned in the EMP are executed to look like common violence."

Although Dina Fernández hadn't named General Espinosa, he answered with an indignant public letter denying her charge and portraying himself as an offended and faithful Catholic. He even invited her to his office for an interview. When Fernández arrived, General Espinosa, his chest bristling with medals, was sitting behind a vast desk flanked by three other military offiers and a soldier who was videotaping the meeting. At one point, Fernández commented on the general's collection of elephant figurines, about a hundred and forty of them, made of marble, glass, ivory, and so on. "The elephant has a long nose to sniff out danger," General Espinosa said to her by way of explaining his collection, "big ears to be able to listen to everything going on around him, strong tusks for defending himself, a thick skin for resisting dagger thrusts, and a very short tail that nobody can grab hold of." It could have been a maxim for operational survival in the cutthroat world of Guatemalan Military Intelligence.

General Espinosa had come out of the Air Force, and it was said that President Arzú had chosen him to lead the EMP because that branch of the military was less politicized than others, less contaminated by the military excesses and power struggles of the past. Colonel Rudy Pozuelos, Espinosa's successor as head of the EMP, had also come out of the Air Force, as had other officers now at the top of the organization. Pozuelos was Espinosa's relative by marriage.

SENSING THE WAY THE WIND was blowing, Fernando Penados had made several attempts to speak with Father Mario, and to offer him help from ODHA in arranging precautionary legal representation. After Mario Menchú's insinuations appeared in the press, Ronalth Ochaeta also tried to reassure the priest. But Father Mario tersely rebuffed all of ODHA's initiatives. In June he announced that he had contracted the services of Vinicio García Pimentel, one of Guatemala's most prominent defense attorneys. García Pimentel had defended the EMP guardsman for the murder of the milkman Sas Rompich. He also represented the elderly Olga Novella, whose kidnapping for ransom by guerrillas on the eve of the 1996 Peace Accords had nearly derailed the signing. Olga Novella was quickly freed, and the guerrilla commandant who had carried out the kidnapping became the last "disappeared" person of the war, a circumstance for which the EMP's anti-kidnapping commando unit was later revealed to be responsible.

Threatening telephone calls arrived regularly at ODHA's offices. Nery Rodenas's wife had recently given birth again, and when he picked up the phone—he had one now—it was often to hear a recording of a desperately wailing child. Threats were called in against the archbishop, who publicly denounced the obvious tapping of his private telephone line and the fact that ever since Bishop Gerardi's death his mail had been arriving opened. Everyone in ODHA had always known that they were subject to surveillance and infiltrators, but the dangerous-looking men posted on the sidewalk outside their doors were becoming more brazen. A priest who had worked on REMHI and whose parish was in the notorious La Limonada slum began to receive threats and was forced to leave the country.

IN HIS FRUSTRATION that none of the blood evidence or the few fingerprints taken from the crime scene had been matched in the FBI labs to Carlos Vielman or anyone inside the parish house—the priest, the cook, the sacristan—Special Prosecutor Ardón requested that fingerprints be taken from every corpse that turned up in the Guatemala City morgues. A buried body missing both hands and the head was exhumed, and Ardón sent tissue samples from the corpse, known as "XX," to the FBI as well.

One night in late May, at an evidentiary procedure conducted at the church of San Sebastián, Ardón turned up with the two protected witnesses, Rubén Chanax and El Chino Iván, to reenact what they had seen on the night of April 26. A policeman played the role of the man without a shirt. Father Mario, other members of the prosecutor's office, and people from ODHA and MINUGUA were also assembled outside the garage.

The small metal door in the garage scraped open, and the subdued fluorescent light from inside penetrated the darkness. A policeman-actor stepped into the narrow doorway, naked from the waist up, in jeans and boots. He hesitated and then took off, running across the park toward Second Street, just as Chanax had described.

The young Untouchable Rodrigo Salvadó, the anthropology student, told me later that the performance gave him goose bumps.

On June 18 Otto Ardón returned to the church of San Sebastián to take a statement from Father Mario, the fourth the priest had given. Two forensics specialists, one medical and the other dental, accompanied him. They tossed a blue plastic ball to Baloo, and after the dog had retrieved it a few times, the dental forensics specialist examined it and, apparently satisfied, placed the ball inside a plastic bag. They dipped the dog's paws in ink and pressed them onto a piece of paper to make prints.

In July, Ronalth Ochaeta traveled to Madrid with Bishop Gerardo Flores to present the REMHI report there. It was a trip he had intended to take with Bishop Gerardi. In response to a reporter's question about whether he thought the Guatemalan government was seriously investigating Gerardi's murder, Ochaeta said that he feared the government was engaging in a cover-up, and that so far it had refused to investigate any of the information ODHA had passed on to it through the High Commission: the license plate, and the anonymous tips implicating the Limas. It was the first time that these pieces of potential evidence against the Limas and the military had been mentioned publicly. Archbishop Penados was said to be frantic with worry that when Ochaeta returned to Guatemala, he would be arrested for his comments. But he came back into the country without incident.

Declassified U.S. embassy diplomatic cables from 1998, dating from the immediate aftermath of the murder, reveal that early on in the case embassy officials regarded ODHA and its claims with skepticism. They regularly expressed sympathy and respect for President Arzú, and even seemed unsuspecting of the military: "The military vigorously denies that any of its members were involved in the murder."

On July 21, UN Secretary-General Kofi Annan visited Guatemala and called for a thorough investigation into Bishop Gerardi's "abominable murder." He warned, "We don't want to give the impression that impunity is something that Guatemalan society tolerates or will tolerate." The next day, a detachment of some 150 special-forces policemen in black berets, armed with automatic rifles and wearing bulletproof vests, surrounded the park and the church of San Sebastián. It was as if they had come to lay siege to a terrorist cell. Otto Ardón was there too, of course, with a warrant for the arrest of Father Mario for the murder of Bishop Gerardi. But

Father Mario wasn't at home. It was his day off and he was at his parents' house, having lunch. He was reached there by telephone and told to return to the parish house immediately, which he did, although the police wouldn't let him past their security perimeter. He insisted that he lived there, but the police said that their orders were to not allow anyone in.

The attention of the assistant prosecutor, Gustavo Soria, was directed to the police line at the edge of the park and the tall, pudgy man wearing large-frame designer glasses, a white shirt with bold blue stripes, gray wool trousers, and a brown suede jacket. Pleading confusion and innocence, tears streaming down his face, Father Mario was handcuffed and led into a police van. Margarita López, the cook, was brought out of the parish house, sobbing loudly. She'd been arrested for destroying and concealing evidence, mainly because, on the priest's orders, she'd helped mop up the crime scene. Baloo was also taken in that day, as material evidence. Baloo was a large dog, but his hindquarters were weak and he had to be shoved, practically hoisted, into the back of a pickup by dog trainers from a private security firm hired by the Public Ministry. On the pickup's bumper someone had scrawled the words "MINUGUA OUT" with a black marker.

Portly Nery Rodenas, dripping sweat, and Mario Domingo came running all the way from ODHA's offices as soon as they heard the news. They showed their identification and the police let them pass. Inside the house they found Pablo Coello, a Spanish Civil Guardsman appointed by MINUGUA to work with the prosecutors, directing the police in a search for evidence in the priest's luxuriously appointed bedroom. Mario Domingo heard one of the policemen exclaim, "All these photos of Baloo! He has more photographs of the dog then religious images!"

Gustavo Soria called out that he had made a new discovery, and Mario Domingo joined the crowd outside the bedroom door, craning his neck to see. The assistant prosecutor, with a malicious smile, was pointing his index finger at a little drawer—he'd just closed it after looking inside—in a wooden table near the door. Theatrically, he reopened the drawer and, using a handkerchief, pulled out a black Walther .380 pistol. "Then, without using the handkerchief," Mario Domingo wrote later, "he popped open the cartridge and raised the pistol to his eye." The gun was loaded.

Two days later, Otto Ardón summoned ODHA's lawyers to the parish house for their first formal meeting in three months. The prosecutors' team had practically moved into the parish house by then. Forensics experts and a Public Ministry psychologist who had prepared a profile of the imprisoned priest were gathered there. Ardón, smoking like a film noir detective, gestured toward a table that was covered with photographs from Bishop Gerardi's autopsy. He drew attention to a photograph that showed four small puncture-like wounds, in the shape of an arc, in the skin on the bishop's skull. The arrest of Father Mario and Margarita López, and the incarceration of Baloo, had been precipitated by the conclusions of a forensic anthropologist in Madrid, Dr. José Manuel Reverte Coma, who had studied the autopsy photographs and had concluded that the marks could have been made only by a dog's bite.

The Public Ministry's dental forensics specialist pulled a plaster cast of a dog's upper teeth and fangs, a model of Baloo's teeth made from the plastic ball the dog had obligingly fetched for prosecutors at the parish house a month before. A transparent laminated sheet had been laid over one of the photographs on the table, which showed Gerardi's skull. The locations of the four puncture wounds had been circled with a black marker. The forensics specialist set the plaster cast down on the transparent sheet, and the points of the teeth fit precisely over the arc of four tiny circles marking the wounds. A crushingly convincing presentation!

But there was even more proof, and there were more photographs. The puncture-like wounds at the base of the bishop's index finger and on his thumb were also explained as a dog bite.

The four parallel streaks on the bishop's neck had been caused by Baloo's claws. Some muddy smears on the bishop's jeans had been left by the dog's paws. A chest-high condensation of bloodstains on the inside of the bishop's jacket had been formed by the weight of the dog's front legs and paws. On and on it went. Then the psychologist spoke: the priest had an infantile personality, he reported, and was overly dependent on his mother.

Mario Domingo and Nery Rodenas, the two lawyers from ODHA, sat listening to the prosecution's presentation, incredulous and downcast. Rodenas asked Otto Ardón when he had first begun to suspect the dog. "Don't believe it was just my idea," Ardón replied. He gestured toward his secretary, Noemi, a skinny, large-breasted young woman in a miniskirt. "She was the first to say, 'Look, *licenciado*, I think these are dog bites.'" Just the other day, Ardón related, Noemi had had a dream in which she came to a fork in a dirt path and a man wearing a priest's black cassock, but lacking a face, appeared to her and said, "Go on, go on, you're on the right path."

Along with Dr. Reverte Coma's deductions about Baloo, the cast of the dog's teeth, and the photographs, Ardón had other circumstantial evidence that made it hard to dismiss out of hand his decision to arrest Father Mario. In one of the priest's declarations he had admitted that Baloo, as a young dog in Germany, had "received the normal training they give to any German shepherd that is going to compete in 'shows' for the breed." That included being trained to attack a forearm. A sheet of paper had been found in Father Mario's bedroom with commands in German, spelled out phonetically, and their translations, including, "*Fass!*" "Attack!" and "*Ous!*"—apparently a command to growl. But when asked if his dog had ever bitten anyone, the priest answered, "Never," and said, "The most he's ever done is growl at people he doesn't know when they come close to me, because when I'm with him in the street or the park, he's defending me." In two of his statements, Father Mario admitted that Baloo sometimes growled at people in the parish house, especially the parish secretary, but never at Bishop Gerardi, and in another, his first statement, he claimed that "the dog never growls, even if he hears footsteps nearby"— this was why, he said, Baloo had kept silent while the murder was taking place.

The most damning testimony against Baloo was in an account of an interview given to prosecutors by a *bolito*, Arni Mendoza, alias El Pitti, on June 12. "Monseñor [Gerardi] was a very good person, totally the contrary of Father Mario Orantes," the transcript of the interview said, "because on the twenty-fifth of April of this year Father Mario turned and ordered his dog to attack him [El Pitti] and it bit him and tore through his pants leg." The *bolito* had also testified that on the night of the bishop's murder, at approximately nine o'clock, he had seen a white car, a Mercedes Benz, parked on Second Street. He saw the same car three days later. Getting out of it was "a priest whom he suspects of having been involved in the crime."

Press accounts, which were usually based on fragmentary information and hearsay, about the "mystery witness"—the taxi driver—always described the car with plate number P-3201 as a white Mercedes. It was a closely held secret among the Untouchables and others at ODHA that the white car with the four-digit military plate had actually been a Toyota Corolla. There had been a white Mercedes Benz at the church the afternoon and the night of the murder, but that car, it was eventually discovered, belonged to an elderly, conservative Spanish priest named Amezaga, who had first come to San Sebastián that day on a routine matter.

El Pitti's declaration seemed designed to link Father Mario to the shirtless man whom the mystery witness had seen next to the white car, but his testimony wasn't credible, and not only because of its convenient timing. He had never mentioned being bitten by Baloo in his earlier declarations to police or during an extensive interview with MINUGUA. And this was the same *bolito* who had turned up outside the cathedral during Bishop Gerardi's funeral ceremonies to shout that the murderer was El Chino Iván. Years later, Rafael Guillamón, the investigator from MINUGUA, told me that in his opinion El Pitti's declaration about the dog bite had been entirely cooked up by Ardón's assistant Gustavo Soria.

"WHAT HAPPENED IS THAT Monseñor saw something extraordinary in the parish house that night as he pulled his car into the garage. And that was precisely what led to his death, because what he saw was something that was supposed to be hidden. That started an argument between Monseñor and his assailant, and his assailant ordered Baloo to attack and then he assaulted Monseñor with some blunt instrument, maybe a crowbar. . . . This murder was committed by one person and a dog, because the corpse had a dog bite in the back of the skull." Mario Menchú, the defense attorney, gave this succinct account of the situation four days after the the arrest of Father Mario and one day before his hapless client, the alcoholic and lame indigent Carlos Vielman, was finally released from jail.

Margarita López, the parish-house cook, was also soon given "provisional" liberty. Two years later, in October 2000, Carlos Vielman died of cirrhosis of the liver. El Pitti had died the year before, of AIDS.

2

FATHER MARIO WAS, at thirty-five, still a young priest for such a relatively quiet, genteel, centrally located parish as San Sebastián, the kind usually reserved, I was told, for bishops with overloaded schedules, like Bishop Gerardi, and old priests on the verge of retirement. Yet Father Mario had already been at San Sebastián for eight years. His duties were relatively light. He'd shared four daily Masses, six on Wednesdays, with Bishop Gerardi. His base monthly salary was 500 quetzales, about seventy-four dollars, plus fourteen quetzales for each Mass. He met and prayed with rosary groups, conducted the occasional group catechism class, heard confessions—the routine duties of a parish priest. The first Saturday of every month he made the rounds of the neighborhood to take confession from parishioners who were too old or infirm to come to church. He was said to have a sympathetic bedside manner with the gravely ill.

When I asked the sacristan, Antonio Izaguirre, whom Bishop Gerardi used to affectionately call Tonomono (Tono is short for Antonio, and *mono* means cute, or monkey)—he had the disheveled, sweet-natured, lonesome air of someone who would have had trouble handling a more demanding job—if Father Mario often left the church to do charity work, the sacristan could barely restrain a laugh. Father Mario, he said, rarely left his bedroom. He was "obsessed," the sacristan told me, "with talking on the phone." But Father Mario was also known for the reticent brevity of his sermons. He struck some people as lazy, others as highly intelligent. Many found him unsociable, barely acknowledging Bishop Gerardi's friends when they visited; others recalled him as gregarious and said that when he did go out, he liked to attend the dinner parties of close friends, especially those of an extremely wealthy woman in late middle age, Martha Jane Melville Novella, whom he had chosen to be "godmother" at his ordination and who gave him a birthday party every year.

Father Mario's relationship with Bishop Gerardi was described by some as friendly enough, though perhaps a bit perfunctory, and by others, including by some of the bishop's relatives, as warmly affectionate. They added that Father Mario liked searching the Internet for obscure theological texts that he knew would delight his superior. Once, Fernando Penados told me, when he was working at the Public Ministry, he'd asked Bishop Gerardi for some Franciscan robes for an undercover operation he was organizing near the church of Candelaria, and it was Father Mario who had procured them.

Father Mario's bad health—he had migraines, asthma, colitis, and ulcers—was the usual explanation for his assignment to San Sebastián, along with his intimacy with Monseñor Efraín Hernández, the chancellor of the Curia. During their boyhood, Hernández had been like a second father to Mario and his older brother, Sergio, who was also a priest. Father Mario had studied at the Liceo Javier, a prestigious school run by Jesuits that was a breeding ground for young political activists and radicals in the 1970s and 1980s, but he became a seminarian in the conservative Salesian order. Later he was a simple diocesan priest. His family was connected to the most conservative wing of the Guatemalan Church. His mother was related to a well-known cleric —Archbishop Mariano Rossell y Arrellano, an aggressive anticommunist who collaborated with the CIA in the lead-up to the coup of 1954. An old schoolmate recalled that Mario's brother,

Sergio, was nicknamed El Nazi because of his authoritarian personality and love of all things military.

Father Mario's schoolmates recalled also that he had wanted to be a priest since childhood. Yet something about him seemed poignantly unsuited for the austere demands of the priesthood, at least as most people conceive of that calling. There was the striking babyishness of his speech, including an overuse, even by Guatemalan standards, of diminutives. And though, as Father Mario, in his own defense, later pointed out, diocesan priests don't take a vow of poverty, the disconcerting number of possessions in his bedroom did not seem in keeping with spiritual transcendence of the seductions of the material world. Father Mario slept in a king-size bed imported from England, made up with luxurious sheets and bedding. Most of the furniture in the room was mahogany, including shelves holding some 600 books, mainly theological, and an entertainment unit that supported a JVC television with a thirty-six-inch screen, a VCR, and a Pioneer laser-disk player. When prosecutors and police searched the room on the day of the arrest, they found approximately ninety videocassettes (*Jurassic Park, The Godfather, The Exorcist, Bordello of Blood,* boxed collections of *Lethal Weapon, Frankenstein,* James Bond thrillers, and comedies with the Three Stooges—the last, according to Mario's mother, his favorite performers). He had a Macintosh 6500/300 computer, an Epson Stylus 800 color printer, a collection of fifty CD-ROMS, a JVC stereo with four ambient speakers, and approximately 200 CDs of mainly classical music and soft Latin romantic pop in the style of Julio Iglesias. He had a reclining armchair and a computer chair upholstered in magenta leather. In his closet were sixty shirts, most either from Ermenegildo Zegna or custom-made in London; twelve leather jackets; twelve pairs of Italian shoes; twenty pairs of slacks and fifteen sweaters, all with designer labels; four Dunhill belts; at least six sets of pajamas; and four bottles of Dunhill cologne. He had three expensive watches, one a gold Cartier found with a receipt for more than $3,500. Along with the Walther pistol in his drawer there were several cartons of bullets, which were described as a gift from his brother Sergio and which Father Mario said he had been intending to sell. There was a framed autographed photograph of a beautiful woman who turned out to be his ordination godmother, Miss Martha Jane Melville Novella. But many of the things found in the room reflected Father Mario's affection for Baloo. There was a stuffed felt dog on the striped bedspread, and the bedroom dresser displayed trophies that Baloo had won in dog shows, as well as a number of framed photographs of the dog. Also found in the room were photographs of Baloo with an erection, or, as Fernando Penados phrased it when describing it to an eminent Church figure, "in his maximum expression." Fernando had then held his hands up, wide apart, and asked the prelate, "Do you understand what I'm trying to tell you?"

Otto Ardón confiscated many of Father Mario's belongings during twelve separate searches of his room conducted in the weeks after his arrest. Some of his clothes and a pair of Gucci shoes were sent by Ardón to Washington, D.C., for testing at the FBI crime lab, along with other pieces of potential evidence, including the cushion Baloo had slept on.

BALOO, WHO WAS BORN in Germany and cost $2,500, was also a gift to Father Mario from his brother, Father Sergio. (Bishop Gerardi's nickname for the pricey thoroughbred was Pecado, "Sin.") In 1992, Father Sergio had assumed the prestigious post of rector of the Colegio San José de los Infantes, which stood alongside the Metropolitan Cathedral. During his tenure, which lasted only four years, he ran up mostly unaccounted-for bills, on the school's bank account, of 4,008,000 quetzales (then nearly $650,000). Part of the money was spent on guns: high-caliber Colts, Tauruses, and Jerichos. The priest gave guns away, and he sold them. The guns were now a problem, because a number of those bought and registered in the school's name were missing. Bills of sale for other missing weapons had been found as well, along with a cache of guns that were never registered at all. In the wake of Father Mario's arrest, the chief of police had personally come to the school and taken away all the documentation relating to the weapons.

One reason that Father Sergio had armed himself so heavily, at least initially, may have been a problem he was having with parents over the issue of school military marching bands. Known as "war bands," they had been omnipresent in the streets of Guatemala City—every school seemed to have its own war band—for as long as any living person could remember, marching and rehearsing dreary martial music for the September 15 Independence Day parade and other patriotic events. Father Sergio's predecessor as rector of the Colegio San José de los Infantes had made the mistake of suspending the bands and was driven from his post by angry parents. In 1998, about 50 percent of the school's 1,100 students were the children of military officers. When Father Sergio took over in 1992, he had reinstated the war bands, and he even organized a trip to Miami for teachers and students to buy new uniforms and instruments; it was one of the first outlays that led to the enormous debt he left behind at the school. The rector who eventually succeeded Father Sergio, José Mariano Carrera, told me that the war bands, with their fervent militarism and patriotism, were a powerful symbol of the anticommunist, pro-military, pro-oligarchy Church of the 1950s, epitomized by the Orantes brothers' cold warrior great-uncle, Archbishop Rossell. The war bands were an expression of the peculiar character of certain sectors of Guatemalan society, and the battle over them was a parable of a clash of local values and beliefs, backward versus modern—easy to imagine as a comic provincial novel with sinister undertones.

The parents of the students at Colegio San José de los Infantes must have been happy with Father Sergio at first. But then President Arzú and his education minister, as a gesture toward demilitarizing Guatemalan society, banned school war bands. The Colegio San José de los Infantes moved from its old quarters alongside the cathedral to a new modern complex on the outskirts of the city. Supposedly, Father Sergio began to receive threats from the parents of students angered by the long commute to the new campus, and by the end of the war bands.

But the guns, and the millions of quetzales in debt—these were discovered later—weren't the reason that the young priest was dismissed from his post. Father Sergio "was having problems of the Lewinsky sort," the new rector, José Mariano Carrera, told me. "As I understand it, his being removed was due to denunciations by various female teachers before the ecclesiastical Curia." Teachers and, it turned out, the mothers of some students, had accused Father Sergio of sexual harassment.

Father Carrera, who was in his sixties, told me that he had been looking forward to retiring to a small coffee farm, but after it became clear that Father Sergio had plunged the venerable school into chaos, Archbishop Penados, an old friend, had asked Carrera to take over. At the time we spoke, only 1 million quetzales of the debt had been paid off. Now the school's accounts were being overseen by a board, but when Father Sergio had been there he could write checks drawing on the school's accounts whenever and for as much as he wished, with no oversight. "Sergio was loved here," Carrera said. "Before he left, he gave away four pistols to his friends at the school. And, of course, dogs." (Sergio had bought four pedigreed German shepherds that lived in his house at the school, and he bred them.) The new rector had also discovered an account at the Popular Bank of Florida in the name of both Orantes brothers, Sergio and Mario.

Father Mario traveled to Houston at least twice a year to receive treatment for his migraines and other ailments at the Methodist Hospital there. Carrera told me that Baloo also went to Houston. "I know that dog traveled to the United States one time," he said. "It was paid for with this school's money. Sergio took the dog to Houston on a plane, so that his brother wouldn't be sad." In Houston, Father Mario reportedly stayed in an apartment owned by his wealthy ordination godmother.

Monseñor Hernández, the chancellor of the Curia—the Church's highly placed power broker, the man to see in Guatemala City if you needed a bureaucratic snag resolved, the man with connections and influence everywhere—had handled Father Sergio's dismissal from the post of rector very discreetly, arranging for his transfer to another parish, with a certificate stating that he had run the Colegio San José de los Infantes responsibly. "Monseñor Hernández is like Richelieu," Carrera said. "He's in charge of the ecclesiastical government's business." The new rector paused a moment, as if to reflect silently on the ethical dilemma he was presenting. "Archbishop Penados said we have to show that we're not hiding anything," he continued, as if arguing with himself. "What information we have, we have to give. . . . What seems so strange to me is that, well, these are priests. One has to have confidence in their sanctity. If Hernández knew about what Sergio was doing, he should have told the other bishops. Archbishop Penados should be able to believe in his priests— believe in them and love them. " Carrera paused again. "The archbishop is very tired. I feel bad for him. The man he most trusted was Gerardi. His absence has been very painful for him, with good reason."

Shortly after Father Sergio's problems at the school became known, he left Guatemala. At the time of the murder, he was a Jesuit novitiate at a seminary in Panama. "Sergio is very intelligent," Carrera said. He characterized Father Mario's godmother as "a dangerous woman." And, he said, "I'll tell you that, personally, I am afraid of Sergio."

The rector then gave voice to the thoughts that inevitably arose from the conversation we'd been having. "If you absorb this information, you're going to notice that something like this"—he meant Father Sergio and what had happened at the school—"can seem to have a connection to a crime like that." He meant Bishop Gerardi's murder. "And that's crazy, no?"

Something like this can seem to have a connection to a *crime like that.* That would be the seemingly irresistible logic behind so much of the suspicion, speculation, and tendentiousness that was beginning to envelope the Gerardi case, and that was only a small fraction of what lay ahead. So much could be made and so much would be made to *seem to connect.* That endlessly exploitable situation was what the ODHA lawyer Mynor Melgar was referring to when he said of those who plotted the crime that when they considered who Bishop Gerardi was sharing the parish house with—Father Mario— "they must have felt like they'd won the lottery."

MARTHA JANE MELVILLE NOVELLA, Father Mario's great friend and patron, was an unmarried woman from the family that owns Guatemala's cement monopoly. She was known for her elegant beauty and iron sense of privacy as well as for lavish charity to the most conservative wing of the Church. She also made accomplished recordings of herself singing religious music, which she gave out to family and friends. José Toledo, the lawyer who had soon replaced García Pimentel as Father Mario's representative, told me that Melville Novella and Father Mario met when she audited a theology class in which he was a Salesian seminary student. A Guatemalan who had married into the Novella family and who asked to remain anonymous said that relatives had confided that Melville Novella was obsessed with the priest and that on her frequent trips to Europe she zealously shopped for gifts for him. Melville Novella was the likeliest source—his brother Sergio's bank accounts were another—of the many expensive items found in Father Mario's bedroom. Bishop Gerardi used to tease the priest about the way he "exploited" that "poor woman."

A Guatemalan woman, a self-described "observer" of Guatemalan society, told me that when they were both in late adolescence,

Martha Jane Melville Novella was "the most beautiful woman in all Guatemala." Melville Novella's first boyfriend, the woman told me, was an aristocratic polo player, "with the dark skin and handsome looks of a Bedouin. He was beautiful. He drove a gray Jaguar. You'd see them here and there and they were the most beautiful pair of *novios* anyone had ever seen. They were together from the time she was fifteen until she was in her twenties, but they never married." Later Melville Novella married a man who became a politician. But as soon as they returned from their honeymoon, the Guatemalan society observer told me, the couple separated. An aura of mystery and secrecy subsequently enveloped the heiress.

One evening I phoned Martha Jane Melville Novella. I gave my name to the maid who answered the phone, then listened to a long train of footsteps recede and then return across what I imagined to be a highly polished floor. The maid asked the purpose of my call. I answered that I was a journalist from New York, then listened to the footsteps go away and come back again. The maid said that her mistress wasn't in.

THE FABULOUSLY WEALTHY WOMAN from the family with a cement monopoly, a financial supporter of the most conservative wing of the Church, and the middle-class mother of two priests who was herself the niece of a politically conservative and powerful prelate, Archbishop Rossell, and who perhaps saw the Church as a place where her sons could advance in society just as her uncle had advanced—these were Guatemalans who would naturally prefer the old Church, close to the military and ruling establishment, cozy with privilege, over the modern, more activist one, with its "Preferential Option for the Poor" and its Bishops' Conference that issued pro-reform pastoral letters such as the "Clamor for Land" in 1989.

"The Orantes were always very disrespectful to my uncle," Fernando Penados told me. He said that Father Mario's mother,

Marta Nájera de Orantes, was so angry at Archbishop Penados over the removal of Sergio from the prestigious post of rector of the Colegio San José de los Infantes that she refused to speak to him at Monseñor Gerardi's last birthday party. Two weeks after the bishop was killed, Father Mario went to see the archbishop and asked to be elevated to the post of parish priest at the church of San Sebastián. When the archbishop declined to grant his wish on the spot, Father Mario angrily departed without even saying good-bye.

Fernando Penados knew from experience that investigating the murder of a priest is always a delicate matter. Priests are expected to live purer lives than other people, and when evidence to the contrary turns up it is assumed that such "disappointing" personal behavior must have something to do with the crime. (The *something like this* that connects to the *something like that*.) The investigation of Bishop Gerardi's murder, Fernando knew, wasn't going to be an exception. The "documentation" by ODHA of the murder on behalf of the Church was exposing elements of the lives of the clergy that were not very attractive.

"Our responsibility was to get the facts, but we were worried about what position the bishops would take when confronted with them," Fernando told me. Nevertheless, when he warned Bishop Mario Ríos Montt, Gerardi's successor as the head of ODHA, that a full investigation into the murder meant opening the Guatemalan Catholic Church to further embarrassment and scandal, "Monseñor Ríos said, 'If we have to purify the Church in order to get to the bottom of this crime, then we'll purify the Church.'"

3

OTTO ARDÓN HAD, clearly, decided to pin the murder of Bishop Gerardi solely on Father Mario and to ignore ODHA's insistence that Military Intelligence was involved. It didn't help that in July, following the priest's arrest, Ronalth Ochaeta was quoted as saying, "From the time of Jesus, the Church has always had its Judases." People inside ODHA were annoyed with Ronalth for playing into Ardón's hands. But he told me that he didn't regret his statement about Judases. "I believe that Mario knows more," he said. "Of that I am sure."

Ronalth Ochaeta had been involved in human rights issues since the early 1980s, when he was a young graduate of the law school at the University of San Carlos and was teaching some courses there. Antigovernment guerrilla organizations were recruiting students—"crassly co-opting them," in Ronalth's words—with free flights and junkets to Mexico, and the government was cracking down. More than a dozen student leaders "disappeared" or were simply murdered. Ronalth Ochaeta did legal paperwork for students who were in danger and wanted visas to the United States, and he would spend hours arguing on their behalf with embassy functionaries. Then he realized that he was being followed, that he was under surveillance, and he canceled the classes he was teaching, began staying away from the university, and started a small law practice in Guatemala City.

As a lawyer, Ochaeta traveled frequently to Cobán, the provincial capital of Alta Verapaz, where he had grown up, to work with his brother in the pastoral social office, a charity and aid group. It was there that he met Myrna Mack Chang, the young anthropologist, who frequently came through Cobán to meet with Church officials regarding the plight of displaced internal refugees, the subject of her research and activism. Around this time, Archbishop Penados was looking for young people to work with Bishop Gerardi, who was setting up what would become ODHA. Gerardi had been the bishop of Verapaz when Ronalth was a boy and had given Ronalth his First Communion and had also shut down the school in which he studied. When Ronalth finally went to see Bishop Gerardi for a job interview, he described their last encounter, eighteen years before. "So it's you!" laughed Gerardi. "And what happened to you after I closed your school?" The bishop told Ronalth that working in human rights would be dangerous, and that there wasn't any money yet to pay him. Ronalth said that the money didn't matter, that he had his law practice, and that he would work for the bishop part-time. After nine months, as international donations made ODHA more solvent, the bishop asked what he thought a fair salary would be for full-time work. Ronalth said more than a law professor at the University of San Carlos earned, and less than a judge, and Gerardi agreed.

Ronalth Ochaeta worked with Bishop Gerardi until 1993, when he and his new family were forced by threats into exile. He spent a year studying for a master's degree at the University of Notre Dame law school in South Bend, Indiana, and then returned to ODHA. He said to me that his years with Bishop Gerardi were "a long tortuous path where the occasional joy of saving a life compensated for the daily grind of feeling utterly impotent in our work." Ronalth was worn out. He had assumed that he would leave ODHA after the REMHI report was published, but the murder of the bishop had changed everything. The dark cloud of fear in which years of human rights work had submerged his wife, Sonia, and their two small children at last seemed too much to ask of them, and of himself. One evening, in a moment of unguarded pessimism, he said to me that Bishop Gerardi's murder had left him feeling that everything—the years at ODHA, REMHI, fighting for human rights in Guatemala—had been futile.

OTTO ARDÓN HAD BEGUN suggesting that Bishop Gerardi had actually been assaulted in or on the threshold of Father Mario's bedroom, that the bishop had stumbled on something that Father Mario didn't want him to see. "Who were the people who carried Monseñor Gerardi from the spot where he was attacked to the spot where he died?" Ardón had demanded of Father Mario during the interrogation on the day of his arrest. The priest answered that he didn't know, because he had found the bishop dead in the garage.

I went one morning with Ronalth Ochaeta to the church of San Sebastián, to look at the crime scene. There were lit candles and a vase of flowers along the garage wall, facing the spot where Bishop Gerardi's body had lain, his head in a pool of blood. There had been double streaks of blood smeared to that pool from a larger one near where Gerardi's Volkswagen Golf was parked, indicating that the bishop's body had been dragged about twelve feet. Ronalth speculated that the double streaks were made by the bishop's buttocks dragging along the floor while his body—which was bulky—was hoisted by two people, one holding him under the arms, the other by the legs. The bishop's blood-soaked jeans had been tugged down well below the line of his underpants, as would happen to someone pulled along like that. Ronalth's theory was that the killers were worried that the blood might seep outside, under the garage doors, to where the *bolitos* were sleeping. But the prosecutors were arguing that the blood streaks had been made with a mop, in order to plant misleading evidence.

The small, narrow footprint had been found not far from the body, pointing to the rear of the garage. After it had been wiped away, the footprint had turned up again during the first week of May, when prosecutors—with some assistance from the FBI on at least one occasion—had twice performed tests inside the parish house with Luminol, a chemical that reacts to traces of seemingly invisible blood by emitting a bright blue glow. Luminol detects the iron particles of hemoglobin and also reacts to other organic matter, but with a glow different from that caused by blood. The Luminol had revealed more bloody footprints leading into the small library inside the house, and at the entrance to the ironing room, and traces of bloody handprints on the library's glass-topped desk. There were also blood drops on the floor of the VW Golf. The blue glow took the shape of fingerprints near the garage door, and of splatter marks and wiped smears on the wall opposite the driver's side of the parked car. The Luminol exposed blood drops and smudges along the corridor of the house and in front of Father Mario's bedroom door. The prosecutors claimed that Baloo had left some of those marks. Luminol testing inside Father Mario's bedroom found traces of more blood, or of "organic matter," near his closet, and stains on the soles of his Gucci loafers.

Of course, it was possible that the Luminol reactions in the priest's room indicated nothing more than unsurprising traces of a very bloody crime scene, along with the ordinary secretions of daily life, even something like a forgotten nosebleed. Luminol can identify blood but gives no definite indication of when it might have been deposited. Father Mario had insisted that he'd been very careful not to get blood on his shoes, though it was more than possible that he could have done so anyway, and he insisted that Baloo had not left the bedroom on the night of the crime. From prison, Father Mario, through his lawyer, explained that the drops of blood attributed to Baloo could be a result of the aged dog's multiple infirmities: Baloo's prostate bled sporadically, as did his claws, from the effort of walking on arthritic hind legs.

There had also been traces of blood (surely Bishop Gerardi's blood) found on the steps leading to a short hallway that connects the garage to the sacristy and the church, and a smudge, as if left by the light brush of a fingertip, on the wall of that hallway. That little smudge had remained there, unnoticed or ignored by prosecutors, for a long time. Recently it had been carelessly whitewashed during routine maintenance of the parish house. Ronalth Ochaeta speculated that those traces and the smudge were from the same person who had left the footprint while stepping away from the bishop. The footprint seemed a key piece of evidence in support of one of the few theories on which the prosecutors and ODHA agreed: that there was more than one perpetrator. There was the man who had left his sweatshirt on the floor and stepped out naked from the waist up through the little garage door, and who was wearing boots. Then there was another person, perhaps the owner of the shoe that had left the bloody footprint, who could have fled through the back of the parish house garage into the church and out through any number of exits. But for that to be true, Ronalth explained, someone had to have unlocked the door and gate connecting the parish house to the church.

We were interrupted by the arrival of a group of girls from the Sacred Family School. The students came into the garage double-file, first-graders first, high schoolers in the rear, singing the hymn "*No podemos avanzar sin la ayuda del Señor.*" They carried candles and colorful homemade paper kites, a traditional symbol of communion with the dead in Guatemala. The kites had photographs cut out of newspapers and headlines about Bishop Gerardi and the REMHI report glued to them, and hand-printed messages. The girls laid the kites down in a pile near the candles and the vase of flowers along the wall, and then they went into the church to pray (up the steps and down the hallway where the bloody smudge had been, through the door and gate that were always locked at night). The students were part of the first generation of Guatemalan children being taught to say out loud that it is wrong for the state to murder. The first generation that might actually have a chance to learn about Guatemala's past, and to distinguish old lies from new truths. By the time the last kite had been laid down, Ronalth's eyes were overflowing with tears. He told me that he and his wife still hadn't told their five-year-old son that Monseñor was dead.

Several of the kites in the pile next to the flowers were decorated with photographs of the bishop's funeral Mass. Tens of thousands of spectators had watched a procession of priests and nuns follow the body around the plaza in front of the Metropolitan Cathedral. People fell silent when they saw the coffin, and then broke into long, steady applause as it slowly circled the plaza. One kite was decorated with a newspaper photograph of Father Mario as a pallbearer, staring sternly ahead. I picked up another kite, on which an adult, probably a parent of one of the girls, had written, in crayon, "*¿Y el sacerdote, qué?* . . . And what about the priest? Good if the authorities tie those military men to the crime, but the participation of Father Mario Orantes should not be discounted." That kite was decorated with another photograph of Father Mario, slumped in a chair at the police station, an image of utter misery.

Bishop Mario Ríos Montt, San Sebastián's new parish priest and Gerardi's successor at ODHA, stepped into the garage. Bishop Ríos was a squat, somewhat penguin-like figure, but energetic, with a stentorian voice and a booming laugh. He had a curious history. He was the brother of the former dictator General Efrain Ríos Montt, who had presided over some of the worst atrocities of the 1980s. In interviews, Bishop Ríos refused to discuss his brother in personal terms, instead stressing generally his belief in "reconciliation as the consequence of justice." He had kept out of the public eye for years, and apparently regarded the fight for the truth about the murder as a final mission in life. "If I accomplish

that," he told me later, "I believe I will have finished my work." It
was he who had told Fernano Penados that if it turned out that
the Church was in need of purification, then they would purify it.

Father Mario's insistence that he hadn't at first recognized the
body as that of Bishop Gerardi had always seemed unlikely.
Bishop Gerardi was a tall man in a country where most people are
not. And the description of the body in the police report from
that night is of a man who is recognizably the bishop: "white-
skinned, curly gray hair, wide forehead, long face, bushy eyebrows." Father Mario said that he had retrieved a flashlight from
his room and shined a light on the bishop's face until he realized
who it was. He had needed the flashlight, he said, because the
light in the garage was insufficient. Bishop Ríos and Ronalth discussed that, perplexed, and Ríos flicked on the lights. Two long
fluorescent tubes came on in the garage ceiling, and even by day-
light, with the doors partially open, the garage was illuminated
brightly. He asked us if we thought the light was sufficient.

"Father Mario *sabe algo*," he knows something, said Ronalth.

"*Sabe algo*," Ríos gruffly agreed, and then he flicked off the
light and headed back into the parish house, repeating, in a lamenting singsong, "Mario, Mario, Mario. . . ."

WHAT REALLY HAPPENED that night? If, as everyone at ODHA believed, Father Mario was not the murderer, why did he continue
to give implausible, contradictory accounts of what went on?
What could be so terrifying or shameful that the priest would
endure imprisonment and offer only the most pathetic denials?
Had he let a homosexual lover into his room, and was the lover
one of the killers? Had the killers tricked Father Mario into
collaborating in a less nefarious deed, telling him, for example, that
they were just coming in to steal some papers related to REMHI?
Two of the San Sebastián parish housekeepers told Rafael
Guillamón that a week or so after the bishop's murder Father
Mario had remarked to them that Gerardi had been killed be-

cause "he was the *jefe* of all the guerrillas." That was the sort of flippant comment any right-wing Guatemalan might have made in order to justify the bishop's murder. The bishop himself had told Ronalth Ochaeta and Edgar Gutiérrez some years before that he had heard stories about Father Mario's being an Army informer. He had joked that the priest could do less harm close by, where Gerardi could keep an eye on him. As for Father Mario's sexual orientation, there were only rumors.

On the morning of August 7, copies of a three-page document printed on paper to which UN Refugee Commission logos and German headings had been pasted—including a quotation in German from Euripides—arrived by fax at a number of locations in Guatemala City. The office of the Myrna Mack Foundation received one, as did the newspaper *Prensa Libre*. Reporters from the latter immediately brought it to ODHA's attention. The document was apparently an internal memo, an intelligence analysis of Bishop Gerardi's murder, addressed to a lieutenant colonel in the EMP. It named the Limas and implicated other officers in the execution, bungling, and cover-up of the murder of Bishop Gerardi. The document said that Captain Byron Lima Oliva's mission had been to steal "information related to REMHI" from the parish house, "not the physical destruction of Mon. Gerardi." Captain Lima was described as having lost control of the operation, whereupon he phoned his father, Colonel Byron Lima Estrada, who arrived in a car previously assigned to him, when he was the commander of the military base in Chiquimula.

The document was composed by a person who knew certain information—some details of the crime and the names of officers —that only someone close to the hermetic EMP, if not inside it, would know. (Some of those names would emerge at later stages of the investigation into the crime; others would not.) Perhaps most astonishingly, it mentioned that Captain Lima had "left his sneaker print at the crime scene." How did the writer know that the bloody footprint—which wasn't, in fact, from a shoe in Captain

Lima's size—was a sneaker print? Had the EMP photographer who was alleged to have been in the garage that night photographed it? Had he seen and reported it? The FBI report that would identify this print as having been left by the sole of a NIKE Air Top Challenge—an athletic shoe that was discontinued by Nike in 1991—wouldn't be submitted to Guatemalan prosecutors until January 1999.

Perhaps a military officer who was dismayed by the recklessness of the crime and the risks it posed to the EMP's reputation and position had written the document. It referred to the "degrading of the Presidential Guard" and lamented that "now with this act we are seen as violators of the Peace Accords." Or maybe it was someone who didn't like the Limas and their "faction"—if there was a faction—and their influence inside the EMP. (The document also mentioned the money Lima and others had reportedly stolen when they were in the anti-kidnapping commando unit.) Perhaps, some would charge later, it was the true culprits, intending to misdirect suspicion toward the Limas, who had written the document. Perhaps more than one officer had worked on the anonymous note. Perhaps it was written in revenge by military men, formerly close to President Arzú, whose power and influence had been usurped by General Espinosa and his cohort at the EMP. In any case, the authors knew some things about the crime, but were wrong about others.

The day the document arrived at ODHA, Bishop Ríos personally marched over to the office of Eduardo Stein, the foreign minister, and attempted to show it to him, but Stein was busy. Later, when journalists asked Stein about this, he said that he personally wouldn't give any importance to such a document.

THE UNTOUCHABLES WERE TRYING to identify the two members of the EMP seen at the church on the night of the murder, and they were still looking for the taxi driver. They had driven Father Quiróz, the priest the taxi driver had visited, to taxi stands all over the city in a futile attempt to identify the putative witness. Finally the priest, fed up with the tedium of basic police work, refused to accompany them on any more outings. At the end of August, a taxi driver named Carlos García was found murdered, wrapped in plastic garbage bags, a bullet through his forehead and his body marked by signs of torture; the body had been tossed into one of the deep ravines outside Guatemala City. The taxi driver's family said that García had recently been receiving death threats. It turned out that he had once been briefly imprisoned on a drug charge. When Father Quiróz was shown a photograph of the murdered man, he told Fernando Penados that he was "seventy percent sure" it was the same one who had come to see him in his church. Father Quiróz had himself begun to receive threatening telephone calls and was frightened nearly out of his wits.

A new taxi driver, Hans Pérez, soon surfaced, first inside the prison where Father Mario was being held and then back out on the streets. Pérez had been taped in prison, where he made both credible and ludicrous assertions about the involvement of the military and gangs in Gerardi's murder. He mentioned a white Mercedes Benz and implicated the gang of satanists who used to hang around San Sebastián park and also—more significantly, it turned out—a young delinquent from the so-called Valle del Sol gang. The Untouchables tried to follow up on some of those leads. Looking for a military agent whom Pérez linked to the satanists, Fernando Penados and I went to the second-rate bordello where he was said to hang out and wasted a few hours drinking beers, waiting to see if he would show up. Hans Pérez repeated his story in the press, to the police and the Public Ministry, and to anyone else who would listen, which was highly suspicious. "In a country like this," Fernando said, "it's not credible for someone to be going around implicating the military like that."

Had someone planted Hans Pérez? The same people who had murdered Carlos García? The Untouchables, who had dismissed him at first, tried to find him again, hoping to discover what the real story was. But Hans Pérez had dropped from sight.

NERY RODENAS AND MARIO DOMINGO, meanwhile, had regained their composure after that dispiriting day in the San Sebastián parish house with the autopsy photographs and the casts of Baloo's teeth. They had studied the photographs further and had some questions. If Baloo's upper teeth had made those bites, where were the bites made by the bottom teeth? Dr. Reverte Coma had identified a tear-like bruise in the bishop's earlobe as the spot where the lower teeth had sunk in. But could Baloo unhinge his jaws like a python to envelope nearly the bishop's entire head? And, most strikingly, the top of the arc of the alleged bites was pointed in the direction of the ear.

Mario Domingo was scathing. "So they're saying that this poor *chucho*"—it means dog in Guatemala—"has a snout made of rubber if he can twist it around into a shape like that." The other lawyers laughed at his *chiste*. Domingo physically resembled a cross between Popeye and a Chinese monk, with a perpetually cranky expression and a lively glint in his eye, an effect amplified by his eyeglasses. He often spoke so quickly, swallowing consonants, that people unaccustomed to listening to him had no idea what he was saying. When he laughed, he laughed quietly but with all his body, his face intensely flushing the color of strawberry juice.

The ODHA lawyers were in a difficult position. As co-plaintiffs in the case, they were supposed to be on the side of the prosecution. And they weren't at all convinced of Father Mario's innocence. But on August 24 they asked that Bishop Gerardi's body be exhumed to see if the dog bites were there or not. The Public Ministry blinked first and said that it needed more time to prepare. On September 7 the judge in the case ruled that Dr. Reverte Coma's theory about Bishop Gerardi's having been bitten by a dog shortly before, during, or even after his murder was so compelling that a new autopsy was required.

*　*　*

WHEN PEOPLE IN GUATEMALA said that the murder of Bishop Gerardi was "the perfect crime," they didn't necessarily mean that they didn't think they knew who had done it. Most, at least in 1998, thought the Army had done it. But it was much harder to understand why.

Edgar Gutiérrez told me that it had never even entered his mind that Bishop Gerardi might be killed. "Why would a seventy-five-year-old bishop, on the verge of retiring, become the target of assassins? It made no sense." Only later did he realize what "a complex chess move" the murder had been. Gutiérrez was one of the people who always referred to the murder as "a masterpiece," "a work of diabolical genius."

If one looked at the situation only in the *old* way—the way that preceded the Peace Accords—then the Guatemalan Army had every reason to want to kill Bishop Gerardi: his murder would be interpreted as a warning, as a clear statement that the Army would not tolerate threats to its position. But for the crime to be "perfect," the Army would have to get away with it officially, and it would have to accomplish much more than just terrorize the Army's traditional opponents in human rights circles and the Church. One step toward that goal would be to disguise it as the consequence of a domestic conflict or a robbery or such. This strategy had often worked in the past: the assassination, in 1994, of the president of the Constitutional Court, Epamonidas González (after he had ruled to extradite an Army lieutenant colonel to the United States to face drug trafficking charges), which was made to look like a carjacking gone awry; the assassination of the newspaper publisher and politician Jorge Carpio Nicolle on a lonely mountain road, seemingly the act of a predatory highway robber; the murder of my former colleague the young, elegant Malaysian-British journalist Anson Ng (who had been reporting for the *Economist* on the involvement of some Guatemalan generals in the BCCI banking fraud scandal), apparently a robbery or sexual crime in a hotel room; and, of course, the murder of Myrna

Mack Chang in 1990. The EMP had even employed hot dog vendors to stake out Mack's office and study her comings and goings. Whenever people said that Bishop Gerardi's murder couldn't have been a political assassination because it had all the markings of a domestic or common crime, they were displaying their unfamiliarity with how political murders are carried out in Guatemala. But precisely because such methods were familiar, in order to really create a masterpiece and also get away with the crime, the plotters of Bishop Gerardi's murder would have to be much more inventive.

"I don't like this case, it's *shuco*," gross, dirty, Otto Ardón confided to a courthouse reporter in Guatemala City, and the homophobic content of the remark was obvious to her. It was another little dart, one more strategic salvo. Get it into the press, into the rumor mill, into the public consciousness, and it won't matter when later it turns out not to be true. What people would have been talking about in the meantime was not the content or repercussions of *Guatemala: Never Again*. They would have been debating, joking, and amusing themselves about the man without a shirt and the carnivalesque "dog-and-priest" show. Would people even notice that the Public Ministry was refusing to conduct any serious investigation of the Army's role in Bishop Gerardi's murder?

What if a crime could be created in which as soon as one false scenario was rebutted, another one was ready to take its place? In the case of Bishop Gerardi, there would always be one more thing like *this* that could be made to seem as if it must have had something to do with *that*.

One effect of Bishop Gerardi's murder, whether intended by the murderers or not, was to encourage President Arzú not to pursue many of the Peace Accord reforms that were opposed by the Army and hard-line conservatives. "The president's discourse keeps getting harder and closer to the Army," Edgar Gutiérrez noted. The insistence by human rights activists—and ODHA was not the only such group in the country—on accountability was seen by Arzú as a disruption of the normalization process. The murder of Bishop Gerardi and its aftermath coincided with a ferocious campaign by the government against human rights organizations in general and the Catholic Church in particular. In September, in a speech to graduating military cadets, President Arzú called human rights activists "nearly traitors to the fatherland." It is not only in Guatemala that such language invites and summons violence against its target.

4

BY MID-SEPTEMBER, all across the country, automobiles displayed bumper stickers reading "Free Baloo!" It was reported that prosecutors had sequestered the dog somewhere on the steamy southern coast but that he so missed Father Mario that he had stopped eating, and that this led to such a severe decline in his health that he was brought back to the city for a brief reunion with his master. Now Baloo was being held at some secret location. It was also said that the prosecutor and his men had worn the dog out to the point of death trying to train, or retrain, him to respond to the German attack commands written out on the sheet of paper found in Father Mario's room. This didn't seem completely far-fetched to Father Mario's cheerful, pie-faced young lawyer, José Toledo. "They wanted to retrain him to be a killer, but they couldn't, because the dog isn't any good anymore!" Toledo laughed. Too old and sick to be a killer dog now!

I laughed too, and said I'd thought that was just a rumor. "Rumor!" echoed the lawyer, and then he added, "Of course, if I were the prosecutor, I'd do it too." Another blast of nervous laughter. "To prove my theory. Sometimes in this life, lawyers use strategies that are not totally moral, true? And prosecutors are no exception," he said. "They're convinced that Father Mario has information he doesn't want to give. They want to put pressure on the Father. Maybe he'll get desperate, bored, and give them something. But he doesn't know anything."

A few nights before the exhumation of Bishop Gerardi's body, I took a taxi to the San Francisco de Asís veterinary clinic, in the industrial outskirts of Guatemala City, in the hope of being able to see Baloo. José Toledo had confided to me that the dog was being kept there. There was only one plainclothes security man posted in the small parking lot, and no sign of activity inside the building. I knocked at the door, a small window slid open, and the sympathetic face of the night-shift veterinarian appeared. He said I couldn't see Baloo, that I wasn't even supposed to know Baloo was there, but he agreed to let me come in and talk about the dog. The veterinarian told me that Baloo had been extremely ill when he arrived at the clinic. He was dehydrated and showed signs of neglect. Instead of bathing and grooming the dog as Father Mario used to do, his handlers from the Public Ministry had occasionally just hosed him down. His hindquarters were almost paralyzed from spondylitis, a degenerative, arthritis-like condition of the spinal column, for which he was being treated with regular doses of anti-inflammatory medicines. Baloo was doing much better now.

We talked about what Baloo was fed in the clinic (Purina Proplan), how many times a day he was walked, the size of his cage, and so on. If I wasn't going to be allowed to see the celebrity patient, I wanted to be able to accurately report the conditions of his confinement. In my notebook, the veterinarian helped me sketch the patio where Baloo was being kept. I drew a large cage in the corner. He touched the page with his finger and said, "No, there are four cages," and traced their layout. So Baloo shared the patio with other dogs. "Then people who come to visit their own dogs get to see Baloo?" I asked. And he said, "Yes, but they don't know they're seeing Baloo." I said, "What if I pretend I'm just going back there to visit my sick Chihuahua, and you don't have to say anything? I'll just look around and see if I can spot Baloo."

The veterinarian thought it over for a moment, and then, to my surprise, he said, "*Bien.*"

We walked down a corridor, past the one orderly on duty, while in a rather theatrical voice the veterinarian began giving me a tour of the clinic, including a stop into the postoperative recovery room (dogs with plastic cones around heads, baleful stares), and then into a darkened patio lined with large cages. Three of the cages had dogs in them, and two of the dogs were German shepherds. I walked up to one of them, cooing, "*Hola,*" and "*Qué buen perro,*" and the dog—long, lean, and handsome—jumped up onto the wire mesh, wagging his tail. When I went over to the other cage, where a thick-necked German shepherd sat regally, the dog bared his fangs and growled so menacingly that I stepped back. The veterinarian nodded toward the dog and said, "*Perro bravo.*" Mean dog.

We had agreed that he wouldn't identify Baloo. "Which one of those two dogs is older?" I asked. The veterinarian just laughed.

Mean Baloo or nice Baloo? Had Baloo indeed bitten the bishop's head and thumb, as claimed by Dr. Reverte Coma and the prosecutors? During those days leading up to Bishop Gerardi's exhumation, few people in Guatemala were not taking that question seriously. Not only the issue of Father Mario's freedom but also the course and character of the entire Guatemalan peace process seemed to hinge on the answer.

AT SIX IN THE MORNING on Thursday, September 18, people began assembling in the Spanish colonial courtyard of the building where ODHA has its office. The exhumation of the bishop's corpse and the autopsy were scheduled to last two days. Experts from the United States who had volunteered, pro bono, to attend on ODHA's behalf had flown in the day and night before, but now it wasn't at all clear that they would be allowed to participate. They had been unexpectedly confronted with a hopelessly convoluted credentialing process. The previous morning, Judge

Isaías Figueroa, a wily veteran of the court system, had dropped a bomb, claiming that all experts had to present themselves to him by three in the afternoon, and had to have already been credentialed as members of the Guatemalan professional associations their expertise corresponded to; but this was impossible to do in one day. Meanwhile, Dr. Reverte Coma had quietly arrived in the country ten days before.

"Those shits had this cake already baked," Ronalth Ochaeta fumed. The ODHA lawyers frantically worked the telephones, arguing with various court and government officials that in fact Guatemalan law required such credentialing only for participation as a foreign expert in an actual criminal trial, not for a pretrial evidentiary proceeding. (ODHA's telephones were thoroughly tapped, subject to sudden storms of static and continual disconnections. People there were always slamming down phones and muttering, "*Puta,* they kidnapped the call.")

At this point, only the San Francisco attorney and private investigator Jack Palladino—fresh from a controversy raised by the independent prosecutor Kenneth Starr and congressional Republicans over his role in "opposition research" for President Bill Clinton's 1992 campaign—who had arrived in the judge's quarters before the three PM deadline on Wednesday, could participate, and even Palladino could participate only as a "forensic photographer." Standing by in the courtyard were Dr. Robert Bux and Dr. Norman Sperber. Bux was the deputy chief medical examiner of Bexar County, Texas, which includes the city of San Antonio; he was a veteran of over 1,200 autopsies of homicide victims and of two separate clandestine exhumations from mass graves in Bosnia, and the author of a not irrelevant article published in the December 1992 issue of the *American Journal of Forensic Medicine and Pathology*, "Death Due to Attack from Chow Dog." Norman Sperber was the chief forensic dentist for California's San Diego and Imperial counties, with 2,000 forensic examinations behind him and criminal investigations of more than 500 bite cases, including fourteen involving dogs. Sperber had developed the Dental Division of the FBI's National Crime Information Center, and had been an expert witness in high-profile homicide cases in the United States, including the trials of serial murderers Ted Bundy and Jeffrey Dahmer. Jack Palladino's clients included not only President Clinton but the hip-hop entrepreneur Suge Knight, the cofounder of Death Row records, who in 1998 was in prison for parole violations. Among the murders Palladino had investigated were the People's Temple case, the murder-suicide of more than 900 members of a religious cult in Jonestown, Guyana; and the notorious murder of the Hollywood entertainment company executive José Menendez and his wife by their two sons.

Thursday morning the American specialists huddled with their Guatemalan counterparts, Dr. Guerra of the Judicial Morgue, who had performed the original autopsy, and Helen Mack's friend Doctor Mario Iraheta, who would be ODHA's forensics specialist at this second autopsy. They talked quietly, speculating on the likely condition of Bishop Gerardi's corpse, and on how dry conditions might be in the crypt and inside the coffin.

I spoke to Dr. Reverte Coma in an office off the courtyard. He was seventy-nine years old, bald, and had a white mustache, bushy white eyebrows, brilliant blue eyes, and pale skin that seemed nearly translucent. Leaning back in his chair with arms folded across his chest—a characteristic posture, it turned out— he began telling me of his long history in Central America, particularly in Panama. When the Nicaraguan dictator Anastasio "Tacho" Somoza (the elder) was mortally wounded by an assassin's bullet in 1956, he was flown to the Canal Zone on orders of the White House, and there, Reverte Coma told me, he had participated in the failed surgery to save Somoza's life. In 1992, he was the Spanish delegate to an exhumation sponsored by the UN in El Mozote, El Salvador, where more than 1,200 peasants had been massacred by the Salvadoran Army.

Suddenly our conversation was cut off by a hulking man in a beige suit, demanding to know if I was a journalist. He was a bodyguard from Safari, a private security company. A little later, in the courtyard, I stood next to a pair of Safari's young security agents, outfitted like commandos in full battle gear, as they ostentatiously scrutinized the red-tiled rooftops for signs of a sniper willing to resort to a last-second assassination in order to prevent Dr. Reverte Coma from proving his theory about the dog bites.

Bishops in their dark suits and red caps; prosecutors, including Otto Ardón; people from ODHA and the Church; lawyers and Guatemalan forensics experts representing all parties in the case; the mortician who had originally embalmed Bishop Gerardi; and of course the ubiquitous observers from MINUGUA, including Rafael Guillamón, were gathered around Judge Figueroa and Ronalth Ochaeta—probably the two shortest men present—as they faced off like a pair of fighting roosters in the middle of the courtyard to resolve the issue of the American experts' participation. Judge Figueroa had privately told Ronalth that if he would agree to expel MINUGUA's observers from the proceedings, on the grounds that they would leak information to the press, he would allow ODHA's foreign experts to participate. But Ronalth had rejected any such deal, thinking that MINUGUA's presence would ensure that whatever happened at the exhumation might not be publicly misrepresented later. (I was the only journalist present.)

"We all want the truth," Ronalth said. "This should be between scientists, not lawyers." He pointed out that not letting ODHA's experts take part would damage the legitimacy of the proceedings. The atmosphere couldn't have been more grimly tense as Judge Figueroa nervously began polling those assembled around him. Only Ardón voted to ban the Americans. Figueroa was perspiring, and his resolve was obviously wilting. Suddenly he exploded at Ronalth Ochaeta, "What are you smiling at!"

"Not at *you*, Judge," Ronalth retorted.

They argued back and forth for a moment. Then the judge reversed himself, but only partially. He said the American experts could be present at the exhumation and autopsy, but only as observers. They could not participate alongside the Spanish expert and the others at the autopsy table.

Led by Bishop Ríos Montt, the assembly filed through a door into the cathedral, passed behind the nave into a corridor of the sacristy, went down a stairway into another courtyard ringed by priests' and seminarians' residences, and then through a door into the subterranean crypts. Some of those in attendance put on surgical masks. Jack Palladino later recalled that a chair was brought for Dr. Reverte Coma, as if to assign him a special status. Everyone else stood for the fifteen minutes it took two masons with hammers and chisels to work through the whitewashed plaster and crumbling brick of the crypt wall. Then workers from a funeral parlor—they were wearing white gloves—pulled out the long red-lacquered coffin, with handles that Palladino later compared to those of a Porsche briefcase. The coffin was placed on a stand and wiped off with a cloth, and the part of the lid at the end, the part over Bishop Gerardi's head, was pulled open. Bishop Ríos said an Our Father. He leaned over the coffin to peer through the glass window, and the others pressed in around him.

The coffin's surface and the condition of the crypt had seemed promisingly dry. But now they saw that the bishop had grown a beard of dark green mold; his skin had turned black, but his face was covered with white mold—"like the white makeup in a Kabuki play," Jack Palladino said—and patches of fungus, due to the high level of moisture inside the coffin during those first five months of death. The corpse was in a state of serious deterioration, and beetles, maggots, and other insects crawled all over it.

THE BODY OF THE BISHOP was taken from the cathedral to the San Juan de Dios Hospital, where special-forces police wearing riot-shield helmets at first barred ODHA's representatives and the

American experts from entering. But Mynor Melgar, who had retained his affiliation with the Public Ministry, led the team around to a front entrance and through hospital corridors and finally into the room where X rays were being taken of the bishop's skull and hands. Jack Palladino described the scene to me later. "Reverte was making pronouncements," he said. "He would say, there's a fracture, and then he pointed to the wrong finger. Iraheta got his notes out from the original autopsy and started explaining to him where the injuries were, and at that point I realized, This guy is just not competent."

Later that day, the corpse was transferred to the Judicial Morgue. The leathery, desiccated skin on the bishop's face and skull had already been badly eroded. Both Dr. Bux and Dr. Sperber thought it unlikely that much reliable forensic information could be obtained at this point. No effort had been made to properly clean the head, and the Americans were shocked to see Dr. Reverte Coma use a scalpel to scrape away fungus and debris from the bishop's face. "This is a very poor practice as use of such a harsh mechanical procedure is likely to disturb or destroy any remaining forensic evidence on the skin," Palladino wrote in an affidavit he filed on the exhumation. Prohibited from participating in the autopsy, Bux and Sperber could only protest Reverte Coma's actions through their interpreter, to Dr. Iraheta.

Even as observers, by studying the X rays and photographs, the American experts were able to confirm much that the original autopsy had revealed: the cause of death was blunt trauma wounds to the head, most consistent with the chunk of concrete paving stone or some other hard object. But they also found that a fracture across the bridge of the nose had been caused by a hard, cylindrical object, like a pipe—supporting the theory that there were at least two assailants. Another blow had shattered the bishop's jaw, unhinged it, and driven it back into his trachea. That might easily have caused him to drown in his own blood if the other blows hadn't already killed him. Robert Bux said that there had been a complete crushing of the bishop's facial bones. "He was struck in the face first, to incapacitate him and get him down, and then dragged, and struck again."

The forensics specialist who had presided at the first autopsy, Mario Guerra, had noticed, and Dr. Sperber and Jack Palladino confirmed, that the photograph of the bishop's head used by Dr. Reverte Coma to match the cast of Baloo's teeth had been blown up by 25 percent. In any case, according to Dr. Sperber, the marks didn't have the rhomboid shape of dog bites; nor were there any traces of frenzied tearing. The lesions weren't even alike and could easily have been caused by the irregular edges of the concrete chunk. Nor, as Mario Domingo had first observed, was there any credible evidence of an impression made by the lower jaw, which would have to be present for a bite mark to have been made with the top teeth too. The other contested wounds at the back of the head "were not dog bites," according to the American experts, "but the very common stellate wounds typical of blunt trauma." The wounds on the bishop's hands and thumbs were "found to be consistent with defensive wounds but not to be dog bites."

At the autopsy table, Dr. Reverte Coma insisted that lesions caused by bites were still visible in the badly decomposed skin. Sperber asked him to indicate, with steel pointers, the area where this was true. Reverte Coma's Guatemalan assistant kept pointing to a place where no mark at all was visible. "He was literally making this up!" Palladino said to me.

Decisive evidence of a bite would have been marks of penetration in the skull. The dog's two upper canines, each an inch long, were much longer than his very short incisor teeth. For four teeth to have left any mark at all on the skin, the two canines would have had to penetrate the layer of fatty flesh into the skull. A mere peeling back of the skin was enough to prove—at least to the satisfaction of Bux and Sperber—that the bone area in question was completely smooth.

*　*　*

I WAS IN ODHA'S OFFICE later that afternoon when Palladino, in a billowing black suit, clutching his big, black Pentax 6x7 camera, burst in and cried, "Reverte Coma wants to cut off the head and boil it." The Spaniard had kept a large industrial pot at a constant boil on a hot plate during the autopsy. "He wants to get down to what he knows, which is bones," Palladino explained. Bishop Ríos Montt decided that Gerardi's body had already been desecrated enough and adamantly forbade it.

The next day Palladino was astonished when a member of Reverte Coma's team approached him, carrying the bishop's thumb. Palladino raised his camera, thinking the man wanted a photograph, but instead he lifted the lid from the roiling pot and dropped the thumb inside. Nobody seemed to notice that the thumb was missing until the autopsy was over and the corpse had been returned to the coffin. It was Bishop Ríos Montt who asked, loudly, "Where is Monseñor's thumb!" Palladino had seen one of Reverte's assistants take the now skeletal thumb out of the pot and place it in a little transparent vial. He had assumed it was for a forensic procedure.

The prosecution team was gathered in a corner of the room, pretending not to know anything, but finally, with a guilty expression, Gustavo Soria produced a jar filled with alcohol in which scraps of Bishop Gerardi's robes had been preserved. Bishop Ríos Montt was in a fury about the thumb by now, and someone from the prosecution team finally, rather sheepishly, handed over the vial containing the pilfered thumb, and it was laid in the coffin. Apparently—there seemed no other explanation —Dr. Reverte Coma had wanted the sacred scraps of cloth and the historic thumb to take back to Madrid to display in the Professor Reverte Coma Museum of Anthropological Forensics, Paleopathology, and Criminology. As described in a résumé of the Spaniard's many accomplishments handed out to the press by the

Public Ministry, the museum collection included: "historic crani-
ums," "murder weapons," "the skulls of murder victims," and
"historic mummies."

The dog-bite theory would seem to have been demolished, but
at a jammed press conference held at the end of the second and
final day of the exhumation, Dr. Reverte Coma embraced Otto
Ardón and gushed, "What a look of triumph you have! You can
see it!"

Reverte Coma's performance at the press conference constituted, for me, one of the most bizarre episodes in the case. In a
Castillian accent ringing with aristocratic Hidalgo haughtiness, he
referred to the American experts as "very barbaric" and defended
his hypothesis: "That is a dog bite here or in Peking!" He held out
one hand and slapped it with the crooked fingers of the other to
illustrate how a dog can bite with just its top teeth. "It's their word
against mine," he said, defiantly crossing his arms over his chest,
raising his chin, and sitting back in his chair. Then he got up to act
out the crime. First he was Father Mario, saying *"Fass"* to the dog;
next he was Baloo, pouncing; then he was a cowering Bishop
Gerardi, covering his head with his arms to ward off the dog; then
he was Father Mario again, stomping on the bishop's face with his
shoe. "The individual or individuals who kicked the bishop in the
face hated him profoundly," Reverte Coma announced. "They've
wanted to give this the appearance of a political crime. Lie! This is
a domestic crime and that is extremely clear!"

A few days later, there was a story in a Guatemalan newspaper
about how Reverte Coma had been expelled from the exhumation
of the El Mozote massacre site for impeding the investigation with
ludicrous interpretations. All those very small skeletons were not
massacred children, he had suggested, but adolescent guerrillas—
young recruits from a race of small, malnourished men—killed in
battle. Belisario Betancourt, the former president of Colombia,
who had presided over the UN investigation of El Mozote, happened to pass through Guatemala on unrelated business a few

days later and confirmed the story. Reverte Coma was the author of some thirty books, among them *From Macumba to Voodoo, The Curse of the Pharaohs,* and *Medical Anthropology and Don Quixote.* There was nothing in itself revealing, of course, in Reverte Coma's being a Don Quixote enthusiast. But his behavior—honor-obsessed, egotistical, cruel, seemingly deluded, and perhaps a touch mad—did make him seem like a character sprung from the darkest side of the Spanish fantastic imagination, from Cervantes to Goya.

"Maybe Baloo was a ghost dog," Jack Palladino cracked, "or else he was wearing sneakers." The crime scene video of the parish-house garage taken the night of the murder showed a bloody footprint, he observed, but no paw prints.

The American and Guatemalan experts who examined Baloo concluded that he was "extremely tame" and even "meek." Norman Sperber wrote that in all the prior dog-bite cases he'd been called on to investigate, "the dog was sedated in order to accomplish the necessary examinations and impressions. The dog 'Baloo' is the only case in which an examination was accomplished without the need for sedation . . . due to the unusual docile and non-combative nature of the dog." I watched a video of Baloo limping about at the evidentiary proceedings in the patio of the San Francisco de Asís clinic. The overall impression was of a decrepit, ailing, completely dispirited old dog.

Yet this was the same thick-necked dog that had growled at me, the *perro bravo.* Could even the dog be dissembling? Bishop Gerardi's sister, Carmen, who had lived for a time at the parish house while recovering from an illness, told me that Baloo was indeed bad-tempered and that whenever Father Mario was about to walk him, he would shout a warning, and everybody would dash into his or her room and close the door while the snarling dog plowed past—everyone except Bishop Gerardi, that is, because Baloo loved him, loved to sleep at his feet while Monseñor worked at his desk or read.

*　　*　　*

IN THE COURTYARD on the morning of the exhumation, an elderly
social worker from the Guatemalan Church had reminded me of
the many exhumations that were taking place at massacre sites all
over the country. "Even in death, Bishop Gerardi is a good pastor," he said, "sharing the fate of his people, submitting to the
mortification of allowing his bones to be exhumed in the cause of
justice." This had seemed more appropriate to the solemnity of
the occasion than other remarks I'd heard that had strained for
eloquence. But if Guatemala teaches you anything, it is never to
poeticize or idealize reality. The prosecution, and its allies in the
press, especially the newspaper *Siglo Veintiuno,* whose board of
directors was made up of a small clique of the country's wealthiest
and most conservative families, tenaciously clung to Dr. Reverte
Coma's theories, which they claimed had been vindicated. "Char-
latans, those gringos are *charrrrr*-latans!" the little lawyer Mario
Menchú shouted when I visited him in his office, where, on the
floor by his desk, he kept a plaster copy of the jagged triangular
chunk of pavement that his client, the hapless *bolito* Carlos
Vielman, had once been accused of wielding.

Judge Figueroa decided that neither side had proved its case.
How was he supposed to know who was right? Father Mario remained in prison, and Baloo went on living at the San Francisco
de Asís clinic. The judge had ninety days from the date of Father
Mario's arrest in July to decide whether to charge the priest with
murder and send the case to trial. The exhumation and dismem-
berment of the bishop's cadaver seemed to have resolved nothing.

During the following weeks, the press continued to report on
Baloo's confinement. When the dog's health took a turn for the
worse, it was reported that veterinarians thought it best that
Baloo be put down. But the decision belonged to Father Mario,
and he insisted on sparing the dog he affectionately referred to
as *mi gordito,* "my little fatty." A cart with wheels and a leather

harness was built to help Baloo get around on his withered hindquarters.

When the rumors of homosexuality and a crime of passion in the San Sebastián parish house had first appeared in June, an unprecedented "black snowfall" of ashes had blown over Guatemala City from the simmering Pacaya volcano, burying the town under an inches-deep blanket of soft, sooty powder that required a titanic cleanup effort. On the day after the exhumation, the phenomenon repeated itself. Though the ashes fell more lightly this time, looking like desiccated insect wings slowly drifting down from the sky, they were sufficient to close the airport. Helen Mack was going to drive Jack Palladino to El Salvador so that he could catch a flight from there, but before they set out we had lunch. Helen Mack was usually self-effacing and, in the Guatemalan manner, quaintly formal, though when discussing her foes and their provocations she often unleashed astonishing torrents of profanities, as she did at lunch that day.

A few days earlier, a small plane registered in Colombia had crash-landed in flames on an airstrip on the Mack family's sugar farm on the south coast, and the story, with incriminating insinuations, was trumpeted on the front page of *Siglo Veintiuno*. No cocaine was found, but that could have been because the fire had consumed it, or the police had made off with it. Like a practiced animal tamer, Helen Mack had moved quickly to defuse the situation: she contacted the U.S. embassy, with its busy DEA operation, so that officials could authoritatively clear the Mack family of any suspicion of having narco airstrips on their farm. Ronalth Ochaeta's wife, Sonia, had recently sold her car through a used-automobile dealer, and right after it was sold, packages of cocaine were supposedly found in the car's trunk. This, too, was broadcast in the press with suggestions that the Ochaetas were cocaine dealers and had carelessly left some of their product behind in the car before selling it. Later, Ronalth would endure something similar when ludicrously inflated assessments of the worth of a country house he was building would be used to suggest that he had embezzled funds from ODHA. However false the charges, the damage to public reputations was real and, for Ronalth and his family and others, became a part of the fabric of daily life.

Guatemalans were skeptical about anyone who claimed to—or even seemed to—act from selfless or altruistic motives, certain as they were that such people must be, at best, cynical opportunists. After all, one civilian president after another had turned out to be outrageously corrupt or cowed by the Army and its clandestine crime mafias. The police were so widely regarded to be criminal, cowardly, and inept that across the country mobs were taking the law into their own hands, lynching suspected thieves and delinquents. An especially perverse expression of cynicism was that many Guatemalans preferred to believe the best of those widely regarded elsewhere as monsters. Thus the former dictator General Ríos Montt, who was perceived by most foreigners as genocidal, was one of the most popular and supposedly "populist" democratic politicians in Guatemala, a symbol of "law and order." On the other hand, when my mother visited some of her now elderly school friends in Guatemala, they assured her that Bishop Gerardi had been the *jefe* of all the homosexuals and *maras*—criminal street gangs. They were old women and widows, pious, relatively affluent matrons, gathering over coffee and cake for a sentimental reunion. Where did they get such notions?

"Small countries have big politics," Joseph Brodsky wrote. Some small countries have even bigger intelligence services. Intelligence services, of course, don't just gather information; they also, when it serves their or their government's ends, spread disinformation. Cocaine-stuffed planes, drugs secreted in the trunk of a young wife's car, tapped telephones and threatening calls and opened mail, complicit journalists and judges, ubiquitous informers and infiltrators—the Army had many chess pieces to play with, and a very large board.

At lunch, while specks of volcanic ash floated down around us, Helen Mack spoke about Freemasons. It was like a conversation Guatemalans might have had a century before, in the era of General Justo Rufino Barrios's anticlerical Liberal revolution. In that sense, Bishop Gerardi's murder seemed like Guatemala's last great nineteenth-century crime. It was redolent of Masonic and Jesuit intrigue, and it had propelled the country's two most influential institutions—the Army and the Church—into their bitterest confrontation since the 1870s, when General Barrios, "the Reformer," expelled Jesuits from the country; turned nuns out of their cloisters; converted churches and convents into prisons, post offices, a Masonic temple, a customs warehouse for liquor and tobacco; and invited Protestants from Europe and North America to Guatemala as part of a program for racial improvement and modernization. General Barrios's government seized traditional Maya lands and gave them to immigrants and Liberal Party cronies to convert into coffee plantations, the basis of an economy whose trappings exist to this day. He was the tyrant whom the Nicaraguan exile Enrique Guzmán said had made even the drunks in Guatemala discreet, and who in many ways shaped the society that Guatemalans still reside in. Barrios despised the aristocratic Conservative elite his revolution had driven from power, but those *cachurecos* were too wealthy and entrenched to simply be done away with. So he founded the Escuela Politécnica military academy as the breeding and training ground for a new ruling caste of men cut from the same rough cloth as himself, and the Escuela Politécnica has been at the heart of Guatemalan society ever since, turning out a steady flow of ambitious young military officers to dominate the country.

In certain respects, Guatemala skipped the twentieth century. When I began to see how a society that had taken shape in the nineteenth century was beginning to disintegrate and change into something else—not necessarily less dangerous, though that was what the fight was about—on the cusp of the twenty-first, I also understood how the Guatemalan Army and priests like the Orantes brothers and their associates were, paradoxically, linked, not as co-planners of a murder—though they might yet be proved to have been that too—but through a common stake in the preservation of a culture under assault by forces much broader and greater than, but definitely including, those represented by Bishop Gerardi and REMHI. They were the defenders of a willfully walled-off culture rooted in local ideas about privilege, status, and the militarism and anti-Indian policies of the nineteenth century, which had easily metamorphosed into the cold war militarism and massacres of the twentieth. But as General Pinochet's arrest in London in the autumn of 1998 for human rights violations in Chile, an arrest ordered by a judge in Spain, would show—along with so many other changes in the world—it was getting harder to keep the walls up around small countries.

At lunch that day, Helen Mack listed Masons who were in positions to eventually have an impact on the Gerardi case: five Supreme Court justices, the head of the police, an array of generals and colonels, even the attorney general. "And that's why human rights cases don't get anywhere in Guatemala," Helen Mack said flatly, though of course that wasn't the only reason.

I TOOK A TAXI to Colonia Lourdes, in Zone 17, one day, hoping to talk to Colonel Byron Lima Estrada. The colonel lived in a two-story, modern, middle-class home that, on its ground floor, had the little grocery store, the sort of *tiendita* that grandmother might run, that the former head of G-2 Military Intelligence now claimed as his main source of income. The store was closed, its steel shutters down, when I arrived. It was a day so bright and sunny that the light seemed to rebound off high, white-washed walls in a way that made me squint. I rang the door-bell. A middle-aged woman with possibly bleached blond hair, pale and puffy-eyed as if from weeping, came to the door. This was the colonel's wife—the woman who had supposedly overheard the conversation between her husband and other retired military officers, who had said to him, "*No te rajes, Lima*"—Don't get cold feet.

The colonel's wife told me that her husband wasn't in, and before I could say anything else, she wrote down a telephone number in my notebook and invited me to call. She asked, nervously glancing up and down the street, "You're with MINUGUA, no?" I said no, that I was a journalist. She gaped at me, a bit abashed. Then I wrote down the number of my rented cell phone and gave it to her.

I'd noticed, while reporting this story, that if I managed to conduct myself with a certain peremptory air, as if I was one of those people who have the right to ask things, people assumed that I must be involved with the UN mission. Which suggested that MINUGUA was really getting around.

That evening, I stopped by the offices of *elPeriódico*, Guatemala's small but best newspaper, as I did on most days, to talk with the reporters covering the Gerardi case. The paper's owner and editor, José Rubén Zamora, was from a famous publishing family and he had upheld and even surpassed the family legacy. Thus he had been the target of several assassination attempts, which he had survived with the weird luck that the very brave sometimes have. He'd founded *elPeriódico*, funding it mainly with donations from a wide circle of admirers and friends in and outside Guatemala. That evening at the office something unsettling happened. I was talking to the editor of the newspaper's literary page when my cell phone rang. I answered, and a deep, florid voice boomed, "I am Colonel Byron Lima Estrada." I'd been having trouble with my phone, which was a clunky, old-fashioned model, and I often got sudden intrusions of storms of static. I heard very little of what the colonel said next, but he sounded worked up. I could hear him yelling behind the storm, his words obscured. I said loudly into the phone that I couldn't hear him, and asked if we could talk later or meet, but the static, and his incomprehensible shouting, went on for quite a while. All I could make out was Colonel Lima saying, in his deep, lowing voice, "There will come a day, there will come a day, and it won't be long from now . . ." and then the static storm swept in and drowned out the rest. After I hung up, the editor I'd been visiting with said that I'd turned pale. I tried phoning back a number of times, that night and the next day, and finally was able to explain to a younger-sounding man who answered that I hadn't been able to understand what the colonel had said when he called. The young man said that the colonel had already said everything he had to say to me.

Knowing that I'd put myself on Colonel Lima's radar made me uneasy, although I didn't really think that anything was going to happen to me, an American citizen. With the world community watching, it would be very hard for the Army to get away with a homicide even against my friends at ODHA, no matter how ingenuously it was disguised. I knew that. But when I came home at night I was frightened by the darkness of my room at the Spring, whose only window opened onto a small patio, and I worried about the flimsy lock on the door. Stuck in traffic on gray afternoons in late September, I'd feel overwhelmed by a very particular sadness, something that seemed to come from the unconscious memory of the street itself, of all the people who were driving or just walking to or from someplace—an office, a church, the movies, school—and must have had a last moment of panic or grief or resignation, realizing that there was no escape and that they would never get home. Only one person in the whole country had ever been held accountable or castigated as the person responsible for any of those people not making it home, only *one:* Sergeant Noel Beteta, Myrna Mack's killer.

I was living in Guatemala City in 1984 and 1985, the years when Colonel Lima—though I didn't know it then—was the head of G-2 Military Intelligence. I was living in my late grandparents' house in the old center of the city, near the church of San Sebastián, trying to write my first novel and also doing freelance journalism, mainly in other Central American countries. If I had to go to Managua, San Salvador, or Tegucigalpa, I usually had friends, other freelancers and stringers, whose houses I could stay in, and when they came to Guatemala City, they were welcome to stay in my grandparents' house. My friend Jean-Marie Simon, the photographer and human rights investigator, lived in the house for a while.

One day a black Jeep Cherokee pulled slowly alongside Jean-Marie and me as we were walking to the corner store for a beer. The Jeep came to a stop, and three or four men, in denim and leather jackets, got out, opened the rear door, and reached inside, presumably for weapons. We threw ourselves down behind a row of parked ambulances belonging to a little private hospital, and then, when a bus suddenly drove between the Jeep and us, we got up, ran alongside it, and jumped on. The men got back into the Jeep and took off like a rocket down the avenue, running red lights.

The next day I went to the U.S. embassy to report the incident, which had obviously been aimed at Jean-Marie. The official I spoke to seemed to have already heard about it. His exact words were, "It's what we call a heavy-handed tail, meant to send a message. Believe me, they could have splattered you all over the sidewalk like tomato sauce if they'd wanted to." His advice was to leave Guatemala, but I was too broke. I didn't have the money for a plane ticket, and at that time I had no real place to go home to. Jean-Marie simply had too much important work in Guatemala, and wasn't going to leave. Years later I ran into that same diplomat in Mexico City, when he was attached to the U.S. embassy there. He recalled the incident and said that he couldn't believe we hadn't left.

I'll never forget those months. There were incidents in which "they" broke into homes or apartments and horribly mutilated their victims (a woman from the Swedish embassy, for example, who was rumored to have maintained close contacts with guerrillas). I rigged up homemade alarms in my grandmother's house: glass bottles on chairs beneath every window, an escape rope leading onto the patio. I lost about thirty pounds just from nervousness, and developed a tic in my cheek. This time of fear and sadness—but also of unforgettable intensity—stayed inside me like a dormant infection that can sometimes be stirred back to life, even by a glance.

So I think you will understand how relieved and grateful I was when, fourteen years later, in the fall of 1998, the editor at *The New Yorker* who had said that I could write an article about Bishop Gerardi on spec told me that the magazine would pay for me to move to a better hotel—a hotel with security guards in the lobby, filled with foreign business types and European airline crews and couples who had come to Guatemala from the United States to adopt babies.

DURING THE YEAR THAT Jean-Marie Simon and I were living in my grandparents' old house, Guatemala's first group of relatives of the disappeared, Grupo de Apoyo Mutuo (GAM), which was modeled somewhat after Mothers of the Plaza de Mayo in Argentina, announced itself in the streets of Guatemala City. They disrupted traffic at intersections, banging on pots and pans, holding up placards with photographs of their disappeared loved ones. Through Jean-Marie, I met their leaders a few times, and visited their main office, where the walls were covered with hundreds of photographs of people who were missing. I was particularly struck by a tall, very pretty young woman named Rosario Godoy de Cuevas, the wife of a recently disappeared trade unionist—recently enough that I'm sure she harbored the faith and the hope that her husband was still alive in some wretched Military Intelligence torture hole, and that there must be some way to save him. Godoy de Cuevas and her husband had a two-year-old son. I liked to watch her, banging on her pot, taller than the other protesters holding up traffic, her chin raised as she shouted her slogans, the emotion showing in her lovely face, her long black hair flowing.

Easter Week is a time of solemn religious observances in Guatemala, but it is also a vacation week. The capital shuts down. Congress closes, and most prominent Guatemalans, including journalists, and also foreigners, particularly diplomats, take off for one of the country's lakes or beaches or mountain chalets, or go to nearby Antigua or Miami or wherever it is they go to relax and enjoy themselves. During that Holy Week of 1985, the GAM's small leadership was almost wiped out. Héctor Gómez Calixto, a thirty-four-year-old baker from Amatitlán, near the capital, was abducted and murdered and found the next day by a highway exit. He had been tortured with a blowtorch, his face was brutally battered, and his tongue had been torn out. His sister, who was also abducted, was viciously raped. Another GAM leader barely escaped with his life, leaping over the wall into the grounds of the Belgian embassy, following an escape from a death squad.

Rosario Godoy de Cuevas spoke at Héctor Gómez's funeral, promising that his death would not be in vain. Three days later, Rosario, her young son, and her twenty-one-year-old brother were abducted from the parking lot of a shopping center. The next day her car was found flipped over in a shallow ditch by a road outside the city. The bodies of Rosario, her brother, and her child were inside. The government announced that it had been a tragic car accident, as did President Reagan's State Department spokesman, and the State Department spokesman's declaration, probably unnoticed by anyone in the United States, was repeatedly played on Guatemalan television.

The journalist Mark Fazlollah, later a distinguished reporter at the *Philadelphia Inquirer,* but at the time a young stringer, was staying in my house, and he decided to do some old-fashioned police reporting. He looked at the car the three had died in, and at the ditch where the accident had supposedly occurred, and concluded that the car had been rather gently rolled into it. He spoke to the doctor who had performed the autopsy confirming that the incident had been an accident. The doctor, who was soon murdered, could not bring himself to stand by his autopsy report. When Rosario Godoy de Cuevas's relatives went to claim her body at the morgue, they noticed that there were bite marks on her breasts. Her underpants were stained with blood, indicating rape. At the funeral, people noticed that her infant's fingernails had been torn out. The torturers would have done that, torn out the baby's fingernails while the mother was still alive, to try to get her to say whatever it was they wanted her to say.

The Easter Week murders and attempted murders of the GAM leadership and their relatives must have taken a great deal of careful planning, months and months at least, probably longer. ("We had to do much worse things during the war," Colonel Lima's wife had supposedly heard her husband say shortly before Bishop Gerardi's murder, at the meeting in his garage.) No murders ever shocked or touched me in the way the murders of Rosario Godoy de Cuevas, her baby, and her young brother did. Nobody has ever been found guilty, or officially charged, in those crimes or tens of thousands like them. Accuse me of living in the past if you'd like, but I don't think there should ever be a legal amnesty for whoever planned and executed murders like those.

5

THE TAXI DRIVER TURNED up again one day in September. He went to see Father Quiróz to discuss some domestic problems he was having. The priest asked for a way to contact him, and the taxi driver gave him a beeper number. After four telephone conversations with the Untouchables, the taxi driver agreed to meet with Fernando Penados, who tried to persuade him to give an official witness deposition. But it turned out that he had relatives in the military who had already threatened him about talking. Fernando said that the taxi driver had changed his job, moved houses several times, didn't want to leave his family, and was terrified. The Untouchables moved him to a spot outside the city.

The Untouchable Rodrigo Salvadó said it made him feel a little sad to think that Carlos García, the murdered taxi driver, wasn't the same one who'd seen the shirtless man and written down the plate number. "If this isn't our driver," said Rodrigo, sitting in a cubbyhole office, "doesn't it seem kind of inhuman to lose interest, to say, well, this isn't our taxi driver?" The Untouchables had spent months making the rounds of taxi companies and stands in their hunt for the taxi driver who was a witness—a futile effort, it turned out, because like so many nighttime drivers, the witness had leased his taxi from its daytime driver, and had dealt solely with him, rather than with the owner or any other employee of a taxi company. For a while afterward it was even rumored—

incorrectly, I believe—that Carlos García's killers had found the right taxi, but the wrong driver.

Fernando had a productive couple of days around this time. He spent an afternoon at *Prensa Libre,* looking at archival photographs of the trial of Sergeant Major Obdulio Villanueva, the presidential guardsman accused of killing Haroldo Sas Rompich, the milkman involved in the unfortunate incident that day President Arzú went horseback riding. One of the photographs showed the man he was looking for, the EMP photographer who had also turned up at the church of San Sebastián on the night of the murder of Bishop Gerardi. Fernando told me he felt sure that the photographer and his companion that night had played roles in the operation, that their job was to check up on how the crime had gone, to learn what evidence might have been left behind and what mistakes had been made, and to listen to what people were saying.

THE PRISON, THE CENTRO PREVENTIVO, where Father Mario was being held was situated between steep cliffs and spread over the downward sloping floor of a ravine on the outskirts of the city, in Zone 18. Standing outside the prison gates, you could hardly help imagining a mythological entrance to the underworld. I spent hours outside those gates one day waiting to talk to Father Marios' mother, Marta Nájera de Orantes, who was visiting her son. She'd told me to meet her at one o'clock, but three hours later she still hadn't come out. I stayed, caught up in watching other visitors come and go: a steady trickle of people who, as the visiting hours drew to a close, became more like a crowd emptying out of a packed movie theater. There were schoolgirls in uniforms, and Mayan mothers in traditional dress, and weary-looking mothers and wives in the drab dresses of the mestizo poor or the starchy brightly colored dresses of the somewhat better-off, and mothers and wives hugging stacks of plastic containers and dishes they had brought meals in. (Some women would have been coming out from "conjugal visits" with their husbands in spartan cabins reserved for that purpose.)

Fathers were fewer in number—rural men in straw cowboy hats and frayed clothing, with sad, wrinkled faces. There was one wealthy woman, like a movie star, blond, light-skinned, in dark glasses, holding a swaddled baby, accompanied by her uniformed Indian maid, who carried a cooler in one hand and a bassinet in the other. And then there were the boys, the *patojos,* the *cholos* or *jomies,* gang youths, or wannabe *cholos* and *jomies,* affecting the universal made-in-USA gangster style—baggy clothes, basketball shoes, do-rags—a noticeable spring to their step as they reached the outside air, some of them performing little circling, backward glances at the prison before leaving, as if amazed not to be incarcerated there, or at least not today. Teenage bad girls who hadn't been allowed inside because their clothing didn't meet the dress code (hems had to fall below the knees and no cleavage was permitted, or shorts or even pants) lingered around the gates, with their tattoos and lipstick and attitudes. They flirted with the boys: "*Oye Gato,* you're the one who belongs in there. You're next, *jajajaja.*"

Lawyers, of course, came and went, and the occasional priest. And a group of evangelicals in polyester suits with padded shoulders, carrying Bibles and electric guitars and organs in cases, members of the 30 percent of the population that was now Protestant. (Seventy years ago there were only 2,000 Protestants in the country.) When I asked if they'd come to pray with the prisoners, they made fun of me, reciting a little nursery rhyme. I'd used the verb Catholics use for prayer, *rezar,* apparently implying merely rote recitation, whereas the verb they employed, *orar,* indicated direct communication with God.

Now and then the gates swung open, and a pickup roared in or out in a cloud of dirt, carrying handcuffed prisoners to and from the courts. A kidnap gang called Los Pasaco, just days before condemned to death by lethal injection, returned from a hearing, and two of the members stood up in the rear of the pickup to curse at

the reporters running after them, shouting questions. Two pla-
toons of soldiers, carrying automatic weapons, arrived and filed
inside to carry out a search.

I spent much of the afternoon on a stool at Doña Lucy's, a
food stand facing the gates. Doña Lucy also rented conservative
clothing to female visitors whose apparel didn't pass the prison
dress code. It wasn't a good business, she confided, because
often women turned up in clothes worth even less than those
she rented and then didn't return to claim them, absconding
with Doña Lucy's goods.

Finally Marta Nájera de Orantes came out. She was a diminutive, steely-haired woman, forced by her new circumstances into
a nearly professional air of sharp-eyed, protective reserve. She
apologized for her lateness and said her son wasn't feeling well.
His migraines, ulcers, and colitis had all recently worsened. While
in detention, Father Mario had been moving between prison and
a private hospital where, under heavy guard, he had developed
complications from asthma that led to a pulmonary infection.
He'd lost weight and had been having fainting spells.

Señora Orantes arrived at the prison every morning before
dawn, bringing her son healthy vegetarian meals, and she stayed
until late afternoon, when she had to go home to prepare supper
for her nearly invalid husband. Father Mario had given the impression that he didn't want to talk to journalists, although his
lawyer had tried to schedule a press conference once and it had
been canceled by the prison authorities. Señora Orantes told me
that her son was silent so as not to jeopardize his treatment. He
did receive regular visits from Catholic prayer groups, who came
to declare their belief in his innocence and lend spiritual support.
Even Doña Lucy had been inside to see the priest. She described
him standing on his feet for hours with his mother at his side
while the group she was with, led by a nun, sang and prayed for
his freedom and "for everything to become clear." When he felt
up to it, Father Mario gave Masses for prisoners and heard confes-

sions. I remarked to his mother that they must be very different from the confessions of the genteel congregation at the church of San Sebastián, and she smiled sincerely and said, "Yes, I imagine."

Otto Ardón's difficulties in pinning the murder solely on Father Mario, on the basis of the dog-bite scenario, was the beginning of the end of his term as special prosecutor. Ardón had his supporters, but he had also become a widely ridiculed figure. He finally agreed to at least make a procedural gesture in the direction of investigating the EMP. He summoned all the officers listed in the anonymous document faxed to various organizations in August, the document purportedly from a disaffected military man. The interrogations of the officers took place, officially, at the Public Ministry, but they were actually held in a hotel suite. It was a fairly meaningless and perfunctory event, although much later, when Ardón was no longer the special prosecutor and Judge Figueroa no longer had jurisdiction over the case, the record of their testimony would come back to haunt some of those men.

Captain Lima told his story about having been in the Sports Grill with his friend Erick Urízar until midnight the night Bishop Gerardi was murdered. His father, Colonel Lima, said that he had been at home resting with his wife and youngest son. He claimed that it had been years since he'd set foot in the park and church of San Sebastián. Darío Morales, who had finally been identified as the EMP photographer who was spotted in the parish house that night, could no longer deny having been there, but he said he'd arrived at around a quarter to four in the morning. He identified Major Francisco Escobar Blas, the commanding officer of the Services Division in charge of presidential security, as the man who had accompanied him. This was not true, although that was not known yet. Another member of the EMP confirmed his friend Captain Lima's earlier account of having eaten cake with him at eleven PM, contradicting the captain's most recent version of having returned to the EMP headquarters after midnight.

*　　*　　*

WHEN ARTURO AGUILAR, the youngest Untouchable, went to Otto Ardón's office to deliver some routine paperwork, Ardón came to the door in his stocking feet and launched into a speech about how everyone except him was trying to profit from Bishop Gerardi's death. "Everybody has forgotten about Monseñor," he railed, "and people are only looking after their own interests. I'm fucking angry [*como la chingada*] and I'm going to send you all to shit and you can stuff those papers up your ass." And then the special prosecutor slammed the door. (He'd slammed the door in my face too, when I'd shown up for an interview he'd earlier promised to grant me.)

On October 21, Judge Figueroa formally charged Father Mario with the murder of Bishop Gerardi. Two days later, Jean Arnault, the head of MINUGUA, broke the UN mission's "diplomatic silence" on the Gerardi case when he announced at a press conference that the suspicions of a politically motivated murder and an official cover-up "are a perfectly reasonable hypothesis" that "in our judgement is fully justified. . . . If we think of the recent history of Guatemala, we know that groups exist that have both the capacity and the motive to carry out a political crime that has the appearance of a common crime." Otto Ardón took a month's vacation, and when he returned in December he submitted his resignation.

As 1998 DREW TO A CLOSE, at a ceremony marking the second anniversary of the Peace Accords, President Arzú went through with his long-promised public apology on behalf of the government for the suffering the years of war had inflicted on the Guatemalan people. Although the admission and the apology were in many respects praiseworthy, the timing struck observers as questionable. It was widely interpreted as a ploy to preempt the impact of the UN Commission of Historical Clarification report that was due out two months later. Rumors were swirling that the UN report was going to accuse the Guatemalan Army of genocide. Also in December, President Arzú directed his brother Antonio to contact Bishop Ríos Montt with an offer. Father Mario would be freed if the Church agreed to drop all claims against the Army and the government in the Bishop Gerardi case.

When the ten-volume report of the UN truth commission, *Memory of Silence,* appeared in February 1999, it painted an even darker picture than the REMHI report had, finding the Army responsible for 93 percent of the 200,000 civilian deaths that had occurred during the thirty-six-year internal war. The guerrillas were said to be responsible for 3 percent. The report formally charged the Guatemalan Army with having commited acts of genocide against the rural Maya. Genocide is, under international law, a crime against humanity, for which there can be no amnesty. In March, President Bill Clinton visited Guatemala and, with President Arzú sitting in stony silence beside him, made an extraordinary apology for the decades of U.S. support of military dictatorships. "It is important that I state clearly that support for military forces or intelligence units which engaged in violent and widespread repression of the kind described in the report was wrong," he said. "And the United States must not repeat that mistake."

Unclassified diplomatic cables reveal that the U.S. embassy's opinion of how the Guatemalan government handled the Gerardi case, which had initially been positive, had changed. The cables show that U.S. diplomats did not disagree with MINUGUA's recent public criticisms. One of the cables says that Otto Ardón is "accused of incompetence, malfeasance, and losing evidence during his tenure." Ardón had been replaced as special prosecutor by Celvin Galindo, a sharp-dressing, thirty-nine-year-old former soccer star. Galindo was reputed to be politically ambitious, which might turn out to be a good thing, or a bad one. But ODHA's lawyers and investigators believed that they now had a prosecutor they could work with.

When I went with the Untouchables to visit Galindo in his cramped little office in the suburb of Mixco, he told me he was reluctant to proceed to trial against Father Mario. "So much evidence and potential information has been lost," he said. "Eight months have been wasted. Ardón left me with no case." He admitted that he was feeling pressure to free the priest. "Public opinion is not convinced of the participation of Father Mario," he said. But Galindo still suspected the priest of covering something up. "He knows more than he has told," he said. "We have to find a way to get him to help us." If the priest went to trial and was acquitted, he would be immune from ever again being arrested and tried for Bishop Gerardi's murder, and would lose all incentive to reveal what he knew.

IN THE LAST WEEKS of 1998, a new scenario had emerged that implicated Monseñor Hernández, the chancellor of the Curia, and Ana Lucía Escobar, known as La China, the pretty twenty-four-year-old daughter of Monseñor Hernández's housekeeper. Ana Lucía Escobar turned out to be a figure of lurid tropical melodrama. A year earlier, she had been arrested for belonging to a kidnapping and crime ring, but—as is customary when a young criminal has a powerful or wealthy sponsor or connection, in her case Monseñor Hernández—she and other members of the gang were released for lack of evidence. The new theory about the murder of Bishop Gerardi was that Ana Lucía and her gang, who were called Valle del Sol for the neighborhood that was their base, had been trafficking in stolen Church icons, artwork, and relics, with the complicity of Father Mario. Bishop Gerardi had been murdered by the gang because he had found out what was going on.

A former judge named Juan Carlos Solís Oliva, who happened also to be Colonel Lima's stepson, announced that he was conducting an "independent" investigation of the Valle del Sol scenario. Solís Oliva was chronicling his findings in the afternoon daily *La Hora,* and he had written that the sources of much of his information were four intelligence agents who supposedly had conducted the EMP's internal investigation into the murder. Solís Oliva said that he met with them regularly, although he didn't know their names. They used aliases. He had been introduced to them by Major Francisco Escobar Blas, the man who had been identified, for the moment, as the companion of the EMP photographer who showed up at San Sebastián the night of the murder.

But the most important source of the allegations against Monseñor Efraín Hernández and Ana Lucía, although this was not yet widely known at the time, was a Guatemalan woman who lived in Canada and who went by several names, including Blanca Lidia Contreras, and who had once been married to Monseñor Hernández's brother. In August she had traveled from her home in Canada to testify before Otto Ardón. Her trip had been arranged by a man named Luis Mendizábal, an unofficial adviser to President Arzú.

Blanca Lidia Contreras thought she knew—or so she said—why Bishop Gerardi had been murdered. It was because of two letters that she had written to the bishop and sent from Canada to Guatemala with a friend to be hand-delivered. Blanca Lidia claimed that when she heard of Bishop Gerardi's murder, she'd connected the dots, and realized that her well-intentioned letters could be the source of the crime. After calling the Guatemalan embassy in Ottawa and not receiving the response she'd hoped for, she phoned President Arzú and the first lady directly. That, she claimed, was how she had found herself in contact with the presidential adviser Luis Mendizábal.

Blanca Lidia Contreras said that Ana Lucía's mother, Imelda Escobar, had come to work as a housekeeper for Monseñor Hernández in the early 1970s, when he was parish priest of a church called Esquipulitas. Imelda Escobar was a poor but handsome woman with five children. Blanca Lidia Contreras, by virtue of her position as Monseñor Hernández's sister-in-law, was close to the workings of the parish house, and she noticed that the new housekeeper soon began showing signs of wealth, dressing her children in expensive clothes and enrolling them in expensive schools. Then, in 1974, Imelda Escobar became pregnant with

Ana Lucía, and she implied, Blanca Lidia said, that Monseñor Hernández was the father of the child. What Imelda Escobar actually, allegedly, said to her was: "Congratulations, you're going to be an aunt!"

Blanca Lidia's testimony was rife with tales of lurid happenings years earlier, when Monseñor Hernández was the Esquipulitas parish priest and the Orantes boys were among his parishioners. She described young Mario and Ana Lucía and her friends romping naked on a church altar—an entertaining image, though perhaps not an entirely credible one, considering the eleven-year age difference between Father Mario and the girl. Blanca Lida described young Mario riding around with Imelda Escobar's gangster children in cars full of guns. She said that Mario used to bring Imelda Escobar porno films. She said that Imelda Escobar would let the adolescent Mario and his brother Sergio drink alcohol in the parish house with her sons, and that she allowed "grown women" to lock themselves in rooms with the boys to entertain them. She said that Imelda Escobar practiced witchcraft. That Imelda had placed relatives in housekeeping positions in parishes throughout the country and through that web operated her ring of stolen Church valuables. That Imelda and Ana Lucía traveled to Houston and Egypt, where they had bank accounts and did business. She also said that El Calvario, the church where the Escobars and Monseñor Hernández lived now, was a center of drug trafficking, child prostitution, and gambling, and a criminal lair for Ana Lucía's gangster friends.

Throughout her testimony—apparently culled from decades of family gossip, some of it, I would guess, true, but much probably exaggerated or invented—Blanca Lidia Contreras painted a picture of the chancellor of the Curia, Monseñor Hernández, trapped in an earthly hell, constantly threatened with exposure by his criminal housekeeper and their daughter, and sometimes drugged. Ana Lucía was said to have threatened to identify Monseñor Hernández as her father if he didn't use his influence to help her and her friends. Indeed, people at ODHA had witnessed some of the titanic tantrums the tempermental vixen had thrown when she demanded his help in getting her out of some scrape. They had seen her nearly carried out of his office after having been given tranquilizers.

Blanca Lidia Contreras told the prosecutor that the letters she wrote Bishop Gerardi asked for his help in disentangling her former brother-in-law (she was by then divorced), Monseñor Hernández, from his criminal housekeeper and her gangster daughter. She said she believed that Bishop Gerardi had been murdered because those letters had fallen into the wrong hands. She refused to identify the friend who, supposedly, had delivered the letters, saying that she feared for the friend's safety.

Several people told me that they had heard the stories about Ana Lucía being Monseñor Hernández's daughter. There is a saying in Guatemala, "*Hijo negado, pinto y parado,*" meaning that if you deny that someone is your child, the child will grow up looking just like you. Ana Lucía was small of stature and pretty, and she shared Monseñor Hernández's dark complexion, soft round face, and vivid, nearly Asian eyes.

Ana Lucía Escobar

Fernando Penados's assessment of the church of El Calvario, home of the chancellor of the Curia and his housekeeper's brood, was that "there are several of dubious genetic origin living there." Fernando said that Ana Lucía's identification papers had always listed her father as unknown, but that in the fall of 1998, when stories of her suspected involvement in the Gerardi case got around, a man came forward to say that he was the father. Fernando didn't believe that Ana Lucía had had a direct role in Bishop Gerardi's murder. He remarked that she was guilty of just about every crime but that one.

I talked to Ana Lucía Escobar on the telephone a few times. Her voice was sweetly girlish and lilting. She denied all the accusations against her and said that she had broken up with her boyfriend of several years, a member of the Valle del Sol gang named Luis Carlos García Pontaza who had a history of arrests for such crimes as bank robbery and possession of drugs and unregistered weapons. The only time she seemed surprised was when I mentioned Blanca Lidia Contreras. I realized that Ana Lucía had no idea that Blanca Lidia had come from Canada to testify against her.

Most of the suspicion that fell on Ana Lucía for her role in the Gerardi case centered on her presence at the parish house on the night of the murder. She and her cousin Dagoberto had turned up with Monseñor Hernández, the first person Father Mario had telephoned. Her account of that night—that her mother woke her at about midnight, that she drove Monseñor Hernández and her cousin from El Calvario to San Sebastián, arriving minutes before the firemen—hadn't been credibly contradicted by anybody.

Juan Carlos Solís Oliva, the former judge and stepson of Colonel Lima, continued to write about his independent investigation into Gerardi's murder. But he would soon fall out with his military and government contacts and give a statement to prosecutors explaining how he had sold the theory about Valle del Sol to Otto Ardón, who was an old friend from law school. In September 1998, as the dog-bite scenario was falling apart, a distraught Ardón had met with Solís Oliva in a Burger King. "He had big circles under his eyes, and physically he'd deteriorated tremendously," Solís Oliva would recount of that meeting with the special prosecutor. "He told me that he couldn't sleep, that he was under pressure, and he wept, right in front of me he started weeping, and he said, 'Look, Juan Carlos, you've always been a strategist, I've always admired you,'" and he asked for help. Solís Oliva offered the Valle del Sol scenario.

By May, when he gave his statement to prosecutors, Solís Oliva was claiming that his former collaborators in the EMP, particularly Major Escobar Blas, had threatened to kill him, and he had gone on the run, changing houses every night. Solís Oliva called Escobar Blas "a pathological killer," although he also declared that he remained convinced of the innocence of his stepfather, Colonel Lima, and his half brother, Captain Lima. He identified Escobar Blas as a member of the Cofradía, the elite brotherhood of present and former Military Intelligence officers in which his stepfather was a leader. Solís Oliva testified that his informants at Military Intelligence had shown him the *very letters* that Blanca Lidia Contreras had meant to be delivered to Bishop Gerardi. He said the EMP had intercepted those letters.

That was a curious claim. How had the EMP come into possession of the letters? Had Father Mario found them, and then passed them on to the EMP? But why would the priest do that, if the letters incriminated him? Did the EMP send somebody into the parish house to steal the letters, either shortly before or immediately after the murder? Was it possible that the letters shown to Solís Oliva were forgeries?

Years later, in the spring of 2005, shortly after Monseñor Efraín Hernández's death from cancer, I received a phone call from a woman speaking in French who turned out to be Blanca Lidia Contreras. She had somehow gotten hold of my number, but it was *the wrong number*. She was mistaking me for a French reporter who had by then emerged as one of the military's strongest defenders in the Gerardi case. Blanca Lidia Contreras was highly entertaining to speak to on the telephone, but she did seem to nurture an obsessive desire for vengeance against Imelda Escobar. She said that after the Guatemalan earthquake of 1976, Imelda Escobar had really begun enriching herself, stealing foreign aid for earthquake victims donated through the Church. Ana Lucía, she said, was the sort of little girl who ripped up flower beds and tore the heads off baby ducks.

Blanca Lidia had phoned me (thinking I was the friendly French reporter) because she wanted to draw attention to Imelda Escobar's alleged financial misdeeds in the aftermath of Monseñor Hernández's death. I put her in touch with a newspaper reporter in Guatemala City. Blanca Lidia and the reporter had a number of friendly and animated conversations—it's hard to imagine a dull conversation with Blanca Lidia—but when the reporter tried to press her about the identity of whoever had supposedly delivered the letters to Bishop Gerardi, Blanca Lidia withdrew, and cut off all communication.

Luis Mendizábal, the presidential adviser who arranged Blanca Lidia's trip to Guatemala to testify to prosecutors in the late summer of 1998, was later linked, in a long investigative report published in a newspaper in El Salvador, to the Salvadoran ARENA party leaders who ran death squads and engineered the assassination of Archbishop Romero in 1980. Mendizábal was the liaison in Guatemala for the founders of ARENA; he introduced the Salvadoran Roberto D'Aubuisson to the leader of Guatemala's ultra-right MLN ("the party of organized violence"), Mario Sandoval, who became D'Aubuisson's mentor. ARENA, actually constituted in Guatemala in 1980, was closely modeled on the MLN. In Guatemala, Mendizábal owned a clothing boutique whose back rooms were rumored to have been a meeting place for MLN death squads in the war years. In 2000, the Guatemalan newspaper *elPeriódico* would report that Mendizábal was a member of a clandestine group known the Oficinita, which acted as a liaison between the Army, the government, and powerful hard-line conservatives in the private sector. Allegedly formed by General Espinosa in the late 1990s, the Oficinita was intended primarily to subvert, from inside the legal system, prosecutions that threatened the military and its supporters.

Were the letters that Blanca Lidia Contreras supposedly wrote to Bishop Gerardi actually a ruse in which she collaborated in exchange for being invited by Luis Mendizábal to come to Guatemala and, on the record, wage her vendetta against Imelda Escobar? Solís Oliva *saw* the letters, and he described their handwriting and salutations, although that is not the same as having them examined by a handwriting expert. But suppose Blanca Lidia really did write the letters? Those letters provided powerful supporting evidence for the Valle del Sol scenario, and many people were desperate to discover just that sort of evidence. Why weren't the letters passed to the special prosecutor, Otto Ardón, during the time he was thrashing around for any such evidence? Why did the letters never turn up again in the Gerardi case?

The theory that Ana Lucía Escobar and the Valle del Sol gang murdered, or participated in the murder of, Bishop Juan Gerardi would prove to be the Frankenstein monster in this case. It was a good story, a seductive story, too *good* a story to dismiss, even too good not to wish, as a tabloid editor might, for it to be true. But like ODHA's legal team, some later prosecutors on the case, and others, I eventually—years later—came to believe that the scenario might have been entirely fabricated. Perhaps the sinister Valle del Sol gang was only a group of young delinquents, including Ana Lucía, and not a true organized crime gang at all. The old family ties and perhaps the friendship between Father Mario and Ana Lucía were just another circumstance that would have made the murderers feel they had won the lottery. Solís Oliva's confession that his ludicrous investigation was essentially phony should have been revealed immediately. But it wasn't. He had confided to a judge and lawyers, not the public. The propaganda machine ground on, until the Valle del Sol scenario became the most popular explanation of who killed the bishop.

In early February 1999, Monseñor Hernández resigned as chancellor of the Curia. He said that he was retiring not because of what was being said about the Gerardi case, but simply because "in less than two months I will be sixty-five, and I'm tired." At the same time, in a move that would have repercussions for the case later, Edgar Gutiérrez resigned from ODHA and REMHI.

DURING THE SECOND WEEK of January, the taxi driver had given a deposition to prosecutors. The taxi driver's name was Jorge Diego Méndez Perussina, and he was the nephew of General Roberto Perussina, a former minister of defense. He had quit working and was living at home with his wife and children, receiving support and some protection from ODHA. He was a scruffy, jittery, but affable man with something of the high-strung hilarity, and even the look, of a pudgy Dennis Hopper. He'd been a drug user from the age of twelve.

On the night of Sunday, April 26, 1998, at around ten o'clock, Méndez Perussina had picked up some transvestites who asked to be taken to Ninth Avenue, near the Red Cross headquarters in Zone 1, where there was a seedy gay bar in an alley. Instead of turning down Fifth Street, he mistakenly turned down Third—a fateful error—and when he reached Ninth Avenue his passengers said, "Let us off here, *papito*," and he did. He turned left onto Ninth, and then left onto Second Street, driving toward the church of San Sebastián.

The block-long stretch of street alongside the park was isolated and dark at that time of night. A good place to pull over and smoke some marijuana, perhaps even laced with something stronger, and that is what Diego Méndez Perussina did. He opened up his glove compartment, prepared his joint, lit it, and inhaled, and when he looked up he noticed a strange scene at the end of the block. A white Toyota Corolla was parked with its door open, and some men, including a shirtless man, were standing outside it. The shirtless man had a military-style haircut and was about five feet six inches tall. Another man had his hands on the shirtless man's shoulders, as if detaining him in some way. Méndez Perussina thought he saw a mark, perhaps a scar or tattoo, on the shirtless man's arm. Until very recently in Guatemala, four-digit license-plate numbers, especially in certain combinations, had belonged to police or military vehicles. In an almost instinctual act—in case he should ever see the same car again when the urge was on him to get high in his taxi—he memorized the number. He rolled up his window, and suddenly another car, a gold Toyota Corolla, with no license plates, sped past him on Second Street, through the Sixth Avenue intersection, and turned onto Fifth Avenue, left, against the one-way traffic. He thought that the gold Toyota must be part of whatever police operation was going on.

When Diego Méndez Perussina's family discovered what he'd seen and that he was apparently willing to testify about it, he began receiving visits from relatives he hadn't seen in years, including General Perussina and a cousin assigned to a section of the Ministry of Defense formerly known as "Vulture Central." They suggested that if ODHA released the videotape of the statement he had already given to the Untouchables, he should retract it. When they learned that he had been speaking with MINUGUA too, they said they no longer wanted anything to do with him. The day before he was to give a statement to the special prosecutor, Méndez Perussina was forced into a car by three men who drove him around blindfolded for two hours. When the car stopped so that one of his abductors could place a call from a phone booth, Méndez Perussina managed to fling himself out the door and ran to a nearby hospital. I saw him the next day. He had raw, wet scrapes on his palms and knees.

Méndez Perussina thought that the abduction had probably been more of an attempt to terrify him than an actual thwarted "disappearance," and the idea of having to go into exile for his own safety after testifying seemed to dismay him as much as any other of his current prospects. "I don't want to go," he said to me, his eyes filling with tears. "Why should I have to leave for doing the country a favor?"

THERE WERE OTHER DEVELOPMENTS in the case. Around midnight on December 29, Captain Byron Lima, back from Cyprus for good, had been arrested—after an anonymous telephone call to the police—outside his car on a deserted street for creating a disturbance and carrying a weapon without a license. He was drunk, or perhaps on drugs. He gave false answers about his identity, and he was carrying false identification cards. The policemen who had participated in the arrest told me that he had warned them that they would soon know what it was like to wake up in bed with the barrel of a pistol pressed to their foreheads. They said Lima strode outside the police station, still handcuffed, and announced, "I'm looking for where I'm going to put the bombs when I get out. I'm going to blow all this to shit." He was released to military authorities within hours of his arrest.

During the first week of January, one member of the Valle del Sol gang had been murdered, and the police announced that they had captured two others. The day before, Fernando and I had gone to a police hospital to interview Elser Omar Aguilar, a twenty-two-year-old former member of the gang who was quietly being lined up to testify about Ana Lucía Escobar's criminal past. She claimed that she didn't know him, but Elser said that he'd been her lover. He said that he'd met her when he was stealing cars with Carlos García Pontaza, who became her lover later. He said that Ana Lucía had paid the rent on the house in Valle del Sol that the gang used for kidnappings, and that he used to give her cocaine, to which she was addicted. He implicated her in a kidnapping gone awry, in which Ana Lucía was supposed to distract a security guard while the victim was abducted from inside his office, but the kidnappers failed to capture their prey, and another member of Valle del Sol killed the security guard with an M-16 that Elser claimed to have sold to the gang.

Elser Omar Aguilar was awaiting trial for murder, and he had briefly been in the same prison wing as Father Mario. He described the priest rocking out to tapes of Guns 'n' Roses and teasing gay inmates. When Fernando asked if he thought it was possible that Ana Lucía and Carlos García Pontaza could have had something to do with Bishop Gerardi's murder, Elser said he didn't know. "But to give you an example," he said, "if someone contracts me to murder someone, I'm going to do it the way I like to do it. I'm not going to beat him in the head. Two bullets with an unregistered gun. . . . But these people like money. If they were paid to do it, they were paid well." The price for murdering Bishop Gerardi, he guessed, would be at least 200,000 quetzales ($30,000).

About a year after Fernando Penados and I spoke to Elser Omar Aguilar, he was kidnapped from the hospital where we'd visited him. He turned up murdered, stuffed into the trunk of an abandoned automobile.

ONE AFTERNOON ARTURO AGUILAR, the youngest Untouchable, and I paid an uninvited visit to Father Mario and his mother in his room at the Ciudad Vieja hospital, where he was being treated for a pulmonary infection. An armed guard stood in the stairwell outside. Father Mario was wearing a bathrobe and pajamas and had grown a beard. The bathrobe looked as if it hadn't been washed in a while. There was a sodden air of depression, of barely repressed hysteria, in the room. The priest kept his eyes riveted on the floor the whole time we spoke. He gestured angrily when I mentioned Ana Lucía and insisted that he'd never met her until she turned up with Monseñor Hernández at the parish house on the night of the murder.

On Ash Wednesday, February 17—I was back in New York—
the new judge assigned to the case, Henry Monroy, provisionally
freed Father Mario, saying that he was still subject to investigation. The judge also ruled that the taxi driver's testimony was
pertinent. The ODHA lawyers had advised Méndez Perussina to
leave the fact that he had pulled into Second Street to smoke pot
out of his statement. The day after the judge's ruling, the taxi
driver's name appeared in the newspapers for the first time, and
his mother received a phone call from her brother, General
Perussina, saying that her son was going to be killed and should
flee the country immediately. He left a week later, without his
wife—with whom his relationship was acrimonious and who refused to accompany him—or any of their children.

Father Mario was convalescing at his parents' house. His
mother went to the San Francisco de Asís clinic to pick up Baloo,
and a crowd of reporters watched the dog being led to the car, but
they were not permitted to witness Baloo's reunion with the
priest. The night-shift veterinarian told me over the phone that a
more technologically advanced cart that would help Baloo walk
was being built in the United States.

6

FERNANDO PENADOS HAD LOST Ronalth Ochaeta's confidence. He was too secretive. Whenever Ronalth or ODHA's lawyers asked if they could speak to his sources, or even know who they were, Fernando said no. Then Ronalth discovered that Fernando was using ODHA's money to pay off the sources. Rodrigo Salvadó and Arturo Aguilar, the two youngest Untouchables, knew that Fernando had contacts in Military Intelligence, but even they didn't know who these contacts were. Fernando was trying to be a one-man version, it seems, of the sort of criminal investigations team the Church hadn't allowed him to form in the first place. But it could be that Fernando was paying money to someone who was taking advantage of him. And it would turn out later that there were many important leads that he had ignored or over-looked. Rafael Guillamón, the investigator from MINUGUA, told me he had discovered that Fernando had at one point obtained a record of his cell-phone calls. He had apparently been trying to penetrate MINUGUA's investigation of the murder. Guillamón suspected that Fernando trafficked in information with his sources in the EMP and elsewhere, and not always to ODHA's benefit.

Whatever his mistakes, Fernando Penados had made crucial contributions to the Gerardi case and had helped establish ODHA's investigation as a force to be taken seriously. Nevertheless, when the Untouchables' contract was up, Fernando was told that there was no longer money to pay him. Only Rodrigo Salvadó and Arturo Aguilar were kept on.

I was still in New York. *The New Yorker* published my piece, and I moved on to other things. *ElPeriódico* published an abridged translation. I tried to keep up with the Gerardi case, logging on to the Guatemalan newspapers' Web sites every day. But I knew that the real information wasn't appearing there. Whenever I left Guatemala, the country turned into a ship lost at sea without radio contact. There was no way to keep in touch or to stay informed. People in Guatemala, especially if they were involved in certain kinds of work, always worried that their phones were tapped, that their mail was opened, that their e-mails were intercepted, not entirely without reason. In Guatemala, even late-night drunken e-mailers are discreet.

Major developments in the case, I eventually noticed, were always preceded by an especially frustrating period of silence. I thought I was able to recognize when one of those was occurring, and then I would be anxious for days or weeks. Once or twice a year, at least, I managed to get to Guatemala and would catch up. On one trip I found Fernando Penados flat broke but still trying to investigate the case on his own, borrowing money to pay his sources, and persuading the other former Untouchable, Arturo Rodas, who was now working at Avis Rent-A-Car, to lend him cars so that he could get around the city.

In March, there had been more evidentiary hearings at the San Sebastián parish house. Father Mario was instructed to re-create his movements on the night of the murder. "*Bueno*, Father. Put yourself in your room at ten PM and walk us through what happened from there." The priest reenacted being awakened in his bed by the light in the corridor, going out to turn it off, heading down the corridor to the garage, and discovering the lifeless body he claimed he did not recognize as Bishop Juan Gerardi's. Then Father Mario began to walk in circles. "In circles and circles,"

Leopoldo Zeissig, then one of Celvin Galindo's assistant prosecutors, recalled later. Finally, the priest put on his eyeglasses. For about twenty minutes, in a nonsensical pantomime, Father Mario attempted to re-create not recognizing the bishop and not knowing what to do. Both of Bishop Gerardi's cars had been parked in the garage, indicating that he was home, whether the priest had heard him arrive or not. Father Mario perambulated all over the parish house, back down the corridor to his room to fetch a flashlight, back to the garage, out the front door to ask the *bolitos* if they had seen anybody, finally to the door of the cook's room. "But he never knocked on Bishop Gerardi's bedroom door," Leopoldo Zeissig said, "either to check to see if he was home, or to inform his superior that there was a corpse in the garage." Father Mario never even paused before that door as if to think about whether or not to wake him.

Ana Lucía Escobar also put on a riveting show, leading prosecutors and ODHA's lawyers on a trek through the parish house as she re-created *her* movements on the night of the murder. She said that she was studying to become an actress, and during questioning from the prosecutor Galindo, she provided long vivid accounts of her "mistaken" prior arrests. In response to another question, she replied that at home she referred to Monseñor Hernández as "Dad."

Darío Morales, the photographer from the EMP seen taking pictures inside the parish house that night, was summoned to the proceedings as well. He repeated the account he had given previously to Otto Ardón, saying that he had received a call from Major Escobar Blas at three o'clock in the morning, ordering Morales to meet him in the park across the street from San Sebastián. Morales denied taking pictures or entering the parish house or the garage. There was more than one lie in Morales's account, though not all the lies were yet evident.

Major Francisco Escobar Blas wasn't expected to show up at the evidentiary hearing. He'd been sent to Chile on a military scholarship. But he surprised everyone by appearing on the second night. He had shaved off his mustache and "looked made of stone," Mario Domingo observed. Major Escobar Blas was a karate expert with a tough, menacing presence and a crushing handshake. His stare was so oddly dramatic and cold that he seemed to be wearing eye makeup, like a silent film actor.

"I've been ordered to tell what I know about the murder of Bishop Gerardi," Escobar Blas said in a slow, deep voice. "All I can tell you about the murder of Bishop Gerardi is that I know nothing." He testified that he didn't remember what he was wearing that night at San Sebastián. He said that he'd been sleeping in his home when he received a call at about three in the morning from another commander of a Security Services corps in the EMP, telling him that there had been a fight at San Sebastián and that someone had died and that he should go and check it out.

It was a torturously slow interrogation. After every question put to him, the major arduously copied it into a little notebook he'd placed upon a small wooden table, leaning closely over the table as he wrote, and then he would straighten up and give a curt or evasive answer. He was wearing a watch enclosed in an unusually thick black band made from some synthetic material. The lawyers wondered later if perhaps the thick watchband concealed a listening device or monitor through which the major was receiving instructions on what to say.

The man who had accompanied Darío Morales to the church of San Sebastián the night of the murder, the man in the red baseball cap who was seen talking into a radio, had been described as tall and thin. Major Escobar Blas was square, muscular, and not very tall.

FOUR DAYS LATER, on March 23, Judge Henry Monroy fled into exile. In addition to the Gerardi case he had been presiding over Helen Mack's seven-year attempt, stalled by previous judges, to bring the officers who had ordered her sister's killing to trial.

Judge Monroy had been receiving threats, and he felt that the Supreme Court was not supporting him in his attempts to oversee thorough investigations that could result in bringing military men to trial in either case. Later, from exile in Canada, Monroy revealed that earlier, when he was deciding on whether to free Father Mario or to bring him to trial, he'd received a visit from an emissary of President Arzú, Howard Yang, head of the SAE. "Yang told me that he had instructions from Álvaro Arzú," said Monroy, "that Mario Orantes should be sent to trial, but only him."

The day that Monroy left Guatemala, Special Prosecutor Galindo announced that he was investigating a political motive in the crime.

IN APRIL, the head of the EMP, Colonel Rudy Pozuelos, a strikingly fastidious figure in suit and tie instead of his military uniform, and Artillery Major Andrés Villagrán, also from the EMP, testified before the new judge in the case, Flor de María García Villatoro, a tall young woman with large eyes and luxurious black hair falling to her shoulders. In her brief career she'd established a reputation for strict impartiality, with a record of decisions that left lawyers on both sides of the Gerardi case initially nervous about what to expect. García Villatoro had a diploma on her wall from DePaul University, in Chicago, where she'd taken a course in human rights law. Her office was cheerfully feminine, with vases of flowers, pretty paintings, and a dish of candies for visitors. Mario Domingo said that after his first visit there he experienced a rare, if still guarded, sensation of optimism.

The most important revelation in that hearing was provided by Major Villagrán, who testified that on the night of April 26, he had seen Captain Byron Lima in the EMP headquarters sometime between the hours of eight and ten. This contradicted Captain Lima's statement that after paying his credit card bill at around eight-thirty at the Sports Grill he had lingered with friends for another three hours before heading back to the EMP barracks to sleep.

Major Villagrán would later withdraw his testimony, saying that he had been mistaken.

RONALTH OCHAETA'S DAYS AT ODHA were coming to an end. In early March, he had undergone emergency surgery for severe ulcers and internal bleeding. The operation was bungled, and he was so close to dying that he was given extreme unction. He convalesced at home for a month and a half. His first day back at ODHA was April 16. He was going to stay only a few hours. Nery Rodenas picked him up. Ronalth's wife, Sonia, who was a lawyer, was away from the city on business and the Ochaetas' four-year-old son was at home with the maid. As Ronalth and Nery Rodenas drove away from the house they noticed three men standing across the boulevard, well dressed, with short hair, but tough-looking.

Not long afterward, at ten o'clock, Ronalth was summoned to the telephone. It was his sister, yelling frantically that he should come home immediately, that armed men had broken into his house.

Ronalth Ochaeta and several colleagues from ODHA raced to his house in three cars. His son was in a state of shock, not able to cry or utter a word. The maid told Ronalth that ten minutes after he had left that morning, the men had pressed the buzzer of the house. The maid answered by intercom, and a voice from outside said that they had "work" to deliver to Ronalth Ochaeta. She told them she wasn't allowed to answer the door, and they said, "It doesn't matter, we'll leave it in the living room." The maid responded that the door was locked. Over the intercom, the voice answered, "We have a key."

She ran downstairs and found the three men already inside. They shoved her onto a sofa, struck her, and aimed a pistol at her. Ochaetas' son screamed, "Don't kill her!" and tried to kick one of the men, and they flung him aside. One of the men held a pistol on the boy and the maid and warned that if they didn't stay quiet, he would shoot. They were clumsily tied together with blankets and rope. While one man remained in the living room, the other two ransacked the house. It seemed as if they were searching for something specific, yet all they took were some of Sonia's jewels and the family's passports. They drank beer from the refrigerator. After forty minutes they left, but first they said, "Tell Ochaeta that we left this job for him in this box. He knows what's going to happen if he keeps fucking around." Inside the cardboard box was a concrete chunk similar to the one that had supposedly been used to strike Bishop Gerardi in the garage.

The street out front filled with reporters, police, people from MINUGUA, emissaries from foreign embassies, and so on. The police stayed for seven hours. Later the sloppy manner in which the crime was carried out was commented on by some, and even aroused suspicion—why would the intruders have left behind the beer cans they drank from? But the men may have been confident that they had nothing to fear from a police investigation. Eight years had passed since the murder of the police detective José Mérida, who had tried to investigate the EMP's role in Myrna Mack's murder, and since then no successor—not a single one—had dared to follow any trail of evidence past the security gates on the Callejón del Manchén.

That night, as he held his weeping wife in his arms, Ronalth Ochaeta felt a great emptiness. The house was under twenty-four-hour armed protection, but of course the Ochaetas could not live that way indefinitely. The bishops, Amnesty International, diplomats—everyone was telling Ochaeta that it was time to put his family first, and leave the country, at least for a while.

They moved out of the house, and during the time they remained in Guatemala they lived in the residence of a foreign embassy, with protection provided by MINUGUA. One day an Italian policeman from MINUGUA told Ronalth that Jean Arnault, the head of the UN Mission, said that there was a woman who knew him and who wanted to speak to him about what had happened. "Who is she?" Ronalth asked, and the Italian police-man answered that it was confidential, that she was also under MINUGUA's protection.

A few days later, a meeting was arranged in a café. Ronalth did, indeed, know the woman. She was Arlene Cifuentes, a woman previously involved in progressive political circles. She wanted to know all the details of what had happened during the break-in at his house. Ronalth asked why, and she said that the same thing had happened to her, and she thought the same people were be-hind it.

"Do you remember a woman phoning the archbishop's office and giving the name of Byron Lima?" she asked. "Well, that was me." She told him that Jean Arnault knew the whole story. Cap-tain Byron Lima was her cousin, the son of her aunt, her mother's sister. "He's crazy," she said. One day the captain's father, Colo-nel Lima, had driven to her house and rammed his car into the garage door. Enraged and cursing, he demanded to know why she'd phoned the archbishop. How, he shouted, could she defend that communist son of a whore Gerardi?

The people who had broken into her house hadn't stolen any-thing. She had also been receiving telephone threats, warning that she knew what would happen if she didn't stop talking. Her young daughter was briefly abducted at a shopping center, which drove her to seek the protection of MINUGUA. She and her chil-dren were living now in Jean Arnault's private residence.

Ronalth had the impression that MINUGUA was encouraging Arlene Cifuentes to testify in the case. He also urged her to do so. But Cifuentes said that she was frightened. She didn't believe that anyone would dare to prosecute the Limas; she feared that they would get away with whatever they had done and she would be left vulnerable to their anger.

Ronalth asked why she was so sure the Limas had been involved in the bishop's murder. She repeated the story that ODHA had already heard from another source, about the colonel's distraught wife coming to see her sister, Cifuentes's mother, Meche, after the bishop's murder, and telling Meche about the conversation she'd overheard between other military officers and the colonel in his little shop.

On June 30, Ronalth and his family flew to San José, Costa Rica, where he had accepted a job with the Inter-American Court of Human Rights. Months later, Arlene Cifuentes's story leaked out. Guatemalan newspapers began reporting that a secret witness, supposedly living in Jean Arnault's house, someone close to the Limas, was preparing to testify in the Gerardi case. And then her name got out.

Arlene Cifuentes convened a press conference in the Guatemalan National Congress and announced that she knew absolutely nothing about the Gerardi case or about any involvement on the part of her military relatives. She said that she had no idea why people were trying to implicate her in the case.

As Ronalth wrote to me in an e-mail: "And kaput." Cifuentes retreated back into her private life and silence.

Years later I spoke with Rafael Guillamón, the Spanish investigator for MINUGUA, who had befriended Arlene's mother, Meche. He told me that she had frequently spoken about Captain Lima's extortions, and of his participation in threatened kidnapping plots against her daughter.

During this interregnum in the case the diminutive lawyer Mario Menchú, reemerged in the press, now calling for prosecutors to investigate Ronalth Ochaeta and Edgar Gutiérrez. It was as if, offstage, a new scenario was already being developed to replace Valle del Sol, should that one falter: Ronalth and Edgar Gutiérrez had embezzled money from ODHA, and when Bishop Gerardi found out the two had organized his murder.

Shortly before he left for Costa Rica, Ronalth was warned by an employee of ODHA named Guillermo Monroy that the Public

Ministry was investigating him, along with Edgar Gutiérrez and Helen Mack, for narco trafficking. Perhaps the plane, registered in Colombia, that had mysteriously crashed on Mack's father's farm had been part of this "investigation." Monroy said he had heard that Ronalth and Edgar Gutiérrez were going to be accused of laundering the proceeds of their drug dealing through ODHA and Helen Mack's real estate business.

During the summer of 1999, when Helen Mack and I both, for separate reasons, happened to find ourselves in Madrid, we decided to visit the Professor Reverte Coma Museum of Anthropological Forensics, Paleopathology, and Criminology. The museum was not listed in the phone book or in any tourism guide, but a friend helped us locate it at the Complutense University medical school, where Dr. Reverte Coma was now a professor emeritus. The museum, which consisted of two rooms, was situated at the far end of a long corridor on the top floor of one of the campus's outermost pavilions, adjacent to a room holding a collection of some 2,000 skulls heaped in piles atop long tables. Among the trinkets, fetish objects, and artifacts of crime displayed in the museum were a shriveled human fetus on a leather necklace "confiscated from a hippie," and a long cord made from condoms tied together, ingeniously fashioned by a prisoner to use in an attempted prison escape. Rubber snakes and cheap Indian masks like those sold in the gift shops at Guatemala City's airport were exhibited in a glass case full of objects purportedly connected to witchcraft and voodoo. A mural displayed portraits and rudimentary facts about famous serial killers, including New York's Son of Sam. The phrase "The Greatest Serial Killer of All: Abortion" appeared in bold letters.

The balding, benevolent-seeming Dr. Reverte Coma, with his snowy brows and mustache, was present that day, in a white lab coat. He was clearly delighted to have visitors. An ordinary shop mannequin's detached head, brightly colored like a map to represent different sections of the singular brain of Spain's most notorious serial killer, was on a table. "This is my invention," the eminent forensics specialist proudly announced, pressing a button. The microwave oven dish on which the head was mounted slowly began to revolve.

Dr. Reverte Coma did not recognize me from nearly a year before, when we had met on the morning of the exhumation of Bishop Gerardi's corpse. But as we were leaving, he asked us to sign the museum guest book, and when he saw Helen Mack's clearly printed signature, his bright blue eyes lost their friendly sparkle and he stiffened. I asked about his participation in the Gerardi case, and he asserted that it was at a most delicate stage right now, most delicate and interesting, and that he was not allowed to discuss it.

RODRIGO SALVADÓ AND ARTURO AGUILAR had been unsure how to proceed after Fernando Penados and Arturo Rodas left ODHA, but they started by carefully sifting through boxes filled with random information that had never been followed up, and they found several provocative leads that had somehow been missed. One involved a man who, in 1998, soon after the murder, had turned up at ODHA, presenting himself under the pseudonym Aníbal Sandoval. Fernando had not been interested in the man's information, but Rodrigo and Arturo thought that it was worthwhile to try to find him again. Apparently he was a former military man, and from the way he had introduced himself, it seemed that he worked—or at least had worked in 1998—as a private security guard. On the off chance that the man might use the name Aníbal Sandoval in his working life, they made inquiries with several of Guatemala's numerous private security firms: Wackenhut, Grupo Golán, and Sistemas Israelíes de Seguridad, to name only the most well known. Because of the natural secrecy of private security firms and the hostility with which most of them regarded human rights groups, the two young men received little cooperation.

The man had given an address in the department of Chimaltenango, a few hours' drive from the capital, and Rodrigo and Arturo went out there in ODHA's beat-up Suzuki Samurai minijeep. A woman who answered the door at the house said that Aníbal Sandoval no longer lived there, but that she thought he was employed by Don Bang, an immense Korean-owned textile plant on the Pan-American highway. A uniformed guard at the plant affirmed that Aníbal Sandoval did work there but that it was his day off.

So Rodrigo and Arturo returned on another day. This time when they called at the security gate the guard on duty, a different one, replied that he was Aníbal Sandoval. He was a slight, well-built, self-possessed Mayan-featured man with dark, penetrating eyes. He was clearly disconcerted by his visitors: the lanky, ponytailed Rodrigo, and the burly slacker Arturo, with his close-cropped hair and earring, both in their early twenties. They explained why they were there and he at first denied that he'd ever approached anyone at ODHA, but they persisted, and he finally relented. Yes, he'd come by ODHA's office, he said angrily, and with the good intentions of giving them some information. As a former member of the Guatemalan Army, he'd been taking an obvious risk in doing so, but the person who dealt with him at ODHA had told him that his information didn't have much to do with the case. He said he wasn't interested in another meeting with ODHA now.

Rodrigo and Arturo tried to convince him of their seriousness and of how much they valued whatever he could tell them. Finally the security guard agreed to speak with them, although not there in front of the gates, with cars and trucks roaring past on the highway and workers coming and going. He would meet them on a day when he didn't have to work. Aníbal Sandoval's real name was Oscar Chex López.

They met in a Pollo Campero fried-chicken restaurant in the municipal capital of Chimaltenango, on a corner of the tree-shaded central plaza. Chex's condition was that they buy him a meal and a soda, so that it would look as if they were just meeting for lunch. Over the next month or so they met eight more times in the same restaurant. They always began the meetings chatting about general topics, as Arturo recalled later: "the situation in the country, the high price of basic necessities, *mujeres de tragos"*—loose women—"before getting around to talking, a little more deeply every time, about what Oscar knew in relation to the murder of Monseñor Gerardi." By then they were meeting once or twice a week, and they decided to switch their meeting place to a steak house on the outskirts of town. Oscar Chex told them that he had spent twenty-seven months in El Quiché in the early 1980s, for some of that time under the command of Colonel Byron Lima Estrada, and had participated, he said, in about ten battles, including a guerrilla ambush in which twenty-five of his fellow soldiers were killed. During the latter stage of his tour, he'd been trained to conduct interrogations, especially of wounded guerrillas. Chex was a native Kakchiquel-speaker, but he could also speak K'iché, which has a similar grammatical structure, and he understood Mam as well. It was then that he was recruited into Military Intelligence.

Chex had joined the Intelligence Department of the Army High Command in 1992 and, after a period of training, had been given his first assignments, including tailing people who were under surveillance. Among them was Bishop Gerardi. He was then assigned to the Directorate of Technical Intelligence, located in Zone 13, near the Army's main telecommunications center. Chex was put to work translating and transcribing tape recordings of intercepted telephone conversations of people who spoke in Mayan languages, including the Nobel laureate Rigoberta Menchú and another prominent Indian leader and congresswoman, Rosalina Tuyuc. The telephone espionage, he told Rodrigo and Arturo, was conducted in Department 111 of the Directorate, where fifteen to twenty devices used to intercept and record conversations were kept running night and day. Many of the devices were portable. From the Indian Sector of the Directorate, Chex had been transferred to the Religious Sector, spying on a number of prominent bishops, among others. He was put in charge of monitoring Bishop Gerardi's telephones, both in the parish house and in the ODHA offices.

Chex told the two Untouchables that once, a few days before Christmas in 1993, he'd been on duty, monitoring the ODHA telephones, when he heard someone declaim from the ODHA offices, "Merry Christmas, *orejas*—informers—*hijos de la gran puta!*—sons of a giant whore" and other choice words before slamming the phone down.

"Rodrigo and I freaked out," Arturo said to me. They knew that very story. A friend at ODHA called Panchito had recently told them how every Christmas for years he'd unleashed an obscene tirade into the telephone against the Military Intelligence agents he assumed were listening in on ODHA's calls.

Eventually Chex had been unofficially promoted to the position of analyst in Department 112, where he processed transcribed recordings, converting and summarizing raw information into functional intelligence. File 27, begun in 1992, was assigned to Bishop Gerardi. Chex said that in his experience, such a numbered file was assigned to an individual only when that person was considered "an enemy of the State, and marked for elimination."

Their conversations now entered an especially delicate stage—how to persuade Chex to give a pretrial deposition before the special prosecutor and judge overseeing the case, if doing so also meant that for his own safety he would have to go into exile. The Untouchables suggested Canada, usually a reliable option, and promised to explore that and other possibilities. Canada fell through, however, because it had a policy of not granting political asylum to former military men. Costa Rica declared that it was willing to help out, but it lacked a political asylum program, which usually includes helping to settle the refugee into a new life, with a place to live and, if possible, a job.

Oscar Chex offered to give ODHA documents that he said he'd taken with him from the Directorate, and that would substantiate his testimony. He said they were records of the intercepted communications of civilians who had been involved in the Peace Accord negotiations, possibly including transcriptions or recordings of Bishop Gerardi's conversations. Rodrigo and Arturo agreed that they would like very much to see those documents.

The problem was that Oscar Chex wasn't sure where he'd left them. Maybe they were at his father's house, or he might have hidden them in the house of a landlady where he'd rented a room for a while, or in a house where he'd lived before that. The last-mentioned place was in the municipality of Patzicia, and the three men drove there in the Suzuki jeep, but they found nothing. Next they drove to Chex's father's house, in the rural town of San Juan Comalapa, at the end of a long muddy road that was accessible to vehicles only about halfway.

Chex's father lived with his wife in a small, rustic abode with a dirt floor. Chex introduced Rodrigo and Arturo as contractors who were offering him work as a mason, a ruse that seemed to stoke his father's suspicions. After a thorough search of the little house, Chex concluded that he hadn't left the documents there either. Chex's father insisted on accompanying the three men to their next destination—the woman's house where Chex had rented a room. It was a tight squeeze for the four men inside the Suzuki Samurai mini-jeep. The woman lived in a small hamlet a long distance from San Juan Comalapa, and they drove through a rolling landscape where the harsh poverty of the Maya locals, with their scraggly corn plots, stood in striking contrast to the vast poultry farms, with rows of hangar-like coops, where Pollo Campero, the fast-food chain, raised its chickens.

"When we reached the hamlet," Arturo recalled, "Rodrigo and I noticed that the stares directed our way were intense and suspicious, and that toward Chex they were downright hostile." They found the woman at home. It was a typical little rural *rancho* of the *altiplano,* with cane and mud huts arranged around a dirt patio, one of which was used for storing corn. There, behind stacked sacks of corn, with Rodrigo and Arturo looking on hopefully, Chex found a red-twine net, like those used to carry oranges, stuffed with old papers, audiocassettes, and clothing. This was the cache that they were looking for.

It was late in the afternoon now, and the air had turned heavy, the sky dark and blustery. It began to pour as they were walking back to the jeep, where Chex's father was waiting nervously. They climbed in, but they hadn't driven far when one of the jeep's tires blew out and they came to a halt.

"Now we were really in the shit," Arturo said. "Stuck in the jeep with an Army spy and his father, with documents stolen from Military Intelligence, in pouring rain." They opened the trunk and pulled out the tire and a crowbar, but there was no jack. They trudged from one little house to the next, asking to borrow a tire jack, and finally, about a third of a mile down the road of rushing mud and rain, they found someone who would lend them one, and they trudged back to the jeep to change the tire. Then they realized the jack was missing the lever that cranks the ratchet. Close by was a little store, attended, Arturo told me, by the most beautiful young Indian woman he had ever seen. She lent them a screwdriver, which they improvised into a lever. They returned the screwdriver completely bent, along with a promise— never fulfilled—to come back with a new one later.

They returned to San Juan Comalapa rain-soaked and cold. Chex's father wanted to eat, and Rodrigo and Arturo wanted to look over the documents, to decide what to take back to Guatemala City. There, in a little cafeteria where they stopped for a meal and to go through the papers, the two Untouchables learned the reason for all the hostile looks they'd been receiving. Oscar Chex had had some recent trouble with the law, a confusing incident, he said, in which he was innocent, but which had left him "stigmatized by the community." When the locals had seen Chex with the two scruffy young strangers, they'd suspected that the trio must be up to no good. That was why Chex's father had insisted on accompanying them. "Son, are you *delinquiendo?*"—are you out commiting crimes?—Chex's father had asked him. If Chex's father, known to the community as a solid citizen, hadn't gone with them, they might well have been taken for delinquents on the prowl, attacked by a village mob, and even lynched.

The Untouchables eventually grew close to Oscar Chex and were even invited to his wedding to a young Kakchiquel woman who declared herself ready to follow Chex to the ends of the earth. Chex sometimes expressed remorse about his role in Military Intelligence, and, peripherally, the murder of Bishop Gerardi. "It was a job," he would explain. "You have to eat. . . ." Then he would fall silent, or even choke up. He told of the dirty tricks played in Military Intelligence on opposition political figures and human rights activists—informing wives, for example, about their husbands' extramarital love affairs. He spoke about the training and aid received in the Directorate of Technical Intelligence from a pair of agents from the CIA.

In the first week of November 1999, Oscar Chex testified before Judge Flor de María Villatoro, the prosecutors, ODHA's lawyers, and the requisite public defender. He and his young wife spent their last nights in Guatemala in a Catholic nuns' residence and then were flown into exile, to another Central American country.

Chex's testimony established that the Guatemalan Army had regarded Bishop Juan Gerardi as an enemy and had kept him under illegal surveillance since at least 1992.

ANOTHER WITNESS WOULD HAVE even greater impact on the Gerardi case. Specialist Jorge Aguilar Martínez was a member of the EMP's Presidential Guard, where he said he had served as a personal waiter to President Arzú, and sometimes as a concierge or a janitor. On the night of April 26, 1998, according to his pretrial declaration, he'd been assigned to monitor the coming and going of vehicles from the EMP. He directly implicated Captain Byron Lima and some of his own commanding officers in the EMP in the crime.

But aspects of this witness's testimony made the ODHA lawyers nervous. Among the soldiers Aguilar Martínez named as having probably participated in the murder of Bishop Gerardi was EMP Sergeant Major Obdulio Villanueva. How could that be? Obdulio Villanueva was in the Antigua Prison, serving out his sentence in the case of the slain milkman, Sas Rompich. When Aguilar Martínez finally gave his pretrial deposition before flying into exile, ODHA asked him to repress that dubious bit of testimony.

A number of EMP soldiers and military men, including both Limas, were among seventeen suspects who were required to give DNA samples to be analyzed by the FBI. But solving the Gerardi case, with its utterly contaminated crime scene and missed and mishandled evidence, meant relying on the most unscientific evidence, mainly the testimony of witnesses who each might have seen only a segment of the crime.

Celvin Galindo, several family members, and others in the prosecutors' office were receiving telephone threats, and soon the acts of intimidation worsened. Men stalked Galindo's children outside their school. Arlene Cifuentes had mentioned to Ronalth Ochaeta that targeting children was a signature element of the Limas's modus operandi. Nery Rodenas's children would also be trailed from school by thugs.

On October 6, Galindo and his wife and children suddenly went into exile. Only days earlier he'd announced that he was on the verge of indicting military men in the Gerardi case, but the FBI hadn't provided the supporting evidence he'd been hoping for. There were whispers that Galindo had abandoned the case precipitately—that his life wasn't really in danger, that such threats were a routine part of the job. Most parents, however, once they believe their children are in peril, wouldn't hesitate a second about what to do.

A declassified diplomatic cable of the U.S. embassy from the time says that "Galindo's tenure saw the investigation steadily build momentum as he focused increasingly on the mounting circumstantial evidence implicating the Presidential Military Staff [EMP] and its officers. . . . Early on October 7, HROFF [the embassy's human rights officer] met with Galindo's deputy, Anibál Sánchez, who confirmed that both he and Galindo believe the case is very close to being solved, but that they are prevented from exploring certain leads by lack of support from González Rodas [the attorney general] and the Public Ministry. As if Galindo's resignation were not bad enough, Sánchez informed HROFF that the central offices of the Public Ministry had just ordered the Gerardi prosecutors' security detail to abandon their posts."

The next day, the U.S. embassy publicly expressed its concern for the safety of Judge Flor de María García Villatoro.

A FEW DAYS EARLIER, on September 29, more than a year after being taken into custody by the Public Ministry, Father Mario's dog, Baloo, died. Soon afterward, the priest departed for Houston, Texas. Later in October, thirty-four-year-old Leopoldo Zeissig, the former assistant prosecutor under Galindo, took over as special prosecutor of the Gerardi case.

ALFONSO PORTILLO WAS ELECTED president in December 1999. Portillo was a controversial populist from the FRG Party—a party whose most popular and powerful figure was none other than the former dictator General Efraín Ríos Montt, who was constitutionally barred from running for president himself because of his past as a military dictator who had siezed power in a coup. President Portillo promised that he would resign if within three months his government couldn't solve the Gerardi case. The president-elect named Edgar Gutiérrez, the former executive director of REMHI, to be the new head of the Section of Strategic Analysis, the SAE. Gutiérrez vowed to convert the SAE from a branch of Military Intelligence to a wholly civilian information-gathering and analysis agency at the service of the civilian government. That would make it the first Military Intelligence section to be demilitarized, as mandated by the Peace Accords. Gutiérrez took several present and past members of ODHA with him to the SAE, including Fernando Penados.

There was widespread expectation that the EMP would soon be disbanded, but this hopeful idea would be of short duration. President Portillo, his own considerable personal shortcomings aside, would turn out to be no less beholden to the military establishment and other entrenched murky powers than any of his predecessors. The real strongman of the FRG was General Ríos Montt, who was duly elected president of the Guatemalan legislature.

Ronalth Ochaeta soon joined his old colleague Edgar Gutiérrez in Portillo's government as the ambassador to the Organization of American States in Washington. On visits to Guatemala around that time, I was present at long, noisy, excited, argumentative drinking sessions during which the propriety of accepting posts in Portillo's government was discussed. I definitely agreed with those who said it was impossible for people with a past in human rights to join any government in which General Ríos Montt had such a commanding role. But Edgar Gutiérrez and others argued that Ríos Montt wouldn't be around for long: that, after the UN truth commission's genocide ruling, the several legal proceedings being filed, in Spain and Guatemala, against him and other former Guatemalan military dictators would soon discredit him and drive him from power, and they hoped into prison. They predicted an inside battle between dinosaurs and progressives for control of Portillo's government. It was an unprecedented opportunity to learn the inner workings of power, they said, to move from the periphery to the center of political life.

Fernando Penados had no faith in Portillo whatsoever but, he told me, out of admiration for Edgar Gutiérrez and what he was trying to accomplish, he'd decided to follow Gutiérrez to the SAE. Others, like Mario Domingo and Nery Rodenas, were having none of it from the start. To them the whole idea of collaborating with a government in which General Ríos Montt had any role whatsoever stank of cynical compromise and worse. But even they sensed that an opportune and decisive moment to push for results in the Gerardi case had arrived; that for the time being, at least during these first months of Portillo's government, the investigation into the involvement of elements of President Arzú's EMP, a case so quietly, secretively, and painstakingly developed over the past two years, could finally be pushed forward.

ALTHOUGH RELATIONS WERE CORDIAL between ODHA and the new special prosecutor, Leopoldo Zeissig, and his team, it could hardly have been called a collaboration at first. ODHA had trusted Celvin Galindo, and had felt betrayed when he fled, accepting a grant to study in Germany. (On a brief trip to Germany later that year Nery Rodenas found Galindo depressed, living with his family squeezed into a drab little apartment in a bleak German city, where his child's bicycle had just been stolen from the courtyard.) They initially underestimated the chubby, prematurely silver-haired, goateed, quietly earnest, at times introverted Zeissig. The prosecution team had been moved from the far-flung office in Mixco to one at the edge of the old downtown, in Zone 2, a walled-in house with a yard that was already partly occupied by a Public Ministry organized crime unit. On previous visits there, Mario Domingo had been puzzled to see Rubén Chanax Sontay, the indigent from the San Sebastián park who was now a protected witness, washing cars in the parking lot. "He wanted work," Domingo was told by one of Zeissig's assistants when he asked about it, "and so we gave him some work."

More than two years later, in the summer of 2002, when he was no longer in Guatemala, Leopoldo Zeissig would tell me the story of Rubén Chanax Sontay's emergence as a key witness.

Two weeks after Zeissig had taken over as special prosecutor of the Gerardi case, he was told that the National Police no longer wanted the responsibility of caring for Rubén Chanax and El Chino Iván. Two big-bellied assistant prosecutors—Anibál Sánchez and Mario Castañeda—went to visit the men in their rooms in the Hotel Arlington, a sleazy place downtown. The assistant prosecutors found Chanax and El Chino Iván desperate from boredom and uncertainty about the future. It was then that Chanax said that he wanted something to do, that he wanted to work.

Throughout their confinement Chanax and El Chino Iván had stuck to their respective original stories, in those aspects where the stories coincided but also where they differed. But Chanax's quiet, aloof, yet watchful demeanor left the prosecutors with the nagging impression that there was something he wanted to say. When Zeissig decided to give Chanax work washing cars, he told his assistants: "That son of a whore knows more." They needed to cultivate a relationship with him. They would play good cop, bad cop, Zeissig decided, with himself cast as the bad cop. Anibál Sánchez began taking Chanax to the movies, the former vagrant's great passion. Chanax always arrived at Zeissig's headquarters accompanied by two police guards. But while he was washing cars in the lot, sometimes the police would go off for lunch or leave for other reasons. While the police were away, and later, when Chanax had finished with his chores, the prosecutors would let him come inside to watch cartoons and movies on television.

"He was introverted and timid at first," Zeissig said. "But you could see that he was intelligent. He noticed what people wore. He'd say, 'You've been wearing that tie for a week.'"

One day Chanax said to Anibál Sánchez, "Father Mario knew." But that was all he said.

Special Prosecutor Leopoldo Zeissig

Zeissig called Chanax into his office and accused him roughly of knowing more than he'd told so far. That routine continued for several days. But Chanax remained stubbornly silent.

Then, one afternoon in late November, Chanax responded, "If I tell you what I know, they'll kill us both."

Zeissig waited for Chanax to explain what he meant, but he wouldn't say anything more that day.

"This *cabroncito* has screwed us now," Zeissig told his staff. He suspended their Christmas vacations so as not to interrupt the daily routine with Chanax.

One afternoon, Zeissig sat down with Chanax and showed him grisly crime-scene photographs taken inside the parish-house garage. "Look at Monseñor," Zeissig told him. "He defended a just cause. If you want to have a good conscience, or if you have something to say, then we'll defend you."

After a long while, Chanax broke the silence: "He wasn't the way he is in the photos."

La gran puta, here it comes, thought Zeissig. And he waited.

"What happened," Chanax finally said, "is that they moved him."

"Who moved him?" asked Zeissig. "Did the firemen move him?"

"Not the firemen."

"Who?"

"They'll kill me if I tell."

"Who will kill you?"

"You know who," said the former park vagrant. And then he fell silent again.

"You have to let witnesses go at their own speed," Zeissig told me. "We all choose our moments."

ON JANUARY 17, 2000, a journalist named Pedro Pop published a brief story in *Prensa Libre* about Chanax and El Chino Iván. Pop wrote that they had been living in police custody at the Hotel

Arlington, and that he had spoken to them. In the article, El Chino Iván complained bitterly about the prison-like conditions they were living under and asked to be taken out of the country. He said that he and Chanax feared for their lives. "But without a doubt, of the two indigents Chanax is the one who is most worried about his situation," the reporter wrote, "because he has received threats from people who've said: 'If you keep squealing, you're going to die.'"

The story was a scoop, though it wasn't all news to ODHA. The Arlington Hotel rented rooms cheaply to lovers by the hour, and once, when one of the young men from ODHA had slipped away there with his fiancée in search of that privacy so precious to young people still living at home with their parents, he had spotted Chanax, and police guards, in the lobby. But if it was true that Chanax had been threatened for "squealing," to whom was he squealing, and about what?

ODHA's lawyers were taken by surprise when they received a communication summoning them to the special prosecutor's office at four in the afternoon on the very day the article appeared, to hear the official pretrial deposition of the protected witness Rubén Chanax Sontay. Suspecting a trick of some kind, they filed a motion to block the hearing, at least until they could learn more about what to expect. But Judge Flor de María García Villatoro declared their motion out of place.

The untimely appearance of the article in Prensa Libre—especially its revelation that Chanax was talking—had forced Zeissig to bring Chanax before the judge well before he wanted to. Chanax and El Chino Iván had told the reporter much more than they should have. Only frantic last-second telephone calls from Zeissig had persuaded him to refrain from printing more.

Chanax testified for seven hours that day, until nearly midnight. When he was finished, Judge García Villatoro asked Zeissig when he wanted to issue the arrest orders, and Zeissig asked the judge for a little more time. There was much to prepare. Arrangements had to be made for Chanax to go into exile. (He remained in the country until April.)

ODHA's lawyers left the Public Ministry office that night knowing that what they'd just heard was "momentous." As Mario Domingo later put it, they were feeling so excited but also frightened by what lay ahead that "we were carrying our balls in our hands."

ON JANUARY 19, arrest orders, to be executed the next day, were issued against Colonel Lima Estrada; Captain Lima Oliva; Sergeant Major Obdulio Villanueva, who was no longer in prison; and Father Mario. All of them had been implicated by Chanax's testimony. Another arrest order was issued for the parish-house cook, Margarita López. Leopoldo Zeissig's superior, the attorney general, Adolfo Gonzáles Rodas, a holdover from the previous government—the same man who had backed the dog-bite scenario—wanted to charge the military men with murder, but Zeissig held out for what he considered the more accurate, if slightly lesser, charge: participation in an extrajudicial execution, a premeditated crime of state. Gonzáles Rodas insisted that Father Mario be charged with homicide, and Zeissig relented, thinking that he would be able to modify the charges later.

Usually, a judge sends arrest orders directly to the police, but Zeissig asked if he could deliver them. He wanted to add pressure to the situation. The new chief of police, however, made it clear that he was extremely reluctant to arrest the military men. Zeissig returned to Gonzáles Rodas and asked him to speak directly to President Portillo.

"I can't do that," the attorney general answered. "Go back to the police. You'll see, they'll do it."

"You know how things are in Guatemala," Zeissig responded. He argued that if they didn't move quickly, the men might easily be tipped off and given time to escape.

The attorney general finally agreed to speak to President Portillo the next day, during their weekly Thursday meeting. Edgar Gutiérrez, now a member of Portillo's government, told me what happened. "The chief of police went to the president's office," he said, "and the president called me. When I arrived, he showed us the arrest orders. The president, with the order in his hand, said, 'Look, if you use conventional methods to capture these people, they're going to get away. Choose the most trustworthy people you have, don't use telephones or radios, and order a surprise operation to capture them.'"

It would be President Portillo's most direct intervention in the Gerardi case.

At four o'clock that afternoon, Zeissig received a call on his cell phone from his wife: the news had broken on television that a police operation was under way in Colonia Lourdes. Captain Lima was arrested at home. His father, Colonel Lima Estrada, was apprehended at a house in another part of the city.

The operation to capture Obdulio Villanueva at his small rural farmhouse lasted from five to ten in the morning on January 22, during which time the suspect engaged the police and soldiers who came to arrest him in a gun battle that lasted two hours. Father Mario, who was still in Houston, Texas, returned to Guatemala to turn himself in weeks later, while court orders were being prepared for his extradition.

In the ensuing weeks, Sergeant Major Obdulio Villanueva's lawyers presented proof that their client had been freed from prison, having served his sentence, two days *after* the murder of Bishop Gerardi. But prosecutors found some of his old cellmates who explained that Villanueva had frequently received visits from military officers, and that he was sometimes allowed to sleep outside the prison, in hotels in Antigua—the beautiful old town is a major tourism destination, with majestic ruins of churches and convents from a colonial-era earthquake. Unfortunately, none of the prisoners was willing to say this on the record. Finally, there being no evidence against him other than Rubén Chanax's testimony, the judge ordered Obdulio Villanueva freed.

Mario Domingo and Nery Rodenas had by then sheepishly confessed to Leopoldo Zeissig that the earlier witness from the EMP, the presidential waiter Aguilar Martínez, had also implicated Obdulio Villanueva in the crime, but that ODHA's lawyers had asked him to withhold that information from his deposition, because it seemed incredible. Zeissig was furious. Even if they'd instructed Aguilar Martínez not to mention Villanueva, ODHA *still* should have informed him. Then he and his assistants could have quietly begun investigating months before anyone else learned that Villanueva was a suspect. Chanax's testimony and the subsequent arrest orders, Zeissig presumed, had given Villanueva's protectors enough time to cover their man's tracks and ensure the silence of other prisoners.

But there was one small breakthrough. Zeissig managed to establish that Sergeant Major Obdulio Villanueva had remained on active duty, drawing a salary as a member of the EMP, while he was in prison.

THE LIMAS' DEFENSE TEAM was led by Julio Cintrón Gálvez, an elderly lawyer with a long record of courtroom successes on behalf of military clients. Like many extremely conservative Guatemalans, Cintrón regarded human rights cases against the military as a leftist stealth tactic for continuing the country's internal war by nonmilitary means. "This is an ideological struggle of the communists against the anticommunists," he said. His younger colleague, Roberto Echeverría Vallejo, had been a member of the three-judge tribunal that had presided over the trial of Obdulio Villanueva for murdering the milkman. The judges had so reduced the homicide charges against Villanueva that he'd ended up spending less than a year in prison. Among other lawyers and courthouse reporters, Cintrón was regarded as a master of the kind of legal ploys that had long characterized the practice of criminal law in Guatemala, and Echeverría Vallejo was an adept young protégé.

At a pretrial hearing in March the two defense lawyers, along with Father Mario's defense lawyer, José Toledo, arrived with what Zeissig referred to, metaphorically, as *un gallo tapado,* a hidden rooster. Unveiled, the rooster crowed. Echeverría stunned ODHA's lawyers by presenting Judge Flor de María García Villatoro with a document signed by Archbishop Próspero Penados withdrawing the Catholic Church's backing of ODHA as its legal representative, and thus as a co-plaintiff with the prosecution. It looked as if ODHA was about to be removed from the case. While Judge García Villatoro went over the papers, Echeverría watched the crestfallen Nery Rodenas and Mario Domingo with a satisfied smirk. Cintrón launched into a taunting tribute to the glorious Guatemalan Army, which had defeated the guerrillas, only now to defeat their enemies again—the now "extinct ODHA," he said— in the courtroom.

"Puta muchá, just like that, you're *gone,"* one of the prosecution lawyers cracked sardonically, and there was sympathetic laughter.

Leopoldo Zeissig asked to see the document signed by the archbishop, and he immediately noticed some interesting details. It was a Wednesday, but the document had been signed on Sunday, then notarized that same day. Zeissig pointed out to Judge García Villatoro that lawyers in a case involving the interests of the state couldn't be removed from a legal process, such as the current hearing, without prior notice. Since ODHA's lawyers were already in attendance, they couldn't be removed now.

Zeissig had won ODHA some time. But the lawyers had no explanation for Archbishop Penados's betrayal. Nery Rodenas, tears in his eyes, declared himself ready to resign. During the lunchtime recess, he and Mario Domingo hurried over to see the archbishop. It turned out that he didn't even know what he'd signed. The previous Sunday, Father Mario's mother had gone to visit the archbishop in the company of the three defense lawyers, along with Monseñor Hernández. Since the death of Bishop Gerardi, Archbishop Penados had been in failing health and broken in spirit, probably clinically depressed. Monseñor Hernández explained to him that the document they wanted him to sign committed the Church to desisting from accusing Father Mario of involvement in the murder of Bishop Gerardi. There was no need for him to read the document, Monseñor Hernández said. The archbishop could trust him. And so the archbishop had signed.

The ODHA lawyers went to Bishop Ríos Montt, who issued a new mandate naming ODHA as the Church's legal representative in the Gerardi case, and on April 10, nearly two years after Bishop Gerardi's murder, Judge Flor de María García Villatoro ordered the rearrest of the former EMP specialist Obdulio Villanueva. On May 18, she ruled that the case against the two Limas and Villanueva should proceed to trial. And she immediately became the target of death threats.

RONALTH OCHAETA was still living in Costa Rica when Villanueva was arrested. He read about the arrest in a newspaper than he left spread open on the kitchen table, and his youngest son idly picked it up. The little boy was thunderstruck. The photograph in the newspaper was of one of the thugs who had broken into their house, he excitedly told his father, one of the men who had trained a gun on him and the maid as they sat roped together on the couch.

III
THE TRIAL
WITNESSES

I would have wished to live and die free, that is to say, subject to law in such a way that neither I nor anyone else could shake off the honorable yoke.

—Jean-Jacques Rousseau, "A Discourse on Inequality"

1

NO MILITARY OFFICER HAD ever been convicted of a human rights crime in Guatemala. Nor had any military man ever been charged with participating in a politically motivated crime of state such as extrajudicial execution, the crime for which the two Limas and Sergeant Major Villanueva were to be tried. Father Mario was accused of homicide and Margarita López of having withheld evidence. The trial, which was to be heard by a three-judge tribunal, was delayed for over a year while the defense filed various legal motions. It got under way in March 2001, and I went down to Guatemala a few weeks later.

Mynor Melgar was the lead lawyer representing ODHA, which, as co-plaintiff on behalf of the Church, was permitted to assist the special prosecutor in the case against the military men—although not in the cases against Father Mario or the parish-house cook. "So far, in the context of what you can hope to accomplish in a Guatemalan courtroom, I think we're doing well," Melgar said to me when I arrived. "The crime laboratories here don't have many resources," he explained, "and there's little capacity for doing good forensics. Usually, the only real evidence you take to trial is the testimony of witnesses. And people can buy witnesses, intimidate them, they can kill them. That makes trying cases in Guatemala very complicated." Most of the important witnesses in the Gerardi case had made written statements and then fled the country.

Mynor Melgar had left the country too, along with his wife and children. In 1999, he spent nine months in Berkelely, California, studying at the University of California's Institute of Latin American Studies and giving volunteer legal advice to Guatemalan immigrants in the Bay Area. But Melgar, unlike most of the other exiles, had returned. "How nice that you've come back just to die," an anonymous voice said in one of the first of many threatening telephone calls he received. A few months later, in December 2000, a man held a pistol to Melgar's head while he knelt in the bathroom of his own home, in the presence of his wife and two uncomprehending little sons. The intruder said that he wasn't going to pull the trigger. He had been told just to issue a warning.

Melgar's soft-spoken, cheerfully bantering manner hid a basically reserved nature and a composed and incisive intelligence. When he was intensely engaged, his face settled into an expectant, slightly bemused expression and his eyes held an avid glow. Melgar grew up in El Gallito, Guatemala City's most notorious barrio, where cocaine and crack are sold openly in the dirt streets and where chop shops for stolen cars are dug like caves into the walls of ravines, their entrances covered by day with tin sheeting and brush. In accordance with the sometimes straight moral logic of those living crooked lives—a theme that would figure in the testimony of some key witnesses in the trial—Melgar was something of a folk hero in El Gallito. Not many people from there went to college, and given Melgar's roots and litigation skills, he could easily have become a wealthy narco defense lawyer or even a member of the Oficinita. Instead, he won national and international renown by taking on the Guatemalan Army in case after case. He was the special prosecutor in the Myrna Mack murder case, which resulted in the conviction of the EMP operative who stabbed her to death. He'd won another conviction for murder against Ricardo Ortega, a notorious carjacker who was protected by military officers. And he was the prosecutor in the (stalled) case against military personnel who ordered and carried out the massacre of 350 civilians in the community of Dos Erres in 1982.

It had not been easy to find judges to hear the Gerardi case. Two of the three judges originally selected had fought successfully for permission to resign, essentially out of fear, although they were obligated to provide other reasons. Judge Carlos Chin's last-minute resignation (he claimed a conflict of interest: his son had studied at the Colegio San José de los Infantes when Sergio Orantes was rector) at the beginning of February had caused a postponement of the trial's scheduled opening. One of the Limas' defense lawyers, Roberto Echeverría Vallejo, filed a motion for a mistrial because Judge Chin had already been ruling on evidence and witnesses. The defense lawyers seemed desperate to delay the trial as much as possible, and ODHA's lawyers suspected that they knew why. Archbishop Penados had announced his resignation several months earlier. The defense lawyers were playing for more time because they thought that the Vatican was going to name a conservative as the new archbishop, someone who would remove ODHA from the case and perhaps even close it down.

The three judges finally selected to hear the case were young, in their early to mid-thirties. On the night before the day set for opening arguments, Wednesday, March 21, as Judge Yassmín Barrios was preparing dinner—she had just removed the steamed corn-husk wrappings from the corn meal *chuchitos* she was about to serve to her bodyguards—two grenades exploded in her backyard, shattering windows and destroying a water tank. A month earlier, Captain Lima's defense lawyers had attempted to have Judge Barrios recused from the trial. What made the grenade attack seem especially sinister was that to reach the backyard of the modest home where Yassmín Barrios lived with her mother, in a dense middle-class subdivision, the perpetrator had to have traversed two adjoining properties with walled-in backyards, implying, perhaps, aerial surveillance in planning the attack, and the possible collaboration of neighbors.

Judge Barrios had an air of nervous fragility. Leopoldo Zeissig, the special prosecutor, was among many who didn't believe she would show up in court for the opening of the trial the next day. He expected to learn that she'd been escorted by MINUGUA to the airport for her trip into exile. That would mean yet another postponement of the trial, and weeks or even months of legal fighting over seating another judge. But the U.S. embassy's human rights officer came to Barrios's home the night of the explosion, and the next morning the U.S. ambassador, Prudence Bushnell, and several other foreign diplomats visited the judge in her office. The show of support sent a strong message to the Guatemalan government and military, and it buoyed Judge Barrios. Her resolve was strengthened by her own sense of the historical importance of the case. When she arrived at the courthouse later in the morning, she told Zeissig, "We're going to endure everything, whatever it takes."

An investigator from MINUGUA told me it was likely that the grenades had been tossed into Judge Barrios's yard by her own security detail, which was headed by a police officer named Ronald Manfredo Ruano. Most of the men in the security detail were former soldiers from the EMP. (A year later, Officer Ruano would be arrested for the extrajudicial execution of two young men he and a partner had taken into custody. Their bodies were found with their hands tied behind their backs, a bullet in each head.)

The opening of the trial was nearly postponed again when the accused military men refused to come out of their cell blocks in the Centro Preventivo, on the outskirts of the city, alleging a plot to assassinate them by sniper fire on the long drive to the Torre de Tribunales, in the neo-Mayan complex of government buildings and plazas at the edge of the old city center. "If that happened to her," said Captain Byron Lima, referring to the grenade attack on Judge Barrios, "imagine what could happen to us." But finally, an hour and a half late, the men were led into the courtroom at the

Guatemalan Supreme Court. Captain Lima was wearing a Kaibil T-shirt. Some reporters noticed that there were tears in his eyes.

Judge Flor de María García Villatoro, who had issued the arrest orders and had juristiction over the pretrial investigation, was receiving round-the-clock protection from MINUGUA. Earlier that year Amnesty International had sent letters to President Arzú and the attorney general asking that special protection be provided to Nery Rodenas, who had succeeded Ronalth Ochaeta as executive director of ODHA, but no such protection was offered. The death threats to ODHA accelerated as the proceedings went on. In one day alone, Rodrigo Salvadó reported twenty calls to his home from a man who said that a group was on its way to kill Rodrigo at midnight. Three of the four most important witnesses in the case were in exile as the trial got under way: Diego Méndez Perussina, the taxi driver who saw the shirtless man standing by a parked car and wrote down the license-plate number that was traced to the military; Jorge Aguilar Martínez, the EMP waiter who had implicated Captain Lima and Sergeant Major Villanueva; and Rubén Chanax Sontay. The fourth key witness, a thief who had been in the Antigua prison with Obdulio Villanueva, was still incarcerated.

Oscar Chex, the former G-2 Military Intelligence agent who had listened in on Bishop Gerardi's telephone calls, was in exile, as were Juana Sanabria, the administrator of the church of San Sebastián and the bishop's closest personal friend, and even Father Quiróz, the priest whom the taxi driver had first gone to see. El Chino Iván Aguilar, the *bolito* who had lived with Rubén Chanax in the Hotel Arlington before Chanax made his final statement to the prosecutors, was in another Central American country. A number of people who might have been able to corroborate aspects of the testimony of others or even provide new information of their own had been murdered or had died, including, by then, many of the *bolitos* who used to sleep outside the San Sebastián parish house and garage. Their deaths, perhaps, were mostly attributable to the hardships of life on the streets, but some of the *bolitos* were also rumored to have "disappeared" or been murdered.

No one had endured a steadier volume of threats than the people who worked in the special prosecutor's office. Funeral music would play into their phones. This was a familiar trick. Leopoldo Zeissig once tried to dial his wife at home and an unknown woman's voice came on, speaking to him like a concerned close friend, advising him to resign from the case. All the telephones in the prosecutors' office would start ringing at once, a bombardment of simultaneous calls. Then all the cell phones would start ringing. It was like something out of a Japanese horror movie. Zeissig's wife was a young attorney, and they had a one-year-old child. How could anyone ever grow accustomed to receiving anonymous calls saying, "Your husband hasn't come home yet? Well, he's not coming home."

One day a green ambulance parked outside the special prosecutor's office. It had a four-digit license plate. For several days in succession, the ambulance arrived punctually; sometimes a Jeep Cherokee was parked behind it. Finally Zeissig and some members of his security staff drove a car with tinted windows alongside the ambulance and videotaped it. A few days later Zeissig received a call from someone who said, "Don't be angry. I'm just doing my job. Those people who were watching you? They know everything. We know where your wife works. We know where your parents live. We know where her parents live. We saw that you were filming us, so we left. We're going to do other things now that you won't notice."

Two policemen were stationed in front of Zeissig's house at night—policemen were also stationed outside the homes of the assistant prosecutors—but intruders managed to climb up onto the roof overlooking the patio. Zeissig then sealed off his patio from the rest of the house. By the time the trial began, Zeissig was under twenty-four-hour protection, traveling everywhere in a caravan of three cars escorted by pickups carrying armed police commandos.

At the Centro Preventivo, Captain Byron Lima had had a scuffle with another prisoner, Carlos Barrientos, who was angry over the special privileges Lima and his codefendants were receiving. In the course of the fight, Barrientos somehow made off with Lima's personal agenda notebook, which he turned over to the prosecutors. The noteook contained telephone numbers, records of the visits Lima received, and an accounting of the prison businesses Lima was running. There was even a draft of a letter to a lover, the unmarried mother of their child, in which he complained of the high cost of having to pay off witnesses. The notebook also contained hand-drawn maps and diagrams of the layout of Leopoldo Zeissig's home—drawings indicating possible ways to get into the house and into the bedrooms—as well as the telephone numbers and addresses of his assistant prosecutors.

THE TRIAL WAS HELD in an auditorium-like courtroom with rows of steeply banked seats and walls of polished marble and inlaid tropical woods. (The Supreme Court ordinarily used this courtroom, but it was made available for the Gerardi trial because so many spectators and members of the press were expected.) The three judges—two women, Yassmín Barrios and Amada Gúzman de Zuñiga, and a man, Eduardo Cojulún, who was the presiding judge—sat on a raised dais, behind piles of legal volumes and documents, in the middle of a long table lined with more than a dozen empty chairs. Below, perpendicular to the judges' table, the prosecution team—Leopoldo Zeissig and his assistant prosecutors, and the ODHA lawyers, Mynor Melgar, Nery Rodenas, and Mario Domingo—sat at a table facing the defense lawyers. Behind the defense lawyers' table was a row of chairs where the two Limas and Sergeant Major Villanueva usually sat. Margarita López always sat at the defense table next to her lawyer, as did, at the far end, alongside his lawyer, Father Mario, in a wheelchair, dressed, for most of the trial, in his bathrobe and pajamas. The priest was being kept in custody at a private hospital. (On the first day of the trial he arrived with an oxygen tank and a mask, although it soon became apparent that he was unfamiliar with the way they worked, and he didn't bring them again.)

Except when all three judges leaned close together in intense discussion, the two female judges sat silently while Eduardo Cojulún briskly and elegantly ran the proceedings. Judge Barrios, who had a soft, round face, full lips, and black curly hair, spent most of the trial wearing the expression of a sorrowful Madonna in an old Italian painting, her eyes cast upward at the cloudlike whitewash of the wide, arching ceiling. Judge Gúzman de Zuñiga was so resolute in her seemingly stricken lack of expression that ODHA's lawyers nicknamed her "Santo del Pueblo," after the rustically carved, blankly staring wooden saints of village folk Catholicism.

"I thought the defense would be stronger," said Nery Rodenas of the early proceedings. "I thought it would offer stronger proofs, even if they were false ones." But not many others shared the ODHA lawyers' confidence. Early in the trial the courthouse had been filled with spectators every day, but by the ninth week the crowds had waned, and it had become almost fashionable in Guatemala, especially among those who weren't actually attending the trial, to remark with a knowing air that the case wasn't going well. An influential young columnist from *Prensa Libre* told me, "For all the effort *los muchachos* have put into it"—she meant the boys from ODHA—"it's leaving many doubts." But she hadn't been attending the trial either, so how did she know? Foreign press attendance had dropped off to almost nil except for a few wire services and two European journalists—a Frenchman who had for a while been a press spokesperson for MINUGUA and had previously reported for *Le Monde*, and a Spanish woman who reported for *El País*. They liked to remind Guatemalan reporters that Dr. Reverte Coma, the discoverer of the dog-bite marks in the bishop's skull, was an eminent and respected figure.

Most people one spoke to in Guatemala, whatever they thought of the trial, seriously doubted that the judges would vote to convict. They thought that the judges would be bought or simply wouldn't dare convict, for so it had always been in the past. But those who were attending the trial regularly were hearing things that had never been spoken out loud in Guatemala before. They were receiving an unprecedented tour through some of the inner workings of the covert intelligence units that had sown so much terror in their country.

Over the trial's forty-six sessions, 115 witnesses and experts would testify. It wasn't easy for anyone, certainly not a foreign reporter occasionally dropping in, to follow such a complex and largely circumstantial case. The pretrial depositions of the witnesses who were now in exile were droningly read into the court record. All you had to do was step out of the courtroom for a cup of coffee, or doze off in your seat, or let your attention stray, and you could easily miss, say, the EMP waiter Aguilar Martínez's entire testimony, the first eyewitness account that directly implicated Captain Byron Lima Oliva and the EMP in the crime.

Captain Byron Lima Oliva

* * *

ONE OF THE KEY WITNESSES who did testify at the trial was called by the defense. He was Gilberto Gómez Limón, who in the spring of 1998 was in the prison in Antigua—a drive of half an hour or so from Guatemala City—with Sergeant Major Obdulio Villanueva. In pretrial testimony, Gómez Limón had claimed that Villanueva had been outside the prison on the day of the murder.

"The defense had to try to discredit the pretrial depositions," Mynor Melgar explained. "They thought that Gómez Limón was ignorant, that he'd be easy to destroy. We were afraid they would destroy him—or buy him, or intimidate him. The witnesses who come here feel frightened for their own safety. What guarantee is there that a witness, once he's on the stand, is going to tell the truth? And we were thinking, if they destroy Gómez Limón, or if they destroy Rubén Chanax, they destroy our case." The defense lawyers seemed to believe that in Gómez Limón they had found the prosecution's softest target.

In April 1998, when Bishop Gerardi was murdered, Sergeant Major Villanueva was in the first year of the five-year sentence (later much reduced) he had received for slaying the milkman Sas Rompich. Gómez Limón was serving time for robbery. He and Villanueva were in the same cell block. By looking over a wall in that cell block, prisoners could see down into a passageway that led to the infirmary, the guardhouse, and the prison director's office. But a part of the passageway was blocked from view by a short section of wall in front of a door to the street. If someone walking down the passageway went behind that wall and did not emerge on the other side, it could mean only that the person had gone out the door into the street.

Gómez Limón was the *segundo encargado,* the number two prisoner in charge of the maintenance of the cell block, and his duties included collecting seventy-five quetzales, about ten dollars, from each new prisoner who wanted to be excused from cleaning chores. The money was used (he would testify) to buy mops and cleaning materials. Gómez Limón was the kind of inmate who liked to keep a little domestic order, cooking simple meals for himself with a certain zest that attracted Villanueva's attention. Gómez Limón said that he greatly resented it, that he did not think it was "correct," when Villanueva tried to bully him into cooking for him. Gómez Limón was a bit of a busybody too, the sort of person who would always hoist himself up to see who was going down the passageway with the section of wall hiding the door to the street.

According to Gómez Limón, prisoners at Antigua could come and go by paying the warden and prison mayor 200 quetzales, as long as the prisoner was present at the morning and evening roll calls. The Sunday morning of April 26, Gómez Limón watched Obdulio Villanueva, shortly after the roll call at five-thirty AM, heading down that passageway, and when he did not come out the other side, Gómez Limón knew that Villanueva had gone out the door into the street. Nevertheless, when Villanueva's family came to visit that same day, Gómez Limón, in his role of *segundo encargado,* dutifully went to look for him in the infirmary, the warden's office, and the guardhouse, but he was nowhere to be found. According to Gómez Limón, Villanueva *was* back in time for the roll call at five-thirty PM in the yard. But then he went out again. That night Villanueva's bed, which was only a few feet from Gómez Limón's, remained empty, though by the next dawn's roll call Villanueva had returned. In the morning, Gómez Limón said, Villanueva was anxious to watch the television news. "Since the television is mine," Gómez Limón testified, "you have to ask me for the remote, so that I will lend you the *tele.*"

I watched Gómez Limón's testimony on videotape. He spoke in Spanish, but with the cadences, repetitions, and somersaulting clauses of the Mayan languages, and also with the typical *Ahhhh, sí pues,* and other similar rhetorical expressions through which he narrated his own acts of listening or thinking, and denoted his own reactions and deductions as events unfolded. "*A la gran chucha!* It's time for the news! He was very worried, watching the Channel 7 news," Gómez Limón recounted to the court. "I went to watch a little. He was sitting in the plastic chair, and he looked the way he looks at you, like he wants to punch you." The burly, grim-faced, rough-featured Villanueva, hard lines at the side of his mouth, did resemble a thug from central casting. "Then Villanueva explained, 'That is a priest, and they killed him.' *Ahhhh, sí pues.* And I thought it was my own craziness when I thought, Oh, and it happened when he was out."

Gómez Limón said that he and the other prisoners knew that Villanueva had worked as the president's bodyguard. The day that Villanueva entered the prison, the authorities had warned that he should be left alone: "'Don't touch him in any way, because he works for the State.'"

Gómez Limón claimed that he'd never told anybody about what he saw that day, April 26. But a few months later, without warning or explanation, he was transferred to another prison, Pavoncito. Shortly after he arrived there, a prisoner came into his cell block shouting his name. "What's going on? And he's calling my name again," Gómez Limón recalled. "And I say, 'That's me,' and he says, 'Well, they're looking for you.' *Ahhhhh.* . . . 'The president is looking for you.'" (The president of the Committee of Order and Discipline, who is elected by other prisoners, is a kind of *capo* who runs the prison rackets—narcotics, alcohol, and so on— usually in coordination with the warden and guards.)

The other prisoner asked Gómez Limón if he'd been an *encargado* at the Antigua prison when Villanueva was there. Gómez Limón answered that he had, and the prisoner said, "Well, that's the situation. What more do you need know? They want to kill you. They're offering 65,000 quetzales for you."

They found the prison president, who told Gómez Limón he would take care of him, and he assigned two prisoners as guards. Gómez Limón was ordered into the "well," a dark, solitary cell.

He spoke to a jailhouse lawyer and got in touch with the Public Ministry. Leopoldo Zeissig came to see him at Pavoncito, and Gómez Limón told him his story.

In the courtroom, Gómez Limón, who wore a black ponytail and had broad, expressive Mayan features, sat at a small table facing the judge—from behind he looked like the Incredible Hulk, because of the bulky bulletproof vest he was wearing under his green, imitation-leather jacket—telling his story of how fear and a survivor's wily desperation had brought him to this moment: "I was very worried, because the truth is, Villanueva, they say he's very heavy in his way of doing things. They increased my protection, but in that place where I was, you're always in danger." He then described some of the threats directed against his family, his children and his brothers—presumably by the Army or supporters of the defendants, though Gómez Limón hadn't yet said so. "And they come and tell my family they're paying 20,000 quetzales so that I won't say anything. Well, this was last week, they come again and they're offering 100,000 quetzales so that I won't say anything, won't open my mouth. Yesterday they came for a third time"—to see his brother, Noé Gómez Limón—"and they want to know, 'What's your brother going to say?' They've tried many strategies, to stop me from telling the truth."

The well-tailored *licenciados* of the defense—the far more Indian and mestizo public-sector prosecution lawyers and judges made a striking contrast—questioned Gómez Limón for three hours. The prosecutors betrayed their anxiety by objecting to nearly every question, but Gómez Limón almost always seemed ready to jump right in, signaling, as he looked from Judge Cojulún toward the defense, that he wanted to answer by putting his hand out and turning it palm up with a certain flourish, and then he would hold that posture until the lawyers stopped arguing and the judge finally ordered, "*Contesta.*" Answer.

The defense tried to imply that Gómez Limón's testimony was being given in return for luxuries—a private room in prison, perhaps, or better food—and that he had been coached in his story. He had expressed himself more than adequately in Spanish, but one stubbornly pursued line of questioning, interrupted by objections and *No contesta*'s from the bench, went like this: "Señor Witness, where were you born? What is the Mayan tongue in that place? Do you speak that *lengua*? Do you prefer to speak in Kakchiquel or in Spanish? How do you prefer to testify? In Spanish or Kakchiquel? In which language do you express yourself best when you are with you family?" and on and on. The only point of the questions was to suggest that Gómez Limón was a native Kakchiquel-speaker, and how could a Kakchiquel Indian and criminal have put together such a coherent story on his own?

But it was the cook's lawyer, Ramón González—a small-time defense lawyer and public defender, low-paid, unlike the rest of the defense team—apparently sensing that the witness was wearying from riding the dangerous bull of his own fear and seemingly desperate honesty, and pushing for a courtroom trophy of his own, who accidentally provoked the examination's most memorable revelation.

Defense: "How many times did you talk to Prosecutor Zeissig?"

Gómez Limón: "Twice. People said that Villanueva is *muy matón*, a real killer. 'Get me the prosecutor!' I told my wife, 'Call the prosecutor!' Inside, all the time I had to stay inside. They had me worried about poison. They brought me my food. I couldn't even buy a soft drink. They came to see me. Prosecutor Zeissig. A person from MINUGUA. I didn't ask their names. They put me in this place, a safe place, near the guardhouse. How sad, to live like this. People said, 'Why did you get mixed up in this, if Villanueva is a killer?' If I mention names, more enemies for me!"

Defense: "When did these people come to talk to you?"

Gómez Limón: "I don't know anything. I don't want to involve more people."

Defense (shouting): "How is it that they came three times, offering money? You took an oath! Give me the names!"

Gómez Limón (in a frantic burst, as if thinking out loud): "What I need is to tell the truth. I'm protected here, and the court will find some way that nothing will happen to me."

Defense (shouting): "Can you tell me the names of the people who offered the money?"

Prosecutor interjects: "He said he doesn't know."

Gómez Limón (blurting): "Well, yes, but those people are here, the ones who are offering the money. The first who came was [the jailhouse lawyer] Paco. Then came the lawyer who is right there." (He indicated a defense lawyer, Roberto Echeverría Vallejo.) "He had come right from the Ministry of Defense, they say. Who did they go to? To my brother who is a prisoner in Escuintla, who told my other brother, who is the one the *licenciado* has now come to, at seven-thirty last night. And my brother came to the place where I was being kept and said, 'They're offering money so that you won't say anything and all this will end.'"

Captain Lima's lawyer, Roberto Echeverría Vallejo, had just been accused of attempting to buy the witness. (Later, at the end of the trial, when Goméz Limón's brother Noé was called to testify, Echeverría quietly slipped out of the courtroom. Noé Goméz Limón told the story of the lawyer who had come to buy his brother's silence, and he perfectly described the physical characteristics of the bearish, balding, sallow Echeverría.)

The visit to Pavoncito by the observer from MINUGUA whom Gilberto Gómez Limón mentioned was perhaps the reason he was still alive. The prisoner who had first informed him about the price on his head had no such protection when, during a flash prison riot, he was fatally stabbed, the only prisoner to die in that riot. ("What a coincidence," was Mynor Melgar's dry assessment.)

In Villanueva's defense, his lawyers presented family members, including his wife, who said they had visited him in the Antigua prison on the day his accusers claimed he'd left it. Villanueva's wife was a humble person. She didn't seem like the kind of person who would lie with such an earnest demeanor. The prosecutors and ODHA's lawyers were worried by that testimony. However, Zeissig reminded them, judges know that if anyone is likely to lie in court, close family members are, no matter how out of character that might seem. Under cross-examination, Villaneuva's wife had been forced into several contradictory statements. For example, first she said that there was no phone in her village, but then she said that she'd been informed of her husband's release from prison by phone.

An important revelation came late in the trial. The prosecutors discovered that Villanueva had been eligible to be paroled from prison on April 24, *two days before* the murder, but had chosen not to take his freedom until April 28. Why would someone elect to stay in prison four days more than he was required to? Unless, of course, prison was an alibi.

RUBÉN CHANAX SONTAY, the trial's star witness, had been brought back to Guatemala from the as yet undisclosed country of his exile to testify. Chanax's pretrial statements, if allowed to stand unchallenged, were devastating to all of the accused except Margarita López, the cook, and he seemed vulnerable because of the apparent inconsistencies in his stories, and because of the implausibility of some of his assertions.

Chanax had previously testified, in January 2000, that he'd encountered Sergeant Major Obdulio Villanueva, along with another person he knew only as Quesén, by the park on the Sunday of the murder, at about nine-thirty in the morning. Villanueva warned him to stay away from the park until ten that night, because someone was going to die. He said he felt pity for Chanax and didn't want to have to kill him. Chanax asked who was going to die, but Villanueva wouldn't say.

Why, of all the vagrants who lived in the park, had Villanueva singled out Chanax to warn of a murder that was to occur there that night? The answer Chanax had given during his pretrial testimony was not persuasive: "Later I imagined that it must be because I'm the only one who doesn't drink; the rest are drunks."

For his day in court, Chanax, a boyish twenty-seven-year-old with a halting yet determined voice, wore a shirt, a wide tie with a big knot, and a cumbersome bulletproof vest underneath his jacket. He gave his occupation as carpenter and began his testimony with an account of his nearly thirty months of required military service. He'd had nowhere to go after his discharge, and he had eventually found a home in the park in front of the San Sebastián church and self-employment there as a car washer. Earlier, Chanax had testified that he was able to recognize Colonel Lima on the night of the bishop's murder because the colonel had once broken up a fight between him and a group of high school students in the park, and had then introduced himself as the father of Captain Byron Lima, who was in charge of the president's security.

Now, in court, Rubén Chanax introduced a new story. Colonel Lima, he said, had approached him in the park one day and identified himself as a colonel of G-2, Military Intelligence. (Colonel Lima would not have had to cut his ties in retirement.) According to Chanax, the colonel had asked Chanax to work for him. "I want you to be my informant," the colonel had said, "because of what happens here, being so close to the palace." Chanax said that he accepted the colonel's offer because he needed the money. He was given a phone number and told to call it every Saturday. Three months later, he was asked to watch Bishop Gerardi. When Chanax phoned to inform, he was simply to say the code words "Operation Bird."

That testimony provided a new logic for Rubén Chanax's story. (Villanueva had warned him because Villanueva knew of his role as an informer whose job it was to spy on Bishop Gerardi.) Leopoldo Zeissig would tell a Guatemalan reporter weeks after the trial that he hadn't known everything Chanax was going to say in court, though he'd intuited that Chanax might have been an informer for Military Intelligence, "because only someone who was in on what was going on could have known in such detail about all that happened that night."

Later, I thought that the defense lawyers must have realized the risk to their clients in summoning Chanax back from exile to testify but had reasoned that the witness would still be inhibited by fear—fear of retaliation, and also of the repercussions of incriminating himself. Maybe that was what those lawyers had taken from a pretrial hearing held before Chanax went into exile, when he and Captain Lima had confronted each other. During that earlier hearing, after several heated exchanges— Captain Lima essentially arguing that Chanax was a liar and fabricator, and Chanax steadfastly holding his ground—an irate Captain Lima had finally warned, "And what will you do if a video turns up that implicates *you* in the crime?" The defense must have believed that Chanax, when called to testify in front of the judges and television cameras, would *never* confess to having had any role in the operation that resulted in the murder of Bishop Gerardi.

In the courtroom, Rubén Chanax continued with his account. After Villanueva and Quesén, whom another car washer had once introduced to him as a member of the EMP, gave their warning that morning, Chanax had wandered off and enjoyed an ordinary Sunday: a matinee at a downtown cineplex, an afternoon nap under some trees on a hill in Zone 3. A little after nine o'clock that night, he and El Chino Iván were in Don Mike's little neighborhood store, watching the movie *Congo* on television. It was then that Colonel Lima Estrada came in with at least two men Chanax said he didn't recognize. They were welcomed by Don Mike: "Here come my favorite clients." The men huddled at the counter, drinking beer and talking. A little before ten, Chanax started back to the park. When he saw how quiet and tranquil everything seemed, he decided that what Villanueva had told him wasn't true, or hadn't been carried out. He began to prepare his bedding. Then the man without a shirt appeared in the small door in the garage.

"He used to walk across the park," Chanax testified, "and I'd washed his car once, and he'd told me he worked for the EMP." Chanax said that this man was called Hugo. After a desultory exchange, the man without a shirt ran off, leaving the small door open. Minutes later, said Chanax, a black Jeep Cherokee arrived on the scene, and two men got out through its rear door— Sergeant Major Obdulio Villanueva, carrying a small video camera, and Captain Byron Lima. According to Chanax, Captain Lima said, "'Vos, vos serote, you little shit, come help us'—like that, but with stronger words, I can't say them here." Judge Cojulún said, "No, hombre, go ahead." And Chanax said, "He says, 'Vos, son of a big whore, come and help us,' and he grabs my arm, and pushes me inside. They gave me a pair of gloves, the kind doctors use." There was a body lying facedown on the floor in a pool of blood, though Chanax said that he didn't realize it was Bishop Gerardi until they turned the body over.

In his previous statement, Chanax had said that at this point he was terrified and had run off. But now he admitted that he'd stayed. Villanueva filmed the crime scene, set the camera down on the parked car, and helped drag the body several feet farther in. While the men from the EMP arranged the bishop's body— legs crossed just so, hands crossed under the chin—Chanax, as he'd been told to, scattered some newspapers around in the blood, to create an impression of disorder caused by a violent struggle. Villanueva set the large chunk of concrete in the pool of blood.

Captain Lima told Chanax, "If you talk, you'll end up just the same as this one." He took the gloves back from Chanax, put them into a little bag, and then, with Villanueva, climbed back into the Jeep Cherokee and drove away. The small garage door had been left open. Chanax said that he went to the main door of the parish house and rang the bell several times, but no one answered, until suddenly Father Mario appeared in the small door, wearing a long black leather coat. Chanax said, "Father, they left the door open," and before he could say anything else the priest said, "*Gracias,* Colocho," and kicked the door shut.

Claiming that he didn't know what else to do, Chanax lay down to sleep. If he truly was a Military Intelligence informer, he would have known he had less to fear there, if he did as he'd been told, than by doing or saying anything else, anywhere else. At midnight Father Mario, now dressed in a bathrobe, came out again, and addressed the row of *bolitos:* "Did you see who came in, who came out?" went the now familiar refrain, and Chanax said that he'd answered, "The only one was the *muchacho* who came out a while ago." The priest went back inside. Moments later, Monseñor Hernández's red car drove up. Soon Father Mario came out again and dramatically announced that Bishop Gerardi had been murdered. He pulled Chanax aside and said, "Tell them [the police] what you know, everything except that I came to the door."

Chanax finished his testimony by saying, "If I've hidden some things, it's because I didn't feel 100 percent *seguro*"—he was using the word in the sense of secure, or safe—"just as I don't now, really, but I think I'm all right, this being a courtroom."

What the defense cast as inconsistencies, and thus lies, in Chanax's declarations, the prosecution defended as augmentation. The central progression of events stayed the same; bit by bit, he filled in the picture a little more, until he finally felt *seguro* enough to complete it. During four hours of questions, the defense repeatedly pounded at Chanax's claim to have felt fear, "panic." During his first statement to the police, the defense argued, he had shown no fear. Why was he talking about fear now?

Defense: "Señor Witness. Why didn't you tell the police what you'd seen?"

Chanax: "I believed they'd kill me if I did."

Defense: "But you just said you were an informer. But you didn't inform. Who were you afraid of?"

Chanax: "Of all the G-2 that's around that park."

Defense: "Why, Señor Witness?"

Chanax: "They follow through on their threats."

Defense: "And now you feel more *seguro*." The lawyer wanted to exploit Chanax's use of the word *seguro*, as if the witness were referring not to his sense of safety but to the clarity of his recollection, to being *sure*.

Chanax: "Almost *seguro*."

Defense: "Almost *seguro*! Are you aware your declaration could cost the accused their lives? . . . Do you realize that when you say you went into the garage, you implicate yourself in extrajudicial execution?"

Another line of questioning, by Echeverría Vallejo, implied a material motive to lie: "When you slept by the garage, where did you put your head down?"

Chanax: "On my pillow."

Defense (mockingly): "And where did you get the shoes you're wearing now?" (Objection sustained.) "And what do you work at now?"

Chanax: "I work as a carpenter. And I dressed then the way I dress now, though not with a jacket. Are you asking was I filthy and begging? I wasn't. I bought my own clothes, sometimes new, sometimes secondhand."

The prosecution's cross-examination was mercifully brief.

Mynor Melgar: "When you say *seguro*, what do you mean by *seguro*?"

(Defense objects, claiming witness has already answered that.)

Chanax: "That I'm out of here—out of Guatemala."

2

"CHANAX'S TESTIMONY WAS CONTROVERSIAL," Leopoldo Zeissig said to me as the trial was drawing to a close. "The defense questioned his credibility. They said he was drugged, coached, bought. It's the defense's job to try to destroy him. And it's up to the judges to decide if they did. The defense interrogated him for four hours. If someone's going to lie, it usually shows up fairly quickly. He told what he knew, and he never lost his composure or contradicted himself." Zeissig said that the prosecutors had always suspected that Chanax probably knew far more than he'd told. The Public Ministry could not offer a witness the same sort of protections or deals that such a witness might receive in a federal case in the United States (as when a lower-ranking mafioso testifies against his bosses).

The defense was unrelenting in its efforts to propagate the idea that the entire case depended on Rubén Chanax alone, and that he'd lied. "¡*Chanax miente!*" Chanax lies! (The defense lawyers had shouted it so often, with such theatrical indignation, that it became a drinking toast for ODHA. Lift your beer and cheerfully bellow: "¡*Chanax miente!*") The defense's strategy was not only to play through the media to the public, to plant the idea that "the case is leaving many doubts," but also to leave "handles" in the trial record that a sympathetic judge might want to grab on to if the case was appealed. ("The witness himself admitted he wasn't *seguro*!")

But it wasn't true that the prosecution's case depended on Chanax. There was another witness whose testimony was also crucial—Jorge Aguilar Martínez, the waiter from the EMP. His pretrial declaration, made in the summer of 1999, was read into the record by a court secretary. He was now in exile, in a foreign political asylum program.

ODHA found Jorge Aguilar Martínez because Rodrigo Salvadó and Arturo Aguilar, the two remaining Untouchables, kept looking through old tips and leads that Fernando Penados, for one reason or another, had never pursued. They found an anonymous hand-printed letter from someone who wrote, essentially, that he or she knew someone who knew someone in the EMP who knew something about the Bishop Gerardi case, giving some details. Four months later ODHA had received another letter, unsigned, though it was believed that the author was same person who had written the first one. But this time the letter had been delivered in an envelope that bore the logo of a labor union, and the person who'd delivered the letter had left his name—Luis Flores. (I have changed his name.) The name seemed familiar to Mario Domingo, who before coming to ODHA had worked as a labor lawyer. Rodrigo and Arturo made repeated visits to the union office, but Luis Flores was never in. What followed was like the patient work of ants.

Rodrigo and Arturo finally found Flores, who confessed that he got the letter from his sister, "Doña Lupita," who ran a "people's pharmacy" that dispensed medicine free or at reduced prices in a poor neighborhood. Doña Lupita didn't want to talk to them, nor did the woman who had given the letter to Doña Lupita. But the Untouchables were persuasive, and after six weeks of cajoling they drove out to the pharmacy one afternoon and met a curly-haried woman with a round face and small, frightened eyes who said that she was the wife of a member of the EMP who had been on duty the night of Bishop Gerardi's murder. "I don't want my husband to know I'm here," she said. "This is very delicate." She said that her husband had written the letters because his conscience was troubled over the crime, but she couldn't tell them anything more. The Untouchables pressed their case. "Take your time deciding," Arturo remembered saying, "but we're very interested in what your husband can tell us. They killed a bishop. Our country can't go on this way."

As they drove back into the city, Rodrigo and Arturo savored a thrilling sense of expectation. For the first time, they had a chance to talk to someone who was inside the EMP on the night of the murder.

There were many more frustrating weeks of canceled meetings, meetings that went nowhere, and others that seemed to bring them tantalizingly close to the source of the information—the husband from the EMP. But by then Doña Lupita's husband had forbidden her to host any more meetings with ODHA in their home. Mario Domingo came with them to a meeting in the lobby of the Marriott Hotel—the Untouchables had chosen it because they thought they were unlikely to be recognized there, among the foreign tourists and business travelers. He told the wife of the man from the EMP that if her husband really had information on the crime, he and his family would have to leave the country for their safety. This might be traumatic, but it could also provide an opportunity for a better life, especially for their children. The wife began to weep. She was frightened and confused. She said she didn't know what she was doing there, that she shouldn't have come. The attention she was attracting made the Untouchables cringe. "But I don't want to leave the country!" she wailed.

After the meeting at the Marriott, the wife seemed to have decided to break off communications. The Untouchables waited nervously but patiently. Finally, a call came. There was another meeting in the lobby of another hotel, where they were given a letter sent by the husband. He was President Álvaro Arzú's personal waiter, he said. Sometimes he also had janitorial duty or was sent to work in a little office near an EMP entrance. He'd been on duty in that office the night that Bishop Gerardi was murdered. He named five people from the EMP who he said were responsible for the crime: Major Escobar Blas, Captain Lima, a man named Galeano, the EMP commander Rudy Pozuelos, and Obdulio Villanueva. He also named Howard Yang, the head of the Secretariat of Strategic Analysis, not because he'd seen Yang that night but because nothing happened in the EMP without Yang knowing about it. And he wrote that on the day before the murder President Arzú had been visibly nervous and drinking more than usual.

The next meeting was in the Hotel Camino Real. The Untouchables waited in a little lounge area, facing the pool. Jorge Aguilar Martínez arrived with his wife. He was wearing jeans and a white shirt; his dark, bird-like eyes flitted about nervously. "He looked incredibly frightened," Arturo recalled. Aguilar Martínez was thirty-three years old. His first year in the EMP he'd worked in intelligence, in the Archivo. But before going into the Army he'd been a butcher, and he also knew how to cook, so he was put to work, briefly, as a dishwasher before being promoted into the officers' kitchen. Eventually he'd been a cook and waiter for five consecutive civilian presidents, from Vinicio Cerezo to Álvaro Arzú. He worked in the presidential residence, but also accompanied presidents on their trips around the country and even abroad. Later Aguilar Martínez would produce a photo album with pictures of himself in the company of all those presidents. He would also confess to resentment over the bad treatment he'd lately received at the EMP. Aguilar Martínez may have been motivated to write those first letters out of conscience, but he also had personal grievances.

The Untouchables brought Aguilar Martínez to a priests' residence in the city where he met with ODHA's lawyers and videotaped an unofficial statement about what he'd seen on the night of April 26. They gave a copy of the tape to Jurgen Andrews, the human rights officer at the U.S. embassy. "With this witness the U.S.

embassy was really good," Arturo Aguilar said. The Army would have to think twice before harming him. Nevertheless, soon afterward the Untouchables got a call from Aguilar Martínez. A few days earlier he'd been ordered to do some cleaning in the offices of the EMP's anti-kidnapping commando unit. In one room, taped to the wall, he said, were photographs of ODHA's Suzuki jeep with Arturo sitting in it. One of Aguilar Martínez's commanding officers came up to him while he was cleaning in a corridor. "Listen," he said, "I don't want to find out that you've been talking *babosadas*," stupidities, and added, "You know what happens to people who talk."

The moment had arrived for ODHA to get Aguilar Martínez and his family into hiding. His wife packed in a frantic rush, in half an hour fitting everything she could into a few suitcases. Arturo and Rodrigo drove her and their five children to where Aguilar Martínez was waiting. ODHA had accepted an offer from a group of nuns to hide the family in their residence.

That was a terrifying night for Aguilar Martínez. He heard a car parked outside the nuns' residence, engine idling, men's voices— at any moment, he thought, they would break in and grab him. It wasn't until four in the morning that the car finally drove off. ODHA moved the Aguilar Martínez family to the Archbishop's Palace.

A fews days later, on August 25, 1999, Aguilar Martínez gave his pretrial deposition in the ODHA offices, before Judge Flor de María García Villatoro. The two assistant prosecutors from the Public Ministry who were present were taken by surprise by the testimony. Lawyers for Father Mario and Margarita López, and the ODHA legal team, among others, were present also. The day after that, Aguilar Martínez, his wife, and their children were driven to the airport in a caravan of eight vehicles: two each from ODHA, MINUGUA, and the Public Ministry and one each from the U.S. embassy and the international Interpol police. Throughout the operation, the U.S. embassy's human rights officer phoned repeatedly to check in, presumably knowing that calls to ODHA's cell phones would be heard where it most counted.

The family, along with Rodrigo, Arturo, Mario Domingo, and an armed Interpol agent, were booked on a flight to El Salvador, but they lost the Interpol agent's protection when the airline refused to allow him on the plane with a weapon. At the Salvadoran airport, because of a problem with Aguilar Martínez's daughter's passport, the family was on the verge of being sent back to Guatemala, although finally that terrifying mix-up was resolved too. On the long ride into the Salvadoran capital—they would spend the night in yet another convent there before flying on to their final destination—Aguilar Martínez surprised the young men from ODHA when, describing his feelings at the airport during the contretemps over his daughter's passport, he compared the experience to something he'd read by Jorge Luis Borges: Inside a single moment, you can live many lives.

In his deposition, Jorge Aguilar Martínez stated that he had belonged to the EMP since 1989 and had received training in basic security duties: "the norms which the EMP gives you as a specialist." ("Specialist" is the term used to indicate members of the Army who have stayed on beyond the thirty months of soldiering required of all recruits and have been contracted as office workers, chauffeurs, cooks, mechanics, security guards, etc.) On Saturday, April 25, 1998, the day before the bishop was murdered, Aguilar Martínez had been at the service of the president. The next day, from six in the evening until dawn, he was subchief of Services, under the command of Captain Alvin Dubois, in the Services Office. He said that his job that night was to write down the names of the people who came and went and the license-plate numbers of their vehicles. The Services Office was near the Guard Command entrance to the EMP's central complex. It was a small office, Aguilar Martínez said, with two facing desks.

The soldier who turned the post over to him at six reported *Sin dieciocho,* "No eighteen," military jargon signifying no problems. Sometime between eight and eight-thirty, a red Isuzu Trooper carrying Major Escobar Blas, chief of the EMP's Protection Services Division, Specialist Galeano, and three other men from the unit "that used to be called G-2" stopped at the gate on its way out. Aguilar Martínez clarified: G-2 had long been a name for the military's intelligence and counterintelligence services, but later the EMP began to use other names: the Protection Services and the Center for Analysis. If that seemed confusing, it was undoubtedly meant to be.

Specialist Galeano was driving the Isuzu Trooper. Escobar Blas got out from the passenger side, approached the office's small window, and asked Aguilar Martínez if Captain Dubois was there. He said that he was, and Major Escobar Blas said, "Affirm that we are leaving, and everything is *sin dieciocho.*"

When Aguilar Martínez was about to record Escobar Blas's and the Isuzu Trooper's exit, including the license-plate number, Captain Dubois said, "Please omit that." He told Aguilar Martínez that this night he was not to register the comings and goings of vehicles and specialists, as he normally would have been required to. He was only to man the telephones in the office, which included a private line for Major Escobar Blas. He was also told to make sure that absolutely no one entered the "presidential patio," as the EMP's sealed-off section of Callejón del Manchén, behind the presidential residence, was called.

Shortly after nine, Aguilar Martínez began receiving telephone calls every three or four minutes, reporting, "*Sin dieciocho.*" Finally a call arrived from someone who said, "*Dieciocho* . . . a bomb in front of the José Gil drugstore," which the judges interpreted, they wrote later, as "code words whose meanings were understood . . . by Major Escobar Blas." Between ten-twenty and ten-thirty, a black Jeep Cherokee with tinted windows and no plates drove into the EMP grounds. "In this vehicle were Captain

Lima," Aguilar Martínez testified, "a young man I knew only as Hugo, and three more people who were dressed completely in black, wearing black caps with visors that covered their eyebrows, and dark glasses." When he got out of the jeep, "Captain Lima went down the corridor that leads directly to Colonel Rudy Pozuelos's office." Captain Lima was wearing casual civilian clothes.

Colonel Pozuelos was the head of the EMP. In the chain of command, only President Arzú was higher. Though it was a weekend, and he was off duty, Colonel Pozuelos had arrived at EMP headquarters at five that afternoon. Now he came back down the corridor with Captain Lima, got into the black Jeep Cherokee with the others, and they left. Five minutes later a phone call reported a "*dieciocho*," meaning danger, a problem. Captain Dubois rang an alarm, and everybody in the EMP that night, according to Aguilar Martínez, spilled out into the presidential patio. "It looked like a market," he recalled. At one-thirty in the morning, the men milling outside learned that Bishop Gerardi had been murdered at the church across the street from the Third Street exit of the Callejón del Manchén, just outside the EMP's gates.

That Monday morning, at a meeting in the patio of the presidential residence, Aguilar Martínez said, "They told us, the specialists, that we were strictly prohibited from talking about or revealing anything that had happened the day before. When questioned, Aguilar Martínez also said that in the EMP motor pool there was a white Toyota Corolla like the one the taxi driver had seen, and that it was the custom to switch the license plates of cars used in operations.

Aguilar Martínez recalled that when he'd first met Hugo, in 1990, Hugo was a member of the G-2 and was giving karate classes to the Presidential Guard. He said that Hugo was discharged in 1995 because of problems with drugs and alcohol. Aguilar Martínez described the tattoo on Hugo's arm, which the taxi driver had also perhaps glimpsed—parachute corps' wings around the word "Kaibil," the Army special-forces unit.

Aguilar Martínez's claim that he had seen Obdulio Villanueva get out of the black Jeep Cherokee was not included in the evidence presented at the trial. ODHA had asked him to omit that "problematic" detail in his pretrial deposition, and it wouldn't have seemed credible to introduce it now. In any case, the prosecution was satisfied with Aguilar Martínez's deposition as it was and saw no reason to summon him from exile to testify further. (Much later, of course, when ODHA lawyers learned that Aguilar Martínez, like Rubén Chanax, probably knew even more than he'd told about the operation, they would lament not having called him.) The defense did not want to summon Aguilar Martínez to testify either. Mario Domingo said later that this was beause the defense lawyers were afraid of what he would reveal.

Prior to the trial, the prosecution had subpoenaed the EMP's payroll records and the ledgers and books in which the comings and goings of people and vehicles were recorded. Judge García Villatoro and several prosecutors met at the EMP to examine them. Colonel Rudy Pozuelos had received the visitors. Pozuelos was immaculately turned out, in a crisply ironed uniform and with perfectly combed hair. Even his fine hands made an impression. For a Guatemalan military officer, he seemed to be an unusually refined person. Colonel Pozuelos described the workings of the president's security staff, including the position of personal waiter and chef—the man who cooked for the president also had to serve him—which, for obvious reasons, could go only to the most highly trusted individuals. It was a position, he claimed, never held by Jorge Aguilar Martínez, who never rose above assistant. Aguilar Martínez had indeed been on duty on the night of April 26, 1998, he said, but not inside the EMP. He was working as a concierge in the National Palace, a position to which he'd been demoted as punishment for stealing eighteen pounds of meat from the presidential kitchen.

Judge García Villatoro asked if she and the lawyers could have some time to inspect the records alone, and when they did so they noticed that the punishments meted out to EMP specialists for even minor infractions—fifteen days in the brig merely for answering a telephone incorrectly—were severe. It was hard to believe that Jorge Aguilar Martínez had merely been demoted to concierge for stealing meat from the presidential kitchen. Indeed, the EMP records revealed that Aguilar Martínez, at the end of April 1998, and later, was still on the payroll as a cook, not as a concierge or janitor.

On the night of the murder, the Guardia de Prevencion gates, at the entrances to the EMP and Presidential Guard headquarters, were manned by Presidential Guardsmen at both the Fourth Street and the Fifth Street entrances. But inside those gates, the entrance to the EMP's central complex, known as the Guard Command—where all the comings and goings from the EMP were kept track of and recorded—was under the authority of Artillery Major Andrés Villagrán, the highest-ranking EMP officer officially on duty that night. Major Villagrán was the chief of the EMP's Services Division, which was an entity distinct from the Services Office where Aguilar Martínez claimed to have been. The Services Office was about thirty-five feet farther in, though traffic at the Guard Command checkpoint could be monitored from there. (The hermetic EMP had groups with nearly overlapping names: Security Services, Protection Services, Administrative Services, etc. These services were in turn divided into A and B sections. There were three Services Offices—one in the EMP, a second assigned to the Nationl Palace, and a third assigned to the Presidential Guard. It was like an elaborate shell game. It would take the prosecutors and ODHA years to straighten all this out.)

The judge and the lawyers examined the EMP ledger in which the comings and goings at the Guard Command had been recorded. They showed that nothing unusual had occurred that night. But for the hours between eight and ten—the hours when

Aguilar Martínez said he'd been ordered not to write anything down—the handwriting in the record book inexplicably changed. A court-ordered handwriting analysis established that the record for those two hours had been filled in by another, unknown person. It had been falsified. At the trial, and even afterward, no one from the EMP was put forward or identified as the person who had made the entries.

JORGE AGUILAR MARTÍNEZ'S TESTIMONY was read into the record during the long documentary-evidence portion of the trial. In the sultry warmth of the courtoom, the voice of the young court secretary droned on, although whenever a commercial airliner thundered overhead on its approach to the airport, making it impossible to hear her, she would pause, wipe her brow, and take a sip of water. The bronze disk of the grandfather clock in the corner of the courtroom swung back and forth; many of the spectators dozed. I was glad for the chance to make some notes for the novel I'd left behind on my desk in New York. Claudia Méndez Arriaza, a gifted young reporter assigned to cover the trial for *elPeriódico,* fished a front-page story from the sluggish river of words: the testimony of Oscar Chex, the witness who had testified that from 1992 to 1996 he'd worked for G-2, translating, transcribing, and analyzing information collected from telephone espionage against Bishop Gerardi. If it hadn't been for Méndez's reporting, Chex's testimony would have been noticed by almost no one other than the lawyers at the trial and the judges. In the weeks before the trial and then during it, she also published an enterprising series of prison interviews with the Limas, father and son; with Sergeant Major Villanueva; and with Father Mario.

Claudia Méndez seemed even younger than her twenty-three years. She was a pretty young woman, with dark hair falling past her shoulders, prominent dimples, and large, vivid eyes. Girlishly perky, deferential and attentive yet unthreatening—or so men thought when they first met her—she appeared to be a model of

old-fashioned Latin American femininity, at least if one over-
looked the fact that she was a crime reporter for a Guatemala City
daily. Méndez was also an evangelical Protestant, and thus in
many ways a true social and cultural conservative. The men
Méndez interviewed often called her *nena,* "little girl," and they
sometimes patronized her. She had a way of listening, and of
questioning, so direct that it seemed to disarm her subject's de-
fenses. The men often ended up speaking to her as if she were a
trusted younger sister rather than a journalist.

"Tell me, Captain, are you growing desperate in prison?"
Claudia Méndez began her interview with Captain Byron Lima,
who had already been imprisoned in the Centro Preventivo for a
year and two months. "Hasn't incarceration been frustrating for a
military man whose career had promised such a bright future?"
The photograph accompanying the interview showed an olive-
skinned, athletic figure in a Kaibil special-forces T-shirt, his arms
extended in a spidery reach to grasp the chicken-wire prison
fence as he spoke to the reporter on the other side. Captain Lima
replied to Méndez's bold query with bravado: soon he'd be free,
and he had no doubt that he'd be able to rejoin the Army. On the
other hand, he also wanted the start of the trial to be postponed,
though it had already been postponed more than once.

"And why do you want more time?" asked Méndez.

"Because this isn't going to be easy," the captain said. "The
Catholic Church wants to make more money off the case. . . ."

Méndez interrupted him. "But why do *you* want more time?"
she asked. "Sometimes you seem desperate."

"No. Being in prison doesn't make me desperate. What makes
me desperate is the small amount of loyalty shown by my
compañeros—loyalty and support in the economic and moral
sense. They believe that something like this could never happen
to them."

"What are you referring to? Are you saying that other military
men could fall because of this crime?"

"I'm saying that this is a problem that begins at a certain point, and will explode"—he made an exploding gesture with his hands—"whether it be under the Ministry of Defense's desk or in the Presidential Military Staff."

"What are you trying to say? That they are involved? That the EMP was behind the crime? Because that's what's always been said."

"That. They arrest innocent people to destroy the Army." The captain switched gear, making a display of his own loyalty, taking refuge in the official defense line, but then restating his warning: "When I talk about the lack of loyalty I mean we soldiers should support each other institutionally. . . . They have to wake up and stop thinking they'll never be involved in a case like this one. They have to understand this process, what's going on here, and what can happen to them if they're not careful."

"It seems you're sending a message with that answer."

"Yes, I'm sending one, and I'm saying, Wake up!"

"To whom, Captain? To whom are you sending that message?"

"To all of them! All of them! This subliminal message is for the people who will recognize it as meant for them."

Claudia Méndez took the interview in another direction. "Nobody knew that Carlos García Pontaza, the prisoner who was killed in this prison just a few weeks ago, was to be a witness proposed by you. Was he a key element of your defense?" Captain Lima had included García Pontaza in his list of defense witnesses.

"He knew a lot about the case," Captain Lima replied.

ON NOVEMBER 28, 2000, Carlos García Pontaza, Ana Lucía Escobar's former boyfriend, the young leader of the Valle del Sol gang, who was wanted for bank robbery, had been arrested in a town far outside the capital. Most unusually, a helicopter was sent to fly him back to the city, to the Centro Preventivo prison where the Limas and Villanueva were also being held, the prison in which Captain Lima was said to patrol the cell blocks in a black ski mask, in the company of armed prison guards. Two months later, García Pontaza was found dead in his cell with a single bullet wound in his head. His death was quickly ruled a suicide, but few believed that. (For one thing, García Pontaza was left-handed, and the bullet had been fired into his right temple.) In the weeks before his death, García Pontaza had made a series of increasingly frantic phone calls to MINUGUA, saying that he was afraid for his life. He'd phoned Leopoldo Zeissig too. He wanted protected-witness status and was offering to name public officials involved in organized crime.

Military Intelligence agents from the EMP and at least one emissary from the Public Ministry had visited García Pontaza in prison. They came to pressure him into implicating Ana Lucía Escobar in the murder of Bishop Gerardi, along with other Church figures, particularly Monseñor Hernández. An investigator from MINUGUA told me that Gustavo Soria, the assistant to the former special prosecutor, Otto Ardón, was one of the young gangster's visitors at the prison. Soria was reputed to have ties to Military Intelligence. A report by MINUGUA on the incident said that García Pontaza was told that if he incriminated Ana Lucía, he would be granted "complete impunity and logistical support for his criminal operations." But García Pontaza refused that fantastic offer. He couldn't, the young gangster told MINUGUA, falsely accuse his former girlfriend. MINUGUA's investigation also established that García Pontaza had had contact, personally and by telephone, with Captain Byron Lima.

So there it was: the case's most romantic episode, appropriately fatal. García Pontaza's unexpectedly stubborn integrity must have been extremely frustrating to the defense. Imagine the explosive testimony he could have provided. Imagine being a young gangster, promised complete immunity from prosecution *and* the logistical support of a clandestine intelligence unit in carrying out crimes. (It would be even better than belonging to the EMP, because during time off from committing crimes—kidnapping, extorting, cocaine trafficking, etc.—you wouldn't have to obey orders from officers, or go horseback riding with the president and first lady, or sleep in barracks.) Who fired the bullet into the faithful delinquent's head? Did his killer look him in the eye and give him one last chance to change his mind? Did he count to ten? Did García Pontaza—who in 1999 had enrolled for two semesters to study French in the public university's school of languages—have a chance to reflect on the consequences of his choice as he listened to the countdown?

In the hours before dawn on January 29, 2001, the ringing of cell phones woke a few Guatemala City reporters in their beds. When they answered, they heard the voice of Captain Lima. Given the hour, the place he was calling from, and the gravity of the occasion, that voice must have been unusually solemn and quiet. The captain was dutifully phoning from prison to let reporters know that Carlos García Pontaza was dead. The telephone calls left some reporters with a creepy feeling.

"AND WHAT DID HE"—García Pontaza—"know?" Claudia Méndez asked Captain Lima during their interview.

"I can't say, because it pulls other people in. It would pull them in with a force that not even the police would be able to stop. A force that would pull in many people of all kinds: lawyers, priests, people from organizations that receive money."

Sometimes a murdered witness can do that, leave a gift to the living; he can even leave salvation. But the murdered witness has to have left a record somewhere: a confession, a list of names, a tape recording, *something*.

"How important was his testimony for your defense?"

"Extremely important."

Lawyers and judges, priests, people from organizations that receive money, such as ODHA. All were implicated in the murder, and all were engaged in a criminal conspiracy of fabricated witnesses and testimony. That was the defense, and would remain so throughout the trial and long after. The accusation didn't seem to have much force. Then, later, strangely, it would. The key witness who refused to speak would be forgotten, but his silence would be stolen, as if by grave robbers; the words some wished the gangster had spoken would find zombie-like life, in the arguments of the Limas and their defense lawyers, in newspaper columns written by their supporters in the press, in a book, in Guatemala and beyond.

There had been times when some had thought Captain Lima was close to admitting a role in the murder of Bishop Gerardi. Why had he, for example, announced to the press that he had in his possession—hidden under lock and key somewhere—the watch, the chain, and the keys to the VW Golf and the San Sebastián parish house that had been taken from the bishop's body? He'd mentioned also a receipt for a delivery from Pollo Campero, an order of fried chicken, to the parish house for the night of April 26, 1998—a clear reference and "subliminal" warning to Father Mario.

"And why haven't you presented Monseñor's watch and chain?" asked Claudia Méndez. "You said you had them."

"No, I didn't say I had them. I said someone showed them to me."

"You said you had them. You announced it to all the media."

"No, I said I saw them. I don't have them. If I had them, they'd blame everything on me. I saw them because somebody came and showed them to me."

"And why aren't you presenting that person as a witness?"

"Because I don't have the money. They all want money."

"And with all these misunderstandings, how do you think things are going to go for you in the trial?"

"Good. At least I hope things will turn out all right for my father."

"And you?"

"How long can they keep me here? Five years?"

Claudia Méndez brought up the possibility that he could even face the death penalty if found guilty.

"But if that's how destiny turns out, what can I do?" A few exchanges later, the captain said, "Anyway, look, what does the prosecutor have on me: the declaration of a homeless bum!"

A YEAR BEFORE, in March 2000, the Limas, on the advice of their defense attorneys, had petitioned Judge García Villatoro for a chance to expand on their earlier declarations. The request was granted, and on that occasion Captain Lima had provided a more detailed account of his travels in the ten days before the bishop's murder, coordinating security arrangements for President Arzú's visits to Peru and Argentina. In this new statement, his account of the day he arrived back in Guatemala—Sunday, April 26, 1998, the day of the murder—took an odd and memorable turn.

He had gone from the airport to the presidential residence, where he was picked up by his friend Erick Urízar. They left the EMP headquarters in Urízar's car, heading for Lima's parents' house in Colonia Lourdes. On the way, he said, they stopped for a police roadblock at the Asunción Bridge. Erick Urízar was asked for his papers and then ordered to get out of the car and show the weapon he was carrying. Captain Lima identified himself as a military officer and handed over his credentials. The police insisted that the photograph on Lima's identification card was of a different person. That was because, Lima said, he'd recently grown a light beard. As Captain Lima was trying to explain the situation over the radio to the policeman's superior, he said, another officer from the EMP, Colonel Roy Dedet Catzprowitz, coincidentally arrived at the roadblock in his car and had the same hassle with police over his papers and weapon as Lima and Urízar were having. Two minutes later a security vehicle assigned to Colonel Rudy Pozuelos, the head of the EMP, also arrived at the roadblock and was also detained. Captain Lima said that he phoned the EMP, and that the chief of Protection

Services, Major Francisco Escobar Blas, was dispatched to the roadblock to straighten the mess out.

It was like a slapstick movie scene in which all the main characters unexpectedly converge at one spot for a farcical denouement. The incident at the roadblock, as Captain Lima had told it, was highly unlikely; probably, it never occurred. More likely, Captain Lima had been sending yet another "subliminal message," or a warning. He'd peopled his fictional account of a roadblock with other officers from the EMP, perhaps those who'd had a role in Bishop Gerardi's murder, entering their names in the public record of the case.

In her interview, Claudia Méndez pressed the captain about the roadblock. "There are those," she said, "who say you were trying in that statement to remind them of something. Was that what you were doing?"

Captain Lima said no. But then he mentioned more names. Méndez had asked him whom he admired, and in addition to the Chilean dictator Augusto Pinochet he cited General Otto Pérez Molina, a Guatemalan officer who, Captain Lima said, always stood by his men. Méndez omitted this detail from the article she published, not realizing its potential significance. Rubén Chanax would later claim that General Pérez Molina was one of the officers who had come into Don Mike's little store with Colonel Lima Estrada on the night of the murder. It was assumed by the prosecution that the officers had gathered in Don Mike's to monitor the crime, but there was an even more logical reason for them to be there. The murder of Bishop Gerardi was the most audacious and risky assassination the Guatemalan Army had ever attempted, and it must be perceived as a defense of the institution rather than of individuals. No military man should be able to shirk responsibility. Everybody's tail should be snagged—a ring of tigers holding each other's tails in their jaws.

What did Captain Lima want from all the people he'd named? Was he telling them that he wasn't going to take the fall, silently and alone? Or that if he was, he expected something in return?

Why, asked Claudia Méndez, hadn't Major Francisco Escobar Blas also been arrested and sent to trial?

"Because they wrapped the cord around the littlest ones. Everything has a hierarchy."

"Do you think the truth of the crime will ever be known?"

"No."

"Why not?"

"The investigators aren't interested. They're frightened or too inept to go forward and capture higher-ups."

"But who wouldn't reveal everything they know in order to defend themselves?"

"But then who is going to defend me?"

CLAUDIA MÉNDEZ'S INTERVIEW with Captain Lima's father, the sixty-year-old Colonel Byron Lima Estrada, was published in *elPeriódico* on May 13, 2001. Colonel Lima Estrada explained that he was on trial because his enemies "wanted to win in the political sphere the military war they lost." He said that they were seeking vengeance. "I'm just the point of the spear. Once they've created a judicial precedent, then they're going to go after the others."

"You've been described as the brains of the operation," Méndez said. "The charges say that—"

"No!" interrupted the colonel. "The brains are the señores Edgar Gutiérrez and Ronalth Ochaeta, who, along with Army officers, involved me in this." He was referring to a "new wave" of military officers, some from the provincial capital of Cobán, former ODHA executive director Ochaeta's hometown. "A new wave, constitutionalist, obedient to civilian rule, respectful of human rights, this wave of *patojos*, boys, now colonels, joining up with the little group of legalists from ODHA—they implicated me in this problem."

"Who are you referring to?" Méndez persisted.

"You want me to name names? The names are those in the *apócrifo*." (This was the anonymous document, purporting to be an internal intelligence report, that had been faxed to reporters and human rights organizations in August 1998, and had named the Limas, along with the officers from Cobán.)

"Is there anything in life that you are afraid of?"

"Yes: that the guerrillas could execute me, apply their revolutionary justice."

"I don't understand."

The colonel exploded angrily. "You don't understand because you are just a little girl. You are a *niña*. You are not up to the level of my brain. Write this down: I don't answer a lot of your questions because you are not of my brain level, you haven't lived. . . . *Listen to me:* I'll get out of the Gerardi case. I'll get out of Gerardi. And then what will it cost to do *rrrrrrrrrrrr*." (The colonel gestured with his hands as if they were a pair of pistols.)

The colonel reminded Méndez that, in his view, the Church, or at any rate some of its members, had been allied with the guerrillas in the war.

"And Gerardi?"

"He had his line."

"And what was that?"

"Ask the priests who've been coming to the trial. They'll tell you: liberation theology."

Colonel Lima Estrada had used his interview with Claudia Méndez to put his theory about the crime into play. Everything about the Gerardi case—perhaps even the murder itself—was a continuation of the war by other means. The war wasn't over.

But at the time of the interview, Colonel Lima was facing a less theoretical problem. He didn't have a credible alibi for his whereabouts for that Sunday night, April 26, 1998. His belated efforts to provide one at the trial had only worsened the difficulty. In his first pretrial declarations the colonel had insisted that he'd spent

Sunday night at home with his family. But his wife didn't make an appearance at the trial to corroborate this. His youngest son, a teenager, gave it his best try but was ineffective. He said he'd gone into his bedroom to do homework that night and had fallen asleep. He had no way of knowing who came and went at the house during the crucial hours. So a new witness suddenly appeared at the trial—an old friend and neighbor, Colonel Edgar Carillo Grajeda, who told the court that on that Sunday night, from the hours of eight to eleven, he was sitting on beer crates in Colonel Lima's garage conversing. And what, Special Prosecutor Zeissig asked during a typically patient cross-examination, had he and Colonel Lima been talking about? About the glory days of the war, of course, Carillo Grajeda replied, swelling with proud emotion, when he'd fought under Colonel Lima in the Gumarkaj counterinsurgency battalion. "There was one beautiful day," he recalled, "when we had the cadavers of thirteen guerrillas laid out at our feet, all wearing a disgusting olive green, with red wounds. . . . There is no greater or more beautiful glory for a soldier than to see his enemy lying dead at his feet."

Colonel Lima Estrada did not testify in the trial and so did not face cross-examination by the prosecutors. Thus he did not have to answer before the judges the obvious question that Claudia Méndez put to him in their interview: Why had he never before, in any of his pretrial declarations, mentioned sitting on beer crates in his garage conversing with his friend from eight to eleven on the night of the murder?

Colonel Lima Estrada replied that the judge monitoring the statements had not let him express himself. "She never let me talk. . . . No one handles his interrogation as he ought to. I have only one witness: *him*, and that's enough. And me and my own word are enough! . . . Nobody had better try to corner me, because if I don't want to tell it, then I don't tell it. My word is the truth. *Period*!"

*   *   *

BUT IF, AT APPROXIMATELY TEN O'CLOCK on the night of the murder, Colonel Lima, in the company of two other men, stopped into Don Mike's little store, around the corner from the church of San Sebastián, and ordered some beers, in order to monitor the crime, how would they have done that? According to the prosecution, all that the colonel had to do was leave the shop, cross to the opposite sidewalk, stand on the corner, and look into the park. Maybe he'd had a radio through which he could send messages or even directions—to say, for example, that the shirtless man had come out through the garage and that everything was proceeding "sin dieciocho." Or he might say that now was the moment for the driver of the second Toyota—the one that raced past the taxi driver —to pick up an operative who had fled through a rear exit of the church.

The defense argued that it was impossible to see the parish house from the street corner in front of Don Mike's shop, and an evidentiary procedure was conducted one morning in the last weeks of the trial regarding this issue. Lawyers, judges, police guards, and the press filled the street in front of the shop. It was a fast, tense operation. Zeissig, who'd refused to don a bulletproof vest, was clearly a little frightened; his eyes were wide as he strode rapidly down the street from the shop to the opposite corner. His bodyguards, pressed around him, kept their hands on their pistols underneath their jackets and nervously scanned the rooftops.

I stood on the corner next to Irvíng Aguilar, Obdulio Villanueva's lawyer. He was short and rotund, with a protruding belly, a fat, flushed face, and thick gray hair. From where I stood I could clearly see the parish-house garage through the park and the trees.

"You can't see anything!" the defense attorney yelped in triumph.

"I can see it perfectly," I said. It was absurd that I wanted to argue with him.

"No, no, no!" he shouted. "From here you can't see anything!"

*   *   *

THE GESTURE THAT Colonel Lima Estrada had made during his interview with Claudia Méndez, pointing with his hands as if they were pistols, came up during the trial. During an afternoon hearing Mario Domingo complained that the colonel was making threatening gestures at him.

"I haven't done anything," the colonel responded, "and there are video cameras that record everything." Throughout the trial, he told the judges in a tone of offended dignity, his behavior had been "composed and respectful."

It didn't appear that any of the courtroom video cameras had been trained on the colonel at that moment. But later a reporter, looking over the video footage he'd taken that day, found that his camera had indeed recorded the incident, along with the date and time (April 17, 12:40:25 PM), and he gave a copy of the image to ODHA. Colonel Lima, like a B-movie thug, is miming cocked pistols with his hands, staring across the room.

Major Escobar Blas, the EMP's chief of Protection Services, testified that he had spent all of Sunday, April 26, 1998, from nine in the morning until six that night, at a country club with family members. (That, of course, contradicted Captain Lima's pretrial testimony that Major Escobar had turned up at the famous police roadblock in the middle of the afternoon.) At about three in the morning, he testified, in the first hours of Monday, April 27, he'd received a phone call from Major Villagrán—though in his pretrial statement, he'd said that the call was from Colonel Pozuelos, the head of the EMP. Major Escobar Blas now said that he phoned Pozuelos, who ordered him to go to San Sebastián to check on whatever had happened there. The major, who lived near the church, said that he arranged to meet the photographer Darío Morales by the park at three-forty AM—although several people in San Sebastián that night, including Helen Mack and Nery Rodenas, had seen Morales taking photographs with a flash as early as one-thirty. Major Escobar Blas said that Darío Morales had walked ahead of him, toward the parish house, while he remained behind, talking to firemen. These firemen, said Major Escobar Blas, told him that the person who'd been killed inside the parish-house garage was Bishop Juan Gerardi.

Aside from the glaringly evident fact that the burly, medium-height Major Escobar Blas bore no resemblance to the tall, thin man in a baseball cap whom witnesses saw with Darío Morales that night, there were other problems with the major's testimony. The firemen who'd been called to the parish house by Father Mario at around one in the morning had already returned to their station at the hour Major Escobar Blas claimed to have spoken to them. The firemen wouldn't return until nearly dawn, when summoned back in order to deliver Bishop Gerardi's body to the morgue. So Major Escobar Blas couldn't have spoken to them if he arrived when he said he did.

His testimony was riddled with lies. And under cross-examination the major's arrogant martial façade began to crumble.

"Was it the usual procedure for you, Chief of Protection Services, to go personally to verify an emergency at three in the morning?"

"*Emmmm* . . . No, it's not usual."

He began to stumble and hesitate over his answers, and Captain Lima, apparently trying to buy the major some time, rose to his feet and addressed Judge Cojulún. Lima announced that there were two unknown and suspicious people sitting in the courtroom and asked the judge to make them identify themselves. The men turned out to be two ordinary office workers who'd wandered over during their lunch break to catch a bit of the historic trial. Terrified, they gathered up their things and fled.

FOR THE MOST PART, the officers from the EMP remained consistent in the basic elements of their version of the events of the night of the murder. But low-ranking soldiers provided some surprises. For instance, the EMP specialist Estrada Pérez said that he'd seen Captain Lima inside the EMP grounds, in civilian clothes, between ten and eleven that night, which was when Aguilar Martínez said that he'd seen Lima arrive, dressed casually.

A witness for the prosecution, a prisoner named Hugo Izquierdo Banini, testified that he had shared a cell with Captain Lima for forty-five days in the Centro Preventivo in May and June of the previous year. He said that Captain Lima had confided to him that President Arzú, through an intermediary, had stayed in touch with him over the telephone and provided money for his needs. Colonel Pozuelos and Major Escobar Blas, according to Izquierdo Banini, had intervened to make sure that the captain received special treatment in prison.

Carlos Barrientos, the prisoner who had turned Captain Lima's agenda book and other documents over to the Public Ministry after their fistfight in the Centro Preventivo, also testified. Mario Domingo told me that Barrientos was a former agent with G-2, Military Intelligence, who, in a romantic conflict over a woman, had murdered a policeman. He'd fought with Lima for control of their sector of the prison.

"I'm under death threats," Barrientos told the court, "but I'm here to tell Captain Lima that I'm not afraid of him. I'm telling him that to his face." Barrientos was blunt about his motives: he had stolen the agenda and other papers and handed them over to the Public Ministry because he wanted to "fuck over Lima." After he'd managed to get Lima expelled from the sector of the prison in dispute, a grenade was tossed into the house of his wife and children.

The Limas continued to maintain that the Valle del Sol gang had murdered Bishop Gerardi. When Ana Lucía Escobar was called to testify about what she'd observed at the crime scene that night in April, Captain Lima made a show of being scared out of his wits by the witness, turning to the judges to complain that she was looking at him threateningly. Ana Lucía responded with an embarrassed giggle.

AT THE BEGINNING of the trial it had been widely thought that Father Mario was the key to solving the Gerardi case. Though his behavior remained one of the case's mysteries, it now seemed strangely superfluous. The priest made a sorrowful spectacle in his pajamas and bathrobe, with his great soft slab of a face and his tittering asides to his lawyer. Marta Nájera de Orantes, his mother, was always looking on, sitting in the front row of the spectators' gallery with his nurse. As soon as there was a recess, they would get up and go to him. It occurred to me that the priest might have secrets that he would rather take with him to prison for decades than confess in front of his mother.

Father Mario hadn't needed the wheelchair before his legal troubles began, and during the trial he was occasionally photographed nimbly hopping into and out of it when he was not in the courtroom. Aside from Rubén Chanax's testimony, there was no single piece of conclusively damaging evidence against the priest—there were just lots and lots of little things that added up to an impression of dismaying, baffling guilt. The cook at the parish house, Margarita López, had, in the immediate aftermath of the crime, told Juana Sanabria that when Father Mario came to her door to wake her the night of the murder, he was freshly bathed and dressed. She had said the same thing to another woman. It was partly because she repressed the story later that Margarita López had been arrested for withholding evidence.

Juana Sanabria testified about her frantic and repeated calls to Bishop Gerardi's telephone in the hours after the murder, calls Father Mario claimed that he hadn't heard, though the bishop's room was next to his own. She said that she had phoned three different numbers in the parish house. The sacristan, Antonio Izaguirre, told the court that the telephones could be heard ringing throughout the house, and that at night it was Father Mario's responsibility to answer them.

EDGAR GUTIÉRREZ, REMHI's former director, spoke to the court about the Guatemalan Army's intelligence structures, and their stake, as he perceived it, in the murder of Bishop Gerardi. Gutiérrez was now the head of the only intelligence-gathering agency manned by civilians. He recounted how, weeks after the bishop's murder, President Arzú's High Commission had refused to look into the participation of the Limas in the crime despite several leads pointing to their possible involvement, or to investigate any of the president's security personnel or the so-called Cofradía, the brotherhood of active and former intelligence officers. During the war, Gutiérrez said, "military and paramilitary structures became accustomed to working with total impunity. Then their acts were based on their security functions. When the guerrillas were no longer a threat, those structures went on operating in the same way, but not with any political objectives anymore, now they were devoted to delinquency. . . . Their crime practices grew over the years. And the civilian governments weren't capable of dismantling them. Because this impunity protects them, it intimidates and prevents anyone from denouncing them."

A spokesman for MINUGUA, Terry Delrue, pointed out that crimes like the murder of Bishop Gerardi, if they were not punished, encouraged the growth of organized crime. Guatemalans in the military had gotten rich through criminal activities such as narcotics trafficking, kidnapping, automobile theft, dealing in contraband, extortion, and so on. Bishop Gerardi had been murdered because he threatened the military's hold on the state's overdeveloped intelligence apparatus, its hold on real power—the so-called parallel power that is the clandestine underbelly of official power—and on their criminal rackets, which depended on their being able to commit crimes with impunity.

Bishop Ríos Montt also explicitly connected the state's murky parallel powers to Bishop Gerardi's murder: "The fact that the authorities had these elements of the Army working in the EMP and refused to investigate them shows that they're incapable of confronting problems like the one occupying us now. I've always said that as long as this power behind the throne exists, Guatemala will not be free, nor will it have justice or peace. Here, presidents come, and presidents go. Just when we thought we'd recovered an environment that made it possible to live in peace, they answered: Here, take your dead man, who tried to discover the truth."

I was back in Guatemala for the closing arguments in the case. The prosecution went first. Leopoldo Zeissig reviewed the evidence the prosecution had presented, point by point, but bogged down and couldn't finish within his allotted time. Mynor Melgar, however, closed powerfully. Bishop Gerardi's murder, the prosecution lawyers argued, had been an elaborate, methodically planned extrajudicial execution carried out by a still unknown number of Guatemalan intelligence operatives and specialists, a politically motivated crime of state, sprung into motion like clockwork on the morning of Sunday, April 26, with, among other elements, Specialist Villanueva leaving the Antigua prison, and Captain Byron

Lima flying in from Miami after an overseas presidential security mission.

The prosecution asked that criminal investigations be initiated against, among others, several high-ranking EMP officers: majors Villagrán and Escobar Blas, and the head of the EMP, Colonel Rudy Pozuelos. The prosecutors also asked for the charges against the priest to be downgraded from homicide to participation in an extrajudicial execution. ODHA had resisted enormous pressure from within the Church to drop the charges against Father Mario, or at least to avoid attacking him in the closing arguments. Mynor Melgar insisted that OHDA owed loyalty above all to the law and to the legal case it was participating in, including the evidence against the priest. But ODHA did ask that the charges against the housekeeper be dropped.

In his closing statement, Mynor Melgar, marking the rhythm of his words with a pencil drummed up and down, promised that ODHA would not falter in seeking justice for Bishop Gerardi's murder, no matter how high up subsequent investigations might lead. He even asked for an investigation of former President Álvaro Arzú, who had sent his brother as an emissary to Bishop Ríos Montt, offering to free Father Mario in exchange for the Church's promise to stop accusing the military. Melgar outlined a case for the defendants' complicity based on their "dominion" over the crime: foreknowledge of the crime, and even relatively secondary operational involvement, gave them the option of preventing and denouncing it, thus implicating them as accomplices. Melgar spoke of Bishop Gerardi's decades of struggle for justice and on behalf of Guatemala's poor, which had long ago earned him the enmity of the Army, culminating in the REMHI project.

THE NEXT MORNING, during the defense's closing arguments, José Toledo, Father Mario's dandyish young lawyer—to the amusement of the prosecution, Toledo had dyed his hair a reddish hue and was wearing it in a tiny ponytail—struck a reprehensible note, shouting across the room at ODHA's lawyers that the Church had benefited from the bishop's death by selling copies of the REMHI report and sweatshirts with his picture on them. "Who had the motive to kill him?" Toledo railed. The defense lawyers repeatedly shouted, "Chanax lied!" and accused Rubén Chanax of being the murderer, in league with organized crime (Valle del Sol, etc.). They repeated their argument that Chanax, by having admitted spying on Bishop Gerardi, had admitted a role in the crime, and so should be arrested. But, they said, Rubén Chanax's testimony was also a fabrication, prepared by the Public Ministry, and legal proceedings should be lodged against the special prosecutor for knowingly using false witnesses. Irving Aguilar compared the prosecution's tactics to Joseph Goebbels's strategy of repeating a lie until it became the truth.

Whenever the defense lawyers said something especially outrageous, nuns sitting in a row in the courtroom were unable to contain themselves, gasping in horror, and whispering in chorus, "Shameless!" "¡Qué bárbaro!" "How could he say such a thing?"

The august, silver-haired Julio Cintrón, with his deep velvet voice and ice-blue stare, made a seething and grandiloquent closing argument. His point was that you couldn't convict someone of being an accomplice in an extrajudicial crime if you didn't know who had committed the crime. Who, after all, was this "Hugo" mentioned by Rubén Chanax and Jorge Aguilar Martínez and presumably spotted by the taxi driver?

During a recess, while I stood in front of the spectator section, near the cordoned-off area where the trial was conducted, I heard a stream of expletives spoken in a deep voice behind me: hueco, faggot, and so on. I looked back and saw Captain Lima turning away from me, and I asked, heatedly, if he'd been speaking to me. He fixed me with a cold glare that quickly became contemptuous and said, with forceful but measured diction—as if I'd insulted him but he was determined to display his lofty superiority—that he had nothing to say to a person such as me, and he walked away. A young woman sitting in the front row, horrified, said that I had indeed been the target of his invective, and the women sitting alongside her nodded. They looked at me with frightened expressions. I thought, with a sinking feeling, Oh, no, what have I done now? After lunch, Leopoldo Zeissig told me that Lima's defense lawyers had tried to have me expelled from the courtroom for provoking their client. (I assume that it was my closeness to ODHA and my piece in *The New Yorker*, which had been excerpted in *elPeriódico*, that drew Lima's scorn.)

No matter how inept its arguments might seem, the defense was cheered on by the many right-wing zealots who came to the trial to show their support. One of them was an elderly but sprightly woman—her surname was something like Von Lutten—who, as far as I could tell, never missed a session. She wore her unruly gray hair loose around her shoulders and dressed flamboyantly, like a mad old hippie, in a purple or pink blouse and tights pulled over twig-thin legs. The ODHA lawyers nicknamed her the Pink Panther. In decades past she'd published a newspaper column that people who remembered it described as either extremely right-wing or fascist. She thought the defense lawyers were wonderfully clever. Whenever they unleashed a zinger, she turned her painted face toward the prosecution table and, with a sneering grin, laughed like a Mexican death skull.

The side of the courtroom where presumably leftist supporters of the prosecution sat was called Woodstock by Guatemalan reporters. It was filled with human rights activists, "solidarity" types in sandals, progressive nuns in secular dress, and Franciscan friars in austere brown smocks. Were they as frightening to others as the Pink Panther was to me? Did their passivity hide another kind of violence? Did they (we?) truly want justice or simply another kind of vindication, a symbolic revenge for decades of rampant, unpunished murder?

*   *   *

PROCEEDINGS ENDED on the morning of June 7 with Captain Byron Lima, in uniform for the occasion, addressing the court. He could easily have testified the previous afternoon, following the defense's closing arguments and the brief personal statements of other defendants, but the judges had decided to adjourn until the next morning. Under Guatemalan law, the judges had twenty-four hours after the formal end of the trial's proceedings to write and render their verdict, and it was believed that they had adjourned in order to give themselves an extra night to deliberate.

As he took his seat at the witness table and folded his hands on top of it, Captain Lima was the picture of an officer and a gentleman. He denied the charges against him and spoke with pride of his years of military service. He described how he'd earned the various medals he was wearing and asked how anyone could believe that he would throw away a brilliant military career by participating in such a sordid crime. And then he demonstrated how detached from ordinary human reality soldiers like him must become, inside their violent, paranoid, honor-obsessed world. His statement devolved into what appeared to be a series of personal accusations and threats. ODHA was merely bent on revenge, he said, and Leopoldo Zeissig had joined the case in search of personal fame. Captain Lima went down the line of lawyers at the prosecution table, boring in one at a time with a hard stare. "You, Mario Domingo"—the sweet-natured, emotionally high-strung ODHA lawyer looked as if he were shaking in his shoes—"you're here because you want revenge against the Army for having destroyed your village in Huehuetenango." ODHA, said Captain Lima, "has no integrity. I won't lie; they are people who can be bought." The only lawyer who seemed unaffected by Lima's bizarre performance was Mynor Melgar, who had grown up around tough guys in El Gallito. He stared back at Captain Lima with a cocked eyebrow and a slight wise-guy smirk of his own.

It was late morning when the session ended. Judge Cojulún, wearing a bulletproof vest under his suit jacket, announced that the court would deliver its verdict at eleven-thirty that night. The prosecutors went back to their office and ordered a large paella for lunch. Zeissig told everyone to go home and take a nap. The ODHA lawyers and the Untouchables came to my hotel, and we sat around the pool. As usual, they made *chistes* at each other's expense. Melgar said that Nery Rodenas, who was lying half out of the water in the hot tub, looked like a sad hippopotamus, and everyone laughed. And then they fell silent and seemed lost in their own thoughts. Lima's speech had cast a certain pall.

I was back inside the courthouse, in the press area, by eight. At ten the guards let spectators in through the metal detectors, and the courtoom quickly filled, row after row. A small forest of cameras on tripods had sprung up in front of the area where the lawyers and defendants sat. The foreign press had returned to Guatemala for this night, and everywhere you looked there were Indian women in traditional clothing. There were so many scruffy, mainly North American, spectators who would ordinarily sit in the Woodstock area that they overflowed into the side of the auditorium claimed by supporters of the defendants. Father Mario's mother came down the aisle carrying a magnum of champagne and went through the door into the defense team's private area. Guatemalan reporters passed around sheets of paper on which they marked their predicted verdicts, as if in an office pool. The lawyers and the defendants slowly drifted in, and by eleven-thirty they were at their usual seats. Captain Lima was in full dress uniform, the medals on his chest glittering in the camera flashes. Father Mario had donned his priest's collar. Heavily armed police commandos in bulletproof vests stood in rows against the walls. The U.S. ambassador, Prudence Bushnell, made a surprise appearance.

By two o'clock in the morning, the judges still hadn't appeared. Rumors swirled. Captain Lima was obviously upset, reportedly because he'd just been told that he was the only defendant who hadn't been acquitted. I had a knot in my stomach that kept me

In court for the verdict: Father Mario, Obdulio Villanueva, Captain Lima Oliva, and Colonel Lima Estrada

awake, climbing up and down the stairs, fidgeting in my chair. Indian women slept in their seats the way they do on long bus trips: torso turned sideways, a hand perched on the seat back, a cheek laid atop it. The young American backpacker types had a way of sleeping that made novel use of the rows of raked seating. They sat on the floor, legs crossed beneath the seats, arms crossed on top of the seat in front, head resting on arms. Foreign reporters spread their suit jackets out on the floor and lay down for a nap. Couples slept in embraces. The nuns, used to praying at all hours perhaps, were wide awake. We were like passengers in steerage in a crowded hold, on a long transatlantic crossing. But it felt appropriate, somehow, to have to stay up all night waiting, keeping a weary vigil, to find out whether or not justice was going to be done, and Guatemalan history made.

The U.S. ambassador had slipped away long ago, though the embassy's human rights officer remained. I found Helen Mack and sat beside her for a while. The defense lawyers formed into a belligerent chorus line, arms around each other's waists, and enunciated another bellowing protest, threatening to withdraw their clients. At five o'clock a court employee came out and took away the water bottles in front of the judges' seats. Did that mean something was about to happen?

Half an hour later the judges trooped out, looking exhausted and grim. People were picking themselves up off the floor, standing in the aisles stretching, rubbing their eyes, sitting forward in their seats, crowding into the camera pit, adjusting their tripods and cameras. Soon everyone was back in place. The young court secretary took her place at the raised podium in a corner and, just like that, she began to read out the verdict. Her voice was breathless and rushed. Judge Cojulún looked over at her, made a reassuring gesture with his hand, and gave her a brief smile. She read in an excited, ringing voice. I wasn't sure that I'd caught the words correctly. Was the priest guilty? His lawyer, José Toledo, sat slumped and scowling. Father Mario Orantes was guilty! "*Culpable!*" And then she was reading out the rulings against the military men. Nery Rodenas, dark circles under his eyes, glanced up to where Fernando Penados and I were sitting and sent us a small, fleeting, almost furtive smile.

It took nearly an hour to read the whole verdict, in which the judges' reasoning was carefully laid out, ruling by ruling.

"What was the accused doing in that shop?" the judges asked in the verdict about Colonel Byron Lima Estrada. After taking into account that the colonel, as the leader of a powerful war veterans' group, had been particularly threatened by the REMHI report—which had named him in three places—and that he was connected, as former commander of the Chiquimula military base, to the license-plate number the taxi driver had seen, a license that had originally been assigned to that base, and taking into account as well the colonel's belated and unconvincing attempts to manufacture an alibi for that night, the judges had decided that it was "by all lights logical" to assume that Colonel Lima Estrada "had knowledge of what was happening in the San Sebastián parish house." They wrote that his criminal liability "was not confined to whatever control he had over what was going on in the vicinity, but rather that his participation began much earlier, when he contracted military informers to monitor Monseñor Gerardi." Even if he only had knowledge of the murder happening half a block away, the judges wrote, he also had criminally complicit "dominion" over the crime—i.e., the power to prevent it.

All of the accused except Margarita López, the cook, were going to be found guilty. A unanimous ruling.

A Guatemalan reporter in the row in front turned to me with a frightened expression and said that Captain Lima was eyeing the weapon loosely slung across the front of a policeman behind him, and that he could easily snatch it away. I looked over and saw that this was true: Captain Lima had turned his head and was looking at the weapon. So, even now, crazy fear. Horrified imaginings of a lethally suicidal Captain Lima spraying the courtroom with automatic weapon fire. But the beautiful, full-throated, intoxicating young voice just kept going on, its every vehement *Culpable!* striking like a slap. Thirty years in prison for each of the military men, twenty years for Father Mario Orantes. When Pope John Paul II had declared that hell is not an actual place but a spiritual state of man, he could have been thinking of Father Mario, sitting in his wheelchair while so many stared at him, looking as if he were being consumed by invisible flames.

The young court secretary's rising and falling, resonating voice announced that the court was ordering a criminal investigation to be opened against others, including the possible "intellectual authors" of the crime. Colonel Rudy Pozuelos of the EMP, Major Escobar Blas, and Major Villagrán were among the seven military men named. The three men on trial were convicted not as individual criminals or murderers but of having taken part in a politically motivated act of state-sponsored murder.

It had been a long-planned operation, an elaborately staged crime and cover-up. There were probably stakeouts in the park that night (such as a couple seen snuggling on a bench in the dark) and getaway drivers to scoop up the EMP specialists and intelligence operatives as they fled out through the various exits of the church of San Sebastián while the shirtless Hugo allowed himself to be seen, quietly igniting rumors of a crime of passion. But nobody had planned on an alert, pot-smoking taxi driver with a knack for memorizing license-plate numbers to drive right into the heart of the operation.

Helen Mack, overcome with emotion, burst into tears at the first reporter's question put to her. But we were already rushing out of there. Standing on the curb with the Untouchables in the gray dawn light, we spotted Special Prosecutor Zeissig's three-car caravan. A window came down a bit and a hand emerged to give us a thumbs-up as the cars drove off.

On the way to my hotel we stopped at a convenience store to buy beer, and three of the four original Untouchables—Fernando Penados and the two who were still on the job, Rodrigo and Arturo—and Helen Mack and I celebrated. Helen kept crying. She had been trying to win an investigation of the intellectual authors of her sister's murder for years, and the judges in the Gerardi case had granted it in a single motion. "Their cases go step and step, Monseñor's and Myrna's, one helping the other," she said. We turned on the television to watch the news, and when that was over, a women's breakfast show came on, the female host announcing that it was a day of joy because justice had finally come to Guatemala.

I thought, This is how a country changes. But I also thought, and told my friends, "Enjoy this moment. Another one like it might never happen again." So much had to come together perfectly for this victory to happen. Their courage and competence aside, it was also significant that the prosecution and the judges were relatively young, all under forty, and hadn't believed what older, more experienced people believed: that you could never get a verdict like this in Guatemala. The judges represented a generation of legal professionals many of whom had been at least partially educated abroad, some in the United States. They were too young to have been corrupted, demoralized, or made cynical.

Judge Eduardo Cojulún received a threat as soon as he was back in his office after the verdict. The phone rang, and a voice said "¡Ojo! Watch out!" In the ensuing weeks the judges received so many threats that Cojulún openly discussed with reporters the possibility of leaving the country. But he refused to yield to fear, and even kept going out for his morning jogs, until he was intercepted by a man who jabbed a hand as if it were a gun into Cojulún's abdomen and said, "Hello, Judge, I'm your personal security." Judge Yassmín Barrios—after enduring such provocations as finding thugs with shaved heads inexplicably standing in her patio one day; and another day seeing a man crouching like a gargoyle on the cornice of a neighboring house, aiming a machine gun at her; and finally seeing a military helicopter buzzing and hovering low over her house, with men inside photographing her when she came out into her patio—was escorted with her mother out of the country by MINUGUA on a Sunday in July. They were headed to Spain, where she planned to study for a while. She had rented out her house and sold her car. Two weeks later she changed her mind and came home.

THE EARLY PROMISE—dim as even that had seemed—of President Portillo's government had quickly faded. Portillo had not been able to free himself from the influence of military strongmen and mafiosos any more than any of his predecessors had. Portillo's EMP was as criminal as Arzú's—it was just a different clique of corrupt officers. No one believed that Portillo, whatever his true intentions, had much control over his own administration. Abroad and in Guatemala, the attempts to bring General Ríos Montt to justice for war crimes had stalled, and he remained the president of the Congress and the real leader of the FRG Party. The vice president of the Congress had accused human rights organizations of being "behind a plot to destablize the country."

In 2000, when Edgar Gutiérrez had become head of the Secretariat of Strategic Analysis, he'd found the agency's files on the Gerardi case ransacked and emptied. But President Portillo said that he had ordered an internal investigation into the Gerardi case, and he promised to share the results. If—as seems likely—such an investigation was ever conducted by Portillo's government, no one in ODHA or the prosecutors' office ever saw a report of it. Fairly or not, ODHA's lawyers blamed Gutiérrez for Portillo's failure to deliver on his promise. The government finally issued a two-page report stating that it had no information about the case beyond what had already been produced by the Public Ministry.

Leopoldo Zeissig, after twenty-one months of enduring constant threats, resigned as special prosecutor and left the country with his wife and child. Just before leaving, he granted an interview to Claudia Méndez. "The defense is criticizing you for having on your side a vagrant, a taxi driver, and an EMP specialist who was by turns a waiter and a janitor. The defense is heavily criticizing them for being of such a low level," she said. Zeissig responded, "At ten at night in San Sebastián's park, you're not going to find lawyers and engineers. Let's talk about the military officers, who are supposedly of a higher level. What happened when they testified at the trial? They lied."

The defense lawyers' continual harping through the media about the "low level" of the witnesses—most were men with Indian features and surnames—also played all too easily on widespread and deep Guatemalan class and racial prejudices and insecurities.

WITHIN WEEKS OF THE VERDICT, ODHA was dug in again, preparing for a battle to recuse one of the judges, Wilewaldo Contreras, who would try the appeal. "Because he's a corrupt judge," Melgar said to me, "who has made money in exchange for freeing criminals. Also, he is a personal friend of Cintrón, and of the group of lawyers defending the Limas, and from a good source we know he's disposed to reverse the sentence. What we don't know is in exchange for what."

The Vatican had finally named a new archbishop, elevating Monseñor Quezada Toruño from Zacapa. When Quezada Toruño was bishop of Zacapa, his diocese was the only one that declined to participate in REMHI. Within days of taking his new job, the archbishop convened a meeting of bishops to vote on whether or not to shut down ODHA. Nine voted in favor, nine against—a clear sign of how severely the prosecution of Father Mario and the scandalous revelations surrounding the Gerardi case had split the Church. Archbishop Quezada demanded a full audit of ODHA's accounts, but in the end he ruled that ODHA woud stay open and continue its mission, including its role as co-plaintiff in the ongoing Gerardi case.

IV
THE THIRD STAGE
PURGATORY

For five years. Isn't quick to say. And isn't it long to live. And lonely.
—Jean Rhys, *Wide Sargasso Sea*

1

THE EUPHORIA OF THE SPRING of 2001, when the guilty verdicts were read, did not last long. Almost immediately the results of the trial were called into question. In the fall, two European journalists, Bertrand de la Grange and Maite Rico—the journalists who during the trial had extolled the virtues of Dr. Reverte Coma, the Spanish dog-bite theorist—published an article in the Mexican and Spanish magazine *Letras Libres* accusing the prosecution and ODHA of being "the intellectual authors of a conspiracy" that had made the defendants "sacrificial lambs." The defense lawyers in the Gerardi case, according to the article in *Letras Libres,* considered the prosecution witnesses "less than ideal." The authors quoted one of the Limas' lawyers, Roberto Echeverreía Vallejo: "The whole case rested on fabricated witnesses. It's truly a monstrosity." And they repeated, with no sign of irony, the remark of a military officer to the effect that "it's another Dreyfus case."

In their article and in later writings about the case, de la Grange and Rico seemed unaware of the effort involved in ODHA's search for each of its witnesses. The EMP waiter Aguilar Martínez, the former G-2 spy Oscar Chex, and even the taxi driver were represented by the European journalists as having simply appeared at ODHA's door.

But there was little public response from ODHA to the accusations. Ronalth Ochaeta and Edgar Gutiérrez were large personalities who had known how to present ODHA's position to the public. After they left ODHA, there was no one who could handle such tasks. Even Mynor Melgar, who was implacable in the courtroom, had a shy demeanor outside of it. Melgar returned to the Public Ministry as a prosecutor early in 2002, and the face of ODHA was projected by the soft-spoken, even retiring Nery Rodenas and the excitable Mario Domingo, who swallowed his consonants and spoke so quickly that people had trouble understanding him. The Gerardi case was complex and bewildering. In hindsight, ODHA's failure to cultivate relationships with Guatemalan journalists, to help them understand how the case had been assembled, was a costly mistake.

There was virtually no support for the verdicts in the trial in the Guatemalan press, other than occasionally in *elPeriódico*, where Claudia Méndez worked as a reporter. And this wasn't only because the media were owned and run by conservative elites, people sympathetic to the military and to former president Arzú. President Portillo's government had turned out to be the most corrupt—and that *is* saying something—and despised administration in recent Guatemalan history. Even people on the political left had a grudging attitude toward the verdicts in the Gerardi case after President Portillo tried to claim the outcome as an achievement of his presidency. (Judge Cojulún publicly rebuked Portillo for "taking a bow by tipping someone else's hat.") And many thought that Edgar Gutiérrez, who had been so closely identified with ODHA's investigation, had "betrayed" the human rights community by taking a prominent post in Portillo's government. The terrain had been well prepared for a public-relations disaster when, in November 2003, Bertrand de la Grange and Maite Rico's book about the case, *¿Quién mató al obispo? Autopsia de un crimen politico,* (*Who Killed the Bishop?—Autopsy of a Political Crime*), was published. The book was treated as a major turn of events, and its charges were ceaselessly trumpeted.

In 1998, de la Grange and Rico had published another book, *Marcos, la genial imposture,* that purported to unmask Subcomandante Marcos, the leader of the Zapatista rebellion in Mexico, as a malevolent fraud; this was pretty much the position of the Mexican government. Their central thesis about the Gerardi case was that the Limas and Villanueva had been falsely accused and that prosecution witnesses had fabricated their testimony in exchange for personal gain, usually a one-way trip into a financially well-compensated exile, a life of ease. Ana Lucía Escobar, Monseñor Hernández, and the Valle del Sol gang played a central role. And, of course, Dr. Reverte Coma's dog-bite theory got its due. Edgar Gutiérrez and Ronalth Ochaeta were depicted as corrupt masterminds and conspirators. De la Grange and Rico more or less floated all the scenarios as simultaneous possibilities without offering any serious evidence to prove or connect them. A conspiracy of breathtaking scope was alleged, involving an enormous number of people and without any institutional oversight, any chain of command, or any central authority to enforce their obedience and guard their silence.

In February 2004, Mario Vargas Llosa, one of Latin America's most admired novelists and easily its most famous political pundit, would weigh in on the Gerardi case in Spain's leading newspaper, *El País.* Vargas Llosa, a political conservative and avowed Thatcherite, had run for president of Peru in 1990, losing the election to Alberto Fujimori. Since then he'd resided mostly in Europe, and he had become a Spanish citizen. The opinion essays that he regularly published in *El País* were reprinted throughout the Spanish-speaking world. He seemed to draw the information for his piece on the Gerardi case exclusively from de la Grange and Rico's book, which was like writing about Senator John Kerry's experiences in the Vietnam War if one had read only *Unfit for Command,* the attack by the Swift Boat veterans. It wasn't a formal book review, although it was certainly a rave. Through their "rigorous investigation, tireless comparisons and scrupulous analysis," wrote Vargas Llosa, the authors of *Who Killed the Bishop?* had exposed a sinister scheme at the heart of the Gerardi case to "cover up for the truly guilty ones, sacrificing innocents and engendering a monumental distortion of the truth, . . . an operation in which a handful of little scoundrels, opportunists, and petty politicians reaped excellent personal rewards."

Vargas Llosa accepted the idea that Baloo had left bite marks in Bishop Gerardi's skull and that poor witnesses, particularly Rubén Chanax, had gone, "thanks to the crime, from living on nothing and in the streets to being maintained and protected abroad by the state. Their testimony was continuously molded—altered, twisted, adapted—throughout the process in such a way that they seemed submissively subject to the dictates of the archbishop's human rights group, ODHA, whose actions throughout this story are supremely suspicious, to say the least."

Vargas Llosa wrote that "the first prosecutor of the case, Otto Ardón, who tried to follow this lead"—the dog bites—"received so many attacks and threats that he had to resign and fled the country." It was a through-the-looking-glass version of the Gerardi case. Otto Ardón never "fled" the country, at least not in the sense the word seems intended to imply. He took a brief vacation after the fiasco of the exhumation and then resigned from the Public Ministry. He was never in exile. (Indeed, Ardón was soon spotted working in Guatemala City, in the law office of Irving Aguilar, Obdulio Villanueva's defense lawyer.) The prosecutors Celvin Galindo and Leopoldo Zeissig, who had investigated the involvement of the military in the crime, were the ones who had actually fled real threats, going into exile, although de la Grange and Rico claimed that the threats were exaggerated. They portrayed Zeissig as never having been subjected to anything more frightening than a single ambiguous call, with music playing, on his cell phone.

* * *

IN THE SUMMER OF 2002, I had flown down to the South American city where Leopoldo Zeissig was then residing with his wife and small child. Dry, sandy-looking Andean mountain slopes, like enormous dunes, closely surrounded the city, making it feel like an impermanent place, overly vulnerable to avalanches and winds, though in fact it was one of the oldest cities in the Americas. We met in the lobby of the hotel where I was staying and spoke there for the duration of an entire working day and much of the next. Zeissig had a job with the legal staff of a German foundation and was also attending law school, studying the consolidation of the rule of law in emerging democracies.

After the verdict, Zeissig said, he had phoned the attorney general, Adolfo González Rodas. Zeissig had been promised a job with a lower profile after the trial, and he told González Rodas that his successor would inherit the Gerardi case in good shape. The next morning, however, he was stunned to read in *Prensa Libre* that, according to the attorney general, he would be staying on as special prosecutor of the Gerardi case. He met with González Rodas and was informed that he was the only one qualified to lead the case forward into its next, highly perilous stage, which would include pursuing criminal investigations against Major Escobar Blas, Colonel Rudy Pozuelos, and other EMP leaders that could eventually reach as high as General Espinosa and even the former president, Álvaro Arzú.

Zeissig asked for a vacation to think things over. He was under pressure to arrest some of the EMP leaders immediately—before the verdicts could be appealed—on the basis of evidence that had emerged during the trial. But he didn't feel the case was strong enough yet. He didn't want to ask for arrest orders only to see the EMP officers go free in a few months. If an element of fear also influenced his hesitation, who could blame him? He was still receiving telephone threats. Then, in July, he learned that the Public Ministry was planning to discontinue his security detail. He decided that the time had come to take his family out of the country. They left on a Saturday morning. Zeissig didn't want his security guards to notice he was leaving, so a friend went ahead to the airport, taking their two suitcases. Zeissig left his house carrying just his laptop, and he purchased one-way tickets to El Salvador at the airlines counter.

Zeissig told me, indignantly, that the accusations against him, about fabricating evidence, were completely untrue. There was no stage of the investigation that hadn't been verified by the UN mission. He'd never denied access to MINUGUA at any moment, so there was an independent record of every step he and the other prosecutors had taken. (By contrast, in 1999, in its ninth annual report, MINUGUA had reported that its verification efforts in the Gerardi case had been "obstructed" by Otto Ardón, "who systematically refused access to the case file.")

Leopoldo Zeissig grew up in Mixco, a large urban municipality five miles outside Guatemala City. He worked his way through law school (it took him twelve years), and when he graduated, in 1994, he took a job in the Public Ministry. He was an assistant prosecutor under Celvin Galindo, investigating homicides and kidnappings, when the bishop was murdered. He learned about the killing while watching CNN before going to work. His first thought was that it must be a political crime. "But how could such a thing have happened?" he remembers thinking. In postwar Guatemala, murders like that weren't supposed to occur anymore. Later, when Otto Ardón's dog-bite theory emerged, "it seemed incredibly strange to me. It was becoming a public joke. But I said, I can't judge. I don't know the case."

After Celvin Galindo took over the Gerardi case, on December 17, 1998, he and Zeissig met for dinner several times. They talked about the various scenarios, including the one involving Valle del Sol, the criminal gang. Galindo told Zeissig that the police considered the Valle del Sol scenario "burned"; that is, they had investigated the gang every which way, and as far as Bishop Gerardi's murder was concerned, "there was nothing there." Zeissig asked

Galindo if he intended to investigate a political motive in the crime, and he answered, "Everything is on the table." But Galindo was under pressure to prosecute Father Mario. In a meeting at the Conquistador Ramada hotel, the head of the Secretariat of Strategic Analysis, Howard Yang, pressured Galindo to take Father Mario to trial. (Yang was the man who had been dispatched by President Arzú to intimidate Judge Henry Monroy into charging only Father Mario for the murder.) Galindo yielded to the pressure and proceeded with the charges against the priest. But then Judge Monroy decided to free Father Mario, though provisionally, keeping him under investigation.

On February 17, 1999—the day before Judge Monroy gave Father Mario provisional freedom—the taxi driver, Diego Méndez Perussina, testified before going into exile in Canada. "I think Celvin began to realize it was a political crime when the taxi driver gave his statement in front of Judge Monroy," Zeissig said. It had been widely reported that Galindo was about to arrest members of the military, most probably Major Escobar Blas and Captain Byron Lima. I sensed that Zeissig now regretted not having charged the major himself. He believed that Captain Lima and Major Escobar Blas had been linked in criminal activities before Bishop Gerardi's murder and that Escobar Blas, especially, had a grisly secret history, including, possibly, having been one of the masterminds of the kidnapping for ransom and subsequent murder of a wealthy college student named Beverly Sandoval Richardson, a widely publicized case. Captain Lima, who was part owner of a gun shop and shooting range, was alleged to have engaged in arms trafficking. Zeissig told me that he believed Captain Lima knew Ana Lucía Escobar and that he had provided logistical help to the Valle del Sol gang for bank robberies and kidnappings. (The Spanish investigator for MINUGUA, Rafael Guillamón, told me later that Ana Lucía and her gangster boyfriend, Luis Carlos García Pontaza, used to practice firing their weapons at Lima's shooting range.) One of

Zeissig's early sources in the investigation was an underworld informer who said that Captain Lima and Major Escobar Blas had provided weapons to the gang. But when Zeissig pressed the informer to testify before a judge, the informer refused, because he feared being killed in reprisal.

"That's the big problem with being a prosecutor," said Zeissig. "The truth commission could bring information out anonymously, but we have to bring it before a judge. Otherwise, what good is it?"

We spoke about the often exasperating but dramatic days when Rubén Chanax had finally begun to talk. This was after Chanax and El Chino Iván had been transferred from the custody of the police to that of the Public Ministry as protected witnesses, when Zeissig decided to give Chanax work washing their cars as part of a strategy to gain his cooperation. Piece by piece, his story had come out, or anyway as much of it as he was willing to tell: Father Mario's involvement, Captain Lima and Villanueva turning up in the black Jeep Cherokee to move the bishop's body, and so on. Some days they didn't talk about the case at all. "We'd just watch television," Zeissig said, recalling that Chanax especially liked Pokemon cartoons. "He'd see the first scene, and then tell you the rest of the episode." In the evenings, on the way back to the Hotel Arlington, Chanax's police guards would always ask him what he and the prosecutors had talked about. His answer was always the same—they'd watched movies, watched television, told *chistes*, nothing more.

During that time, soon after Chanax had finally begun to collaborate as a witness, Zeissig had given him another polygraph test, the first one that had been administered to him since the test given by the FBI, shortly after the crime. Chanax was asked four questions:

1. Did you see someone come out of the parish-house garage? When Chanax answered yes, the test indicated that he was telling the truth.

2. Did you see Father Mario Orantes kick the small garage door shut? Chanax's affirmative answer seemed truthful.
3. Did you see somebody move the cadaver? Chanax's yes again seemed truthful.
4. Do you know the person who came out without a shirt? Rubén Chanax answered that he didn't know the shirtless man, and the polygraph machine indicated the symptoms of a lie.

The shirtless man, Chanax finally admitted, was "Hugo," and he told the prosecutors what he knew—at least *some* of what he knew—about him.

But Rubén Chanax was becoming frightened. What if Military Intelligence found out that he'd been talking? Already Chanax had received a warning in the Hotel Arlington from someone who came in off the street and told him that if he kept squealing he was going to die. Sometimes Captain Lima jogged by and tried to catch Chanax's eye when Chanax was at his window or in the doorway. One day Chanax briefly stepped out of the hotel to buy something in the little shop next door, and a man there said, "Be careful, because Byron Lima is watching."

It was the possibility of a stealthy visit from Hugo that terrified Rubén Chanax most. Hugo was apparently a notorious G-2 assassin. One of his nicknames was Multicolores, for his ability to disguise himself. Multicolores might come disguised as a policeman, as a salesman taking a room for the night, or as one of the lovers who used the hotel for inexpensive trysts. He took his victims by surprise, often strangling them with a piece of fishing line. Chanax begged the prosecutors to move him to another hotel. But Zeissig told him that moving would look suspicious. "They'll suspect you've talked to us," he said. "Go on like nothing has happened. Trust us. And whatever you do, don't tell El Chino Iván that you've talked."

Chanax had told the prosecutors that on the night of the murder El Chino Iván stayed behind in Don Mike's store, that is, away from the park, longer than he'd admitted. Maybe El Chino Iván had never even seen the shirtless man. Maybe Chanax had told El Chino Iván about what he'd seen that night, and then El Chino Iván had elaborated his own versions, or so Zeissig suspected. El Chino Iván still dreamed, as when he'd first turned himself into MINUGUA, of going to the United States. It was unclear what Rubén Chanax hoped for, other than to stay alive and out of prison. Up to that point, he hadn't asked to be taken anywhere, other than to the movies. One day he said to Zeissig, "You've given me the importance as a human being that I deserve."

Leopoldo Zeissig said that when Rubén Chanax had to confront Obdulio Villanueva and then both of the Limas at evidentiary hearings in February and April 2000, Zeissig lost any doubt that his witness was telling the truth. He was convinced by the manner with which Chanax held his own, refusing to back down in the face of the military men's often belligerent ire, accusations, and even ill-disguised threats. "I haven't sold myself, and I haven't been told what to say, and I'm not a liar, like you," he'd defiantly retorted to Colonel Lima Estrada. "You were in the store! It's not my fault you were there." Captain Lima tried to discredit Chanax with a garrulous tirade aimed at exposing his confusion about, for example, what uniforms various EMP units wore, and finally, in an exasperated outburst, Lima had uttered his memorable threat, asking the former park vagrant and car washer what he would do if a video turned up implicating *him* in the crime. Chanax had responded, "If you say so, it's because you know." After that hearing, Zeissig had asked Rubén Chanax what he'd been referring to, and he'd answered, "Because they filmed it."

The prosecutors argued—and at the trial, the judges agreed—that Rubén Chanax's *basic* story never varied. Over time he added to it, but without altering its core sequence. Eventually his reason for doing so would become clear. Chanax repressed details to avoid implicating himself in the crime. When he felt safe enough—*seguro*—he told more. These dynamics made him a dangerous witness, but since Guatemala had no equivalent of the U.S. federal witness protection program, he couldn't, in exchange for total immunity, have revealed everything, including his own role in the crime, and then have been provided with a secure new life, even a new identity. Being a "protected witness" in Guatemala meant that he was safe from prosecution as long as there was a special prosecutor who was inclined to protect him. If a prosecutor with a different perspective took over the case, he might lose that protection.

It was Rubén Chanax, Zeissig told me, who'd left the small, bloody sneaker print on the garage floor. (He'd washed the blood from his shoes in the park's fountain.) There had also been footprints at the rear of the garage, not sneaker prints, leading into the sacristy, as if someone had fled that way. "The footprints going into the sacristy were never documented in the investigation," Zeissig told me. "Ardón lost all that stuff."

It seemed strange to me that Otto Ardón, during those crucial first days, had never tried to match the sneaker print to Rubén Chanax. It was as if he knew that this particular witness shouldn't be scrutinized too closely. If Chanax's sneakers had matched the print, Ardón would have had someone to charge in the crime right away. But Chanax was unlikely to keep silent about what he knew while prosecutors marched him toward a possible death sentence as Bishop Gerardi's murderer.

"He was terrified we were going to accuse him too," Zeissig said. "It was delicate. It's not right to threaten a witness with prison if he doesn't tell you the whole truth. It's better to try to win his confidence, let him see that we can keep our word, and that, within what the law permits, we can get him out of trouble."

Once he'd given his pretrial testimony, Rubén Chanax had to leave Guatemala for his own safety. But he was not a promising candidate for any country's political asylum program. He didn't leave Guatemala until April 24, 2000, when the prosecutors finally sent him to Mexico City on a regular tourist's visa. They bought him a suit and tie so that there would be less chance of his encountering any problems at passport control. Zeissig recalled that when he and his staff went to the airport to see Rubén Chanax off, "Some of the assistant prosecutors became sentimental." When Chanax's first ninety-day tourist visa expired, Jorge García of the Public Ministry's Witness Protection Service went to renew it. (García would eventually succeed Zeissig as prosecutor of the Gerardi case.) Ninety days later, García renewed it again, but when that visa expired Chanax would become an illegal alien. Finally he was granted refugee status by the UN Refugee Commission, which provided a temporary solution.

The prosecutors had rented a small room for Chanax in a poor neighborhood in Mexico City and had given him barely enough to live on—eventually they would only pay his rent of eighty dollars a month—but he soon found work, first as a carpenter, and then in a taco stand. The owner of the taco stand found out who he was and become protective of him. The owner also had a fleet of taco trucks that he sent to fairs outside the city, and Chanax sometimes was sent along to work in them. He called Zeissig at his office using a prepaid international calling card in different pay phones. He was happy to be working.

Once Zeissig visited Mexico City and went to the taco stand. "He served us," Zeissig recounted. "To see him working there, at the skillet . . . it made me feel . . . not tenderness. . . . I don't know. Poor Rubén, I thought. There he is, finally working at an honest job."

Zeissig knew that the defense attorneys would call Rubén Chanax to testify at the trial. They were already boasting that they would be able to "destroy" him in court. But nobody could force him to come back to Guatemala, and Zeissig thought he might refuse.

During Zeissig's last visit to Mexico, Chanax asked, "If I testify, then I'll have the opportunity to tell everything?"

"What do you mean by everything?" Zeissig responded.

"I want to clear my conscience," Chanax said.

So there's more, Zeissig thought. "We'd intuited it, of course," he recalled to me. "But how could you get him to say it? You can interrogate, but . . ."

This was when Chanax first told Zeissig that he'd been contracted by Military Intelligence to spy on Bishop Gerardi long before the night of the murder. "Why do you think I slept in front of the garage door?" he asked. "He had to wake and move me to drive his car inside. That's how I always knew when he came and went." He told Zeissig the same story that would later stun (and outrage) the courtroom, about being contracted by "the colonel" to spy on Bishop Gerardi in "Operation Bird." He told Zeissig that the park of San Sebastián was full of informers, though he never knew who they all were, or what role each one had. He said that El Chino Iván was an informer for Military Intelligence as well.

"When he finally said, I was an informer, not a beggar," Zeissig explained, "he was testifying against his own people. He was risking his life. He was taking the risk that they would find him and kill him."

As Rubén Chanax would later reveal at the trial, one of his calls to Zeissig from Mexico City had been intercepted and he heard a voice that he identified as Hugo, warning him against coming to Guatemala to testify. There were other signs that Chanax's whereabouts and routine had been pinpointed. Chanax was forced to leave his job at the taco stand for more boring work as a janitor in an apartment building.

Rubén Chanax had been flown back to Guatemala City, accompanied by Jorge García, on Thursday, April 27, 2001. That night he slept on a couch in the prosecutors' office. Four security policemen from the Public Ministry, machine guns ready, guarded him, sleeping in shifts of two. When Zeissig arrived at seven in the morning he found his witness bathed and dressed in a suit and tie, apparently ready to go. But Chanax seemed extremely nervous. At breakfast his hands shook so much he could barely hold his fork. Zeissig decided that Chanax shouldn't be

sent to the witness stand until Monday. "I wanted him to be serene. I knew it was going to be a brutal cross-examination. 'They
are going to attack you,' I told him. 'You're going to have to be
very alert. We'll be trying to protect you. But the judges will let
them ask their questions. You have to go forward with the truth.'"

They spent that weekend holed up in the office. They rented
movies, sent out for food. Zeissig and his staff began working on
their closing arguments. Monday morning they went to court.
Zeissig left in his three-vehicle security caravan. He had sent
Chanax ahead ten minutes earlier in a car the prosecutors had
never used before, accompanied by three armed guards. When the
court convened that morning, Zeissig rose and announced that
the witness Rubén Chanax Sontay was in the building. Not even
ODHA knew he was coming. Mynor Melgar's mouth, recalled
Zeissig, dropped open in astonishment.

"I HAD A JOB," was how Leopoldo Zeissig summed up his experience as special prosecutor of the Gerardi case. "And if I believe
in what I'm doing, I should do it right." An unwanted exile seemed
a high price to pay for having done that job. Zeissig missed his
parents, relatives, and friends, his house, the camaraderie of the
Public Ministry. He missed Guatemala.

Captain Byron Lima, Zeissig told me, had a signature manner
of announcing himself over the telephone in anonymous telephone calls: birdcalls. In the Kaibil commando unit that Lima had
belonged to, soldiers became adept at mimicking jungle birdcalls.
On the first Christmas Eve of his exile, when Zeissig picked up
the receiver to answer the telephone, he heard a voice making
eerie, high-pitched sounds. He felt certain that it was the captain
phoning from prison in Guatemala City, just to let Zeissig know
that he knew where to find him.

"Merry Christmas, Byron," Zeissig said into the phone, and
hung up.

2

ON SEPTEMBER 25, 2002, a few months after I visited Leopoldo Zeissig in exile and we spoke in the hotel lobby in that arid South American city, the Fourth Court of Appeals overturned the verdicts in the Gerardi case. A new trial was ordered. The appellate court ruled that the three judges in the original trial had "overly relied" on Rubén Chanax's courtroom testimony. It accepted the arguments of the defense about Chanax's changing his pretrial testimony rather than expanding on it. (ODHA had lost the battle to recuse the most notoriously partisan and pro-military of the appellate judges, Wilewaldo Contreras.)

Because a new trial had been ordered, the defendants had to stay in prison. Father Mario remained in custody in a private hospital. In a triumphant statement from the Centro Preventivo, Captain Lima proclaimed, "Organized crime killed Gerardi, and now it will be proved. . . . It should also be noted that the Public Ministry is contemplating criminal charges against the prosecutors Mario Leal and Leopoldo Zeissig for manufacturing false witnesses." Lima called ODHA "a group of communists who don't understand that the war has ended."

That night in New York, when I checked the messages on my answering machine, I heard a voice making strange noises, whooping and celebratory, somewhat like New Year's Eve noisemakers—wooo-eeeeeee! wooo-eeeee—and drawn-out enough to sound mocking too. A jungle birdcall, possibly. Whoever made the call, without saying a word, hung up.

It turned out that the ruling by the Fourth Court of Appeals was deeply flawed. For one thing, the appellate court was not supposed to rule on the quality of the proof that led to the verdicts but solely on whether the defendants' right to a fair trial had been violated. This legal point aside, it was also soon shown that the appellate judges had not actually examined the testimony they deemed contradictory. Tipped off by MINUGUA, the prosecution lawyers discovered that the records of Rubén Chanax's testimony had never even been requested by the appellate judges. They were still in the files. The judges had ruled on the substance of proofs they had never seen. Judge Wilewaldo Contreras's court had issued a precooked ruling.

On October 3, another Guatemalan court—Yassmín Barrios was one of the judges—found the former head of the EMP Archivo, Colonel Juan Valencia Osorio, guilty of having ordered the murder of Myrna Mack in 1991. (The man who stabbed her to death, Sergeant Noél Beteta, had been convicted in 1993.) But two other officers—another colonel and a general—were acquitted at the trial. Mynor Melgar was the prosecutor in the case. Helen Mack, after an eleven-year struggle, had at last won an unprecedented conviction against an active-duty colonel for being the "intellectual author" of a politically motivated crime of state, however diluted the victory was by the acquittals. Mack's murder did not fall under the Army's self-granted amnesty from prosecution for wartime crimes against human rights because it was a civilian homicide that had occurred outside any military context.

Four months later, in February 2003, the Supreme Court reinstated the verdicts in the Gerardi case. The Fourth Court of Appeals was ordered to hear the appeal again, and this time to conduct the proceeding properly. ODHA initiated a new battle to recuse Judge Wilewaldo Contreras, who'd publicly referred to ODHA's lawyers as his "enemies."

Judge Wilewaldo Contreras and the appellate court struck again in May, when they overturned the verdict in the Myrna Mack case, freeing Colonel Valencia Osorio. Later the Supreme Court reinstated that verdict too, but the damage was done. A truckload of soldiers arrived at the colonel's house just before the prosecutors, including Mynor Melgar, got there to rearrest him. The colonel was smuggled aboard the truck, which drove off to an unknown destination.

THE SAME DAY, February 12, 2003, that the Supreme Court upheld the verdicts in the Gerardi case, a riot broke out in the Centro Preventivo prison. Inmates in Sectors 1 and 2, members—*cholos* —of the infamous Central American youth gangs known as *maras,* attacked Sector 7. The *cholos* were armed with machetes, knives, and guns. Their target was Sector 7's leader, Captain Byron Lima. By the end of the rampage, six prisoners were slain, three by decapitation, including the former EMP specialist Sergeant Major Obdulio Villanueva.

The Limas' supporters had portrayed them in the press as having cleaned up the prison and imposed a wholesome but tough military discipline on their fellow inmates. It was true that Captain Lima had been elected head of all the prison sectors, that he'd put up signs barring spitting, and that he insisted that prisoners follow new rules regulating at what hours they could play their stereos and radios. In the mornings he made inmates assemble and shout out, "Good morning, Guatemala." The lethal riot could be seen, then, as a rebellion by depraved criminals against spit-and-polish military discipline.

But there were other versions, other explanations, about what set off the riot in the Centro Preventivo that day. A full year before the incident, in January 2002, while the Gerardi case was in its first appeal stage, the president of the Penitentiary System Consulting Commission had received a letter from guards at the Centro Preventivo. The guards, who withheld their names, explained that they felt "obligated to denounce to you the corruption of our superiors and also we don't want to be blamed for what could happen." They accused the subdirector of the prison system, Colonel Barahona, of granting the Limas special privileges. "The Limas, being the military men they are," the guards wrote, "have an ally in Colonel Barahona, who allows them to bring in prohibited items for the business they run in their sector. They gave an order allowing them to bring in as many such things as cigarettes as they want, but what the colonel doesn't know is that inside those cigarettes they bring in drugs."

Two hundred *cholos* had recently been transferred to the Centro Preventivo following an outbreak of intergang warfare in another prison. In Guatemala, as elsewhere, narco capos go on directing their criminal enterprises from inside prisons, as do the heads of kidnapping, extortion, and car-theft rings. In the past, inside and outside the prisons, the *maras* worked for these often military-run mafias, providing foot soldiers, assassins, and such; in recent years, they had been asserting a new autonomy. The *cholos* in the Centro Preventivo wanted control over the prison crime rackets. They wanted those lucrative rackets for *themselves*. They didn't want to submit to the Limas' brutal reign. They wanted the Limas to submit to *their* brutal reign. Some had seen it coming: *elPeriódico,* citing prison authorities who refused to be identified by name, had earlier described the tension created by Captain Lima in the Centro Preventivo as a "time bomb" that had long been waiting to go off.

The *maras* are usually described as having their origins in the gang culture of Los Angeles. Young combat veterans, deserters, orphans, the children of parents fleeing the Central American civil wars, especially El Salvador's, formed gangs in Los Angeles to protect themselves and forge an identity of their own. After serving prison terms in the United States, many of them were deported back to their countries of origin. But *maras* have been a presence in Guatemala City since at least the 1970s, when the city's poorest squatter slums began to be filled with people fleeing war and poverty in the mountains.

Central America was flooded with weapons from the United States, the Soviet Union, and their allies during the cold war. Thirteen-year-old boys hold up convenience stores with grenades, and adolescent carjackers and kidnappers go around armed with M-15s, Gallils, and AK-47 assault rifles—"logistical support" often supplied by their partners and crime bosses in the police and the military. In 2005 there were some 100,000 Central American gang members operating across five countries, including Canada and the United States, with at least half of them based in Guatemala, El Salvador, and Honduras. On both the Guatemalan-Mexican and Mexican-U.S. borders, *maras* have established dominion over the lucrative and treacherous business of transporting illegal migrants, while simultaneously preying on them. *Maras* are also employed by the Mexican and Guatemalan cartels on the narco routes through the same territories. They have a reputation for favoring weapons of stealth and silence over guns: machetes, daggers, lead pipes, even Asian martial arts weapons.

The gang members rarely seem to splurge or launder money by purchasing ostentatious vehicles, houses, or other luxury goods. Instead, they reinvest their money in their businesses and the subsistence of their gangs. In Guatemala City there were said to be approximately 350 separate *mara* cells, embedded like spider nests in individual neighborhoods. There are gang members who tattoo their entire faces with Goth lettering and symbols. Other cells forbid tattoos that can't be covered by clothing. The newspapers are full of stories about teenagers murdered by *maras,* who kill, it is often said, just for fun. Initiation rites often seem to require murdering a female victim, usually an adolescent girl. That was one reason that 665 women were violently murdered in Guatemala, mostly in the capital, in 2005. On the other hand, some *maras,* or at least some cells, claim to forbid violence against women.

A twenty-one-year-old *cholo* known as El Bocón ("Big Mouth") told police investigators that the riot in the Centro Preventivo had been planned for two months. El Bocón described how the *cholos* made their way from Sectors 1 and 2, smashing open holes in the fortified doors. "Then the *cholos* got into Sector 8 and they opened a hole to get into 7 and that's where Villanueva and another *maje* made their stand, fighting with the *cholos,* while the rest of us got out of there. And when I was out I realized that Psycho and Chopper from the Salvatrucha gang were decapitating Villanueva. When he tried to crawl out through the hole, he couldn't because he was too fat and he got stuck, and then they grabbed his hair and cut off his head."

Colonel Valencia Osorio, who had been convicted of ordering Myrna Mack's killing (this was three months before that verdict was overturned), crawled to safety through a hole smashed in a wall. But where were the Limas? The *cholos* were chanting, "We want Lima! We want Lima!" They hacked off the top of Villanueva's skull with a machete. Psycho scooped up Villanueva's brain matter with his hands and flung it into the faces of the cornered Sector 7 prisoners, screaming, "Bring us Lima!" But Lima was nowhere to be found. They seized on a felt soldier doll that Lima kept by his bunk. The *cholos* decapitated the doll and shoved its head inside Villanueva's decapitated head, in through the neck and up, so that the doll's face showed through the brain matter.

Later Captain Lima said that when the riot erupted, he'd been in the administration building taking an engineering class. His father, the colonel, was in the infirmary.

Some people found it suspicious that the riot in the Centro Preventivo had occurred on the very same day that the Supreme Court upheld the convictions in the Gerardi case. Amnesty International issued a statement speculating that Obdulio Villanueva's murder was related to his potential as a witness against his as yet uncharged military superiors. Maybe the former EMP specialist had been killed because he was considered the weak link in the

chain, the likeliest to talk? So much rested on the continued silence of the three convicted military men. But such speculations
smacked a bit of wishful thinking and denial of certain nearly
incomprehensibly dark realities (the *maras*).

In the aftermath of the riot, Captain Lima announced that five
cholo prisoners would be executed every day unless the gang
members in Sectors 1 and 2 were transferred out of the Centro
Preventivo. The prison authorities quickly acceded. Captain Lima
and his father were to be transferred to another prison too, for
their own safety, but the captain refused to abdicate his fiefdom.
He insisted that he was needed in the Centro Preventivo, and that
"a good captain doesn't abandon his ship." Despite his protests,
the Limas, son and father, were transferred to El Boquerón, a
maximum-security prison thirty miles west of Guatemala City.

Nobody was ever indicted for the death of Obdulio Villanueva
and the others murdered that day in the Centro Preventivo. Prosecutors at the Public Ministry and the police couldn't find a single
witness willing to testify before a judge. El Bocón, who had given
his statement to the police in the immediate aftermath of the riot,
refused to be a witness. More than two years later, on August 15,
2005, a nonaggression pact between incarcerated *maras* was broken in a prison in Escuintla, setting off nearly simultaneous attacks, coordinated by cell phone, in prisons across the country.
Thirty-four gang members were killed that day, including the two
who'd beheaded Villanueva: Psycho and Chopper.

Legal authorities were too frightened of the Limas and their
allies—when not colluding with them—to expose their illicit
prison activities. Journalists, fearing reprisals, censored themselves. But the Public Ministry and the homicide division of the
Criminal Investigations Section of the National Police produced
a substantial file on the case. That file sheds some light on the
Limas' retail businesses in prison. The Limas sold everything from
cell phones to bottled water. Prepaid phone cards that cost ten
quetzales outside the prison cost double that inside. Inmates had

to pay the Limas two quetzales per minute to use the prison's public pay phones. There were 1,800 prisoners in the Centro Preventivo, and one can deduce how, over months and years, the prison businesses could accrue significant revenue. A prosecutor assigned to the case of the Centro Preventivo riot, who didn't want to be identified, estimated that Captain Lima was earning 50,000 quetzales a month, approximately $8,000, from his prison shopkeeping alone.

He may have been earning considerably more. After all, Captain Lima had been elected sector chief of all sector chiefs. By his own admission, he controlled the prison, all but the *cholos* of Sectors 1 and 2. After the riot, the police reported that the entire prison was infested with weapons. Who, logically, had control of weapons trafficking inside the prison? In the summer of 2004 an assistant prosecutor assigned to the Gerardi case told me that when Lima was still a prisoner in the Centro Preventivo he'd been spotted during a stakeout, dressed in street clothes, entering a warehouse allegedly used by drug traffickers.

Before the trial, Captain Lima had seemed to come close to confessing his role in the Gerardi case several times. He was one of only three military men arrested in a plot that had undoubtedly involved many more, including higher-ranking officers. Compared with his father, Colonel Lima, who was probably one of those in on the plot to kill the bishop from the start, the son might have had a relatively minor operational role. In the captain's interview with Claudia Méndez before the trial, you can sense his anger, self-pity, and frustration. Only four days after the bishop's murder, he had been sent abroad to join the prestigious UN mission to Cyprus. Then he'd suddenly been recalled, and forbidden by his superiors to leave Guatemala. About a year after the murder, Rafael Guillamón, the chief investigator for MINUGUA, received a telephone call in his office from Captain Lima, asking for a meeting. They agreed to meet in the Hotel Melia, where Captain Lima asked Guillamón what he could do to fix his situation regarding the Gerardi case. Guillamón answered that if he was willing to tell all he knew, MINUGUA would guarantee his protection. Lima insisted on speaking personally with the mission chief, Jean Arnault. But no such meeting ever occurred. Guillamón had a theory about Captain Lima. It was just a theory, but a compelling one. He speculated that Lima had received an offer similar to the one the doomed Valle del Sol gangster Carlos García Pontaza had received: a free hand to commit crimes, in Lima's case from prison, with a guarantee of impunity and logistical support. For García Pontaza, the deal had been contingent on his agreeing to implicate his former girlfriend, Ana Lucía Escobar. In Captain Lima's case, the quid pro quo was his continued loyalty to the military and his silence regarding coconspirators in the crime. It seemed likely that sooner rather than later the military men convicted in the Gerardi case would win an appeal from a corrupt court and go free. Captain Lima would leave prison a fairly wealthy man, his honor intact. Powerful men would be indebted to him.

IN THE PROSECUTORS' OFFICE, as in ODHA, the pessimism and anxiety hanging over the case were palpable. Month after month went by, and no ruling had been issued on when the Fourth Court would hear the appeal for a second time, or who the judges would be. ODHA was still fighting to recuse Wilewaldo Contreras. Meanwhile, in the Sunday columns that she published in Prensa Libre, Maite Rico, the coauthor of the article and later the book defending the Limas, stayed on the attack. Many of the country's other media figures, including the host of an influential political talk show on television—whose family owned the Pollo Campero fried-chicken empire—were also relentless in their accusations. Defense lawyers had been waging a campaign through the media since even before the appearance of de la Grange and Rico's article in Letras Libres in 2001. Noé Gómez Limón, the brother of the prisoner who had testified that Obdulio Villanueva was not in the prison the day of the bishop's murder and that Villanueva's lawyer, Roberto Echeverría, had tried to bribe him, was murdered in December 2002. After Villanueva's death in the Centro Preventivo riot two months later, Echeverría told the Guatemalan press, "It grabs your attention that first they murdered the witness and now Villanueva. Let's see if ODHA and President Portillo will turn the body over to his relatives."

Aggressive criticism in the media was daily fare at ODHA, engendering a state of perpetual strain. It seemed as if whenever I dropped in on Mario Domingo in his office I found him indignantly pounding away at his computer's rattling keyboard, working on his ever-growing compilations and annotations of all the errors and falsehoods in de la Grange and Rico's book. After Mario Vargas Llosa's piece appeared, Mario Domingo wrote a six-page single-spaced letter to *El País* that the newspaper did not print, even in an abridged version. During a visit to the office of the new special prosecutor, Jorge García, in the Public Ministry, an assistant prosecutor said to me, "Vargas Llosa's column has given the judges all the cover they need to let the Limas go free without any public controversy." He spoke as if the outcome of the appeal was no longer in doubt.

Nevertheless, the Untouchables and ODHA's lawyers pressed forward with their investigation. They were saying that if they lost the appeal and had to build a new case from scratch, they would be ready. That may have been just bravado, since it was doubtful that the prosecutors would want to start over, especially if they were forced to forgo Rubén Chanax's testimony.

The fate of the Gerardi case seemed to rest more heavily than ever on whether or not Rubén Chanax had told the truth. Since the trial, the defense attorneys and their supporters had been portraying all of the prosecution witnesses as liars who had given fabricated testimony, but they focused their arguments on Chanax. He had been the prosecution's star witness. But he was Leopoldo Zeissig's witness, and now Zeissig was in exile. Before the trial,

ODHA had no relationship with Chanax at all. After the trial, ODHA and the prosecutors devoted much of their energy to investigating Chanax's story from the beginning.

From his very first statement to the police on the morning after the murder, Chanax had claimed to have served in the Army. Much later he had told investigators of being selected for a training course to enter Military Intelligence, and of failing it. His military past explained why he'd been recruited to be an informer, practically an undercover intelligence operative, if he was to be believed. In November 2002, Mario Domingo and Jorge García had gone to Mexico City to interrogate Chanax more thoroughly. Chanax told them that when he was a ten-year-old boy in San Cristóbal Totonicapán, his mother, Rosa Sontay, had sold him to a childless couple—a woman and her much older husband—in Chiantla, Huehuetenango. Chanax would never forgive his mother for this. The wife had been especially cruel to him. Finally, Chanax had run away—this was his first taste of life on the streets, and he fell into petty crime. After a brief incarceration in a prison for juvenile offenders, he had gone to live for a while with his grandparents in San Cristóbal, and then with his father and stepmother. He learned some carpentry, his father's trade. He was fond of his stepmother, Julia Gómez. It was while he was living in San Cristóbal, in 1990, that he was conscripted into the Army and driven in a pickup with other boys to the military base in Jalapa, in Military Zone 9. Later he was assigned to the Fourth Engineering Corps, in the capital.

Told that he'd been selected for a course to enter the Military Police, young Rubén was taken with a few other soldiers to a secret subterranean detention center. Chanax recalled descending iron stairs into pungent darkness and seeing small cells crowded with six or seven prisoners, filthy and neglected, their hair grown wild and long, some of them obviously victims of torture. An officer explained, "This is what happens to traitors." It turned out that the Military Police course was a ruse. Chanax and the others had been selected for a Military Intelligence course in "espionage," which meant that they were to learn how to follow people and vehicles, how to infiltrate a subject's home, and so on. Chanax's first assignment was to spy on a judge, under the tutelage of his instructor, Major López Rico. (All the names of the military officers Chanax had provided later checked out.) After the course, Chanax said, he returned to the Fourth Engineering Corps, and he began to suffer from a chronic sinus problem. His face swelled up, and he had a long stay in a military hospital.

Chanax had "failed" his course in the sense that he was not selected for a career in Military Intelligence, but he was being prepared for the life of a trained informer. When he returned from the hospital, General García González sent him to live in San Sebastián park and gave him 2,000 quetzales to spy on Bishop Gerardi. He was to report to the nearby EMP. That assignment lasted six months. In July 1994, at the age of nineteen, Chanax was discharged from the Army. He took a series of jobs, including one as a construction mason. His mother now lived in Guatemala City, and he tried to live with her and his little sister for a while, but the relationship with his mother was stormy. He began to live in the streets, and he discovered that he liked the freedom. He drifted back to the San Sebastián park, although in those days he slept in cheap "whore hotels" at night. Eventually he was contacted by a "colonel"—apparently not Lima Estrada—and offered his old job back, spying on the bishop. The colonel took him to a house in Zone 6 where he would sometimes give his information. That house would turn up in later revelations about the planning of Bishop Gerardi's murder.

People might argue for or against the truth of anything else Chanax had subsequently said, but if he'd lied about having been in the Army, nothing else about his story made much sense. Mario Domingo was able to locate Rubén Chanax's mother, Doña Rosa Sontay, a decrepit-looking, angry woman with black teeth who lived in a shack in one of the most squalid areas of Guatemala

City. She told Domingo that she used to go to the Jalapa base to collect the small monthly payments the Army issued to the families of conscripts. The first time she went, there was some confusion over her son's name, and she discovered that Rubén was using his stepmother's name, Goméz. After returning from the Army, his mother said, Rubén had a girlfriend named Angélica, with whom he'd fathered a child. Doña Rosa didn't display much maternal affection or concern for her son. Rubén, she said, used to hit her.

Mario Domingo managed to find at least one other former soldier who'd been in Jalapa, in the so-called Tiger Course, with Rubén Chanax. This soldier said that Chanax was good at firing a rifle, but bad at other things. The macabre trials the Guatemalan Army contrives to test recruits, especially in elite combat battalions and intelligence units, are notorious. Over the years the same horrific anecdotes have repeatedly emerged, including one about recruits' being given a puppy to care for through basic training, then having to slash its throat. Some young soldiers vomit, or feel pity or sadness. But Chanax, said the former soldier, had coldly cut his puppy's throat.

Rubén Chanax, in Mexico City, had told Mario Domingo a much more disturbing story about his G-2 training course. At the end of the intelligence course, he said, as a kind of final exam, the trainees had to commit a murder. Considering that it was a course for the Guatemalan Army's most murderous entity, this was not incredible. Chanax described an incident he said had occurred in May 1992 on the Incienso Bridge, spanning a deep ravine outside Guatemala City, resulting in the double homicide of a young couple selected at random. The weapon was a pistol, he said. "And then," said Chanax, "we graduated, if you want to put it that way." Later Mario Domingo found brief newspaper reports from May 10, 1992, of a couple found dead at the bottom of the ravine underneath the Incienso Bridge.

* * *

AFTER THE PUBLICATION of the book about the case by Bertrand de la Grange and Maite Rico, in which they said that a thorough search of military records turned up no documentation whatsoever of Rubén Chanax's military service, Rodrigo Salvadó and Arturo Aguilar went to San Cristóbal Totonicapán and found Chanax's grandfather, who gave them photographs of a young Chanax in uniform. ODHA provided those photographs to the press. Jorge García had for months been petitioning the Ministry of Defense for documentary proof of Rubén Chanax's military service. Inquiries for Rubén Chanax Sontay turned up nothing, but now, on the basis of the conversations with Chanax and with his mother, Rosa Sontay, the prosecutor asked for records for Rubén Chanax Gómez. On May 3, 2004, he received a one-page signed and stamped document that read: "After searching the archives, we confirmed that there is only information about a señor Rubén Chanax Gómez, who was on active duty in the Army Corps of Engineers 'Lieutenant Colonel of Engineers and Engineer Francisco Vela Arrango' from 1 February 1992 to 31 July 1994, when discharged for having completed his required tour of duty." The document also described his treatment for a chronic sinus condition in 1993. Rafael Guillamón told me later that once, during the first months after the bishop's murder, he'd sat Chanax down in front of some disassembled weapons, including military assault rifles. Chanax had reassembled them with an easy, familiar confidence.

Bertrand de la Grange and Maite Rico were no longer living in Guatemala, but Rico was quick to respond to the discovery of the new information supporting Chanax's contention that he had Army experience. She published a column in *Prensa Libre* complaining that the photograph of Chanax in uniform, which had also been published in *Prensa Libre,* was hopelessly blurry (although ODHA had given the paper several legible photographs).

Maite Rico also found the idea that Chanax would use his stepmother's maternal surname ridiculous. But there was a

Rubén Chanax Sontay in uniform, circa 1993

greater problem. The document Jorge Garciá had successfully subpoenaed from the Ministry of Defense, she said, gave Chanax's age when he left the Army as thirty-one: "The problem is that that is Chanax's age now, not his age at the time of his military service. All these absurdities lead one to think that this document was introduced into the Defense information system after October 31, 2003, the date on which Chanax turned thirty-one. The objective: an attempt to give credibility to his testimony. Who did it? That is what has to be verified. . . . Rubén Chanax Sontay is a false witness, as we demonstrated in our book, *Who Killed the Bishop?*"

That particular column by Maite Rico is a key document, I believe, for understanding the nature and context of the campaign waged against the verdicts in the Gerardi case, and against the witnesses, the prosecutors, and ODHA. Rico's account of the military document she saw is especially provocative. It was *not,* in fact, the same document that the Ministry of Defense gave to Jorge García. That document, Report 2418, contains no mention of Chanax's age. I have seen, and have in my possession, a photocopy of that document. (Chanax's age at any time had never been an issue and, anyway, it made no sense to suggest, as Rico's mystifying document did, that Chanax would have been conscripted at such an advanced age, nearly thirty.) So where did Rico get her document? Who sent it to her and why? I asked Mario Domingo about this and he replied, by e-mail, "That was what made us deduce that the authors of that book must get their information from Military Intelligence."

SOME OF THE MOST WORRISOME ISSUES in Chanax's testimony went back to the very first moments of the crime. Mario Domingo had long been troubled by the question of how El Chino Iván could have immediately returned to the park after retrieving his cigarettes from Don Mike's and not seen the black Jeep Cherokee in which Captain Lima and Sergeant Major Villanueva arrived at the church of San Sebastián. In the first week of March 2003, Arturo Aguilar and Rodrigo Salvadó were sent to Costa Rica to talk to El Chino Iván. All they had to go on was an unspecific address in the outskirts of San José, "near a red bridge." They walked the streets, knocking on doors; finally Rodrigo and Arturo called at a door answered by a man who said that El Chino Iván did live there, but that he wasn't in. The house was near a reeking sewage canal. After several more visits and phone calls, it became obvious that El Chino Iván was avoiding them. Several unrelated people seemed to be living at the address, and one finally directed Arturo and Rodrigo to a young woman named Wendy Cascante, who had met El Chino Iván in a computer class soon after he'd arrived in Costa Rica. She had become pregnant with his child, and they had tried living together in her mother's house, but that domestic arrangement hadn't lasted very long. Since leaving her, El Chino Iván came to visit only sporadically, sometimes bringing money for their little daughter's support. Cascante didn't know where he lived now or how he supported himself, but she suspected that he'd returned to a life of street crime. She recalled that El Chino Iván had been especially nervous during the months just after the trial in 2001, repeatedly saying that he was going to be killed. Once she'd answered the telephone and a male voice said, "Tell the Guatemalan that we're going to kill him."

Arturo and Rodrigo finally found El Chino Iván. They met with him twice, and he told them a new story about what happened after the shirtless man stepped out of the garage at the parish house. Chanax had testified that he'd rung the parish-house doorbell to inform Father Mario that the little garage door—from which the shirtless man had emerged minutes before—had been left open. But El Chino Iván said that *he*, not Chanax, rang the bell that night, and that no one had answered. He said that *he*—not Father Mario, as Chanax claimed—had then closed the little door of the garage.

For the most part, El Chino Iván stuck to his original narrative about the night of Bishop Gerardi's murder, but he now said that he had seen some men gathered in Don Mike's store that night. He didn't know who they were. And he admitted that he'd seen Rubén Chanax speaking with Obdulio Villanueva in the park on the Sunday morning of the murder. He also said he suspected that Bishop Gerardi hadn't been murdered by "Hugo." He didn't even believe that Hugo existed. El Chino Iván said that he thought Villanueva and Captain Lima were the murderers, and that they had been helped by Rubén Chanax.

When the Untouchables asked why he'd revealed none of this at the trial, El Chino Iván said that it was because before the trial he'd received a telephone call from Ardón's former assistant, Gustavo Soria (who Rafael Guillamón, MINUGUA's chief investigator, emphatically insisted worked for Military Intelligence). Soria, El Chino Iván said, had wanted him to alter his original story at the trial, and had offered money. El Chino Iván claimed that he'd refused the offer and had instead stuck to the original story. This would explain his fear and the death threat that Wendy Cascante said he'd subsequently received.

In May, Mario Domingo and Jorge García returned for a second time to Mexico to talk to Chanax, who said that somebody from the Guatemalan military had visited him recently and offered him $10,000 if he would return to Guatemala and retract his testimony. "Look, I've already told you plenty," Chanax said, "and I know you want to implicate me, but I promise you this: I'm never going to prison and nobody is going to kill me on account of this case." The military visitor had apparently told Chanax that El Chino Iván was living in luxury in Costa Rica and that the Public Ministry was preparing to betray Chanax. Jorge Garciá, upset to learn that Chanax's whereabouts had been discovered, reassured him that none of this was true.

Rubén Chanax clarified one of the puzzling elements in the witnesses' testimony. In their separate statements to the police on the night of the bishop's murder, Chanax and El Chino Iván had contradicted each other about what had happened after the shirtless man had left the park. In Chanax's version, the man had returned, walking down the avenue, buttoning on a white shirt; in El Chino Iván's version, it was a beige shirt and he walked directly into the park. El Chino Iván even claimed to have sold the stranger cigarettes. In his conversations in Mexico, Rubén Chanax revealed that the shirtless man had never returned at all; he said that both versions were untrue. "I made that part up," Chanax confessed. "El Chino and I had the mission of confusing the investigation."

ONE WAY of possibly resolving the contradictory accounts about the crucial minutes following Bishop Gerardi's murder was to bring Rubén Chanax and El Chino Iván face to face. In November 2003, Mario Domingo, Jorge Garciá—who had recently become the special prosecutor in the case—and two observers from MINUGUA went to Mexico City. They told Chanax to meet them near the Zócalo, the city's enormous central plaza. The lawyers arrived with El Chino Iván, who'd been brought from Costa Rica for the surprise reunion. While El Chino Iván behaved as if he were overjoyed to be reunited with his old friend, Chanax clearly felt betrayed and fell into a sulk.

The lawyers took the witnesses to a hotel suite they had rented nearby. There, El Chino Iván recited his original story. He'd left Don Mike's minutes after Rubén Chanax had. When he reached the park, he'd glimpsed Chanax speaking with the shirtless man in front of the garage door. Realizing that he'd left his cigarettes behind in the store, he'd turned back, retrieved them, and then returned to the park. El Chino Iván said that he was away from the park only two or three minutes. That, he claimed, was when he had his encounter with the shirtless man. (Now, faced with lawyers and UN representatives instead of scruffy young Untouchables, El Chino Iván didn't repeat the suspicion he'd voiced in Costa Rica, that Hugo didn't exist.)

Rubén Chanax said that the shirtless man was barely exiting the park, on the Third Street side, when the black Jeep Cherokee entered the drive on the Second Street side. According to Chanax, it had all happened—the shirtless man exiting the garage, Lima and Villanueva arriving—within a few minutes. So if El Chino Iván was away only two or three minutes, as he insisted, how could it be that he hadn't seen Captain Lima and Obdulio Villanueva arrive to alter the crime scene? Because, insisted Rubén Chanax, El Chino Iván was away from the park much longer than two or three minutes.

Mario Domingo was convinced that Chanax's version was the true one, or at least the truer one, and he had a private conversation with El Chino Iván in which the *bolito* finally admitted that he might, actually, have been away from the park longer than he originally stated. He said he didn't remember. "Maybe I was away longer," he stammered. "Maybe ten minutes." El Chino Iván had probably never seen the shirtless man. His claim that he'd seen the man now known as Hugo may have been premeditated disinformation, or simply a lie.

Rubén Chanax said that the original plan had been for Hugo and El Chino Iván to fake a robbery in the church, but El Chino Iván panicked and ran away. He returned to the garage at the San Sebastián parish house, but only after Captain Lima and Obdulio Villanueva had come and gone. The plan was that he and Chanax would say nothing, but when the police arrived, El Chino Iván told them that Chanax had seen everything, and the police took Chanax away. During those first interrogations, Chanax had revealed little more than his encounter with the shirtless man. Then El Chino Iván, once he was in custody too, had invented his own contradictory version.

El Chino Iván now repeated the story about how he, not Father Mario, had closed the door of the garage. Chanax, he said, had warned him, "You don't know what just happened there inside the garage. And now you've left fingerprints and your DNA on the door." Worried, El Chino Iván had spat on a piece of cardboard to wipe the door clean. His tone grew nearly hysterical as he insisted on his version. Chanax diffidently shrugged and agreed: "*Así fue.*" That's how it was. But later he said, "If you want to believe him, believe him. If you want to believe me, believe me."

Of course it was maddening, for the story made little sense. That El Chino Iván had tried to wipe away his "DNA" with his own spit seemed plausible. But it was harder to believe that he hadn't at least peeked through the open door, into the illuminated garage, to see what had happened there. On the other hand, might Rubén Chanax have lied after all when he said that he'd rung the doorbell, and that Father Mario had come to the little garage door in his long black leather coat and closed the door? Was that story completely credible? What was Father Mario, in his black leather coat, doing in the garage, alone with the bishop's corpse?

What if both El Chino Iván and Rubén Chanax were lying about that particular moment and incident? Rafael Guillamón later told me what he thought had occurred immediately after the murder, after Hugo (if indeed Hugo existed), Captain Lima, and Villanueva (and whoever else) had come to and gone from the scene of the crime. Rubén Chanax, he believed, had then entered the parish house from the garage and walked down the corridor to Father Mario's bedroom door. He had knocked at the door to let the priest know that the gruesome deed had been accomplished. That would explain, Guillamón surmised, the traces of blood found later outside Father Mario's door. Of course if that *was* what had happened, it was not something Chanax was going to admit. Chanax would have found another way to reveal the priest's involvement, while suppressing his own. It wasn't as if Father Mario would then counter that "lie" with the true, equally incriminating version.

Chanax did not lack imagination. A good, even trained, observer, he noticed people, how they spoke, how they moved, what they wore. He knew how to shape his information (factual or not) into a narrative. He withheld information to protect himself, but also others. One key to deciphering Chanax was to decipher his secret loyalties, some emotional and others tactical. Whatever else it was, Chanax's saga was also about staying alive. Any number of missteps might have cost him his life. By the spring of 2003, nearly two years after the trial, it seemed that Guatemalan Military Intelligence knew exactly where to find him. Yet Rubén Chanax was still alive.

Chanax had told the interrogators from MINUGUA that El Chino Iván was in "G-2 counterintelligence." Those who believed that El Chino Iván was working for G-2 also believed that his and Rubén Chanax's roles were complementary. Chanax's job had been to watch and inform on Bishop Gerardi. El Chino Iván's job had been to watch and inform on Chanax. If Chanax told the Public Ministry or police interrogators one thing, it was El Chino Iván's role to tell them another.

As witnesses they were, indeed, "less than ideal." It was all enough to drive an earnest, dogged lawyer like Mario Domingo crazy. Often, when talking about the two witnesses, he grew outraged, and his squinty expression became contorted. "They're both *hijos de puta*," he'd exclaim, "and they were both in on the plan. But one kept quiet and stayed in his role. The one who talked because he finally got bored and fed up was Rubén Chanax!"

In April 2004 Helen Mack won her case against the Guatemalan state. The Inter-American Court of Human Rights—the Hague of the Americas—ruled unanimously that the murder of Myrna Mack had been planned and carried out by a clandestine intelligence unit within the EMP. In a landmark decision, the judges outlined the modus operandi by which the Army and government had employed state institutions and even civilian entities to stall and misdirect criminal investigations and prosecutions. They addressed the manner in which courts were incorporated into the military's strategies and examined the role of judges who knowingly abused the appeals process and who applied specious arguments in their rulings. The decision identified courts and judges that had acted in concert with the military throughout the long history of the Mack case, including Wilewaldo Contreras's Fourth Court of Appeals.

The judges of the Inter-American Court of Human Rights described the various stages of a politically motivated homicide as typically carried out by the Guatemalan Army, especially by Military Intelligence. First came the preparation and planning, followed by the second stage, the actual execution of the victim. But there was a third stage, which the judges described as a continuation of the murder itself, as much a part of the crime as the prior stages. That third stage included the methods used by Military Intelligence to subvert the courts and the role of complicit judges in preventing justice from being done; and also the crucial role of misinformation, especially disseminated through the media, used to discredit opponents and create confusion.

It was in the long post-execution stage that the murder of Bishop Gerardi was especially masterful. I do not know whether particular journalists consciously spread misinformation or actually believed in the integrity of their Military Intelligence and government sources. It is reasonable to assume that when Mario Vargas Llosa wrote his essay on the Gerardi case and on the book *Who Killed the Bishop?* for *El País,* he was convinced of the truth of what he was writing. It may have been overly eager, unguarded ideological sympathy or prejudice; or the vanity of a Great Man of Letters, seduced, after many decades of adulation, into a sense of his own infallibility; or a case of what Borges had in mind when he wrote that no man, outside his own specialty, is not gullible; or some combination of these that led the distinguished novelist to accept at face value an extraordinarily controversial book's most far-fetched assertions as facts not requiring independent verification, and then to join his voice to the book's smears and accusations.

3

"BUENO, ITS NOW ALMOST ELEVEN *in the morning on monday who knows why i'm writing this because if i don't get out of this i hope that this gets to the press so that they will know who i was in truth and that i'm not how they say . . . if i end up dead or far from here because now i only have two roads in all this but like i said that's life but i'm not afraid because there's no reason i should be. but if they capture that rat i hope he suffers because what he did has no pardon because someone like el padre didn't deserve that kind of death. the way they gave it to him.*"

That, with no attempt to faithfully translate misspellings—although the writer's forgoing of most capital letters has been retained—is from a twenty-six-page diary kept by Rubén Chanax from July to August 1998, when he and El Chino Iván had been in police custody for three months. Across its first page was scrawled the title: "*Thoughts and memories from the Hotel Monterrey.*" In those pages, Chanax more than once asked himself if he'd done the right thing by becoming a witness, wondered what the future held for him, and acknowledged the risks he was taking. "*i get out of this, or they'll kill me.*" Repeatedly, he wrote about being depressed and bored by his confinement. "*You don't even notice if there's any sun . . . one day they took us to the police station and there was sun but when we came out everything was black with ashes from the volcano and like i said one of these days it will rain fire and i won't even notice."*

Sometimes Chanax wrote about how much he missed his friends in the San Sebastián park, whom he considered his *"true family."* He wrote, *"Tried to find my mother with the police with mimigua* [MINUGUA] *but they came and told me she didn't want to know anything about me. that i'm a thief but that's a lie because none of the people in the park who know me would make those kinds of comments about me . . . i'm too deep into all this and how am i going to get out of this i have no one unlike the other* [El Chino Iván] *he has family they visit . . . a while ago they celebrated his birthday he said come with me and my family and i didn't accept for one reason because with me from the day i was born nobody ever celebrated mine nor do I think they ever will. Bueno, i'll go on tomorrow."*

New entry: *"Bueno Here i am again and i'm too angry and sad . . . it's now three months that i've been shut in and i'm too bored what i need is simple some T-shirts, some pants some shoes and to go to the movies three times a week . . . before I write more I want to make clear i am not doing this out of any interest and as for being a false witness, i am not that. and anyway, i don't care who ends up guilty whoever it is i don't care. bueno, this is what i saw that night, at around 6 i got to san Sebastián park."*

Here Rubén Chanax dutifully scrawled the familiar story: his instant soup, Don Mike's, going back to the parish house, the shirtless man stepping from the garage. *"i didn't know that person so I didn't give it much importance . . . characteristics of that person height about one meter seventy* [five feet eight inches] *color of skin brown a round face hair cut in a military style large eyes normal nose and beard in the goatee style. he was wearing black caterpillar boots blue pants discolored old without a shirt. he came back with a shirt. then the other one came and everything ended i didn't sleep that was about ten thirty p.m."*

His writing changes when he gives his description of the shirtless man (to whom he didn't give *"much importance"*), suggesting a practiced method of remembering and writing down people's physical characteristics and attire. Of course he knew that prosecutors or investigators were likely to read his little diary; he had to be careful what he wrote there. But who, after all, was "Hugo"? Why couldn't, or wouldn't, Chanax tell prosecutors who he was, or where to find him? They were little closer to identifying him than when he'd been known only as the "shirtless man." He was believed to be an assassin from Military Intelligence, his identity closely guarded, protected by several aliases.

One of the most convincing suggestions about Hugo's true identity was produced by none other than Fernando Penados, when he was working as an investigator for Edgar Gutiérrez, the first civilian head of the Secretariat of Strategic Analysis. Fernando wrote a report on one "Roberto Rodríguez García, alias 'Hugo' el Karateca. Identity card number e-05 47015," born in 1966 in Santa Lucía Cotzumalguapa, Escuintla, in the hot southern lowlands. He was a former Kaibil counterinsurgency soldier, a parachutist, and, reported Fernando, "a member of the EMP under Arzú and for a while under Portillo, until he began to feel '*localizado*,'" or close to being identified. "But they tell me he's still on active duty in Military Intelligence."

No photograph of Hugo el Karateca was found, but a tiny photo taken for Roberto Rodríguez García's identity card when he was eighteen was located. Leopoldo Zeissig blew it up on his computer screen and called Rubén Chanax into his office. An assistant prosecutor later told Mario Domingo that Chanax went stiff with fright at the sight of the image. But Zeissig told me that he hadn't noticed any reaction in Chanax at all. At any rate, when Zeissig asked, Chanax said he didn't recognize the person. The photo, however, depicted a "Hugo"—if he was the same man—at about half the age he'd been on the night of the murder.

RUBÉN CHANAX WAS LIVING in a notoriously seedy barrio in Mexico City, a city of more than 23 million inhabitants. To say that he was working again as a *taquero* is not to give much away. The number of taco stands in that city could be a metaphor for infinity; a lifetime might not be long enough to visit every one. I first met Chanax in February 2005. I was just passing through and had to be back in New York the next day. A friend from Guatemala, someone Chanax trusted, was there for the weekend. We went to the taco stand and found Chanax at work.

Rubén Chanax was smaller of stature than I'd imagined, but also brawnier. The backs of his strong, knotty hands had several large warts. He had classic Mayan features—the sloping nose and forehead—and a melancholy air. His large, black, deerlike eyes gave him a boyish aspect. That day we spoke only briefly. He had to return to work. I told Chanax that I would be back in a few weeks, and that I hoped we'd be able to talk. Chanax said it was best to look for him before he started work in the afternoon. He lived in a shabby little apartment building directly across the street from the taco stand.

I didn't have a chance to return until three months later, in May. Because Chanax's apartment had no doorbell, he'd told me that I should stand on the sidewalk and call up to his window. The pane was broken, covered by black plastic garbage bags. I was worried that he wouldn't remember me. From the sidewalk, I shouted his name, and after a while the black plastic was tugged back and Rubén Chanax's face appeared. He called down that I should go around to the front. He came to the door in floppy shorts and a baggy T-shirt. It was eleven in the morning, but he seemed sleepy, and his eyes were bloodshot. He glanced nervously up and down the street. I suggested we go somewhere nearby to talk and invited him to breakfast, but he seemed hesitant to accept the offer. As we stood in the door talking, two men appeared, one middle-aged, the other young, and took him aside and spoke with him out of my earshot. They were neighbors. They knew something about his situation, apparently, and looked out for him. I remembered that these same men, or at least the younger one, had appeared during that first visit three months before.

So I followed Chanax inside and climbed the stairs to his apartment—two small rooms, dark and sparely furnished. Empty beer bottles on a plastic table. An old, small couch and plastic chairs. Posters of Thalia and other bikini-clad nearly preadolescent-looking Mexican female pop stars were hung on the walls overlooking his tiny, almost criblike bed. On this visit and subsequent visits I noticed that the lights—if indeed he had working electricity—were never on. We sat in facing chairs in the dark front room. At first, we mainly went over the known, familiar story.

But some of what he talked about that day, if not new information to the prosecutors or to ODHA, was new to me. The information fit with what I was learning elsewhere during that spring and summer of 2005, when, in some ways, the Gerardi case finally seemed to be cracking open, as if pressured from inside by fermenting gases kept too long in airless dark.

The night of April 26, 1998, in Don Mike's store, Chanax told me, he'd thought it was just a coincidence when the three military men came in: Colonel Lima; a powerful general and former head of the EMP, Otto Pérez Molina; and another man. "Later I learned that he was Colonel Reyes Palencia," said Chanax. Reyes Palencia was head of the Presidential Guard, third in the EMP's chain of command. A few months after my first encounter with Chanax, when I met in Europe with Rafael Guillamón, he confirmed that Chanax hadn't known who Reyes Palencia was that night. Later Guillamón had shown Chanax photographs of military officers, asking him to pick out the men he'd seen in Don Mike's. Chanax was able to name Colonel Lima and General Pérez Molina, but when he identified Colonel Reyes Palencia by his photograph, he didn't know he'd picked out one of the EMP's highest-ranking officers.

General Pérez Molina had been head of the EMP during the presidency of Ramiro de León Carpio, from 1993 to 1996, coin-

ciding with Rubén Chanax's military service. Chanax was discharged in July 1994. Rafael Guillamón believed it was not Colonel
Lima but Pérez Molina, or EMP operatives under Pérez Molina's
command, who had originally recruited Chanax as an informer. If
Chanax felt loyalty to General Pérez Molina, it would explain why
he'd suppressed the name from his official testimony. (Captain
Lima had pointedly included General Pérez Molina among those
he was sending "subliminal messages" to during his interview
with Claudia Méndez in March 2001.) Rubén Chanax didn't tell
me that General Pérez Molina had recruited him. He spoke about
meeting the general when he was in the Army Corps of Engineers,
"and what an honor it was to meet a man like that." Ever since he
was a little boy, living in Huehuetenango with the family that had
bought him from his mother, Chanax told me, he'd looked up to
soldiers and liked being around them.

General Otto Pérez Molina represented the military during the
Peace Accords negotiations. He was one of the principal architects
of the amnesty. In 1996, the year the accords were signed, the
New York Times reported that in the early 1990s, when then-
Colonel Pérez Molina was the head of Military Intelligence, he'd
ordered the murder of the captured guerrilla Efraín Bámaca. He
issued the orders *after* Bámaca's wife, the American lawyer Jennifer Harbury, had begun a highly publicized campaign to pressure
the United States and Guatemalan governments to reveal her
husband's whereabouts. Nevertheless, in 1998, during Arzú's
presidency, Pérez Molina was appointed the Guatemalan delegate
to the Inter-American Defense Board in Washington, DC. A few
nights after Bishop Gerardi's murder, Pérez Molina had dinner in
Guatemala City with Jean Arnault, the UN Mission chief. Arnault
told Rafael Guillamón that he was struck by the general's stony
reticence when the subject of the murder was raised.

Rubén Chanax told me that on the day Bishop Gerardi was murdered, he'd met Villanueva and Quesén in the park in the morning
and they'd instructed him to return at ten that night. They were

going to give him some things that were to be stolen from inside the church. (Later that summer Guillamón told me that Quesén had belonged to the EMP's anti-kidnapping commando unit.) *"Una carota de Indio,"* a big fat Indian face—that was how Chanax described Hugo to me, holding his hands wide apart as if to emphasize what, he reiterated, "a big black ugly Indio face" it really was. *"Bien mamado, con brazotes"*—super well-built, with great big arms. We went through that whole story again. Mere minutes after the shirtless Hugo stepped out of the garage, the black Jeep Cherokee had driven up, and Captain Lima and Obdulio Villanueva had both gotten out of the backseat. Chanax didn't see the driver. "Come here, *hijoeputa*," said Lima, "you're going to help us." Lima gave him rubber medical gloves. So much blood! They turned the bishop's body over on his back, and pulled the body farther in. . . . Captain Lima, said Chanax, picked a lens from Bishop Gerardi's eyeglasses off the garage floor and put it in the leather pocket inside the VW's front door. When they were done, Lima collected Chanax's rubber gloves, put them into a little bag with the others, and said, "If you talk, there's this"—and Rubén Chanax mimed Lima wagging the little bag of gloves.

I asked him about his job as an informer in Operation Bird, spying on Bishop Gerardi. He was paid every fifteen days, he told me, sometimes 1,000 quetzales, sometimes less—the amount varied. Sometimes he went over to the Secretariat of Strategic Analysis on Callejón del Manchén and was paid by a secretary named Alejandra (supposedly the same woman who'd borne Captain Lima's child, to whom he'd written a letter explaining that he couldn't send child support because he was spending all his money paying for witnesses). He wrote reports and took them to the secretary; sometimes he phoned them in. "The bird has flown," he was supposed to say, when Bishop Gerardi had left the parish house. Sometimes, said Chanax, he went out to the house in Zone 6 to give his reports and collect his pay.

Chanax described his education as an informer for Military Intelligence, back when he'd been in the Army Corps of Engineers and had been selected for the course. "First, came the theoretical," he told me, sounding like a diligent student. The theoretical included learning how to befriend people one was to spy on. "You have to reach them slowly. First, you find a way to help them in something." Or, he said, you might come by their house looking for work. What if, theoretically speaking, the spy wants a job as a gardener in order to infiltrate the house, but the subject already has a gardener? "Then I pay that person to leave," said Chanax. But what if the gardener doesn't want to leave? "I tell someone else, and that person disappears," said Chanax. "Then I come by and ask for work."

After Rubén Chanax had graduated from the theoretical, he was taught to murder in the stealthy manner of an intelligence agent. He described how you tie two knots into a length of rope, about two inches apart, so that, once you've mastered the technique, you can wrap the rope around a victim's neck and break his windpipe in five seconds. Fishing line, tied between two pieces of wood, was also effective for a fast, silent kill. As I watched Chanax illustrate how to strangle by that method, with his strong, warty hands, my mood changed. I felt frightened of being alone with him in the dark little apartment. When he got up to go to the bathroom, I waited, tense with irrational fear.

We spoke also about the incident at the Incienso Bridge, the "final exam" he'd told Mario Domingo about, in which he and his fellow trainees had been ordered to murder a couple. Their instructors, said Chanax, drove him and two classmates to the bridge in the jeep that night. Chanax told me that he'd turned back and let the other two murder the couple. As punishment for his cowardice, he was punched and beaten all over his body, right there in the jeep.

According to Chanax, one of his former instructors, an officer named Eric Lainfiesta Cáceres, had recently tracked him to the little street where he now lived. At the corner newsstand, Lainfiesta Cáceres had told the old woman vendor that his friend Rubén Chanax had been arrested, and that he needed to know where he lived so that he could fetch his identification papers and

get him out of jail. But the news vendor refused to help the in-
quisitive stranger. Lainfiesta Cáceres, said Chanax, cornered him
soon after outside a nearby movie theater. Chanax said that he
offered him money to change and retract his testimony. He only
had to say that he'd been pressured into giving false testimony at
the trial. Lainfiesta Cáceres acknowledged that Chanax would
probably have to spend about two years in jail as punishment for
giving false testimony, but promised, "Don't worry, we'll take care
of you." When Chanax got out of prison, he would be well set up
financially. Chanax knew who to contact when he decided; they
would help him cross back into Guatemala from Chiapas. It would
look as if he'd acted of his own volition.

Rubén Chanax said that he'd told his former officer, "I'll think
about it. Give me two days." Then Chanax didn't show up for
their next meeting.

"If I went to prison," Chanax flatly asserted, "they'd kill me
there."

A subsequent check of Lainfiesta Cáceres's immigration records
revealed that he did frequently travel to Mexico and as of 2005 was
still doing so. Later I was able to confirm that in President Arzú's
government, Lainfiesta Cáceres had belonged to the SAE. He was
second in command under Colonel Otto Spiegler in a unit of intelligence operatives.

In response to my perhaps unavoidably leading question of
whether he felt any guilt about Bishop Gerardi's death, Chanax
softly answered, "*Parece que sí*—it seems that way. I owed something to Monseñor. He was always good to me. . . . It was so cruel
the way they did it. He'd never harmed anyone. He was just trying to write his book." Chanax possessed a somewhat crude
understanding of what the Recuperation of Historical Memory
project and report had been about. "They say Colonel Lima killed
400 people inside a church. And that was going to come out, and
he didn't want it to."

Chanax was aching to return to Guatemala. He had no family
he could rely on, yet said he missed his family. He beseeched me

to ask Jorge García, when I was next in Guatemala, to get in touch with his mother and let her know that he was OK. But he admitted that he was too frightened to go back.

"Be careful with him," Mario Domingo had warned about Chanax. "He's very crafty and able. He's always playing misinformation off against the truth." I suspected that some of what Chanax had told me wasn't true. (I didn't believe his self-exculpatory account of what had happened at the Incienso Bridge.) But I didn't doubt that if Chanax were willing to further implicate himself in the murder of Bishop Gerardi, he could also implicate others. Chanax was full of secrets. His secret information, in his lonely world, must, by then, have been entwined with his most intimate sense of self, providing him with a sense of power and control, even of movie-like glamour and drama.

Rubén Chanax said that he sometimes had nightmares about what he'd seen in the parish house garage on the night of the murder, that he woke up sleepwalking in the little apartment, trying to escape, to run away. He recalled how frightened he'd been that first night when he'd returned to Guatemala City to testify in the trial. He'd slept on a couch in the prosecutors' office. There were trees in back of the office, and all night he could hear the rustling of wind in the leaves, and he'd felt frightened.

MUCH HAD CHANGED IN GUATEMALA, and much had remained the same. The former PAN Party Mayor of Guatemala City, Oscar Berger, had been elected president in December 2003. He'd switched places with his former mentor, President Álvaro Arzú, who was now mayor. Berger's predecessor as president, Alfonso Portillo, was in Mexico. The Guatemalan courts were seeking to have Portillo extradited to face corruption charges. Before leaving office, Portillo, pressured by his foreign minister, Edgar Gutiérrez —as well as by MINUGUA and the U.S. embassy—had at last come through on his promise to shut down the Presidential Military Staff, the EMP. It was replaced by a new entity, called the Secretariat for Administrative and Security Matters, which was under the command of a former guerrilla. Conceived as a highly professional and apolitical security service, the new unit had received training from Spain, the United States, Israel, and other countries.

Why had Portillo waited until the end of his term to close down the EMP? Because it served as a source of secret funds for him, and was also the operational center of his own covert political operations. Now there was no longer an EMP, with its clandestine presidential intelligence unit. But Military Intelligence and the Cofradía, current and former high-ranking officers from the G-2 (or whatever it was calling itself at that moment), remained entrenched at the heart of power and organized crime.

Most significantly for Guatemala, MINUGUA's mandate had expired at the end of 2004. Though few of the terms of the Peace Accords had been implemented, the UN mission had closed its doors. MINUGUA's aggressive monitoring in the Gerardi case had protected witnesses, judges, prosecutors, and others. MINUGUA had helped Guatemala's fledgling apparatus of justice, however wobbly, to go forward. The justice system's few successes, such as the convictions in the Gerardi case, could be seen as a validation of the multilateral "democratic institutions building" in which the UN mission, along with the United States and European Union donor nations, had been engaged. But the overall weakness of the Guatemalan justice system and its other institutions; the seemingly ineradicable culture of impunity, corruption, and abuse of power; the ever-worsening violence engulfing the country; and the mostly stagnant reform process underlined the limits of such efforts. Real change had to come from Guatemalans themselves, from those who were willing to fight for it, risking everything. As the Gerardi case had shown, sometimes individuals and groups were up to that nearly impossible and dangerous task.

ONE EVENING IN THE SUMMER of 2004, I had met in a café in Zone 10 with Claudia Méndez, from *elPeriódico*, and the two Untouchables, Rodrigo Salvadó and Arturo Aguilar. All three had come of age during the years of their involvement in the Gerardi case, nearly a quarter of their lives so far. Claudia Méndez had gone from being a novice reporter to an award-winning, internationally respected professional journalist, while also pursuing a master's degree in literature. Rodrigo Salvadó was finishing his university thesis for his master's degree in anthropology, and Arturo Aguilar, no longer living at home with his parents, was soon to graduate from law school. Arturo was married and Rodrigo was soon to be.

That night I asked my young friends how they would feel if the convictions were invalidated and the Limas were set free. After having devoted so much of their lives to the case, would they feel that their work had been in vain? Would they think that they had wasted years in a futile battle? Not at all, they answered. They all agreed: even if the Limas went free, they would have no personal regrets. Working on the Gerardi case had been the great and transforming experience of their lives so far. Of course it was all worthwhile, no matter what the outcome.

ON MARCH 11, 2005, nearly seven years after the murder of Bishop Gerardi, attorneys for the defense, the prosecution, and ODHA, along with the imprisoned surviving defendants, finally convened in a courtroom for the decisive appeals hearing. During the transition from the Portillo government to the Berger government, there had been a reshuffling and restructuring of the courts. The Fourth Court of Appeals had simply been renamed the Second Court of Appeals, but Wilewaldo Contreras, whom ODHA had fought a four-year battle to recuse, was no longer one of its three judges. Three hundred spectators packed the courtroom that day. Outside and inside, people carried posters demanding justice for the bishop's murder, or for the Limas to be freed. The crowd included a large and noisy contingent of military men, prominent figures of the Guatemalan right, and the U.S. ambassador, John Hamilton. (His predecessor, Prudence Bushnell, was now the dean of the State Department's School of Foreign Service.)

The defense attorneys, as expected, made Rubén Chanax the center of their arguments: Chanax had lied. Later I was told—and saw for myself on videotape—that both Mario Domingo and Jorge García were nervous and hesitant. They were intimidated by the show of military force in the courtroom.

The Limas were allowed to speak. The blustery Colonel Byron Lima Estrada, who went first, said he couldn't understand a word that the special prosecutor, Jorge García, had said. The courtroom exploded in derisive laughter and shouts, especially from the front row, which was lined with military men. When Jorge García rose and addressed the judges, he was livid, shaking with anger. He'd treated the defense attorneys and the defendants with respect, he said, and demanded the same.

The presiding judge, Thelma del Cid, warned against any more provocations from the defendants or the spectators. Colonel Lima continued, denying his involvement in the murder. Waving his finger in the air, the colonel thundered: "In the Army we don't kill with rocks. In the Army we kill with bullets!"

Captain Lima spoke next. He accused Ambassador Hamilton of exerting pressure on the court. Again Judge del Cid interceded. Captain Lima indignantly responded, "What? After five years of prison, I don't have the right to talk?" Jorge García had prepared false witnesses, he said. And Monseñor Efraín Hernández, "who claims to preach the word of God, is dying of cancer in the hospital while his daughter [Ana Lucía Escobar] travels to Spain. And with whose money? Alfonso Portillo's money. Edgar Gutiérrez is the one who is responsible for everything! He and his second in command, Ronalth Ochaeta!"

Captain Lima continued, "God has forgiven me for what I had to do in prison to maintain my family," and the courtroom erupted in emotional applause. He then turned his attention to ODHA. Nery Rodenas, warned the captain, was the one who would suffer God's vengeance. "Not now, but when your sons are grown. The punishment comes in the fourth generation!"

Captain Lima also said, "Father Mario Orantes doesn't know anything. I can assure you that if the Father knew something, he'd already be dead."

Lima's defense of Father Mario was interesting. It was, I think, a clumsy attempt to cover one of the most gaping holes in the thesis that Ana Lucía Escobar and the Valle del Sol gang had played a role in the murder. That scenario, as Captain Lima had reiterated, remained central to his defense. But in every hypothetical version the scenario depended on a connection between Father Mario and Ana Lucía. Blanca Lidia Contreras, who had come from Canada to give the testimony from which the Valle del Sol scenario emerged, had portrayed the two as linked in depravity and criminality since Ana Lucía's childhood. (In their book, de la Grange and Rico even cited private telephone calls between Father Mario and Ana Lucía that they said had been intercepted by Military Intelligence. "Of the intercepted phone calls, one in particular had caught their attention: a morbid dialogue, with strange sexual insinuations, that the priest had with the girl tied to organized crime.") Yet, for the duration of a long court trial and five years of prison, the Limas and their attorneys had never challenged or called attention to Father Mario's incredible account of his nonparticipation in the crime, or pressured him to admit a connection to Ana Lucía and her gang. Why was that? Because there was little they dreaded more than Father Mario's confessing what he really knew about the murder?

THE COURT ANNOUNCED its verdict eleven days later, on March 22, Holy Tuesday. Private planes flew over Guatemala City trailing banners that read, "Free the Limas," and "Edgar Gutiérrez did it." Outside the courthouse, dozens of children stood holding signs calling for the Limas to be freed. They turned out to be street children who'd been hired by Álvaro Arzú, the current mayor. *ElPeriódico* reported that they were each paid fifty quetzales (about six dollars), nearly double the legal minimum wage for a day's work in Guatemala.

The appellate court ruled that day in a way nobody had expected. In a plea bargain of sorts with the defense, the charges against the Limas were downgraded from their being coauthors to accomplices, and their sentences were lowered from thirty to twenty years. (Father Mario's status remained the same.) The prosecution's and ODHA's fundamental accusation—that Bishop Gerardi's murder was a crime of state—was upheld. The degree of the Limas' culpability had been called into question, but, still, ODHA felt vindicated. This was much better than what they had been steeling themselves for. Shortly afterward, when I returned to Guatemala, I could sense, viscerally, what a relief the ruling had been. Mario Domingo seemed physically transformed, more relaxed. His rosy-cheeked complexion had returned. Now, finally, all that was left was for the Supreme Court to affirm the appellate court's ruling, and the case could finally, four years after the original trial, proceed to the potentially explosive next stage, in which more important and powerful men than the Limas could be charged with the murder.

THE PROSECUTORS AND ODHA were getting closer to an understanding of what had happened inside the EMP on the night of the murder: who had been on duty and who hadn't, what divisions, what subdivisions, which officers and specialists, and so on. Penetrating the miasma of secrecy and deception had been a long and daunting struggle. But when Portillo had finally closed the EMP at the end of his term, many low-ranking EMP specialists found themselves without jobs. A few of them had begun to talk.

One was Osmel Olivares Alay. In September 1999, he'd been asked by his commanding officer to assert publicly that Jorge Aguilar Martínez, the EMP waiter who was a key witness about who came and went from the EMP the night of the murder, couldn't have been at the security office then because he'd been with Olivares Alay in the National Palace on janitorial duty—just as Colonel Rudy Pozuelos, the head of the EMP, had insisted. But during a visit to ODHA five years later, after the closing of the

EMP, Olivares Olay told Arturo Aguilar, the youngest Untouchable, that now he wanted to tell the truth, which was this: "Ninety percent of what Aguilar Martínez said is true." Olivares Alay was extremely nervous about having come to the ODHA office. What if Military Intelligence found out? Arturo Aguilar agreed to wait for Olivares Alay to contact him again, to arrange another time and place to speak. Months passed, and he wasn't heard from.

It turned out that Olivares Alay had done what some 10 percent of Guatemala's population of 14 million had done. He'd struck out for the United States, making the long illegal journey across Mexico. Olivares Alay was in Washington, D.C. Mario Domingo's wife, Jessica, was from West Virginia and Mario took advantage of a family visit to contact Olivares Alay to arrange a meeting. Mario was instructed to go to a certain street corner and look for someone in jeans, a red T-shirt, and a baseball cap. Olivares Alay had found a job painting houses in the suburbs of Washington. They went to a nearby coffee shop and Olivares Alay told Mario that, on the night of the murder, he and Aguilar Martínez had indeed been scheduled for janitorial duty in the National Palace between eight PM and one AM. But Aguilar Martínez had left soon after arriving for his shift, and he didn't return until precisely one, in an agitated and sweaty state. He then told Olivares Alay that Monseñor Gerardi had been murdered. Olivares Alay didn't make much of that information, because he didn't know who Gerardi was. He said he didn't give it more thought until August 1999, when Aguilar Martínez, having given his testimony, left the country.

Colonel Rudy Pozuelos had held meetings with a few EMP specialists after Aguilar Martínez testified. "We felt like a privileged group," Olivares Alay told Mario Domingo. The men agreed to allow their names to appear on a newly drawn-up *ordenes de cuerpo,* a list of men who supposedly were on duty in the EMP on the night of the murder. Olivares Alay was asked to sign a notarized document attesting that Aguilar Martínez had been with him throughout their shift in the National Palace. He gave Mario Domingo a photocopy of that document. So where was Aguilar Martínez between eight and one in the morning, hours during which the operation to murder Bishop Gerardi was taking place? Was he exactly where he'd said, in the Security Services office near the EMP Guard Command gate? Or, like Rubén Chanax, had even he, in his depositions implicating others, suppressed his own greater participation in the crime? At the trial the defense lawyers had never attempted to call Aguilar Martínez as a witness, as they had Chanax and Gómez Limón; nor had they drawn attention to the account of the crime in his deposition. They hadn't even summoned Olivares Alay to repeat his story about both men being on duty in the National Palace.

JUST AS JORGE GARCIÁ AND ODHA seemed ready to push ahead, armed with new information against high-ranking figures, the Public Ministry suddenly disbanded the office of special prosecutor for the Gerardi case. Jorge García remained, technically, in charge, but he had to report to another prosecutor, a former military man, and his team of assistant prosecutors was broken up. President Berger's government would not support prosecutors who wanted to go forward with the Gerardi case. Berger had been elected as head of a new party filled with old Arzú loyalists and backed by General Otto Pérez Molina. Berger's vice president, Eduardo Stein, had been Arzú's foreign minister and a member of the High Commission he appointed to oversee the Gerardi investigation.

BY 2005, EDGAR GUTIÉRREZ, who had been the coordinator of the REMHI report and then had served in President Portillo's government, was running his own small political consulting firm, writing a newspaper column, and publishing an online political journal that mixed reprinted articles by renowned American and European intellectuals with articles by Central American writers. Gutiérrez was jokingly referred to by his friends as "Dr. Satan." No one had been more demonized than he by the critics of the Portillo government. So far, a dozen members of that government had been imprisoned or were under indictment on a variety of corruption charges, including Portillo himself, yet Gutiérrez had not been targeted. It was hard to believe that he would have escaped the wave of criminal investigations and indictments if there were any evidence against him of any type of malfeasance. He was living like a man who had nothing to fear from the law, although he had the most tensely alert, jumpiest bodyguard I think I've ever met.

MINUGUA's final report on Guatemala said that under Gutiérrez's leadership the Secretariat of Strategic Analysis had been transformed into a civilian information-gathering and analysis agency that no longer engaged in covert operations. Indeed, Fernando Penados had been fired by Gutiérrez from the SAE for engaging in activity that transgressed the new mandates for behavior. In late 2000, when Captain Lima held a press conference in prison, Fernando had dispatched a pair of agents to impersonate reporters. Lima had quickly noticed the imposters—who were dressed preposterously, like the Blues Brothers, in black suits and dark glasses—and demanded to know what newspaper they were from. They responded by naming a newspaper that had gone out of business years before. The incident was widely reported. Amusing photographs were published of the unmasked fake reporters trying to cover their faces with their notepads as they retreated from the conference. Lima represented the incident as an ominous threat against him. Edgar Gutiérrez, who hadn't authorized Fernando Penados to indulge in any such ploys, was furious.

In early 2003, when Gutiérrez was serving as foreign minister in the Portillo government, agreements were signed establishing a special commission under UN auspices to investigate criminal networks in Guatemala—the clandestine "parallel powers" alleged to have their roots in Military Intelligence. It was to be called the Commission for the Investigation of Illegal Bodies and Clandestine Security Apparatus and was generally referred to as the CICIACS (pronounced see-syaks). It would be another international truth commission, but one legally empowered to investigate and take on the issue of impunity for organized crime linked to the Guatemalan military, police, and government. As foreign minister, Edgar Gutiérrez was deeply involved in the project, and the government was unlikely to have agreed to it without his urging. But the Guatemalan Congress, which was led by General Ríos Montt, rejected CICIACS as a violation of national sovereignty. (It certainly loomed as a violation of the impunity from prosecution of many members of Congress who were complicit in clandestine crime mafias.) President Berger had resurrected the CICIACS initiative but couldn't yet overcome the predictable resistance. Berger was perceived as a weak civilian leader even by Guatemalan standards.

Edgar Gutiérrez and I met for lunch in Mexico City during the Christmas holidays at the end of 2005. He reflected on the Limas' obsession with him. "People like the Limas can conceive of using political power in only two ways," he said. "For personal enrichment and vengeance against enemies. That's how power has always worked in Guatemala. So when I was at the SAE they looked at me and said, This guy is so clever we can't even see what he's doing. They imagined I was everywhere." They couldn't comprehend that an individual might have a concept of political power—never mind convictions—different from theirs.

I FELT AS IF I WERE LEARNING as much about the Gerardi case as I had learned in all the preceding years combined. Sometimes important sources who were indignant about the credibility given to a campaign of propaganda and smears against ODHA and the prosecutors, and who otherwise would not have talked to a journalist, decided to speak. Some of the new information centered on the role of the fearsome Major Francisco Escobar Blas, who had been implicated in the murder by Aguilar Martínez. Escobar Blas had been one of the prime movers behind the efforts to promote the Valle del Sol scenario—that Ana Lucía and her cohort had murdered the bishop when he discovered they had been trafficking in items stolen from the church.

It turned out that Father Mario, who was known for his comforting bedside manner when visiting ill and elderly parishioners, used to regularly give communion to Major Escobar Blas's ailing grandmother in her home. Leopoldo Zeissig was the first to tell me that, and it was corroborated by Rafael Guillamón. Escobar Blas's mother and grandmother both lived within a few blocks of the church of San Sebastián, and he sometimes lived with one or the other of them. His mother told Rafael Guillamón that on the night Bishop Gerardi was murdered, people from the EMP were phoning the house deep into the early morning hours, looking for her son. Later, when it became impossible to deny that there had been at least two men from the EMP at the San Sebastián parish house and park that night, it was officially claimed that the photographer seen there was Specialist Darío Morales and that the tall thin man in a red baseball cap accompanying him was Major Escobar Blas—who was neither tall nor thin.

Major Escobar Blas had been a legendary figure in the war zones back when he was a pilot with elite airborne counterinsurgency units. A former combat veteran described him as the kind of soldier who liked to strut around with the head of a decapitated guerrilla dangling from each hand. A few months after Bishop Gerardi's murder, he was sent to take an advanced military course in Chile. Escobar Blas told his mother that it was "a presidential order." The mother told Rafael Guillamón that her son was receiving threatening phone calls before he left for Chile. On the very day he went away, she said, Captain Lima had come looking for him in person, but had just missed him.

Why was Captain Lima looking for, and possibly angry with, Escobar Blas? Maybe because Captain Lima's role in Bishop

Gerardi's murder had been secondary to Major Escobar Blas's, yet it was the captain who was in trouble, the captain who had been recalled from the prestigious UN mission to Cyprus, the captain whose name was in the newspapers. Meanwhile lawyers from the Oficinita were supplying Escobar Blas with an alibi and he was being sent off to Chile.

Major Escobar Blas found out that his mother had been talking to MINUGUA. He phoned her and told her to stop talking *babosadas,* foolishness.

Escobar Blas was summoned back from Chile when the court-ordered evidentiary hearings were held at the church of San Sebastián and witnesses and some suspects were asked to reenact their movements and tell what they had seen on the night of the murder. Escobar Blas was reluctant to return to Guatemala, and a message, of sorts, was conveyed to him. (MINUGUA knew the details of this incident, as did the prosecutors.) His mother came home late one night and saw a young couple embracing in the dark shadows near her front door. They pushed themselves into her house behind her. She was very brutally assaulted. As they left, one of her assailants said, "A message from Valle del Sol." If his mother couldn't recognize the message behind those words, her son, one of the creators of the Valle del Sol fiction, certainly would.

So Major Escobar Blas flew back to Guatemala and turned up at the San Sebastián church and gave his weird performance at the evidentiary proceeding as the tall, thin soldier in a red baseball cap seen by witnesses. But what was Major Escobar Blas really doing that night? Chepito Morales, a military defense lawyer, once confided, or boasted, to Rafael Guillamón, "We had to put Escobar Blas somewhere that night." He needed an alibi, and the Oficinita provided one, placing him at the crime scene. It was not illegal, after all, for the EMP to have sent agents to look in on an occurrence within its security perimeter.

"HOMOSEXUALITY WAS DEFINITELY THE KEY that opened the San Sebastián parish house to the killers," Rodrigo Salvadó said to me one rainy afternoon as we sat in the corridor by ODHA's court-yard going over details in the crime one more time. But how? To understand how the killers got into the parish house, one had to go back perhaps twenty years. Another story, as if long hidden inside one of the smaller boxes in a Chinese box—a box of fear inside a box of prudence inside a box of patient time-biding—had emerged.

In 1984, Military Intelligence had become aware of a house in Zone 4 where homosexual officers and civilians mixed at secret parties. It was known as Club Rosa. Few national armies openly tolerate homosexuality among troops, and it isn't hard to imagine how difficult it must be for a gay officer to accommodate his nature to the Guatemalan Army. The swaggering Colonel Lima, who could be described as a personification of the Army's culture of strident machismo, must not have been pleased to learn that promising young officers and cadets from the Escuela Politécnica were partying, even cross-dressing, at Club Rosa. But how to stop this activity without bringing scandal and embarrassment down on the Army at a time when it was at war and when foreign governments and the international press were keeping such a close eye on the country? This was how: a member of Club Rosa, surnamed Muñoz Martínez, was murdered, and in a particularly gruesome manner. The message was understood. Two young officers deserted and fled the country, reportedly to California, where they still reside, one operating a karate dojo there. The rest were quietly transferred to other commands and units. Some served their time in the military and eventually fell by the wayside. But others, managing to hide or master their vulnerability, marrying, producing children, went on to successful military careers. One or two turned up in the nucleus of President Arzú's EMP. (Two EMP officers mentioned in this chronicle of the Gerardi case are known to have been lovers, and were even discovered in bed together by the wife of one of the men. She then, as one former soldier told me, "shouted it from her rooftop in Colonia Lourdes.")

Twelve years later the war was over, and in those new times homosexuality was tolerated a little bit more in some sectors of

Guatemalan society, if not actually in the military or among those associated with the conservative wing of the Catholic Church. And a new incarnation, in a sense, of Club Rosa came into being. Closeted homosexuals were meeting in an elegant home in Zone 2, a neighborhood of belle epoque mansions only a few blocks from the home of Major Escobar Blas's mother. When Captain Lima was interviewed by Claudia Méndez, after his arrest, he told her about "a tryst house near the Morazán Park" in Zone 2. "They say Monseñor Hernández used to go there with Father [Mario] Orantes, along with some very wealthy lesbians." Father Mario's close friend and ordination godmother, Martha Jane Melville Novella, was said to be the owner of the house. At least one other EMP officer, a veteran of the first Club Rosa, occasionally attended the gatherings. Diego Arzú, the son of former president Arzú, was also said to be a member of the group. Diego, who was in his early twenties, had dated a niece of Martha Jane Melville Novella, which was how he was introduced into her aunt's circle.

A leaflet was circulated in Colonia Lourdes, the military officers' residential neighborhood, only days after Bishop Gerardi was killed. It claimed that on the night of the murder Captain Lima had been sent to the San Sebastián parish house to extricate Diego Arzú. In his interview with Claudia Méndez, Captain Lima denied that accusation, but he also introduced into the conversation the allegation—without refuting it—that Diego Arzú belonged to the circle that met in what he referred to as the Zone 2 *casa de citas,* which can mean a bordello, or a place of illicit trysts.

"There was definitely something going on between Diego Arzú and Father Mario Orantes," said Rafael Guillamón. Several of the park vagrants, including Rubén Chanax, had mentioned Diego Arzú's visits to the San Sebastián parish house. And a diplomat, a great admirer of President Arzú, told a former member of ODHA that Diego's "double life" was "a strong rumor among the cabinet and in the corridors of the palace." But what could the relationship have been between the priest and the aristocratic president's young son? Father Mario had worldly enthusiasms but also a spiritual side. Perhaps the priest understood the youth's travails and gave him support and counsel. Leopoldo Zeissig said that he believed, but hadn't been able to corroborate, that Bishop Gerardi's murderers had somehow exploited the link between Father Mario and Diego Arzú, especially afterward, during the cover-up.

In a press conference from prison, Captain Lima had revealed that he had in his possession receipts for the delivery order from Pollo Campero to Father Mario on the night of the murder. Father Mario had told prosecutors that he had ordered a meal from Pollo Campero; so why would Lima use the receipts in order to issue, presumably, one of his subliminal warnings? Axel Romero, Bishop Gerardi's nephew, was shown those receipts not long after the murder. The order was for two large *combos*— sixteen pieces of fried chicken and eight orders of fries. Who might have eaten all that fried chicken with Father Mario in the hours before the murder? A lover? More than one of the murderers? Did his guests surprise Father Mario? Or did they arrive at the parish house according to plan?

There are two terms that one repeatedly hears in Guatemala, especially in discussing the blend of paranoia, stealth, ruthlessness, betrayal, corruption, violence, and cunning that characterize the exercise of real and secret power. One term is *machucar la cola*— to snag the tail, step on the tail, grab hold of the tail. (General Espinosa, who collected elephant figurines, especially admired elephants because, among other reasons, they have "a very short tail that nobody can *machucar*.") Finding ways to *machucar* a rival's, a superior's, a colleague's, or a subordinate's tail is a key to getting ahead, and to survival. The second term is *chantajear*—blackmail. It's what you can do to people when you have them by the tail.

Protecting his son Diego was hardly President Arzú's only problem. The reputation and even legitimacy of his presidency were threatened by the murder of Bishop Gerardi. And there were other things that the president would not wish to see disclosed or publicly exploited by his rivals. A few of these involved his son Roberto, who had become ensnared, according to Rafael Guillamón, in the goings-on at a disco nightclub owned by EMP officers in Zone 14, where narcotics were trafficked and heavily consumed. Someone who possessed information about all this, and who was himself in a powerful position—a general, for example—would be able to bend a number of people to his will, including the president.

When Bertrand de la Grange and Maite Rico's book *Who Killed the Bishop?* was kicking up a storm in Guatemala, President Portillo asked his intelligence officers to find out what they could about who had been helping the authors. (Rico had told an admiring Guatemalan television interviewer that during the two years she and her partner spent investigating and writing the book they had lived off their savings.) Portillo was told that President Arzú had helped to fund the journalists' endeavors. The source of that information being Military Intelligence, I repeat it with natural skepticism. But it does seem worth considering in light of the strikingly proprietary manner with which Arzú displayed his enthusiasm for the book, copies of which he handed out in great numbers. Soon after the new U.S. ambassador to Guatemala, James Derham, assumed his post in 2006, he had a private meeting with Arzú, who was then the mayor of Guatemala City. The ambassador was given a copy of *Who Killed the Bishop?*

FOR ALL THE EFFORT deployed to keep them silent, people—some people—talk anyway. Not long before the murder trial got under way in the spring of 2001, a woman named Elida Mancilla Meléndez held a barbecue to celebrate the inauguration of her new house in San Lucas Sacatepéquez, near the city of Antigua. Among the guests were Archbishop Próspero Penados, two priests who'd graduated from the Adolfo Hall military academy in Cobán, and a nun, the sister of the hostess. The sisters' nephew, an EMP specialist named Julio Meléndez Crispín, was also a guest. He was tall, thin, hook-nosed, sad-eyed, and glum.

Julio Meléndez Crispín turned out to be the real reason for the barbecue. His aunts wanted their nephew to have a conversation with the archbishop. Julio Meléndez Crispín was worried about the potential repercussions of his role in the Gerardi case, and his aunts had urged him to tell Archbishop Penados "what happened that famous night." So Meléndez Crispín, as they say in Guatemala, turned over his bowl of soup. He told the archbishop that all the officers in the EMP knew what was going to happen. That many people had been contracted to monitor what went on around the park: indigents, taxi drivers, shoeshine boys, newspaper vendors, and so on. That there had long been an intelligence operation in effect against the Catholic Church and ODHA. That the murder plan was channeled through the EMP. That during the operation all the on-duty members of the EMP were confined to quarters before, during, and immediately after the murder (as the waiter specialist Aguilar Martínez had reported). And that he, Julio Meléndez Crispín, not Major Escobar Blas, was the tall man in the baseball cap who accompanied the photographer, Darío Morales, to the parish house to observe the murder scene.

Julio Meléndez Crispín said that in Captain Lima's operational group on the famous night there were only fellow veterans of the Kaibil special forces. Lima's job was to monitor the crime. Meléndez Crispín said that Father Mario had long been an informer and that both Rubén Chanax and El Chino Iván were informers too. He said that he had informed on the archbishop's nephew, Fernando Penados, with whom he had first made contact through a family friend. He said that Colonel Lima Estrada and other prominent retired combat officers had been advisers to the EMP's anti-kidnapping commando unit. He identified the person—Danilo De León Girón—in charge of deleting and burning the files on the Gerardi case in the SAE after Alfonso Portillo became president and before Edgar Gutiérrez took control of the agency.

And then Meléndez Crispín revealed to Archbishop Penados the identity of the shirtless man: Obdulio Villanueva. That too made sense. Many thought it doubtful that the planners of the crime had contrived to bring the burly Villanueva from the Antigua prison only to make a video and drag Bishop Gerardi's corpse farther into the garage.

Details of the confidential conversation between the archbishop and Meléndez Crispín reached Rafael Guillamón at MINUGUA through another guest at the barbecue, but the UN did not have a mandate to interfere in the criminal investigation. It is not known what the archbishop did with the information. Apparently nothing. Investigators at ODHA heard only a very vague description, from a nun who also attended the barbecue, of what was said.

MONSEÑOR HERNÁNDEZ, the former chancellor of the Curia, died in the spring of 2005. Archbishop Penados, who had been declining in spirit and health since the murder of Bishop Gerardi, died soon after. That same spring, during a meeting of presidents from Central America and the Dominican Republic, George W. Bush declared that he was "preoccupied by the proliferation of pressure groups in Central America, predominately aligned with the left, who are putting the stability of democracy at risk." So the primary danger to democracy didn't come from narco-militaries or government corruption or institutionalized lawlessness or the violence perpetrated by the *maras*. It came from leftist "pressure groups," by which Bush could mean only nonviolent labor union and peasant organizations, human rights organizations, elements of the Catholic Church, and so on. He didn't specify how such groups were threatening regional democracy.

The *New York Times* and other publications reported that the U.S. Drug Enforcement Administration estimated that 75 percent of the cocaine reaching the United States was being transshipped through Guatemala and that "high-level military and national police were linked to the trade." The FBI reported that thirty former Guatemalan Army Kaibiles had been hired by the Mexican "Zeta" drug cartel as assassins and instructors. In the summer of 2006, Mexicans were scandalized by a series of gruesome murders carried out against that cartel's rivals and enemies. Reporters attributed the murders to the hired Kaibil assassins. Beheadings, the reports said, were carried out in a special manner associated with the Kaibiles, using razor-sharp bayonets.

In the fall of 2005, an enormous secret-police archive of data going back for more than a century, and especially rich in information about the disappearances and political assassinations carried out during Guatemala's thirty-six-year internal war, had been found in a bat-infested, musty old munitions depot in Guatemala City. A government ombudsman, the Human Rights Procurator, took control of the mildewed archive, which promised to provide countless clues and evidence of Guatemalan atrocities. Leopoldo Zeissig had quietly returned to Guatemala that spring and was working with the ombudsman's office as a legal adviser. He was part of the team dealing with the formerly secret archive, which was said to hold sufficient files, if laid end to end, to span the length of 130 football fields.

I met with Zeissig one evening in the Austrian pastry café at the Hotel Camino Real. It was the first time we'd seen each other since I'd flown down to South America to see him when he was in exile there. We reminisced about the investigation into Bishop Gerardi's murder. "I loved the prosecutor's office and thought it was important to do a good job," he said. "I was still a dreamer about justice." But, in the end, Zeissig's motives had been called into question. The backlash against the case had been political, he said, "because of all that Monseñor Gerardi represented, and because of the forces moving around back there who wanted to kill him." Zeissig denied that he and his prosecutors had a political agenda. "Our work was strictly juridical, by the letter of the law," he said. "What personal gain have I gotten out of any of this?" Tears welled up in Zeissig's eyes. "It's idealistic maybe, but I want this country to improve. Is that like Quixote attacking windmills?"

It was hard to predict what, finally, the Geradi case would

mean for Guatemala: historic breakthrough or anomaly, precedent or fiasco? The Army and its accomplices had fought hard, cease-lessly—if not exactly courageously—to cover up their role in the murder, to spread smoky layers of confusion over every aspect of the crime, and to turn the tables on their accusers. "I have no doubts that the military did it," Fernando Penados said to me. "The problem is, go ask the people about the Bishop Gerardi case now, and they have no fucking idea what happened there."

IN THE SUMMER OF 2005, I had visited Rubén Chanax in Mexico again. I'd been warned that he was still in touch with Military Intelligence and I was nervous about being alone with him and his warty strangler's hands in the dark little apartment. So when I called up at his window and he came down—again with blood-shot eyes, and wearing basketball shorts and a big dirty T-shirt—I suggested rather strongly that we go to a restaurant. He hesitated, looking warily up and down the street, and I saw that he was as frightened of me as I was of him, although his caution was nearly instinctual. He couldn't allow himself to trust anybody.

We stepped onto the sidewalk. As before, a vigilant neighbor immediately appeared. I sensed something more than routine about the neighbor's concern this time, and in the brief, whis-pered conversation between them. As we walked down the side-walk, Chanax said that he had been trying to get transferred to another country. Maybe Argentina would take him. He wanted to be someplace else, he said, far away.

I had something on my mind that I wanted to ask him, and I decided to try to catch him off guard. "Rubén," I said, as we walked along, "people are saying that Obdulio Villanueva was the shirtless man, that he was Hugo. Is that true?" Chanax's reaction was in-stantaneous and spontaneous. He laughed, and said, "No, it was Hugo." He held his hands wide apart and asserted, as he had be-fore, that Hugo had a "big, fat, dark Indio face."

Later, when I spoke to Mario Domingo at ODHA—he harbored his own suspicion that the shirtless man might have been Villanueva—he was unsurprised by Rubén Chanax's denial. Chanax, he said, couldn't change his story now. Doing so would only raise questions about how much more he knew and had withheld and further implicate him in the crime. Mario was convinced that Rubén Chanax was in the garage and saw Bishop Gerardi beaten to death, whether by Hugo or by Villanueva, or by both of them, assuming they were not the same person. Investigators— including Jack Palladino, the private eye from San Francisco—had always maintained that there had been at least two people inside the garage, probably more. One or more men could have been inside the parish house before Bishop Gerardi arrived home that Sunday night in his VW Golf. Another man might have been outside, hiding among the *bolitos,* and followed the car inside. Then someone would have had to swing the cumbersome garage door shut. That person might even have been Rubén Chanax. Aguilar Martínez had described seeing at least three other operatives, dressed in black, getting out of the black Jeep Cherokee, along with Lima and Villanueva, when it returned to the EMP. Julio Meléndez Crispín had told the archbishop that those operatives were Lima's former fellow Kaibiles.

Rubén Chanax and I sat down in the restaurant. He ordered soup, some tacos, a Coke, but barely touched his food. We went on talking, and he began to relax. Matter-of-factly, Chanax said that he'd known Bishop Gerardi was going to be murdered months before it happened. I asked him why he hadn't mentioned that when he'd testified.

"Prosecutor Zeissig knew about it," Chanax said. But, of course, he couldn't admit that in his testimony. Hadn't I seen, he asked, how the defense attorneys had clamored for him to be arrested only on the basis of what he'd revealed in court?

"Look," said Rubén Chanax. "I'm going to tell you how it happened." Hugo, he said, had gone into the church just after the evening Mass and hidden, probably inside a confessional, waiting for the sacristan to lock up. Later, El Chino Iván was supposed to go in and steal something, or else receive stolen artifacts from Hugo, and then those artifacts from the church of San Sebastián would turn up for sale a few days later in the Zone 4 stolen goods market. "And there it would all end, and they'd be able to say it had been a robbery." But El Chino Iván had become frightened, and run away, and the robbery had never come off.

Father Mario's job, Chanax told me, had been to unlock the door connecting the church to the parish house so that Hugo could easily come into the garage.

Well, that was what many people had always suspected.

Rubén Chanax said that the day before the murder, he and Colonel Lima met briefly with Father Mario, as Mario was walking his dog in the park, to coordinate arrangements one final time. Now, I had the feeling that Chanax was fabricating a scene. It could have been someone other than the colonel, I thought, someone he doesn't want to mention. Or it might never have happened at all.

Where, at least up until 1998, one could always find Hugo, Chanax said, was at the barracks of the Fourth Corps of Engineers in Guatemala City. "He comes out for a sandwich at the stand in front every day," said Chanax. "He comes out, with that big black Indio face of his."

Chanax's tone had become easy, familiar. There was an animated light in his eyes. He was like some old, nearly forgotten actor, I thought, sought out by an admirer, the attention restoring his old glory. He even boasted a little. It had always been easy for him to win people's confidence, Chanax told me, and to make people like him. That had been his great talent as an intelligence agent. Later, as we were walking back to his building, I sprinted ahead a bit to avoid some traffic, and Chanax laughed and said, "Only Indios run in the street." He caught up and fell into step beside me, as if we were buddies, as if we were just going to see a movie together.

V
Deciphering the Truth
VICTORY AND DEATH

And courage is a rarer thing than evil, after all.
—Salman Rushdie, *Shame*

1

"We won, we won!" That was all Arturo Aguilar wrote in his e-mail message to me in New York on January 12, 2006. A few minutes later another e-mail arrived from Claudia Méndez. "*Confirmaron*"—They confirmed it. The Supreme Court had upheld the convictions and the twenty-year sentences for the Limas. Brief messages for such a big victory, and after such a long wait, but I thought I could feel their astonished joy and relief.

The court had stalled for months, and there had been much speculation that the charges against the Limas would be reduced again, this time to covering up evidence, which carried a maximum three-year sentence. They would then have been freed and the legal basis for proceeding with a criminal investigation against higher-ranking EMP officers would have been erased. But now the case could finally move ahead, with investigations against Colonel Rudy Pozuelos, Major Andrés Villagrán, and Major Francisco Escobar Blas, among others. Everyone I spoke to assured me that there were no more realistic legal loopholes for the Limas to exploit, though one should expect, I was told, a few last *patadas de abogado*, lawyers' kicks (like the thrashing of a drowning man, *un ahogado*), from the defense attorneys.

Mario Domingo was in West Virginia, in his wife's hometown, and I made plans to meet him to celebrate. I pictured it snowing there, probably because it hadn't snowed all winter and in New

York everyone was nostalgic for snow. Mario deserved to feel victorious and vindicated. Bertrand de la Grange and Maite Rico had described him in their book as "tormented," and he liked to joke that this was one thing, at least, they'd gotten right. He was suffering from nearly every stress-related ailment imaginable and was taking a few months' respite, studying English at a local community college. Mario had been planning to go back to Guatemala City in March for the next round of legal battles, whatever those would be.

In some ways, Mario Domingo's life story exemplified Guatemalans of his generation. He grew up in the Río Azul valley, in the village of Buxup, part of the municipality of Jacaltenango, which is situated in the western mountains, near the Mexican border. His family are Popti Indians (though Mario had a paternal grandmother who was mestizo, the source of his somewhat lighter complexion). Mario's childhood was spent in extreme poverty. He could remember long stretches of time when he and his siblings were fed nothing but tortillas and a soup of *chilis* and water. A younger sister died of malnutrition.

When Mario was a teenager, he went to live in Huehuetenango, the departmental capital, to study at the Normal School there. He was visiting his family and helping his uncle and other men from their village harvest corn in January 1982 when the Army massacred the inhabitants of a neighboring village, El Limonár. The men saw smoke rising from burning houses and heard gunfire and explosions. Soon afterward, most of Mario's family joined the exodus of people from Jacaltenango who crossed the border to refugee camps and settlements in Mexico. Mario stayed behind and graduated from the Normal School the following year. He had no money and didn't know what to do or where to go. His hometown, Buxup, was by then pretty much deserted, so he decided to join his family in Mexico. But he was turned back at the border, twice, and even ended up spending four days in a Mexican jail.

Mario made his way to Guatemala City, where an American Quaker group provided him with a scholarship and a loan so that he could study law at the University of San Carlos. By the time his parents returned from Mexico, Mario was working as a labor lawyer, and he helped his family settle and gain land titles in what eventually became Central America's largest squatters' barrio, the Colonia Mario Alioto López, on the outskirts of Guatemala City. One after the other of his younger brothers (he had eight siblings) followed in Mario's footsteps, attending the public university and becoming activists.

I planned to meet Mario in West Virginia at the end of January, after I returned from a business trip. But on January 26 he telephoned my apartment in New York. My wife answered. An unspeakable thing had happened. Mario's youngest brother, Darinel, a twenty-one-year-old law student, had been murdered. Darinel had been tortured and shot. Not just tortured—his limbs had been torn from his torso.

Mario said he was going back to Guatemala to take care of his family. He couldn't bear to think that his little brother had been murdered in retaliation for his work on the Gerardi case, that the killing might be a warning about future investigations. It had occurred less than two weeks after the verdicts against the Limas were upheld. Mario insisted that he didn't want to jump to conclusions. Guatemala, after all, was awash in violence. The police were carrying out one of their *limpiezas social*, social cleansings, targeting delinquents and randomly killing poor urban youths on the chance that they might belong to gangs. Perhaps his brother had been accidentally caught up in that. But mutilating their victim? That was what the *maras* sometimes did, and it seemed unlikely that Darinel had somehow made himself an enemy of such a gang.

Like the murder of Bishop Gerardi nearly eight years earlier, the murder of Darinel Domingo *looked* as if it might be a common crime. But, behind our silence, we all—Mario, his friends, and the people he worked with—knew what such a murder could have been meant to accomplish. Mario Domingo was the only litigation lawyer at ODHA working on the Gerardi case. No one else had the experience and knowledge that he possessed. The Public Ministry had abolished the office of the special prosecutor. Arturo Aguilar, Mario's only legal assistant, hadn't even graduated from law school yet. Fear and doubt struck those working on or associated with the Gerardi case. They all had wives, children, and families to worry about.

I went down to West Virginia to see Mario when he returned from Guatemala. We had dinner with his in-laws in a Mexican restaurant and drove back to their house, where Mario and I sat in the kitchen until dawn with a bottle of bourbon. Darinel had gone out to meet friends on the morning of January 21, Mario said. It was a Saturday, and that night he phoned to tell his parents he wouldn't be returning until the next day. The call—Mario was able to determine this with the help of someone in the telephone company—was made from a pay phone in Zone 1, downtown. Darinel had a girlfriend, also a law student, so it didn't seem strange that he wasn't coming home. But that was the last his family heard from him.

Darinel was a cheerful extrovert who had never been in trouble with the law; nor did he have a reputation as a troublemaker, and he wasn't known to have enemies. On weekend nights, he liked to drink beer with his friends. His family were frantic when they hadn't heard from him by Monday. On Tuesday, when they read a brief notice in *Prensa Libre* that the mutilated body of a young man had been found by a ravine in Zone 12, they ruled out the possibility that it might be Darinel because the paper reported that the body was tattooed. Darinel had no tattoos.

The mutilated body had been taken to the morgue in Amatitlán, just outside the city, and on Thursday, when some of Mario's brothers learned that three more corpses had been taken there, they decided to have a look, just in case. None of the three bodies that had come in most recently was Darinel's, but the morgue attendant suggested that they look at the other body that nobody had claimed—the one that had been described in the newspaper, erroneously, it turned out, as tattooed. One of Mario's brothers went in to see. The face was too decomposed to recognize, but there was a bracelet around the ankle of a leg that had been detached from the body. Mario's brother instantly identified the ankle bracelet as one his little brother used to wear. He recognized the T-shirt on the torso too. Both legs had been torn from the body, and one was still missing.

The family took Darinel Domingo's remains home to Jacaltenango for burial. ("We *jacaltecos* are like elephants," Mario told me. "In the end we always want to return to where we were born.") A few days later, on Monday, February 6—Mario had by then arrived in Guatemala—the police found the other leg in the weeds about two hundred yards from where the torso had been found. Next to it was Darinel's *morral,* an Indian-style woven shoulder bag that he used as a kind of knapsack, and lying on the ground beside it was his identification card. Whoever had murdered Darinel had wanted the body to be identified.

Darinel had probably been killed on Monday. Mario told me that it had been determined that Darinel's legs had been hacked off when he was still alive or very soon after he was dead, before rigor mortis could set in. Often a victim's legs will be cut off after they have stiffened, in order, for example, to be able to fit a corpse into a car trunk. While in Guatemala, Mario also discovered that before the murder, another of his brothers, a social worker, had received death threats by phone.

On Mario's first night back in Guatemala, a friend drove him home from the airport. He'd just stepped inside with his suitcases when the walls lit up with the lights of an ambulance that was followed by police cars. Mario went outside, stopped a police car, and asked what was happening. The policeman told him they had just found two bodies nearby and were looking for another two.

Over the next week, twelve bodies in all were found in the surrounding hillsides, ditches, and fields. Four of the victims were simple construction masons. An eleven-year-old boy had been tortured, his teeth yanked out.

During the previous six years, Mario reminded me that night we sat drinking at the kitchen table in West Virginia, there had been 23,000 homicides in Guatemala. It was a wartime casualty rate. Females accounted for 20 percent of all homicide victims, and over the last three years the number of murdered women and girls in Guatemala had doubled. A lead editorial in *elPeriódico* on March 16, 2006, deplored the violence. "The blood-frenzy with which killings are occurring in Guatemala is exceeding the limits of our imaginations," the writer said. "People talk about macabre initiation rites for armed gangs, of conflict between mafia capos and *maras,* about destabilizing actions carried out by the parallel state, of violent acts of revenge by illegal groups or the clandestine security apparatus, of psychopaths who kill for pleasure. . . . Although it sounds like a litany, we never tire of repeating that the only way to humanize our society is through the rule of law."

Half a century after the United States intervened in Guatemala and created the modern Guatemalan Army, and after the United States supported armed forces of similar character in El Salvador and Honduras through decades of conflict, those three countries had this in common: they were societies that had some of the highest murder rates in the world, and in which the powerful and well connected acted with impunity.

After thirty-six years of internal war and ten of so-called democracy and peace, Guatemala's best hope for warding off the chaos of a totally failed state still lay in the creation and enforcement of an independent legal and judicial system. Functioning democratic institutions—hadn't these been promised in exchange for an abruptly altered national destiny and all the violence and death that ensued whenever the United States intervened in another country? If such a project couldn't be achieved in a speck of a country like Guatemala, how could it be achieved anywhere else?

With MINUGUA gone from Guatemala, ODHA and other human rights groups had come to rely on the U.S. embassy for vigilance and support. In the kitchen in West Virginia, Mario Domingo acknowledged the historical irony of that. "Sometimes," he mumbled wearily, "it seems ridiculous."

Mario had decided to go back to Guatemala. It would be a temporary stay. His immediate concern was to get his terrified family members—as many as were willing to go—out of the country, into foreign asylum programs. After that, he wanted to do what he could about his brother's case. But he had his wife and small child to worry about too. Maybe he'd be able to find a job or a scholarship in some other country. He didn't think it was very likely that he would be returning to ODHA and the Gerardi case. Maybe it was time, he said, for someone else, a new generation, to carry the case forward. Arturo Aguilar would soon be getting his law degree. Arturo had talked it over with his wife. They were both aware of the dangers involved, but he was determined to stay at ODHA, and stay on the case.

"YESTERDAY I WAS in a café-bar in Zone 1 until very late, one near the corner of the National Palace," Claudia Méndez wrote to me from Guatemala City. "I decided to follow the route the taxi had taken that night on those same streets. It was around eleven. I went around the block several times and past that *callejón*. I drove around the church again. Everything looks so different now. . . . I felt so sad. How is it possible that we still can't decipher the truth about those last moments?"

Who killed Bishop Juan Gerardi? Most of the men—Colonel Lima seems the only certain exception—who had planned the murder remained free, as did many of the men who had actually taken part in the operation. How many people, in the end, participated in the crime? It depends, I think, on what one means by "participated." There are those who think that such a controversial and risky assassination could never have been carried out without the collusion of at least a few people from each of the country's most powerful sectors—military, private, and governmental—with the Oficinita as the likely conduit. For many months before the murder, influential rightist voices had been publishing opinion pieces denouncing the threat Church activists such as Bishop Gerardi represented. By some measures, the murder was a logical and even inevitable expression of the values of broad segments of Guatemalan society—a "culture of death . . . of fear," as Pope John Paul II described it a few months after the bishop's murder.

IT DIDN'T TAKE LONG for the *patadas de abogado*—the attorneys' last desperate kicks—to manifest themselves. Following the Supreme Court's ruling, the defendants and their lawyers had thirty days to contest it before the Constitutional Court, which is the highest court in Guatemala and which rules on the constitutionality of lower courts' verdicts. Contesting a verdict is done through an *amparo*—a common legal term throughout the Spanish-speaking world—which is neither an appeal nor a mere motion. It has no exact equivalent in the U.S. system. On February 12 the defense lawyers filed their *amparo,* which recycled old arguments, such as that their clients' constitutional rights had been violated because Rubén Chanax's "contradictory testimonies" had been accepted as evidence; that the Church shouldn't have been granted co-plaintiff status; and that the defendants should be convicted for covering up and not as accomplices, because no one could say exactly whose accomplices they were (i.e., Hugo remained a mystery).

Meanwhile, there was a new allegation of corruption in the case, supported by a supposedly incriminating video that was broadcast on Guatemalan television. Escobar Blas, who just before his recent retirement from active duty had been promoted to colonel, had been personally making the rounds of newspaper offices with copies of the video. It showed a meeting, taped by the Public Ministry, between Celvin Galindo, when he'd just become the special prosecutor, and his predecessor, Otto Ardón, along with other Public Ministry officials, as well as a major from Arzú's EMP, who shouldn't even have been there. The tape showed them watching a television monitor on which videotapes purportedly from Father Mario's collection were being shown. You couldn't actually see what they were watching, but when the tape was shown on television an off-camera voice portentously announced that they were porno videos. You could hear, in a barely audible voice, Ardón defending his scenario of a domestic crime and dog bites. Because Galindo subsequently disregarded Ardón's scenario in his own investigation, the Limas' lawyers were alleging a conspiracy. That was it.

Juan Luis Font, *elPeriódico's* managing editor, was one of those who received a visit from Escobar Blas. Font is a journalist in his thirties, conscientious and devoted to his profession. He told me that Escobar Blas frequently contacted him, and that Captain Lima occasionally phoned from prison as well. They perceived Font as sympathetic to their cause because he had been an early advocate—to his subsequent regret—of de la Grange and Rico's theories about the Gerardi case. Font admitted that his own knowledge of the complex case was superficial, especially compared with that of his main reporter on the story, Claudia Méndez. That was why, when Escobar Blas turned up at the newspaper's office bearing his video, Font summoned Claudia, even though he knew that doing so would irritate his visitor.

Escobar Blas sat facing Font's desk, and Claudia took a seat in a rear corner of the small office. "Throughout the meeting," Font told me, "Claudia peppered him with questions." Escobar Blas had to keep turning in his chair to deliver his menacing stare and curtly evasive answers. But Claudia wasn't intimidated. At the trial, she said to Escobar Blas, the prosecutors had proved their case and anyone who closely followed the record could see that. Escobar Blas had perjured himself when he'd testified that he was the tall thin man in a red baseball cap who had shown up with the EMP photographer at the San Sebastián parish house on the night of the murder. Really, Claudia said to Escobar Blas, it was EMP specialist Julio Meléndez Crispín who'd been there. Wasn't that true?

Escobar Blas, Juan Luis Font told me, lost his composure. Glaring at Claudia, he snarled, "Meléndez Crispín is weak! He's weak! He wasn't going to be able to hold up!"

Moments later, infuriated and flustered, Escobar Blas stalked out of the office.

THE CONSTITUIONAL COURT scheduled a public hearing of the defense's *amparo* for May 16. That morning the spectators' seats in the courtroom were nearly filled, mainly with supporters of the prosecution and the Church. When ODHA's lawyers arrived, there was a surprise. Mario Domingo was there. Instead of going back to West Virginia, he had decided to resume his duties as head of ODHA's legal team. But the defense lawyers didn't show up. They had apparently realized, or found out beforehand, that with such weak arguments—obvious *patadas de abogado*—their efforts would be futile. The court's five judges remained out of sight while everybody waited, and finally the courtroom emptied. The judges now had three days to sign their ruling. It seemed that the case, or at least its nearly eight-year first stage, was finally over.

But the ruling didn't come down. Four months later, on September 22, 2006, *Prensa Libre* reported that the court had upheld the verdicts, and anecdotal evidence—conversations with some of the judges—indicated that this was true. The five-member court decides its cases by majority, and four judges had signed the decision against the defense, which now awaited only the signature of the fifth judge—the court's president—to become official. The president was a rightist, however, and he had the power to stall for time. How long he might be able to stall—if, indeed, that was what he was doing—was a matter of opinion, but Jorge García said that he feared the Gerardi case might devolve into one of those blizzards of legal challenges that were slowly resolved, one at a time, over years and years. Others insisted that the Gerardi case had already progressed too far for anyone to be able to permanently thwart it in that manner.

The most pragmatic opinion was that the character of the next Guatemalan president and government would determine whether or not the Gerardi case would be given a chance to go forward. The new government would—or would not—foster an environment in which prosecutors felt institutionally supported in continuing the fight. There was no political will in President Berger's government to support the prosecution of the case, even though Berger was said to have acrimoniously split with Arzú. Under Berger's rule, the military was reconsolidating its position in the centers of power. The EMP no longer formally existed, but its reincarnation was said to be functioning out of the installations of the so-called Equestrian Unit of the Campo Marte military base in Guatemala City. The main intelligence group of the Guatemalan Army's High Command (G-2) had never gone anywhere.

President Berger's term would end with the dawning of 2008. Rigoberta Menchú had announced that she was a candidate for president, and the Guatemalan press was already tracking the alliances between politicians and behind-the-scenes power brokers. Most potential candidates for president were making pilgrimages to the Miami-based Mexican television magnate Ángel González, owner of almost all of Guatemala's television stations. Dionisio Gutiérrez, of the Pollo Campero fried-chicken family and host of the country's singularly influential political talk show on television, was reported to be allied with General Otto Pérez Molina, the former head of the EMP whom Rubén Chanax had identified as having been in Don Mike's store on the night of Bishop Gerardi's murder, along with Colonel Lima and the EMP's Colonel Reyes Palencia. But this information was not public knowledge. Billboards loomed over Guatemala City's traffic arteries, advertising the candidacy of General Pérez Molina. They featured the general in what looked like a prizefighter's pose, clenched fist raised, with a killer stare. His opponents were sinister *mara* thugs with tattooed faces. A slogan promised *mano dura*, a "hard fist," against street gangs.

RUBÉN CHANAX HAD MENTIONED General Otto Pérez Molina's role in the murder of Bishop Gerardi confidentially, to MINUGUA's Rafael Guillamón, among others. And Captain Lima, during the interview with Claudia Méndez in which he sent his "subliminal warnings," had praised Pérez Molina as an officer who "stands by his men." Lima alluded to other "higher-ups," who might logically include, for example, General Marco Tulio Espinosa, but he didn't identify them. Neither Chanax nor Lima ever mentioned General Pérez Molina in any of their official legal statements. Was their silence a tactic employed to guarantee their own protection? Lima probably employed several such strategies simultaneously. Did he really know the location, for example, of the videotape of the murder scene, with which he'd threatened Chanax? And if he did, who else might be threatened by what was on that tape? What other pieces of compromising evidence and information might Lima have?

"In all the prisons where he has been confined, Lima has been one of the principal leaders," *Prensa Libre* had reported on September 30, 2006, during a week when Lima suddenly lost his aura of Machiavellian invincibility. Guatemalan journalists who'd been to the Pavoncito prison, where Captain Lima and his father were inmates, said—but didn't dare write—that the captain lived apart from the general inmate population, in private quarters, with two golden retrievers; that his control of prison businesses was so complete that he even charged for the use of the plastic chairs visitors sat in. All of this began to change on September 25, when 3,000 Guatemalan soldiers and police conducted a dawn raid at another prison, the Pavón Penal Rehabilitation Farm. In news reports all over the world, the raid was characterized as a successful attempt by the beleaguered Guatemalan government—and by its intrepid new director of prisons, Alejandro Giammattei—to wrest control from the inmates and put a stop to a corrupt system. Newspapers were filled with descriptions of incarcerated crime bosses living in relative luxury while running their enterprises and rackets, and of criminals on the outside using the prison —which was said to have its own brothels and even a disco—as a hideout.

During the raid, seven prisoners, described as heavily armed inmate leaders, were killed. Among the dead was a Colombian drug trafficker, Jorge Batres, who had nearly completed his sentence and was soon to have been released. Captain Lima's old nemesis, Carlos Barrientos, the man who had fought with Lima in the Centro Preventivo and stolen his agenda notebook, was also killed. The raid was such a public-relations success that Alejandro Giammattei resigned as director of prisons and announced that he was running for president on the ticket of President Berger's party.

After the raid, most of the surviving prisoners from the Pavón Penal Rehabilitation Farm were transferred to the Pavoncito prison —Little Pavón. On the day of the transfer, several reporters saw Alejandro Giammattei engage Captain Lima in a brief, seemingly amicable conversation. The story in Prensa Libre on September 30 asserted that, although Captain Lima had been a prison leader throughout his seven years of incarceration, "on this occasion, the military man has failed to win the support of the 1,650 prisoners transferred from the Pavón Rehabilitation Farm, who accuse him of being an extortionist." Inmates were said to be upset that Lima wanted to charge them for bringing cell phones or even food into the prison. Thus Captain Lima and his father were to be isolated from the prison population for their own safety and to prevent the captain from "fomenting instability."

By then, stories were circulating that the seven prisoners slain in the Pavón raid had been murdered by a police death squad. Reporters as well as inmates with cell-phone cameras had photographed a group of heavily armed men in police commando uniforms, wearing ski masks, who were said to have picked out several prisoners who were lined up with others, their hands tied behind their backs. Most of the men later found dead were among those who had been pulled out of line by the masked commandos. They were apparently executed at close range.

Claudia Méndez of *elPeriódico* broke the story about the executions of the seven prisoners. The office of the Guatemalan Human Rights Procurator—who is appointed by the government—investigated and confirmed that there had been extrajudicial executions at Pavón. Throughout the spring of 2007, *elPeriódico* and other papers ran stories about the police death squads that were carrying out the "social cleansing" campaign supposedly aimed primarily at *mara* youth gangs. Members of these death squads also often worked as assassins for organized crime bosses, and it was in this role—one gang of narco-traffickers attacking another—that they carried out the executions in Pavón. *ElPeriódico* identified two members of the police death squad that participated in the prison raid: the Benitez Barrios brothers, wealthy young men who had been invited by Erwin Sperisen, the director of the National Police, to work as unpaid advisers. After the publication of the stories, *elPeriódico* and its director, José Rubén Zamora, once again became the target of an array of virulent threats, specious legal motions, and the usual Guatemalan agitprop.

Alejandro Giammattei, now the governing party's presidential candidate, was furious about the reports. The negative stories included comments from Captain Lima, who wrote a regular column from prison for a small Mixco newspaper, *El Metropolitano,* in which he often attacked his foes in the Gerardi case. Lima wrote that the slain Colombian drug dealer had been taken secretly from Pavoncito to Pavón the day before the raid, implying that there was a plan to kill him. On December 22, four men in civilian clothes and ski masks had visited Captain Lima at Pavoncito. Lima claimed in his *El Metropolitano* column to have recognized at least three of his visitors. They were military men, including a lieutenant colonel named Carlos Santisteban Zárate, who had threatened him before. Lima wrote that his hands and feet were tied and that he was taken to a garbage dump in back of the prison. "They stripped me naked and beat me all over my body with sticks," he wrote, "introducing one of these up my anus, causing me wounds and lacerations." While he was being tortured, Lima said, his assailants asked if General Otto Pérez Molina had paid him to discredit the prison system (and by extension Alejandro Giammattei, who was then Pérez Molina's rival as a presidential candidate, although there is no evidence that Giammattei had prior knowledge of the Pavón assassinations). The masked men also demanded to know if Lima had provided Claudia Méndez with information for her articles in *elPeriódico* about the prison raid. Lima said he wasn't the source. (Méndez says that she relied on other sources for her reports.)

Lima wrote that he was thrown into a filthy isolation cell infested with rats and without light, sanitation facilities, or running water. Then he was transferred to Infiernito—Little Hell— the most notorious prison in Guatemala, where he was again isolated. A former military man who had worked as a security adviser to MINUGUA and to the United States embassy contacted ODHA and Claudia Méndez and told them that *mara* gang members— including a man known as Bam Bam, who had participated in the decapitation of Obdulio Villanueva—had been moved into a cell adjoining Lima's. *ElPeriódico* published an article calling attention to Lima's plight. Leopoldo Zeissig, who was still working with the office of the Human Rights Procurator, declared that the office was monitoring Lima's situation. The consensus was that Captain Lima's powerful protectors had decided it was time to abandon him, especially if his elimination would seem unrelated to the Gerardi case.

In November 2006, *elPeriódico* had published an investigative piece reporting that thirty military officers, many of them veterans of the war and of Military Intelligence, held command posts in the National Police, in clear violation of the Peace Accords. Some of the officers had served in the EMP. One colonel was linked by the paper to the Oficinita; another was described as having worked until recently in Mayor Arzú's office. General Marco Tulio Espinosa, head of the EMP and minister of defense when Arzú was president, was reported to be running a clandestine unit that included telephone espionage from the basement of Arzú's mayoral office. One of Espinosa's main tasks, according to a well-connected source, was monitoring the Gerardi case.

Who was directing the police in the "social cleansing" being waged against presumed urban delinquents? These activities resembled the clandestine military terror of the war years, and it was easy to see how such an operation could be used for political assassinations. "Social cleansing or extrajudicial execution," said Mario Domingo. "The line between crime and politics here can be so fine as to not even exist."

RODRIGO SALVADÓ, one of the last two Untouchables, was leading ODHA's new exhumation team. He was an anthropologist, and that kind of work was closer to what he'd trained for. His college thesis had been an exploration of how the war had affected the observation of traditional religious customs in Maya communities. Rodrigo would sometimes spend weeks at a time in remote mountain areas, but he said that if the Gerardi case ever went forward, he was willing to resume his job as an investigator. "Maybe it's some suicidal urge on my part," he joked softly.

Rodrigo told me about a witness who had been pretty much overlooked—one of the car washers who had been in San Sebastián park on the night of Bishop Gerardi's murder. Rodrigo wasn't sure he could find the witness but was willing to try. Once more we set out on the short walk from the cathedral complex to the church of San Sebastián. Rodrigo said he hadn't talked to the car washer in a while, and that if we found him it was uncertain what condition he'd be in. He wasn't always lucid. We found him bent over a bucket of sloshing water, sponge in hand, busily washing a parked car. He was a tall, dark, middle-aged man with the stark thinness of a terminally ill person. His hollow-cheeked face was wrinkled and scrunched-looking, like a lost leather glove, and his few remaining teeth were crooked brown shards. Yet from under a soiled New York Yankees cap, black hair fell boyishly over his forehead, and he had attentive, glittery eyes. Rodrigo introduced us and then left us alone. The car washer's name was Víctor. He said that after he finished washing the car, he would meet me in the park. I waited. It wasn't long before I saw him approaching, with a lurching gait. Víctor seemed to be lame in one leg.

His full name was Víctor Hugo Godoy Cojulún, and he was forty-two years old. He'd been born in the Guatemalan city of Antigua and had been working as a car washer and living in and around San Sebastián park since he was twenty-three. In 1998, when Bishop Gerardi was murdered, Víctor slept at night in a little storage room—it looked like a concrete bunker—that belonged to the municipality; it was at the corner of the park and the driveway on the Second Street side. We walked over to it so that he could show me. A steel door to the storage space was now kept locked, but back then, in 1998, it had had a wood door behind a barred gate. Since then the storage room had been divided, one half converted into public restrooms.

On the night of Bishop Gerardi's murder, Víctor said, he and a man who shared the storage room with him, Isaías, had been joined there by a third person, Pablo. They'd made a few trips from the storage room to a nearby store to buy liquor, and at around ten o'clock they were inside, drinking. The door was open to the street. Then Víctor heard a sound from outside that he still vividly recalled, a kind of hyperventilated snorting, and when he looked up he saw a man passing, shirtless, muscular, with a military haircut, his body tensed, bent arms moving forward and back in short, abrupt thrusts, and all the while making that noise, as if, Víctor said, the man "was trying to expel his euphoria"—the adrenaline-charged exhalations, perhaps, of someone who'd just beaten somebody to death. Víctor was frightened. "That person gives me an ugly feeling," he told his friends when the shirtless man abruptly reeled around and went past the door again. "Shut the door," he told them, and they did.

But that wasn't all Víctor had witnessed that night in the park, which had been his domain for two decades. Early on, he'd seen a man giving beer and food to the *bolitos* who slept in front of the garage at the parish house; and then, a little later, when he and his two friends went out to buy their liquor, crossing the park, he'd seen Captain Byron Lima and two other men on a bench. The other men were sitting and the captain was standing with one foot up on the bench, his hands resting on his thigh—authoritative, alert. That demeanor seemed, in retrospect, in keeping with the captain's persona. Víctor said that Captain Lima was wearing a white T-shirt, jeans, and sneakers.

Captain Lima, like other soldiers from the nearby headquarters of the EMP, was a familiar figure to the denizens of the park. It wasn't until much later, when allegations about the captain's participation in the crime appeared in the newspapers, that Víctor realized the significance of what he'd seen.

Rodrigo had suggested to me that Víctor had seen the father, Colonel Byron Lima, in the park that evening as well, but Víctor said no. Another of the park's vagrants, Héctor Rivera, had seen the colonel. Héctor and his brother, Marco Tulio, the wayward alcoholic sons of a former director of the National Police, had lived in the park. Víctor said that he hadn't seen Héctor in a while.

About ten minutes before he saw the shirtless man, Víctor had seen El Chino Iván, who said hello when he walked past the open door to the storage room, on his way out of the park.

By now we'd left the park and were in a small café across the street. So why, I asked Víctor, hadn't he and the others in the park ever told what they'd seen?

The people in the park didn't talk, Víctor said, because they were afraid of the *militares*. Didn't I know about "the incident" in the park soon after the murder? He told me about someone who'd pulled up in a white van and stood outside it on Third Street with a wad of bills in his hand, offering money to anyone who had information about Gerardi's murder. "Nobody said anything," Víctor said, "because we knew he worked in the G-2." The visit was understood, in the language of the park denizens, as a serious warning to keep quiet. Nobody had been foolish enough to come forward.

Víctor, like the Rivera brothers, was related to a police chief. Ángel Conte Cojulún, chief of the National Police at the time of Bishop Gerardi's murder, was his cousin. Could that be just a co-incidence? Or were the *bolitos* and car washers of San Sebastián, infested with informers, a peculiar extension of the state's security apparatus, the lowest of the low but with roles and rules that they understood?

Víctor had told Otto Ardón and his prosecutors, when they'd held the first evidentiary proceeding at San Sebastián, on May 17, 1998, a few weeks after the murder, that he'd seen the frightening stranger go past his door, and El Chino Iván leaving the park—essentially corroborating Rubén Chanax's first statements—while maintaining that he'd seen nothing else. Later I looked at a photocopy of the record of the proceeding. The sole entry about Víctor in the official record of the Gerardi case took up just a few lines. Ardón and his prosecutors had never questioned Víctor again.

But now years had passed, and Víctor was giving out more information than he had offered before. Maybe he felt he no longer had anything to fear. Maybe he felt the end of his life approaching, and the twisted story of the Gerardi case provided him with a sense of meaning. He was surprisingly well informed about the case and had his own opinions about various aspects of it. He believed in the innocence of Father Mario. And he expressed his indignation that the appeals court had shortened the Limas' prison sentences by ten years.

Víctor told me that he'd once seen Obdulio Villanueva out on the streets when he was supposed to have been in the Antigua prison—at about four in the morning, months before the murder, just down Sixth Avenue, at the beginning of Zone 2, across the street from the Supreme Electoral Tribune building, near the house of Major Escobar Blas's mother. There were three Chevy Suburban SUVs parked in a row, and Obdulio Villanueva was looking at his image reflected in the black tinted windows of one, adjusting his necktie. Víctor walked past with some friends from the park and said hello, and Obdulio Villanueva looked at them. He raised his fingers to his lips, and said, *"Ustedes se callan."* You all keep quiet.

Later, back at ODHA, I asked Rodrigo Salvadó if the prosecutors who'd come after Otto Ardón—Celvin Galindo and Leopoldo Zeissig—had interviewed Víctor, and he said that he guessed they had. Then why hadn't they called Víctor as a witness at the trial? Rodrigo said that probably Zeissig had decided that with Rubén Chanax he had all he needed, and that Víctor would make an unreliable witness, easy for the defense to discredit, with his obvious drug and drinking problems, and so forth.

MARIO AND I HAD GONE, one afternoon not long after the murder of his young brother, to visit the headquarters of the police detective units, downtown, at the edge of Zone 1. Earlier in the day we had dropped in at the Constitutional Court to see if there was any news about its ruling, and then we'd gone to lunch in the market. I wanted to interview some homicide detectives, and Mario agreed to come with me. We walked down long corridors of modular offices with hand-drawn signs on the doors—Extortion, Kidnapping, Fraud, etc.—until we came to Homicide, located in two adjoining, bleakly austere rooms, with metal desks in rows and cheap computers that didn't seem to get much use. There were only four detectives present, in street clothes, pistols shoved into their pants. They were startlingly young, the beneficiaries, apparently, of recent reforms requiring that detectives have more rigorous training and at least a high school diploma. Mario said he would take advantage of the visit to check up on his brother's case, and he went to speak with an officer in the next room.

The young detectives were a demoralized bunch, understaffed and underfunded, despite the ballyhooed reforms. There were only seventy detectives in their section, they told me, for a city currently experiencing seventeen homicides a day. And look at the grim, shabby condition of their office, one said. How was that supposed to affect their morale? As in decades past, there was such a dearth of patrol cars that they often had to ride public buses to crime scenes.

When I came out of the room I found Mario Domingo staring down at a thick folder of papers he held open in his hands. A detective was sitting on the corner of a desk opposite him. Mario's face was somber, and there were tears in his eyes. We left and were well down the corridor when Mario said, huskily, "They are saying that Darinel's murder was political."

In a way, it was what Mario had most dreaded—confirmation that his brother's murder might be related to his work at ODHA. Still, he told me, he hadn't seen any evidence in support of the conclusions in the folder. And the prosecutor's office was not likely to take action anyway.

When we got back to the ODHA office, one of Mario's brothers was waiting for him. They had agreed, it so happened, to meet that afternoon to compose some phrases for a plaque on Darinel's gravestone. They set to work, but after a while Mario couldn't take it. He went out of the room and walked away somewhere.

In the covered corridor running around the patio and the offices off it, ODHA's employees were occupied with routine duties. The Indian mayor of Nebaj—in the Ixil Triangle, far away in the mountains, one of the areas most affected by the war's violence—had arrived accompanied by three women in traditional dress. They went into a little conference room with another young lawyer who was the newest member of ODHA's legal team. I ran into Rodrigo Salvadó near the front door. He introduced me to a hulking, big-bellied youth with long hair and a beard whose name was Christian Ozaeta and who was developing a program for teaching the REMHI report in Guatemalan schools. Out in the corridor, ODHA's executive director, Nery Rodenas, was taping an interview for a documentary film about the upcoming tenth anniversary of the signing of the Peace Accords. "Can a state of war that has divided a country for decades really end," the interviewer asked, "with just a signature on a piece of paper?"

The sky had darkened and a heavy downpour splashed the old stone tiles of the patio. I sat on a bench, watching it rain. Water rushed from drains and eaves and thunder rumbled in the sky. In his quiet voice, Nery had launched into a reply to the reporter's question that sounded as if it might go on forever.

IN LATE APRIL 2007, a new judge took over as president of the Constitutional Court, and within days—on April 25, the day before the ninth anniversary of the murder of Bishop Gerardi—the Public Ministry was notified that the guilty verdicts against the Limas and Father Mario had finally been upheld. "After six years, the sentences are firm," Leopoldo Zeissig wrote to me in an e-mail. "At last the second stage of the investigation can begin."

He meant the investigation, ordered by the judges in the original verdict, of other suspects in the murder, particularly higher-ups in the EMP. Prosecutors, Zeissig said, would have to establish the crime's chain of command. "Don't forget that the Gerardi crime and the extrajudicial executions carried out during the armed internal conflict have the same pedigree." The murder's operational structure, what he called the "intelligence channel," was the same one, Zeissig believed, that the military had employed throughout the war.

Six years earlier, during the trial, Colonel Lima had drawn a similiar connection when he'd warned: "I'm just the point of the spear. Once they've created a judicial precedent, then they're going to go after the others." He didn't mean just the other murderers of Bishop Gerardi, or only the other war criminals whom the amnesty was meant to protect. For half a century the military's clandestine world had seemed impregnable. The Gerardi case had opened a path into that darkness.

Dramatis Personae
(In order of appearance within categories)

The Church

Bishop Juan Gerardi Conedera, auxiliary bishop of Guatemalan archdiocese, founder of the Archdiocese's Office of Human Rights (ODHA), parish priest of church of San Sebastián. Murdered April 26, 1998.

Father Mario Orantes Nájera, assistant priest of church of San Sebastián. Arrested for Bishop Gerardi's murder, January 2000.

Archbishop Próspero Penados del Barrio.

Archbishop Mariano Rossell y Arrellano, conservative prelate; great-uncle of Father Mario and Father Sergio Orantes.

Monseñor Efraín Hernández, chancellor of the Curia. His housekeeper's daughter, Ana Lucía Escobar (La China), is suspected of being involved in gangs and in the murder of the bishop.

Father Gabriel Quiróz, priest to whom the taxi-driver witness came first.

Father Sergio Orantes Nájera, Father Mario's brother. Loses prestigious job as rector of Colegio San José de los Infantes under cloud of financial and sexual irregularities.

Bishop Mario Ríos Montt, Bishop Gerardi's successor at San Sebastián and ODHA. Brother of General Ríos Montt, president of Guatemala, 1982–1983.

San Sebastián church

Margarita López, parish-house cook.

Juana Sanabria, parish administrator, close friend of Bishop Gerardi. Witness for the prosecution.

Antonio Izaguirre, sacristan.

Monseñor Hernández's household

Ana Lucía Escobar (La China), daughter of Monseñor Hernández's housekeeper. Said to be involved in gang activity. Suspect in murder.

Imelda Escobar, La China's mother, Hernández's cook. Said to traffic in items stolen from church.

Dagoberto Escobar, Imelda's nephew.

ODHA (Guatemalan Archdiocese's Office of Human Rights)

Ronalth Ochaeta, executive director until 1999.

Edgar Gutiérrez, coordinator of ODHA's "Recovery of Historical Memory" report, *Guatemala: Never Again,* published in April 1998. Becomes head of government's Secretariat of Strategic Analysis in 2000, in administration of President Portillo.

Mario Domingo, investigating attorney.

Fernando Penados, chief investigator in Gerardi case (Untouchable). Nephew of Archbishop Penados. Later works in Portillo government.

Nery Rodenas, coordinator of legal team. Succeeds Ochaeta as director.

Arturo Aguilar, "El Gordo" (Untouchable).

Arturo Rodas, "El Califa" (Untouchable).

Rodrigo Salvadó, "El Shakira" (Untouchable).

Mynor Melgar, coordinator of legal team.

MINUGUA (United Nations Peace Verification Mission)

Jean Arnault, French chief of mission.

Rafael Guillamón, Spanish head of police investigation.

Military

Presidential Military Staff (Estado Mayor Presidencial, or EMP), in charge of personal security of president and his family. Included elite anti-kidnapping commando unit and an intelligence unit known, during the civil war, as El Archivo. In charge of interrogation and torture. Shut down by President Portillo in 2003 and replaced by Secretariat for Administrative and Security Matters.

Military Intelligence (G-2).

Secretariat of Strategic Analysis (SAE), an intelligence-gathering branch of the military. Put under civilian control in 2000.

Noél Beteta, EMP operative convicted of the murder of Myrna Mack.

General Marco Tulio Espinosa, head of EMP, then head of the Army High Command, and minister of defense under President Álvaro Arzú.

Captain Byron Lima Oliva, member of EMP. Arrested and convicted of participating in the extrajudicial execution of Bishop Gerardi.

Sergeant Major Obdulio Villanueva, member of EMP convicted of murdering the milkman, Haroldo Sas Rompich, who had run afoul of President Arzú's horseback outing. Later arrested and convicted of participating in the extrajudicial execution of the bishop. Murdered in prison February 12, 2003.

Colonel Byron Disrael Lima Estrada, former counterinsurgency commander and head of G-2, Military Intelligence. Arrested and convicted of participating in the extrajudicial execution of the bishop.

Darío Morales, EMP photographer at crime scene.

Major Francisco Escobar Blas, member of EMP. Head of Protection Services, the former Archivo. Implicated in the murder of the bishop.

Colonel Rudy Pozuelos, head of EMP. Implicated in murder.

Artillery Major Andrés Villagrán, member of EMP. Highest-ranking officer officially on duty the night of the murder.

General Otto Pérez Molina, former head of EMP.

Colonel Reyes Palencia, member of EMP. Head of Presidential Guard.

Public Ministry (prosecutors' office)

Otto Ardón Medina, special prosecutor in Gerardi case, 1998.

Gustavo Soria, assistant prosecutor.

Attorney General Fernando Mendizábal de la Riva, head of Public Ministry until May 1998. A political appointee.

Celvin Galindo, special prosecutor who replaces Ardón. Goes into exile in October 1999.

Leopoldo Zeissig, takes over from Galindo as special prosecutor. Goes into exile in July 2001.

Attorney General Adolfo González Rodas, head of Public Ministry until 2002.

Mario Leal, special prosecutor who replaces Leopoldo Zeissig in 2001.

Jorge García, special prosecutor who replaces Leal in 2003.

Defense lawyers

Vinicio García Pimentel, Father Mario's first lawyer.

José Toledo, Father Mario's second lawyer.

Julio Cintrón Gálvez, lead lawyer for the Limas.

Roberto Echeverría Vallejo, lawyer for the Limas.

Ramón González, lawyer for Margarita López (the cook).

Irving Aguilar, Sergeant Major Obdulio Villanueva's lawyer.

Key witnesses

Rubén Chanax Sontay, homeless car washer in San Sebastián park. Central witness for prosecution. Claims to be informer for Military Intelligence. Testifies and then goes into exile in April 2000.

El Chino Iván Aguilar, homeless *bolito*. With Rubén Chanax the night of the murder. In exile.

Jorge Diego Méndez Perussina, taxi driver who memorized the license-plate number of the Toyota Corolla seen near the church of San Sebastián the night of the murder. Also saw shirtless man. Testifies in February 1999 and goes into exile.

Oscar Chex López (Aníbal Sandoval), former G-2 intelligence agent who spied on Bishop Gerardi. Witness for the prosecution.

Specialist Jorge Aguilar Martínez, EMP waiter. Witness found by ODHA. Incriminates Captain Lima, Major Escobar Blas, and others. Goes into exile before trial.

Gilberto Gómez Limón, imprisoned thief who testifies that Villanueva was not in the prison the night of the murder.

Noé Gómez Limón, brother of Gilberto Goméz. Testifies that Limas' lawyer tried to bribe them. Murdered December 2002.

Government

Álvaro Arzú Irigoyen, president, 1996–2000. Becomes mayor of Guatemala City in 2004.

General Efraín Ríos Montt, president from 1982 to 1983. Presided over some of the worst atrocities of the civil war. During presidency of Alfonso Portillo, 2000–2004, Ríos Montt heads the Congress.

Luis Mendizábal, security adviser to President Arzú.

President Alfonso Portillo, populist elected in 1999. Presides over especially corrupt government.

Oscar Berger, elected president in 2004.

Judiciary

Judge Isaías Figueroa, first judge to have jurisdiction over Gerardi case. Presides over exhumation of the bishop's body.

Judge Henry Monroy, assigned to Gerardi case early in 1999. Goes into exile shortly thereafter.

Judge Flor de María García Villatoro, judge who takes over from Monroy. Presides over pretrial investigation.

Judge Yassmín Barrios, trial judge.

Judge Amada Gúzman de Zuñiga, trial judge.

Judge Eduardo Cojulún, trial judge.

Wilewaldo Contreras, appellate judge.

Judge Thelma del Cid, appellate judge.

United States

Prudence Bushnell, ambassador to Guatemala, 1999–2002.

John Hamilton, succeeds Bushnell as ambassador.

James Derham, ambassador in 2006.

Journalists and writers

Fernando Linares Beltranena, conservative lawyer and journalist.

Dina Fernández, columnist and editor at *Prensa Libre*.

José Rubén Zamora, publisher of *elPeriódico*.

Claudia Méndez Arriaza, reporter for *elPeriódico*.

Bertrand de la Grange, coauthor of *Who Killed the Bishop?*

Maite Rico, coauthor of *Who Killed the Bishop?*

Mario Vargas Llosa, Peruvian novelist and conservative columnist. Writes article critical of the prosecution in *El País*, February 2004.

Miscellaneous characters

Martha Jane Melville Novella, Father Mario's wealthy friend and patron.

Blanca Lidia Contreras, married to Monseñor Hernández's brother. Came from Canada to make a statement against Ana Lucía Escobar and Father Mario.

Luis Carlos García Pontaza, Ana Lucía Escobar's boyfriend. Reputed leader of Valle del Sol gang. Killed in prison January 21, 2001.

Arlene Cifuentes, Colonel Lima's niece. Makes anonymous phone call to archbishop's office implicating the Limas in murder.

Chronology of Events

1944 Democracy established in Guatemala.

1954 President Jacobo Arbenz, the second democratically elected president in Guatemalan history, is overthrown in a coup engineered by the CIA.

1959 Cuban revolution.

1960 Civil war in Guatemala begins when a large portion of the army attempts an unsuccessful coup against a government backed by the United States. Young Army officers take to the countryside to wage guerrilla war. A counterinsurgency campaign supported by the United States will lead to the deaths of some 10,000 civilians in the next decade.

1965 Pope John XXIII opens first session of Second Ecumenical Council of the Vatican. Limited use of the vernacular in the liturgy was endorsed and relation of the Church to the modern world was explored.

1967 Juan Gerardi Conedera appointed bishop of Verapaz.

1968 Pope Paul VI opens the Latin American Bishops' Conference in Medellín, Colombia, which encourages the Church's role in socioeconomic reform.

1974 Gerardi made bishop of El Quiché diocese.

January 31, 1980 Thirty-six protesting Mayan peasants from El Quiché are massacred in the Spanish embassy in Guatemala City.

March 24, 1980   Archbishop Romero is assassinated by ARENA (El Salvador's ruling far-right party) while celebrating Mass.

July 1980   Gerardi escapes assassination attempt and closes El Quiché diocese.

November 22, 1980   Returning from a trip to the Vatican, Gerardi is denied entrance into Guatemala and goes into exile in Costa Rica.

1982   Military coup in Guatemala. General Efraín Ríos Montt, an evangelical Protestant, takes power. Worst human rights violations of the civil war period take place during his regime.

1983   Ríos Montt deposed by his defense minister, General Oscar Mejía Victores.

1983   Archbishop Próspero Penados del Barrio appointed by Pope John Paul II as chief Guatemalan prelate. Bishop Gerardi, who comes back from exile in Costa Rica, is made auxiliary bishop and general vicar of the Guatemala City archdiocese.

1986   Vinicio Cerezo elected president; first civilian president in thirty years.

1989   Founding of Archdiocese's Office of Human Rights (ODHA).

1990   Myrna Mack Chang, young activist anthropologist, is murdered.

1994   Historical Clarification Commission, a UN-sponsored truth commission for Guatemala, is established.

1994   Recovery of Historical Memory Project (REMHI) established under Bishop Gerardi's direction.

1995   Last known massacre by Guatemalan Army, in Xamán, Alta Verapaz. Twenty-five Mayan peasants are killed.

December 1996   UN-monitored Peace Accords for Guatemala are signed.

September 1997   Historical Clarification Commission begins its work in Guatemala.

April 24, 1998   REMHI report, *Guatemala: Never Again,* formally presented.

April 26, 1998 Murder of Bishop Gerardi in garage of San Sebastián parish house.

April 30, 1998 Carlos Vielman, a homeless man, is arrested for Bishop Gerardi's murder.

May 18, 1998 Adolfo González Rodas becomes attorney general and head of Public Ministry.

July 22, 1998 Father Mario Orantes and Margarita López, the cook at the parish house, are arrested. Father Mario's German shepherd, Baloo, is also taken into custody.

July 27, 1998 Carlos Vielman is freed from prison.

September 17–18, 1998 Exhumation of bishop's body to check for dog bites.

December 17, 1998 Celvin Galindo takes over as special prosecutor for the Gerardi case, replacing Otto Ardón.

January 12, 1999 A taxi driver, Diego Méndez Perussina, testifies to ODHA about what he saw the night of the murder.

February 1999 Monseñor Efraín Hernández resigns as chancellor of the Curia; Edgar Gutiérrez and Fernando Penados leave ODHA.

February 12, 1999 Taxi driver testifies before judge.

February 18, 1999 Father Mario is provisionally released.

February 25, 1999 Final report of the UN Historical Clarification Commission, *Memory of Silence,* is published.

May 28, 1999 Ronalth Ochaeta's resignation as director of ODHA is announced. Nery Rodenas becomes new director. Ochaeta moves to Costa Rica.

August 25–26, 1999 Jorge Aguilar Martínez of EMP (the presidential waiter) testifies before judge and goes into exile.

September 25, 1999 Baloo dies.

October 7, 1999 The special prosecutor Celvin Galindo and his family flee into exile.

October 15, 1999 Leopoldo Zeissig becomes special prosecutor.

December 26, 1999 Alfonso Portillo, a populist, wins runoff election for president. General Ríos Montt is elected president of the legislature. Edgar Gutiérrez will be appointed head of the government's Secretariat of Strategic Analysis.

January 17, 2000 Rubén Chanax testifies about what he saw the night of the murder.

January 19, 2000 Arrest orders are issued for Colonel Lima Estrada, Captain Lima Oliva, Sergeant Major Obdulio Villanueva, and Father Mario. Arrest order is reissued for the parish-house cook, Margarita López.

January 21, 2000 The Limas are arrested.

January 22, 2000 Obdulio Villanueva is captured in a gun battle.

February 9, 2000 Father Mario, threatened with extradition, returns to Guatemala from Houston, Texas, and checks himself into a private hospital to avoid prison.

April 24, 2000 Rubén Chanax goes into exile.

September 14, 2000 Third Sentencing Court decides that the Limas, Sergeant Major Villanueva, Father Mario, and Margarita López should be tried together.

November 28, 2000 Carlos García Pontaza of the Valle del Sol gang is arrested.

January 29, 2001 Carlos García Pontaza dies in prison.

March 23, 2001 Trial begins.

June 8, 2001 Trial ends. Colonel Lima Estrada, Captain Byron Lima, and Sergeant Major Villanueva are each sentenced to thirty years in prison. Father Mario gets a twenty-year sentence. Margarita López is freed.

July 2001 Leopoldo Zeissig goes into exile. His assistant, Mario Leal, succeeds him as special prosecutor.

August 2001 The European journalists Bertrand de la Grange and Maite Rico publish an article in the Mexican and Spanish magazine *Letras Libres* critical of the prosecution and in support of the defendants.

October 3, 2002 Colonel Juan Valencio Osorio is convicted of intellectual authorship of the murder of Myrna Mack.

October 8, 2002 Verdicts in the Gerardi case are overturned on appeal.

November 30, 2002 Mario Domingo and Jorge García visit Rubén Chanax in exile in Mexico City.

February 12, 2003 Supreme Court reinstates the verdicts in the Gerardi case. A new hearing of the appeal is ordered. Obdulio Villanueva is killed during riots in Centro Preventivo.

September 2003 Jorge García becomes special prosecutor.

March 2003 Rodrigo Salvadó and Arturo Aguilar visit El Chino Iván in exile in Costa Rica.

May 7, 2003 Verdict against Colonel Osorio in the Myrna Mack case is overturned.

November 2003 Bertrand de la Grange and Maite Rico's *Who Killed the Bishop? Autopsy of a Political Crime* is published in Mexico.

December 2003 Oscar Berger, former mayor of Guatemala City, wins presidential election. Former president Álvaro Arzú becomes mayor of Guatemala City.

February 22, 2004 Mario Vargas Llosa publishes an article on the Gerardi case in *El País*.

April 26, 2004 Inter-American Court of Human Rights finds the Guatemalan state guilty in the Myrna Mack case.

March 22, 2005 Appellate court upholds verdicts against the Limas, although it lessens their culpability.

January 12, 2006 Convictions in the Gerardi case are upheld by the Supreme Court.

January 23, 2006 The mutilated corpse of Darinel Domingo, the younger brother of the ODHA lawyer Mario Domingo, turns up in the morgue.

May 16, 2006 The Constitutional Court meets to hear final defense motions (known as *amparos* in the Guatemalan legal system). The defense lawyers do not appear.

September 25, 2006 Three thousand government troops conduct a dawn raid on the Pavón prison. Seven prisoners are killed.

April 25, 2007 Constitutional court uploads verdicts against Limas and Father Mario.

Photo Credits

Sources and Notes

The material presented in this book is the result of eight years of firsthand reporting. I returned to the same questions, incidents, and testimony and discussed them, time and again, with individuals whose understanding of the case developed and changed. Most of the evidence has been, at the least, double-sourced. I tried to stay as close as possible to the people most intimately involved in investigating the case. They include members of ODHA, especially from the legal team and the Untouchables, and members of the Public Ministry, particularly Leopoldo Zeissig, the prosecutor most responsible for developing the case presented in 2001 at the trial. Another important source, beginning with our first conversations in the summer of 2005, was Rafael Guillamón, MINUGUA's chief investigator. Guillamón had never spoken to a journalist before, at least not for attribution. With the exception of his comments of January 2000 to *Prensa Libre's* Pedro Pop, the witness Rubén Chanax had also not spoken to a journalist prior to our conversations. Nor had Leopoldo Zeissig told his story "on the record" before we met in South America, where he was in exile.

Guatemalan journalists, especially those from *elPeriódico*—including Claudia Méndez and the newspaper's owner and editor, José Rubén Zamora—were enormously helpful to me.

The unpublished manuscript of a richly detailed account of the case, *El Caso Gerardi—crónica de un crimen de estado,* by Mario

Domingo, was an indispensable source of information. I am extremely grateful to him for sharing it with me.

The official, court-certified transcripts of statements and depositions given by witnesses and, in some cases, suspects, to judges and prosecutors were crucial for assembling an accurate account of the legal process, as was the 292-page verdict—which provided a complete record of the trial—written by the tribune of judges who tried the Gerardi case in 2001.

The *Annual Reports of the UN Verification Mission in Guatemala* (MINUGUA) provide an authoritative record of the Gerardi case and of developments and incidents in Guatemala, especially pertaining to the peace process and human rights generally, from 1997 to 2004.

The U.S. State Department Annual Country Reports on Human Rights in Guatemala can be read at http://guatemala .usembassy.gov/.

The REMHI report. *Guatemala: Nunca Más. Informe del Proyecto Interdiocesano de Recuperación de la Memoria Histórica,* 4 vols., Oficina de Derehos Humanos del Arzobispado de Guatemala, 1998. An abridged one-volume version is available in English: Archdiocese of Guatemala, *Guatemala: Never Again,* Orbis, 1999. The report is available online in Spanish, French, and German, at www.odhag.org.gt/INFREMHI/Default.htm.

Guatemala: Memory of Silence, Report of the UN Commission for Historical Clarification, February 1999, is available online at http://shr.aaas.org/guatemala/ceh/report/english/toc.html.

Important background readings on Guatemala's civil war include the following.

Ricardo Falla, *Masacres de la Selva: Ixcán Guatemala (1975– 1982),* Editorial Universitaria, Universidad de San Carlos de Guatemala, 1992. (English edition, Westview, Boulder, Colo., 1994.)

Greg Grandin, *The Last Colonial Massacre,* University of Chicago Press, Chicago, Ill., 2004.

Robert H. Immerman, *The CIA in Guatemala,* University of Texas Press, 1982.

Stephen Schlesinger and Stephen Kinzer, *Bitter Fruit: The Story of the American Coup in Guatemala,* Doubleday, Garden City, N.Y., 1982. (Rev. and expanded ed., Harvard University Press, Cambridge, Mass., 2005.)

Steven Kinzer, *Overthrow: America's Century of Regime Change from Hawaii to Iraq,* Times Books, New York, 2006.

Beatriz Manz, *Paradise in Ashes,* University of California Press, Berkeley, 2005.

Jennifer Schirmer, *The Guatemalan Military Project: A Violence Called Democracy,* University of Pennsylvania Press, Philadelphia, 2000.

Jean-Marie Simon, *Guatemala: Eternal Spring, Eternal Tyranny,* Norton, New York, 1987.

David Stoll, *Between Two Armies in the Ixil Towns of Guatemala,* Columbia University Press, New York, 1993.

Daniel Wilkinson, *Silence on the Mountain: Stories of Terror, Betrayal, and Forgetting in Guatemala,* Houghton Mifflin, Boston, Mass., 2002.

I. The Murder

The information about the Alliance for Progress years and the murders of Guatemalans who studied in the United States under U.S. AID study grants comes from Stephen M. Streeter, "Nation-Building in the Land of Eternal Counterinsurgency: Guatemala and the Contradictions of the Alliance for Progress," *Third World Quarterly,* vol. 27, 2006. Regarding anticommunism as the pretext for antireform repression in Guatemala, Streeter wrote: "The communist threat was in fact a rationalization for bolstering armed forces against a popular revolution against the oligarchy."

In *Bitter Fruit,* Stephen Schlesinger and the *New York Times* reporter Steven Kinzer wrote: "As the 1980s began, the position of Guatemala's ruling generals and their civilian backers remained unchanged. By now, the 14,000-member Guatemalan armed forces had become a wealthy caste unto itself. It claimed its own bank, ran an investment fund for its members, and launched industrial projects. Its leaders owned vast ranch acreage and regularly sold protection to large landowners. . . . Meantime, death squads linked to the Army reached into every sector of national life. Street-corner murders of lawyers, schoolteachers, journalists, peasant leaders, priests and religious workers, politicians, trade union organizers, students, professors and others continued on a daily basis. . . . The intention of the military leaders was essentially to destroy the political center. Anyone not supporting the regime was almost by definition a leftist, and therefore an enemy."

Regarding the Guatemalan Army's counterinsurgency strategy in the countryside, Jennifer Schirmer, a scholar who seems to have had unique access inside the Guatemalan military establishment, wrote that although "[t]he guerrillas were not irrelevant to the Army's plans . . . it didn't matter if the guerrilla was present in the area of a 'killing zone' or not: all were to be eliminated" (*The Guatemalan Military Project*).

The quotations from Bishop Gerardi's early writing are from *Monseñor Juan Gerardi—Tesitigo Fiel de Dios*, Guatemalan Episcopal Conference, 1999.

An interview with Archbishop Quezada Toruño that includes his account of going to meet Bishop Gerardi at Guatemala City's airport was published in *30 Dias*, April 2004. This periodical is a Spanish-language version of the Italian Catholic church magazine *30 Giorni*.

There was some confusion regarding the arrival of Monseñor Hernández and Ana Lucía Escobar at San Sebastián on the night of the murder. Monseñor Hernández identified the car in which he was driven to San Sebastián as a red Mazda 323. However, Ana Lucía Escobar said at the trial that it was a Nissen 323 (a model that does not exist). Rubén Chanax apparently misidentified the Mazda and said that the car he saw drive up to the parish house was a reddish Toyota. Chanax also described seeing two young people get out of the car: a youth and a young woman with straight hair worn in a ponytail. Apparently the woman was Ana Lucía Escobar. But before parking, Escobar said, they had let Monseñor Hernández out of the car and he'd gone directly inside. Those minor discrepancies were later invoked to raise suspicions about Monseñor Hernández and Ana Lucía's involvement in the crime.

II The Investigation

The National Security Archive at George Washington University, www.gwu.edu, is particularly useful. See especially the archive's *Electronic Briefing Book* No. 11, on U.S. Policy in Guatemala, 1966–1996, http://www.gwu.edu/~nsarchiv/NSAEBB/ NSAEBB11/docs/. For a report on Colonel Byron Lima Estrada, written by Kate Doyle and Michael Evans from declassified U.S. documents, see *Electronic Briefing Book* No. 25, www.gwu.edu/ ~nsarchiv/NSAEBB/NSAEBB25/index.htm. For the Death Squad dossier, see *Electronic Briefing Book* No. 15, http://www.gwu.edu/ ~nsarchiv/NSAEBB/NSAEBB15/press.html.

The illegal activities of the EMP anti-kidnapping commando unit were described in MINUGUA's seventh annual report (1997) and in *Inforpress Centroamericana,* October 10, 1997. Since 1972, *Inforpress Centroamericana* has published a weekly information bulletin, with an English-language counterpart, *Central American Report*. Both are available at www.inforpressca.com.

Narco trafficking: In 2003, when the United States revoked the visas of a group of powerful generals and others reputedly linked to narco trafficking and crime mafias, Fernando Linares Beltrana was included in the group. The visa of General Francisco Ortega Menaldo, who was a former head of the EMP and the Guatemalan military officer most frequently linked to narcotics trafficking, was also revoked. Linares Beltrana was General Ortega Menaldo's defense attorney. The official reason given for revoking his visa was that he was "a known helper, assistant, or conspirator with others in the illicit trafficking of controlled substances or chemicals."

See Washington Office on Latin America, Special Report, "Guatemala Decertified," April 2003; see also *elPeriódico*, March 1, 2003.

Following the assassination in 1994 of Chief Justice Epamonidas González, who—using evidence provided by the DEA—had ruled to extradite a Guatemalan lieutenant colonel to the United States for narcotics trafficking, the Constitutional Court reversed the extradition order. Since then no Guatemalan court has extradited any military man to the United States on drug charges. See "Bush's Brush with Latin American Drug Lords," Frank Smyth, *The Nation*, March 9, 2007.

Envio, April 2002, a publication of the University of Central America, Nicaragua, contains an account of Arzú's incendiary speech calling human rights activists "traitors to the fatherland."

Dr. José Manuel Reverte Coma: Invited to El Salvador in 1993 by the right-wing president Alfredo Cristiani, Reverte Coma contradicted the findings of a UN anthropological team investigating the massacre of civilians at El Mozote. He was removed from the team at the request of the head of the Salvadoran Truth Commission, former Colombian president Belisario Betancourt. See *Prensa Libre*, September 24–25, 1998; and *Proceso* 827, University of Central America in El Salvador, October 21, 1998.

A memorable account of the Holy Week murders of the GAM leaders and the death and torture of Rosario Godoy de Cuevas and her relatives, by a writer who experienced those episodes firsthand, is provided by Jean-Marie Simon in *Guatemala: Eternal Spring, Eternal Tyranny*.

Luis Mendizábal: An article in the Salvadoran newspaper *La Prensa Gráfica*, on August 29, 2004, described Luis Mendizábal as a Guatemalan liaison to El Salvador's ARENA party and to the ARENA leaders accused of running death squads and of the assassination of Archbishop Romero. From a series, published in ten installments, on ARENA's leader Roberto D'Aubuisson. In *elPeriódico,* July 4, 2000, Mendizábal was described as one of the founders of the Oficinita and as a security adviser to President Arzú.

For Judge Henry Monroy's flight into exile, see, among other sources, the U.S. State Department Country Report on Human Rights in Guatemala, 1999.

Regarding the position of the "populist" Alfonso Portillo within the FRG Party: In an interview with the reporter Claudia Méndez of *elPeriódico* in 2005, General Ríos Montt recalled that FRG hard-liners had wanted to replace Portillo with the vice president. "They came to me and proposed elevating Paco Reyes to president and naming someone else vice president," Ríos Montt said. "Get rid of Portillo, and put in Paco. The plan was to switch the chairs: 'We have to get rid of him,' they told me."

I have quoted from several declassified communications of the U.S. embassy and the State Department from 1998 to 1999. They show that embassy officials, diplomats, and foreign-service officers went from supporting the Guatemalan government and believing the military's denials about its role in Bishop Gerardi's murder to fully sharing MINUGUA's assessment that the government was covering up a political crime. See the cable from the U.S. embassy entitled "MINUGUA Puts Government to Test on Gerardi Murder Investigation," Guatemala 001279, April 1999.

III The Trial

Various human rights groups documented the threats received by investigators, judges, prosecutors, and members of ODHA who were involved in the Gerardi case. For example, the U.S. Department of State Country Report of 2001 on human rights in Guatemala reported, "On June 14, and again on September 18, a military helicopter circled over the house of Judge Yassmín Barrios at a very low altitude. The police detail guarding the house reported that the helicopter did not belong to the Interior

Ministry, which oversees the police, but to the military." The report also confirmed other threats against her. By the end of 2001 in Guatemala, the U.S. Country Report also noted, "80 cases of threats to justice workers had been reported, approximately half of which were associated with the Gerardi trial."

Threats against Rodrigo Salvadó and Mario Domingo were reported in Amnesty International's *Submission to Param Cumaraswamy Special Rapporteur of the United Nations Commission on Human Rights on the Independence of Judges and Lawyers,* May 2001. Param Cumaraswamy, in his report on Guatemala to the UN Human Rights Commission, April 2000, expressed particular concern about two problems in Guatemala: the pervasive practice of impunity for those who violate human rights and the frequent threats against judges and prosecutors involved in such cases. Human Rights Watch, Lawyers Rights Watch Canada, and other groups also reported in detail on threats against prosecutors and judges.

Future trials: The judges in the trial of the Limas, Sergeant Major Villanueva, Father Mario, and Margarita López did not close the case with their verdict. They called for further investigation into the material authorship of the crime; investigation of the role of the EMP chain of command; and investigation of those who obstructed justice, including seven military officers, two civilians, and four prison officials. They named Rudy Pozuelos, Andrés Villagrán Alfaro, Francisco Escobar Blas, Darío Morales Garcia, Julio Meléndez Crispín, Edgar Carrillo Grajeda, Carlos Rene Alvarado, Erick Urízar, Luis Alberto Lima Oliva (Colonel Lima's youngest son), Hugo Nájera Ruiz, Santos Hernández Perez, Erick Medrano Garcia, and Misael Chinchilla Monzon.

IV The Third Stage

Maite Rico and Bertrand de la Grange published their article on the Gerardi case in *Letras Libres,* August 2001. Their book *¿Quién mató al obispo? Autopsia de un crimen politico* was published in 2003 by Random House, Mexico. Rico and de la Grange dedicated only one passage in the book to the special prosecutor Leopoldo Zeissig. In that passage, which is representative of their journalistic method, they described Zeissig as having received a telephone call, during which a "cloying melody" played, that he considered part of a pattern of threats. "Investigators never succeeded in determining the source of that supposed threat," they write, dismissively. It seems most improbable that there would have been an investigation into just one telephone call in which "cloying" music played. There has never been a serious investigation into any of the countless telephone threats, or the telephone espionage, against Guatemalans. That Guatemalan military intelligence units employ telephones in such a manner is not in doubt. The U.S. State Department Country Report for 2002 expressed concern about the EMP's telephone espionage without mentioning any investigation against such acts.

Rico and de la Grange quote a rival prosecutor's opinion of Zeissig: "'Aside from being stupid, he was paranoid,' commented Berta Julia Morales, in charge of bank robberies and a friend of lapidary phrases. 'He's only a man because the midwife said so.'" The authors do not mention that Berta Julia Morales is the prosecutor who prematurely classified as a suicide the probable murder of Carlos García Pontaza, the leader of the Valle del Sol gang who refused to implicate his ex-girlfriend, Ana Lucía Escobar, in the crime. Her conclusions were strongly disputed by MINUGUA and the Public Ministry. The U.S. State Department's Country Report of 2001 on human rights in Guatemala criticized Berta Julia Morales's performance in another politically charged case of multiple murders, that of Francisco Aguilar Alonzom and his wife: "The prosecutors assigned to the case, including Berta Julia Morales, failed to develop plausible motives for the murders despite evidence of a pattern of killings conducted by a sophisticated and well-coordinated organization."

As to whether or not someone contributed financially to Maite Rico's and Bertrand de la Grange's three-year investigtion, there is some confusion. During an interview with Dionisio Gutiérrez on the television show *Libre Encuentro* on April 25, 2004, Rico said "We financed the book ourselves. Specifically, from our savings and . . . royalties from our book on Marcos." Three years later, in a letter to *elPeriódico* published on June 20, 2007, in response to an erroneous account that this book claims that President Arzú paid them (a claim that was made by Military Intelligence during the Portillo administration), Rico said, "Arzú did not pay us. We were paid, and very well, by our publishers."

Escobar Blas: Allegations of Major Escobar Blas's role in the kidnapping and murder of Beverly Sandoval Richardson emerged during the trial, in the summer of 2000, of Gustavo Carranza, who was accused of the crime and was sentenced to death for it. Carranza said that the real kidnappers had been killed by the intellectual leaders of the crime, Major Escobar Blas and two other EMP officers. He said that Escobar Blas, a former air force pilot, had disposed of the slain kidnappers by dropping them from a small plane into the crater of the Pacaya volcano.

The Limas in prison: The Public Ministry and the homicide division of the Criminal Investigations Section of the National Police produced a substantial file on the fatal riot at the Centro Preventivo. File number 20030212 describes the Limas' retail businesses in prison.

Chanax's military experience: When I visited him in Europe, Rafael Guillamón took out a notebook with notes of his interview of 1998 with Doña Rosa Sontay, Chanax's mother. She had told Guillamón that when she went to the Jalapa base to claim her payment as the closest relative of a soldier, she'd discovered that her son was using the name Chanax Gómez.

For independent corroboration of the Inter-American Court's description of a "third stage" in crimes of state, including manipulation of the legal process and defamation campaigns: A United Nations report of December 2002 by the special representative of the secretary-general, on the situation in Guatemala, stated: "95 percent of the alleged violations against human rights defenders are death threats and acts of intimidation, such as following vehicles, surveillance in front of the victims' homes and offices, anonymous and malicious telephone calls, searching offices and homes, wiretapping and theft of computer files. Defamation campaigns were also reported." The U.S. State Department's Country Report of 2001 on Guatemala observed: "There were also credible allegations of parallel investigations by Military Intelligence—in the Bishop Gerardi and Ordonez Porta murder cases—that interfered with the justice system's efforts to investigate and prosecute those responsible."

For General Otto Pérez Molina's alleged murder of Efraín Bámaca, see *New York Times,* March 24, 1996, "Guatemalans Covered Up Killing of an American, U.S. Aides Say," by Tim Wiener. The article discusses the deaths of Michael DeVine in 1990 and of Bámaca after his capture by the Guatemalan Army in 1992. General Pérez Molina was also linked by human rights organizations to another notorious murder, the 1994 assassination of Judge Edgar Romero Elías. For that and more on Pérez Molina, see Washington Office on Latin America, *Hidden Powers in Post-Conflict Guatemala,* December 2003. The ODHA lawyer Mario Domingo was among those who heard Rubén Chanax claim that Pérez Molina was in Don Mike's store the night of the murder. Domingo thought that Chanax could be mistaken, but Rafael Guillamón of MINUGUA, who had much more contact with Chanax than Domingo did, felt that Chanax was telling the truth.

Where was Jorge Aguilar Martínez on the night of the murder? The attorney who notarized the document that Osmel Olivares Alay showed Mario Domingo was the military defense and Oficinita lawyer José "Chepito" Morales. Olivares Alay, at the request of Colonel Pozuelos, signed the document, which attested that Aguilar Martínez was on janitorial duty with him in the National Palace between eight PM and one AM. But in reality, Aguilar Martínez, sweaty and somewhat agitated, turned up there at one AM. Where was he during the previous crucial hours? Was he where he originally claimed, in the Services Office near the Guard Command, or did he have some other, more direct, role in the crime? After the EMP closed, ODHA and Jorge García spoke with another EMP specialist, Benjamín Alvarenga, who was in the Services Office that night. Alvarenga gave nearly the same account as Aguilar Martínez. He identified Captain Lima, Obdulio Villanueva, and Specialist Galeano among the men he saw arrive after the murder. Mario Domingo now believes that Aguilar Martínez was directly involved in the operation, probably in a security role. The defense lawyers didn't summon him to testify at the trial because they feared what his testimony would reveal.

President Oscar Berger: Berger was regarded as a weak and ineffective president. A nationwide opinion poll on his presidency in January 2006 recorded an 80 percent disapproval rating.

"Club Rosa": According to an anonymous source, a former member of G-2 Military Intelligence, officers and cadets from the prestigious Escuela Politécnica were linked to the first Club Rosa.

The house in Zone 6: It was owned by José Morales Solares, a construction contractor. It is likely that beginning at least in November 1997, Colonel Lima, Chanax, and others met there to plan some aspects of the operation to murder Bishop Juan Gerardi.

Narcotics and government: In the fall of 2005 the Guatemalan government's chief antinarcotics policeman, Adán Castillo, was arrested, along with two subordinates, on a visit to Washington, D.C., and charged with narcotics trafficking (*New York Times,* November 17, 2005). For more on the Guatemalan military and the narcotics trade, see Frank Smyth, "The Untouchable Narco-State: Guatemala's Military Defies the DEA," *Texas Observer,* November 18, 2005.

Kaibiles: From the report of the UN-sponsored Commission for Historical Clarification, February 1999. "The substantiation of the training of the Army's special counter insurgency force, known as *Kaibiles,* has drawn the particular attention of the CEH. This training included killing animals and then eating them raw and drinking their blood in order to demonstrate courage. The extreme cruelty of these training methods, according to testimony available to the CEH, was then put into practice in a range of operations carried out by these troops, confirming one point of their Decalogue: 'The *Kaibil* is a killing machine.'"

Reports of General Espinosa's clandestine activities in Mayor Arzú's office appeared in the October 2005 issue of *Envio*, published by the University of Central America, Managua, Nicaragua, and in the March 30, 2007, *Inforpress Centroamericana*. It was also reported by *Inforpress* that Espinosa, while head of President Arzú's EMP, had organized the anti-kidnapping commando unit that Captain Lima belonged to. Like the police death squads in 2007, Espinosa's commando unit was implicated in illicit operations.

Another possible explanation for the mystery of Hugo: In a conversation in October 2006, the prosecutor Jorge García told me, without providing any other details, that he had found a source from the old EMP who claimed that Captain Lima's job on the night of the murder had been to "eliminate" Hugo after the crime had been committed.

V Deciphering the Truth

See the article "Pavón Journal: Eulogy for an Outlaw Prison (It Was a Jungle in There)" by Marc Lacey, *New York Times*, October 26, 2006, for an account of the Pavón prison raid that did not question the government's account of the inmates' deaths. For the most thorough account of the prison raid, see Claudia Méndez's article, "*La república de los presos*" or "The Prisoners' Republic," in the March 2007 issue of the Mexico City–based magazine *Gatopardo*.

On March 7, 2007, Interior Minister Carlos Vielmann; the director of the National Police, Erwin Sperisen; and the new prison director, Víctor Rosales, submitted their resignations following the murder, on February 25, of four Guatemalan policemen in the

Boquerón maximum security prison, six days after the policemen were arrested for killing three Salvadoran politicians, including the son of ARENA founder Roberto D'Aubuisson, and their driver. It seems clear that the policemen were murdered so that they could not name who gave the orders for the hit. Witnesses among the inmates at Boquerón described a death squad coming into the prison, passing through seven security gates, to murder the policemen. The Guatemalan government maintained that the policemen were murdered by *mara cholos*.

As the commissioner of presidential security in Berger's government, until his resignation in mid-2004, General Otto Pérez Molina had run Military Intelligence, the Interior Ministry, and the SAE. Then Carlos Vielmann became the new interior minister. Vielmann had, during the war years, been an associate of Mario Sandoval and the far-right MLN "party of organized violence," which ran the notorious *mano blanco* death squad and had ties to Military Intelligence. Under Berger, Vielmann and his Salvadoran assistant Víctor Rivera, alias El Don, launched the "social cleansing" program that drove the Guatemalan homicide rate up to an average of twenty a day. Rivera was suspected by the DEA of involvement in narcotics trafficking and had been linked to other organized crime figures arrested in El Salvador and Guatemala.

Acknowledgments

So many people, in Guatemala especially—not all can be named—shared their insights, information, work, friendship, and trust with me during the time I spent reporting on the Gerardi case. To all, my heartfelt gratitude.

Sharon DeLano was my editor when I first wrote about the murder of Bishop Gerardi for *The New Yorker* and she also edited *The Art of Political Murder*. This book could not have had a better or more indefatigable friend. I was also fortunate to profit from the editing of the dearly missed Barbara Epstein at the *New York Review of Books*. I am grateful to my friend Morgan Entrekin and everyone (Amy, Andrew, Jamison, Charles et al.) at Grove/Atlantic for their support and hard work, and especially to Amanda Urban, whose encouragement and interest in the Gerardi case helped sustain my own commitment over many years.

The quotation from *Don Quixote* is from Edith Grossman's translation.

Mama Lotti and Lotti Torres Garza in Guanajuato, Mexico, provided me with shelter, sustenance, and unforgettable conversation and affection during a crucial period of writing in the summer of 2005. Mama Lotti, we miss you so much.

To Aura Estrada—I strike the board and cry, No more! You lived with this obsession for several years. Throughout, you were the light. Thank you.

Index